THE Amazing 1000

Puzzle Challenge 2

Material in this book has previously appeared in:

Mensa Crossword Puzzles (Phil Carter & Ken Russell)
Mensa Mega Mazes (Robert Allen)
Mensa Brainwaves (Dave Chatten & Carolyn Skitt)
Mensa Logic Brainteasers (Philip Carter & Ken Russell)
Mensa Mind Assault Course (Dave Chatten & Carolyn
 Skitt)
Mensa Covert Challenge (David Colton)
Mensa Enigmas (Peter Jackson)

Printed in Dubai

ISBN 184442 356 5

THE Amazing 1000

Puzzle Challenge 2

CARLTON
BOOKS

HOW TO SOLVE PUZZLES

If you're new to all this there are a few things you need to know before you get started. First, stay alert at all times! Puzzle setters are a tricky breed and prey on the unwary. Second, in puzzles numbers can be letters and letters can be numbers. Write down the alphabet and number it A = 1, B = 2, C = 3, etc. Then number it backwards (Z = 1 ... A = 26). Keep this list beside you at all times and it will save you a lot of trouble.

The simplest formula becomes difficult to solve if you don't know what to look for. For example, place three numbers under 10 at the points of a triangle, then add them together and put the sum in the middle. Simple. Any child could do it. But if you don't explain what you've done it is surprisingly hard for others to follow your reasoning.

As a general rule there is very little in this book that children under 10 could not work out if they had the secret formula. Think simple. Good puzzles are not complicated, merely tricky. Good luck! You'll probably need it.

There is a theory that being good at puzzles proves you are a being of superior intelligence. This is pure piffle. Some of the biggest lummoxes you could come across are puzzle fanatics. On the other hand, puzzles are loads of fun if you have a certain amount of patience, ingenuity and sheer low-down cunning. If you don't take them too seriously they can help while away many a pleasant hour or make tedious journeys pass quickly.

The aim in putting this book together was quite simply to give you, the puzzler, some good old-fashioned fun. This book *won't* improve your IQ, it *won't* qualify you for entry to anything and

INTRODUCTION

it *won't* tell the world anything it doesn't already know about your intelligence. So relax and let your mind slowly come to grips with the work of some of the world's most creative and successful puzzle compilers, who have been published in just about every corner of the globe.

You are cordially invited to join that happy band of brothers and sisters who have nothing better to do with their time than wrestle with puzzles. OK, you may never save the world but, on the other hand, you will do it very little damage and, in these strange days, there is much to be said for that.

1 DAZZLING DIAMONDS

Divide the diamond into four identical shapes, each containing one of each of the following five symbols:

SOLUTION ON PAGE 276

2 TRICKY TRIANGLES

Look at the three shapes. Does option A, B, C, D or E continue the sequence?

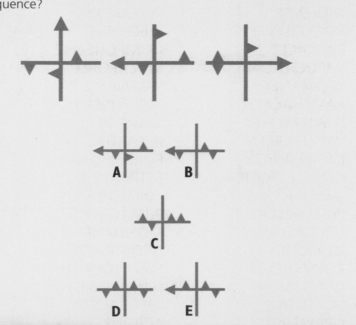

SOLUTION ON PAGE 276

3 ROVING ROBOT

Scientists have produced a robot that contains a simple program for crossing a quiet road (not a one-way street) in the UK.

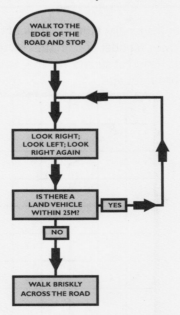

But they made a cardinal error and the robot still hasn't crossed the road after eight hours. What is the error?

SOLUTION ON PAGE 276

4 TALL STORY

A man turned off the light and went to bed. The next morning he turned on the radio and heard of a dreadful tragedy in which more than 100 people had been killed. He realized it had all been his fault. Why? He did not wake in the night and he did not sleepwalk.

SOLUTION ON PAGE 276

5 LETTER LOGIC

What letter appears once only in each of the first two words but not at all in the last two words?

FRUITAGE	INTERPLAY	*but not in*	INTERMISSION	OSTEOPOROSIS
RIPCORD	SHIELDING	*but not in*	WISTFUL	OCTAGONAL
PINNACLE	COMPLAISANT	*but not in*	PINCERS	MATCHBOX
IMPLICATION	MULTIFORD	*but not in*	STAMINA	WARDSHIP
YEOMANLY	VALENCE	*but not in*	SPADEWORK	CARAMELIZE
RAMSHACKLE	MARSHMALLOW	*but not in*	STARDUST	OCCUPATION
PAWNBROKER	SINKAGE	*but not in*	WONDERFUL	SACRIFICE
WINDSCREEN	IMPARTIAL	*but not in*	FICTITIOUS	CAMPAIGN
INCRIMINATE	FINGERPRINT	*but not in*	ALPINE	BLUEBELL
COBBLESTONE	ESTIMATE	*but not in*	GRANITE	IGNORANCE
JAVELIN	ABRASIVE	*but not in*	PROMPTITUDE	RHOMBUS
PICTURESQUE	IMMACULATE	*but not in*	SITUATION	HIDEOUS
EDUCATIONAL	MUNDANE	*but not in*	STEADILY	RIDGEPOLE
RICOCHET	GEOLOGICAL	*but not in*	OSPREY	POLYCARBON
ROBUSTIOUS	SPELLBOUND	*but not in*	THUNDERCLAP	MOUTHPIECE
LYRICISM	HAMSTRING	*but not in*	THISTLEDOWN	WORDLESS
SORTILEGE	DISGRACED	*but not in*	PRIESTHOOD	SOPRANO
GRAPEFRUIT	ACIDIFIES	*but not in*	HEADLAND	INVENTIVE
SPECIFY	INVARIABLE	*but not in*	LAMINATION	STANDARD
AROMATHERAPY	INSPECTION	*but not in*	MAGNIFICENT	DIRECTOR

SOLUTION ON PAGE 276

6 WORD SWITCH

Remove one letter from the first word and place it into the second word to form two new words. You must not change the order of the letters in the words and you may not use plurals.

What letter needs to move?

SALLOW	BAIL	WRING	FIST
PITCH	SALE	TWINE	COME
PRIDE	SLOE	PROUD	BOND
SWAMP	CLAP	DARTED	BEACH
STILL	FACE	CURVED	SHOE
THREE	NICE	CREASE	BAND
VALUE	CASE	BUNGLE	CATER
WHEAT	FAST	BRIDGE	FINER
MONTH	GLAD	TWAIN	HUNT
METAL	HOLY	STOOP	FLAT

SOLUTION ON PAGE 276

7 DIRECTION CROSSWORD

Answers run horizontally, vertically, or diagonally, either to the right or the left. Each solution starts on the lower number and finishes on the next higher number, i.e. 1–2, 2–3, etc. Finish at square 18. The completed puzzle will not have any blank squares.

Clues

1 – 2 Stood out
2 – 3 Ruined
3 – 4 Ascertain
4 – 5 Powers
5 – 6 Light of the sun
6 – 7 Match a feat
7 – 8 Bewitch
8 – 9 Exhausted
9 – 10 Haberdashers
10 – 11 Narrow bands
11 – 12 Relative by remarriage
12 – 13 Require
13 – 14 Short and thick
14 – 15 Affirmative
15 – 16 Woven
16 – 17 Tidy
17 – 18 Metal

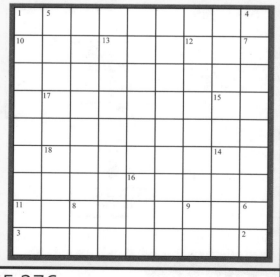

SOLUTION ON PAGE 276

8 CHINESE CHASE

START

FINISH

9 THREE CIRCLES

Draw three complete circles so that each circle contains one ellipse, one square and one triangle. No two circles may use all the same elements.

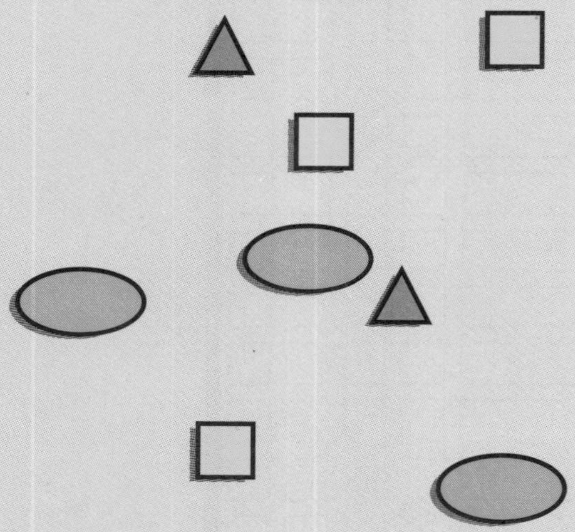

SOLUTION ON PAGE 276

10 COUNTERFEIT COINS

Most counterfeit coin puzzles assume you have balance-type scales available with two pans, where one object is weighed against another.

In this puzzle you have a single scale with only one pan. You have three bags of large gold coins with an unspecified number of coins in each bag. One of the bags consists entirely of conterfeit coins weighing 55g each; the other two bags contain all genuine coins weighing 50g each.

What is the minimum number of weighing operations you need to carry out before you can be certain of identifying the bag of counterfeit coins?

SOLUTION ON PAGE 276

11 WORD MATCH

What word has a similar meaning to the first word and rhymes with the second word?

CRACK	—	**DRAKE**
BOTTOM	—	**CASE**
RELAX	—	**BEST**
TRUMPET	—	**CUBA**
TRUE	—	**MEAL**
REAR	—	**LACK**
HOOP	—	**SING**
CORROSION	—	**MUST**
GRIT	—	**HAND**
THREAD	—	**GRAND**

SOLUTION ON PAGE 276

12 OBSTACLE

Look at the shape below and answer the following questions on it.

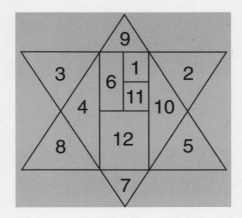

1. How many triangles are there in the diagram?
2. How many rectangles are there in the diagram?
3. How many hexagons can you find?

SOLUTION ON PAGE 276

13 OBSTACLE

In the supermarket, the aisles are numbered one to six from the entrance. Washing powder is next to bottles and it is not the first item you see when entering the supermarket. You will see the meat aisle before the bread aisle. Tins are two aisles before bottles and meat is four aisles after fruit.

1. **What is in the last aisle (aisle six)?**

2. **In which aisle can bottles be found?**

3. **What is in the first aisle?**

4. **In which aisle can tins be found?**

SOLUTION ON PAGE 276

14 QUADRUPLE ALPHABET CROSSWORD

Using all 26 letters of four complete alphabets, 104 letters in all, complete the grid. To help, 27 letters have been given and the word FEZ appears twice.

ABCDEFGHIJKLM

ABCDEFGHIJKLM

ABCDEFGHIJKLM

ABCDEFGHIJKLM

NOPQRSTUVWXYZ

NOPQRSTUVWXYZ

NOPQRSTUVWXYZ

NOPQRSTUVWXYZ

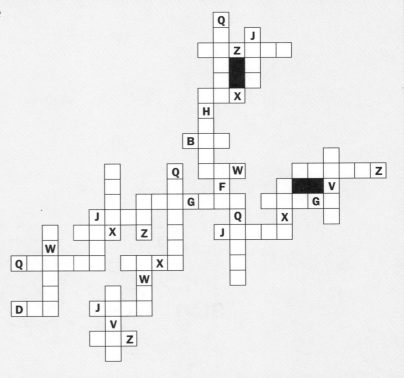

SOLUTION ON PAGE 276

15 CELTIC CONUNDRUM

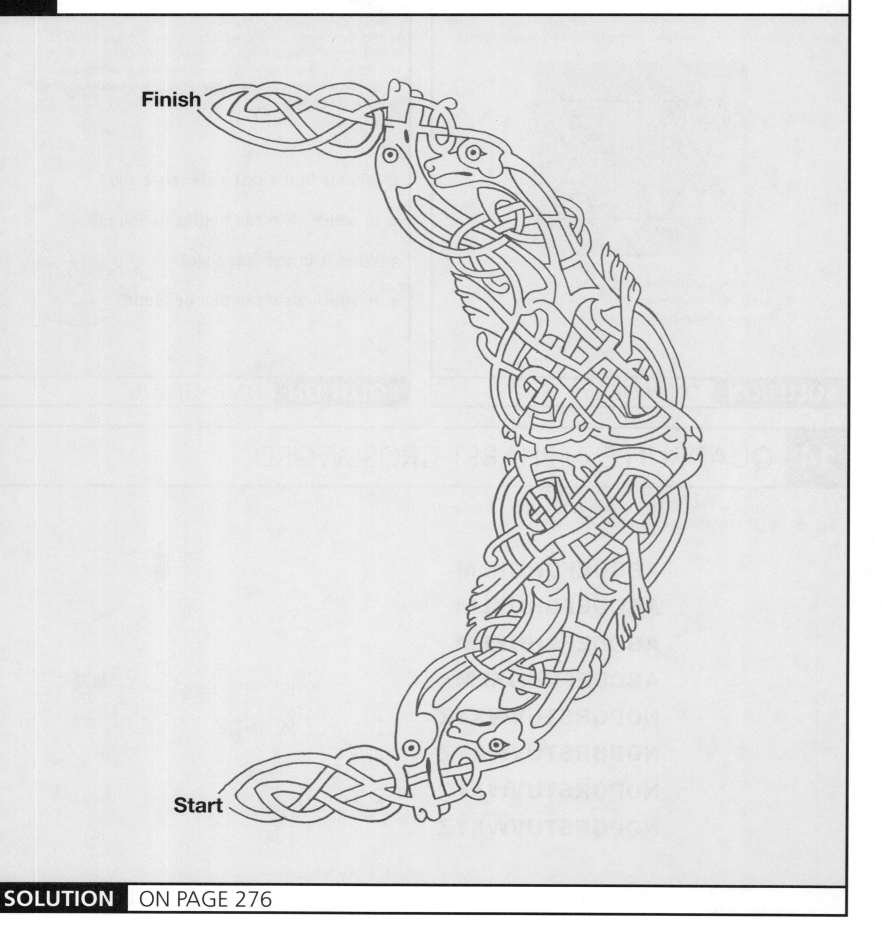

Finish

Start

SOLUTION ON PAGE 276

16 SITTING PRETTY

At the school the boys sit at desks numbered 1–5 and the girls sit opposite them at desks numbered 6–10.

1. The girl sitting next to the girl opposite no. 1 is Fiona.
2. Fiona is three desks away from Grace.
3. Hilary is opposite Colin.
4. Eddy is opposite the girl next to Hilary.
5. If Colin is not central then Alan is.
6. David is next to Bill.
7. Bill is three desks away from Colin.
8. If Fiona is not central then Indira is.
9. Hilary is three desks away from Jane.
10. David is opposite Grace.
11. The girl sitting next to the girl opposite Alan is Jane.
12. Colin is not at desk no. 5.
13. Jane is not at desk no. 10.

Can you work out the seating arrangements?

SOLUTION ON PAGE 277

17 MAKING EYES

Look at the five drawings. Does A, B, C, D or E continue the sequence?

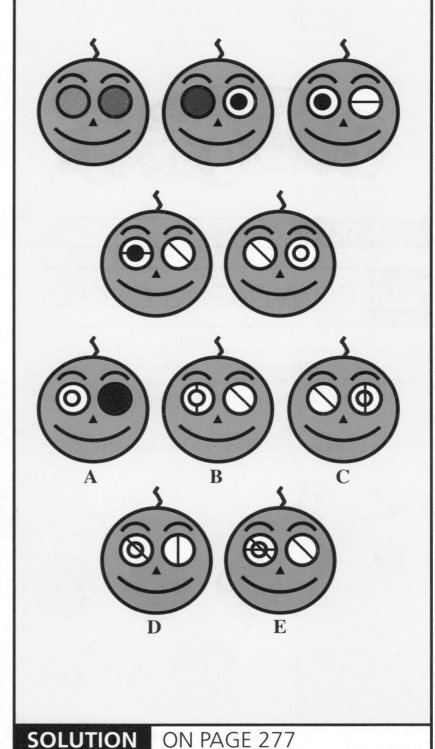

A   B   C

D   E

SOLUTION ON PAGE 277

18 CAR SORTER

In a car showroom, the white car is at one end of the showroom and the purple car is at the other. The red car is next to the black car and three places away from the blue car. The yellow car is next to the blue car and nearer to the purple car than to the white one. The silver car is next to the red one and the green car is five places away from the blue car. The black car is next to the green car.

1. Is the silver car or the red car nearer to the purple car?
2. Which car is three places away from the white car?
3. Which car is next to the purple car?
4. Which car is between the silver and the blue?

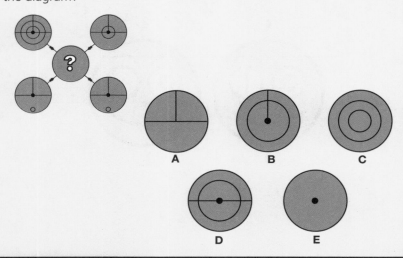

SOLUTION ON PAGE 277

19 FIGURE OF FUN

Look at the five figures. Which of the following options continues the sequence?

A   B   C   D   E

SOLUTION ON PAGE 277

20 CONVERGING CIRCLES

Each line and symbol in the four outer circles is transferred to the middle circle according to a few rules. These are that if a line or symbol occurs in the outer circles once, it is transferred; twice, it is possibly transferred; three times, it is transferred; four times, it is not transferred.

Which of the five circles should appear in the middle of the diagram?

A   B   C

D   E

SOLUTION ON PAGE 277

21 SHOOTING RANGE

Three military marksmen – Colonel Present, Major Aim and General Fire – are shooting on the range. When they have finished, they collect their targets.
Each makes three statements:

Colonel Present:
"I scored 180."
"I scored 40 less than the major."
"I scored 20 more than the general."

Major Aim:
"I did not score the lowest."
"The difference between my score and the general's was 60."
"The general scored 240."

General Fire:
"I scored less than the colonel."
"The colonel scored 200."
"The major scored 60 more than the colonel."

Each marksman makes one incorrect statement. What are their scores?

SOLUTION ON PAGE 277

22 LAND OF ZOZ

In the land of Zoz there live three types of person:

Truthkins, who live in hexagonal houses and always tell the truth;
Fibkins, who live in pentagonal houses and always tell lies;
Switchkins, who live in round houses and who make true whatever they say.

One morning 90 of them gather in the city in three groups of 30.
One group is all of one type; another group is made up evenly of two types; the third group evenly comprises three types. Everyone in the first group says, "We are all truthkins"; everyone in the second group says, "We are all fibkins"; and everyone in the third group says, "We are all switchkins".

How many sleep in pentagonal houses that night?

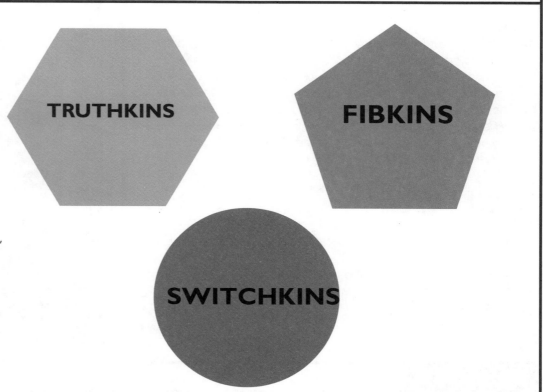

SOLUTION   ON PAGE 277

23 NO FANTASY

Answers to eight of the clues are four-letter words, which, when placed correctly in the grid, will form two Magic Squares where the same four words can be read horizontally and vertically. A bonus clue is given. It is a seven-letter word that appears across and down at the connecting lines of the two squares.

Clues (in no particular order)
Actual
Current
Inventory
Mark left by a wound
Mix
Notion
Peruvian native
Small pie
Bonus clue:
Someone who faces up to the facts

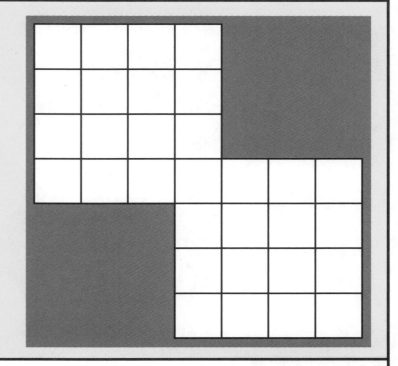

SOLUTION   ON PAGE 277

24 TENT TROUBLE

A survey has been conducted on the types of holidays people have taken over the last twelve months. Five more people had one holiday only and stayed in a self-catering accommodation than had one holiday and stayed in a hotel. Eight people had a camping holiday only and five people took all three types of holiday. Fifty-nine people had not stayed in a hotel in the last twelve months. Four times as many people went camping only as had a hotel and a camping holiday but no self-catering holiday. Of the 107 who took part in the survey a total of 35 people took a camping holiday.

1. How many people only had a hotel holiday?
2. How many people stayed in self-catering accommodation and a hotel but did not camp?
3. How many people did not stay in self-catering accommodation?
4. How many people stayed in only two of the three types of accommodation?

SOLUTION | ON PAGE 277

25 FLOWER FRENZY

SOLUTION | ON PAGE 277

26 KEY CLUE

Which key exactly fits the tumbler in the lock below?

SOLUTION ON PAGE 277

27 SAFE ASSUMPTION

Find the two missing numbers to crack the safe.

MONEY 3

DOCUMENTS 6

NECKLACE ?

BRACELET 5

RINGS ?

SOLUTION ON PAGE 277

28 CONFUSION & LIES

There was once a family that was well known for being awkward. The males in the family always told the truth but the women in the family never made two consecutive true or untrue statements.

When met by a visitor, the father and mother had one child with them. The visitor asked the child, "Are you a boy?" but the visitor could not understand the reply. One of the parents said that the child responded, "I am a boy". The other parent then said, "The child lied, she is a girl". Was the child a boy or a girl and what did the child say?

SOLUTION ON PAGE 277

29 SPY SATELLITE

You are agent 25, on a mission. You need to send a message to base 239 via your laptop computer and a satellite link. However, you need to choose the correct satellite.

Which one do you choose?

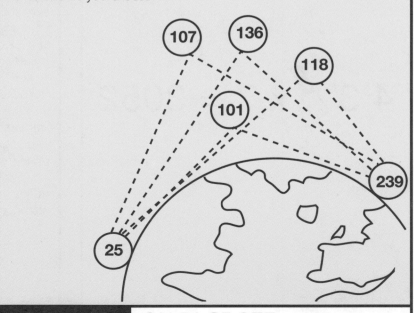

SOLUTION ON PAGE 277

30 CRIME SCENE

These six words below are associated with the murky underworld. Can you unravel them?

NICELOVE

GILLINK

LULUFAWN

GILLALE

TEANG

RIMICLAN

SOLUTION   ON PAGE 277

31 SPYWARE

Merged together here are two items an agent should have when going abroad. What are they?

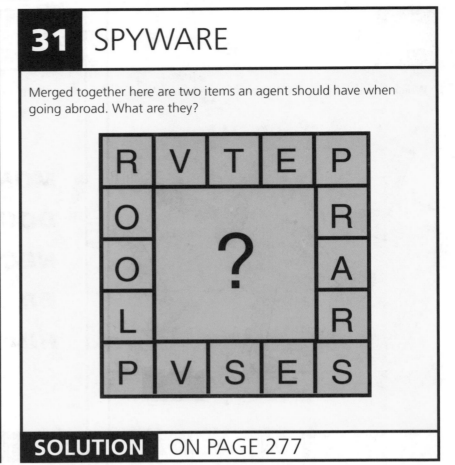

SOLUTION   ON PAGE 277

32 KNIFE NOTE

What is the value of the knife?

$$4\ 3\ \text{} \times 7 = 3052$$

SOLUTION   ON PAGE 277

33 JUNGLE JAUNT

You are on a jungle mission when you reach a river. The only way to cross it is by carefully stepping from stone to stone, from one side to the other. Pick the wrong stones and you'll fall in. The river is full of crocodiles.

Starting at A, and stepping on only one stone from each row, which sequence of stones should you choose?

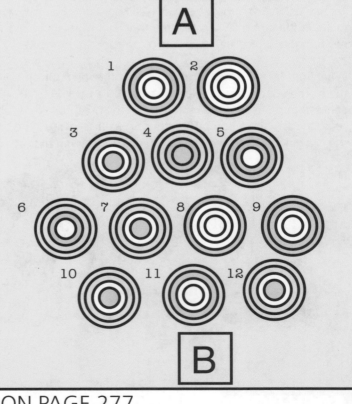

SOLUTION   ON PAGE 277

34 SHAPE SHENANIGANS

Which shape is the odd one out?

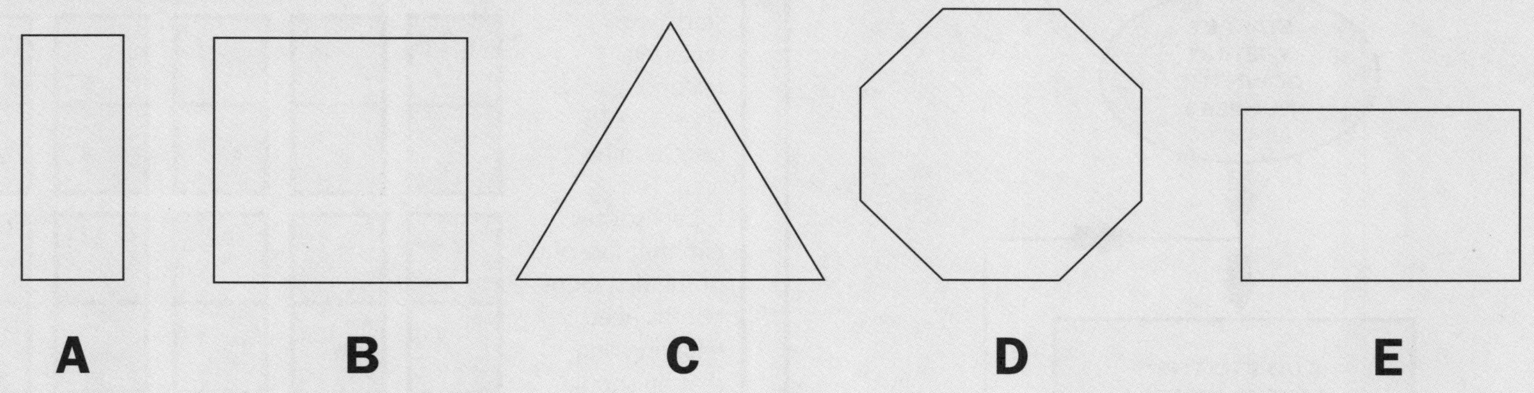

| A | B | C | D | E |

SOLUTION ON PAGE 277

35 WHICH WORD?

What word, which is alphabetically between the two given words, answers the clues?

CURIOUS	—	CURRANT	Twist or roll
BARRICADE	—	BARROW	Obstruction
CABRIOLET	—	CAMPAIGN	French village famous for cheese
CALM	—	CALVARY	Unit of energy
DAUGHTER	—	DAY	Beginning
DUO	—	DUPLICATE	Deceive
EPIC	—	EPIGRAM	Widespread disease
EPISODE	—	EPITAPH	Letter
FAINT	—	FAITH	Fantasy world
FALSE	—	FAME	Waver
GOLD	—	GONDOLA	A sport
GRAFT	—	GRAMMAR	Cereal
HEROINE	—	HERSELF	Fishbone pattern
HESITATE	—	HEW	Coarse fabric
IMMATURE	—	IMMERSE	Instant
JOG	—	JOKE	Junction of two or more parts
KIOSK	—	KISMET	Smoked fish
LEAF	—	LEAK	An association
LIMBER	—	LIMIT	Rhyme
MEDDLE	—	MEDICAL	Intervene

SOLUTION ON PAGE 277

36 FANCY FIGURES

START BY WRITING DOWN THE NUMBER 2

↓

ADD 3 TO THE LAST NUMBER

↓

WRITE DOWN THE NEW NUMBER OBTAINED

↓

ADD 2 TO THE LAST NUMBER

↓

WRITE DOWN THE NEW NUMBER OBTAINED

↓

HAVE YOU WRITTEN DOWN SEVEN NUMBERS? → NO

YES

STOP

What have you written down?

SOLUTION ON PAGE 277

37 BOOTH BONANZA

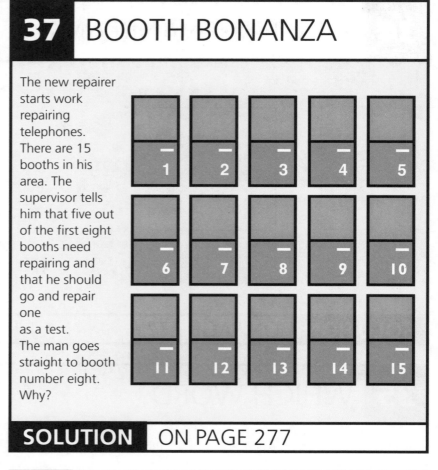

The new repairer starts work repairing telephones. There are 15 booths in his area. The supervisor tells him that five out of the first eight booths need repairing and that he should go and repair one as a test. The man goes straight to booth number eight. Why?

SOLUTION ON PAGE 277

38 HEXAGON HARMONY

Look at the three hexagons. Which of the following four options continues the sequence?

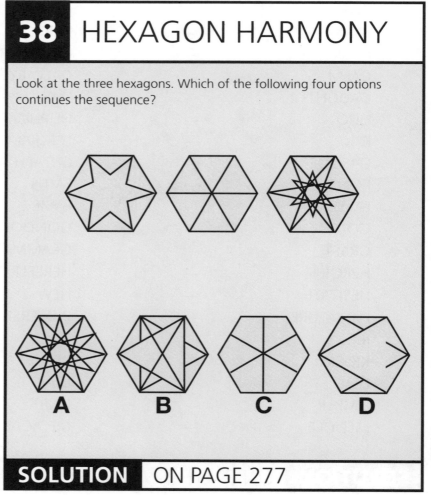

SOLUTION ON PAGE 277

39 RICE PAPER RIDDLER

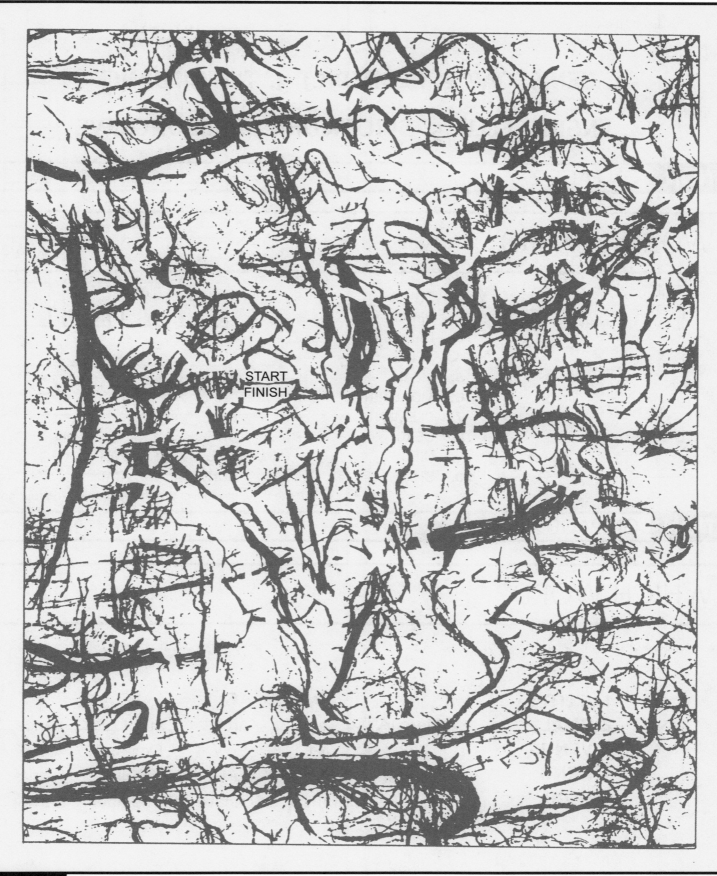

START
FINISH

SOLUTION   ON PAGE 277

40   SPY QUEST

Below are six words associated with spying.

Can you unravel them?

1. GENIESOAP 2. PEONEDICT 3. TINFOILDANCE
4. ENGINECELLIT 5. SPICYACORN 6. REDONCURVE

SOLUTION   ON PAGE 277

41   WORD WIZARD

Join the letters of the given words to form a single word using all of the letters.

1.	DRUM	+	MIMES		
2.	REPAY	+	LIT	+	SON
3.	DANCE	+	SIT		
4.	SPITE	+	ANTIC		
5.	MEAN	+	ATE		
6.	MONSTER	+	RATE		
7.	CLEMENT	+	RAPE		
8.	DEAD	+	CITE		
9.	NIECE	+	GILL	+	NET
10.	SHINE	+	SUIT	+	CAT

SOLUTION   ON PAGE 278

42   WHICH WORD?

Match the word groups below with the given words.

1. EXTRA	A	B	C	D	E
2. WALL	Mercury	Zero	Arch	Surplus	Fence
3. VENUS	Pluto	Nil	Bow	Excess	Gate
4. BEND	Jupiter	Nought	Curve	Residue	Hedge
5. NONE	Saturn	Nothing	Concave	Remainder	Barrier

SOLUTION   ON PAGE 278

43 WORD MATCH

Match the word groups below with the given words.

1. **WAYNE**	A	B	C	D	E
2. **FOXGLOVE**	Dusk	Brando	Durable	Poppy	Trimmings
3. **GARNISH**	Sundown	Bogart	Strong	Crocus	Accessories
4. **TOUGH**	Sunset	Travolta	Sturdy	Peony	Frills
5. **TWILIGHT**	Nightfall	Swayze	Hardy	Aster	Extras

SOLUTION   ON PAGE 278

44 WORD MATCH

Match the word groups below with the given words.

A	B	C	D	E	
Ernst	Borodin	Reduce	Baffle	Cover	1. **JACKET**
Rembrandt	Vivaldi	Decrease	Bewilder	Wrapper	2. **CONSTABLE**
Dali	Liszt	Lessen	Confuse	Sleeve	3. **PUZZLE**
Picasso	Elgar	Curtail	Flummox	Envelope	4. **CHOPIN**
					5. **CUT**

SOLUTION   ON PAGE 278

45 ALPHABET CROSSWORD

Insert the 26 letters of the alphabet once each only to complete the crossword.

ABCDEFGHI
JKLMNOPQR
STUVWXYZ

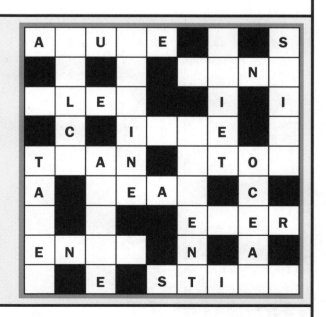

SOLUTION   ON PAGE 278

46 WORD SEARCH

Find at least 20 insects, bugs, or creepy-crawlies in the grid. Words can go in any direction, but a letter can only be used once in a word. Letters must be joined to make a word. For instance, the "H" at the bottom joins the "N" and the "C" but not the "B" or the "A."

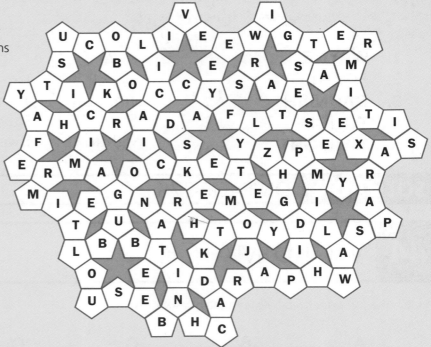

SOLUTION   ON PAGE 278

47 DYNAMIC DOG

Russell Carter lives on a remote ranch in the Australian outback with his dog, Spot. Several times a week he sets off with Spot for a long walk. This morning he is walking at a steady 4mph and when they are 10 miles from home he turns to go home and, retracing his steps, lets Spot off the lead. Spot immediately runs homeward at 9mph. When Spot reaches the ranch he turns around and runs back to Russell, who is continuing at his steady 4mph. On reaching Russell, Spot turns back for the ranch, maintaining his 9mph. This is repeated until Russell arrives back at the ranch and lets Spot in. At all times Russell and Spot maintain their respective speeds of 4mph and 9mph.

How many miles does Spot cover from being let off the lead to being let into the ranch?

SOLUTION   ON PAGE 278

48 ROBOTIC RACE

START

FINISH

49 WORD MATCH

Match the word groups below with the given words.

1. **FRANKENSTEIN**
2. **COUNTRY**
3. **ANISEED**
4. **FEELING**
5. **TRANQUIL**

A	**B**	**C**	**D**	**E**
Calm	Cumin	Kingdom	Werewolf	Theory
Peaceful	Nutmeg	Realm	Demon	View
Restful	Thyme	State	Dracula	Belief
Serene	Saffron	Nation	Vampire	Opinion

SOLUTION ON PAGE 278

50 COMPASS CLUES

1. Which town is at point 1?
2. Which town is furthest west?
3. Which town is south-west of A?
4. Which town is north of D?
5. Which town is at point 6?

SOLUTION ON PAGE 278

51 DAY DILEMMA

A certain month has five Wednesdays and the third Saturday is the 18th.

1. How many Mondays are in the month?
2. What is the date of the last Sunday of the month?
3. What is the date of the third Wednesday of the month?
4. On what day does the 23rd fall?
5. On what day does the 7th fall?

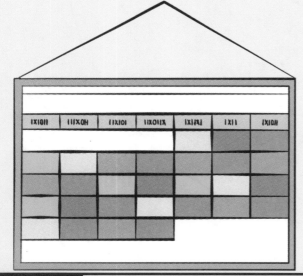

SOLUTION ON PAGE 278

52 THE MAGICIAN

The magician's table is smoking with carbon dioxide gas, produced from dry ice in water. The mystery increases as he taps a smoking metal ball with his wand and places it in a wooden box, which is just big enough to enclose it. The box is placed on a tray for all to see and a few moments later the ball is gone. What was the scientific explanation for this?

CLUES

1. It was a solid metal ball.

2. A small hole at the bottom of the box existed.

3. The ball was 30 times too big to go through the hole.

4. The box was hot.

SOLUTION ON PAGE 278

53 RESIDENCE RIDDLE

The grid represents apartment blocks in a city. Each block has a letter. They are arranged like this: D is just below T, L comes just after K, and Q is between B and M.

Your task is to follow the witness statements below to discover finally where the burglar is hiding.

1. I saw him run out of the apartment just after F.

2. I saw him in the one which is just before the one that is two below that one.

3. I thought I saw him in the one that comes just after the one that is just above that.

4. You must have been mistaken, because I saw him in the one that is just behind the one that is behind the one below that.

WHICH APARTMENT BLOCK IS HE IN?

R	T	Y	U	O
S	D	F	G	H
K	L	Z	X	C
B	Q	M	W	A
E	N	P	J	V

SOLUTION ON PAGE 278

54 SPY CODE

Each field agent needs two code numbers to contact the command centre. What are the two missing one-digit code numbers?

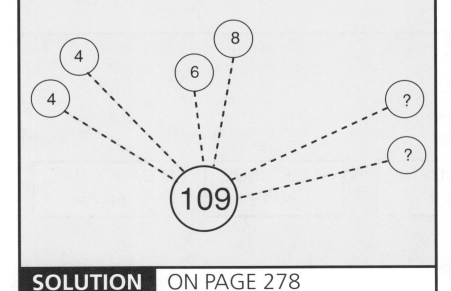

SOLUTION ON PAGE 278

55 DEAD ZONE

The length of crime scene tape needed to go all the way round this area is 18 yards. How many square yards is the area?

SOLUTION ON PAGE 278

56 SWITCH SOLUTION

Which piece will connect up this circuit?

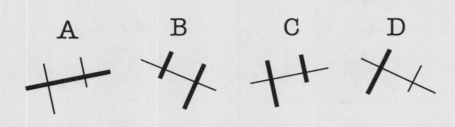 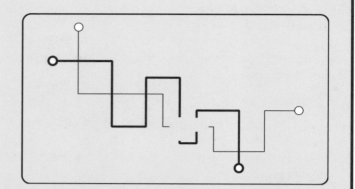

SOLUTION   ON PAGE 278

57 WRONG NUMBER

Find the number that doesn't fit in the sequence:

| 7 | 10 | 14 | 20 | 25 | 32 |

SOLUTION   ON PAGE 278

58 ODD APARTMENT

Which is the odd apartment out in this building?

| ACJK DNEE Ap 21 | AJCK BNEA Ap 28 | JCOK DENA Ap 7 | CAJK NEDE Ap 14 | CAJK DNAE Ap 35 |

SOLUTION   ON PAGE 278

59 HURRY, HIDE!

Can you find which path leads to a door?

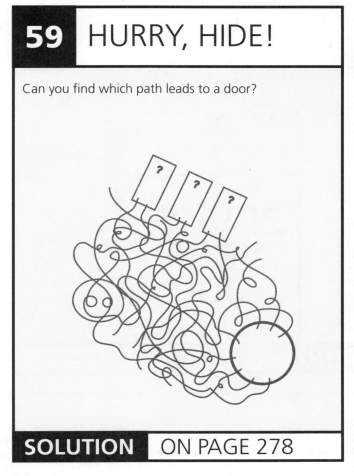

SOLUTION ON PAGE 278

60 WRONG NUMBER

Find the odd number out.

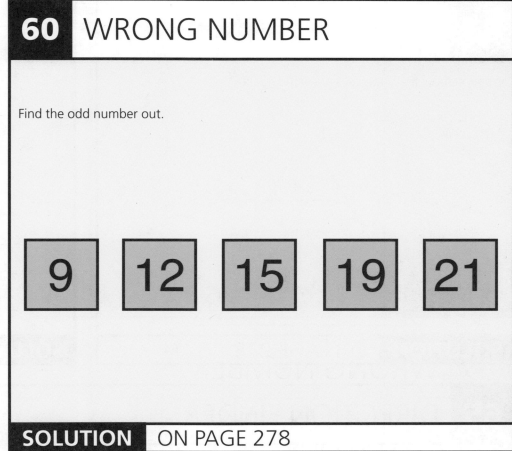

SOLUTION ON PAGE 278

61 SYMBOL SOLUTION

Work out the missing symbol in the sequence.

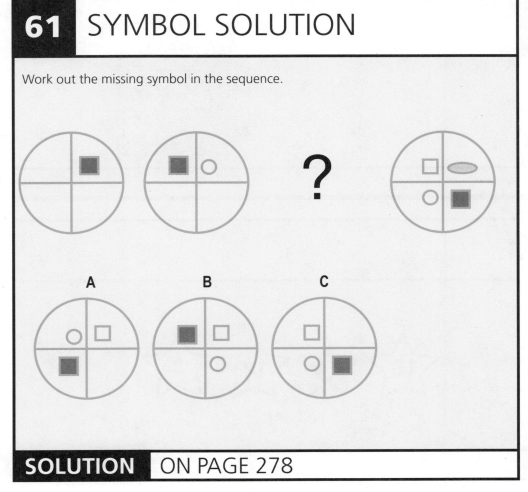

SOLUTION ON PAGE 278

62 NOT FOUND

Look at this list of words and work out which one does not belong with the others.

A) SECRET

B) DISGUISED

C) HIDDEN

D) SPYING

E) CONCEALED

SOLUTION ON PAGE 278

63 SAFE SOLUTION

Work out how many triangles are in this image.

SOLUTION   ON PAGE 278

64 DECODER

What does this message say?

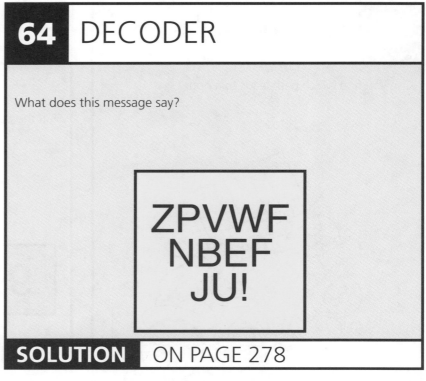

ZPVWF
NBEF
JU!

SOLUTION   ON PAGE 278

65 DIRECTION FINDER

To de-activate this explosive device you must press the correct sequence of buttons until you reach "PRESS".

You must press each button exactly once. Each button is marked with U for up, D for down, L for left and R for right. The number of moves is also on each button.

Which button is the first one you must press?

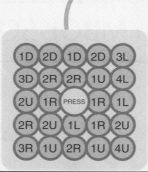

1D	2D	1D	2D	3L
3D	2R	2R	1U	4L
2U	1R	PRESS	1R	1L
2R	2U	1L	1R	2U
3R	1U	2R	1U	4U

SOLUTION   ON PAGE 278

66 CODE CONUNDRUM

Crack the code to find the word:

2   4   3   2   18   4   14   3

SOLUTION   ON PAGE 278

67 PERPLEXING PLATES

Which of these car number plates is the odd one out?

- A FAC 316
- B HDE 548
- C GBH 327
- D AED 451
- E DCA 134

SOLUTION ON PAGE 278

68 COKE CASH

This week NYPD detectives raided a warehouse and unearthed 12 half-pound bags of cocaine. Three months ago these would have had a street value of $250 each, but this month they are worth 50% more.
What is the current street value of the haul?

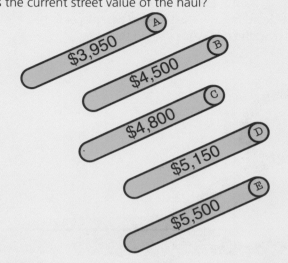

A $3,950
B $4,500
C $4,800
D $5,150
E $5,500

SOLUTION ON PAGE 278

69 MANOR HOUSE

In the English countryside is a traditional manor house. Five staff work there, each of whom has a different hobby and a different rest day.

1. The man who has Tuesday off plays golf but is not the janitor, who is called Clark.
2. Jones is not the butler who plays squash.
3. Wood has Wednesday off and is not the butler or the gardener.
4. James is the cook and does not have Thursdays off; Smith also does not have Thursdays off.
5. Bridge is played on Monday; the chauffeur does not play chess; and James does not have Tuesdays off.

What are their names, how is each employed, what is the pastime of each, and on which day of the week does each have a rest day?

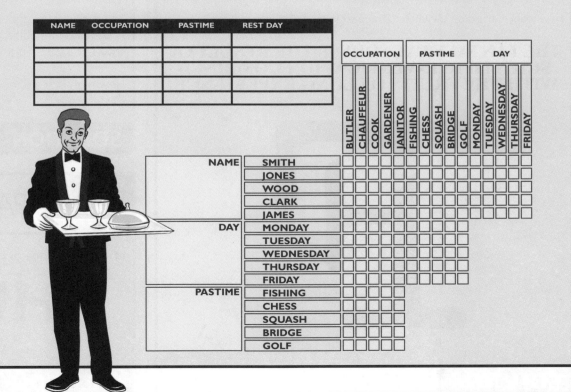

NAME	OCCUPATION	PASTIME	REST DAY

		BUTLER	CHAUFFEUR	COOK	GARDENER	JANITOR	FISHING	CHESS	SQUASH	BRIDGE	GOLF	MONDAY	TUESDAY	WEDNESDAY	THURSDAY	FRIDAY
NAME	SMITH															
	JONES															
	WOOD															
	CLARK															
	JAMES															
DAY	MONDAY															
	TUESDAY															
	WEDNESDAY															
	THURSDAY															
	FRIDAY															
PASTIME	FISHING															
	CHESS															
	SQUASH															
	BRIDGE															
	GOLF															

SOLUTION ON PAGE 278

70 ALL TIED UP

Take an ordinary tea cup and tie it to the handle of a door with a piece of string. Now, can you cut the string in two places without letting the cup fall? Once the string is tied to the door you may not touch it except with the scissors.

You must cut clean through the string in two places.
You may not hold the cup while you do this.

SOLUTION ON PAGE 278

71 TOWN CLOCK

From my window I can see the town clock. Every day I check the clock on my mantelpiece against the time shown on the town clock. It usually agrees; but one morning a strange situation occurred: on my mantelpiece stands my clock and it showed the time as 5 minutes to 9 o'clock.

1 minute later it read 4 minutes to 9 o'clock; 2 minutes later it read 4 minutes to 9 o'clock; 1 minute later it read 5 minutes to 9 o'clock.

At 9 o'clock I suddenly realized what was wrong.

Can you tell what it was?

SOLUTION ON PAGE 278

72 F COUNT

How many times does the letter "f" appear in the following sentence?

THE FANTASY FACTORY IS THE RESULT OF SCIENTIFIC INVESTIGATION COMBINED WITH THE FRUITS OF LONG EXPERIENCE.

SOLUTION ON PAGE 278

73 SEARS TOWER

The national headquarters of Sears Roebuck & Co. in Chicago, Illinois, is the tallest inhabited building in the world. Better known as Sears Tower, it is 225m high plus half its height again.

How high is Sears Tower?

SOLUTION ON PAGE 278

74 JAPAN HOTEL

In a hotel in Nagasaki is a glass door. On the door it says:

PHUSLULq

What does it mean?

SOLUTION ON PAGE 278

75 | CLINK COUNT

A jailer has a large number of prisoners to guard and has to seat them at a number of tables at mealtimes. The regulations state the following seating arrangements:

1. Each table is to seat the same number of prisoners.
2. The number at each table is to be an odd number.

The jailer finds that when he seats the prisoners:
3 per table, he has 2 prisoners left over;
5 per table, he has 4 prisoners left over;
7 per table, he has 6 prisoners left over;
9 per table, he has 8 prisoners left over;
but when he seats them 11 per table
there are none left over.

How many prisoners are there?

SOLUTION | ON PAGE 278

76 | PICK A PATTERN

is to ... as ... is to

A   B   C   D

SOLUTION | ON PAGE 278

77 | SPY CAPER

You are agent 7, on a mission. You need to send a message to base 77 via your laptop computer and a satellite link. However, you need to choose the correct satellite.

Which one do you choose?

SOLUTION | ON PAGE 278

78 CREATIVE CIRCLES

Look along each line and down each column of this shape. Which of the following eight options is the missing square?

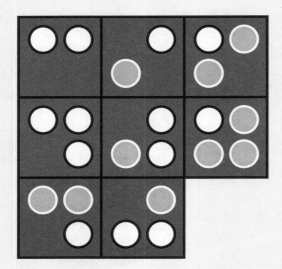

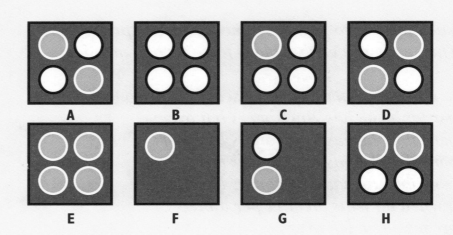

SOLUTION   ON PAGE 278

79 LETTER LOGIC

Join the letters together using straight lines, without crossing over a line, to find the name of an American TV detective.

S   W   N   I

T   O   E   F

J   B   K   E

K   A   S   P

SOLUTION   ON PAGE 279

80 VERY VENOMOUS

There are ten deadly poisons hidden in this square. Can you find them?

```
L X E V N G I X D L Z M P D H H J M P O
Z S K G Y N Y O S W I S X O V Z W A I R A
K Y C W I W I C I N E S R A S F X I V K
C F E O R I Z A R V F I S C Y V C S W K
I K T A P G T T R A D U X O Z I O H X N
M F U E Y O S B R G U K S N N A D C X S
V A C I O P L B J G A Z V I C K T J H U
B C R S I E Z A R R V N S T I H O A I K
U O C I N E K J M B M F S I N R A D N M
Q V Y X N P S U P I E E D N C G S V E Q
I O A L U I T M S S N Y J E C A N F S T
B W N Y X F N L K N I E Y K S R Y I T M
Y W I R M N D O O G S P M O R P H I N E
M V D L A T D O S D I G I T A L I S Q N
V I E N B U C W L N D P E V R T T R T I
Z R O S S P P N L Q Y B I J P R T I S C
E S T U V A G J P B O M H P G E E Y Y S
U X S T R Y C H N I N E M Z R V W R P O
P Y X T J V Z M U I L L A H T H Q S O Y
I S J S B N L L O E V F W Q B W F   N H
```

ACONITINE, ARSENIC, CYANIDE, DIGITALIS,
HYOSCINE, SCOPOLAMINE, MORPHINE
RICIN, STRYCHNINE, THALLIUM

SOLUTION   ON PAGE 279

81 FORMULATION

The numbers on the right are formed from the numbers on the left using the same formula. Find the rule and replace the question mark with a number.

4 ⟶ **13**

7 ⟶ **22**

1 ⟶ **4**

9 ⟶ **?**

SOLUTION ON PAGE 279

82 SHAPES

How many different sections are there in the drawing?

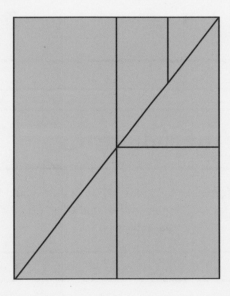

1. How many different sections are there in the drawing?
2. How many triangles are in the drawing?
3. How many rectangles are in the drawing?
4. How many right angles are in the drawing?
5. If the vertical middle line is central, how many similar triangles are there?

SOLUTION ON PAGE 279

83 PARK PUZZLE

	MONKEYS	LLAMAS	LIONS
WILDLIFE PARK A	42	25	16
WILDLIFE PARK B	35	21	14
WILDLIFE PARK C	48	32	10

1. Which park has twice as many monkeys as Park B has llamas?
2. Which park has one quarter of the total lions?
3. At which park does the sum of the llamas and lions total the number of monkeys?
4. Which park has three times as many monkeys as Park A has lions?
5. Which park has twice as many llamas as one of the parks has lions?

SOLUTION ON PAGE 279

84 A IS A

Can you find a word that begins with the letter "A", which is opposite in meaning to the given words?

1. **VANISH**
2. **FORFEIT**
3. **SWEETNESS**
4. **IMAGINARY**
5. **OPPRESSIVE**
6. **BELOW**
7. **CONVICT**
8. **PRESENT**
9. **EXTEND**
10. **IMMATURE**

SOLUTION ON PAGE 279

85 CIRCULAR LOGIC

Calculate the values of the black, white, and shaded circles and the sum of the final set.

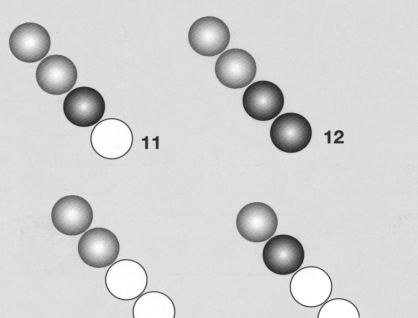

11

12

6

?

SOLUTION ON PAGE 279

86 TEC TOTAL

A Los Angeles private detective has been involved in a number of activities over the past year:

MISSING PERSONS 4

TRACKING 6

COURIER 12

SURVEILLANCE ?

How many surveillance jobs has he had?

SOLUTION ON PAGE 279

87 SQUARE METERS

If the perimeter of a rectangular field was 3000m, what would be the maximum area that you could contain within that perimeter if you could reorganize it into any configuration?

SOLUTION ON PAGE 279

88 FACT & FICTION

The early Roman calendar originated in the city of Rome about 7 to 8 centuries before the Christian era. It was supposedly drawn up by Romulus, brother of Remus, in the February of his 21st year. Today modern historians dispute the validity of this. Do you know why?

SOLUTION ON PAGE 279

89 MOVING WATER UPHILL

You are given a dish of water, a beaker, a cork, a pin, and a match. You have to get all the water into the beaker. You cannot lift the dish of water or tilt it in any way, and you cannot use any other implement to move the water into the beaker. How is this achieved?

SOLUTION ON PAGE 279

90 CIRCULAR LOGIC

Calculate the values of the black, white, and shaded circles and the sum of the final set.

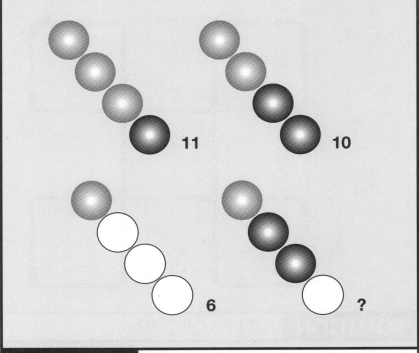

SOLUTION ON PAGE 279

91 MYSTERIES OF TIME

A young man proclaims, "The day before yesterday I was 17, but I will be 19 this year." Is this possible?

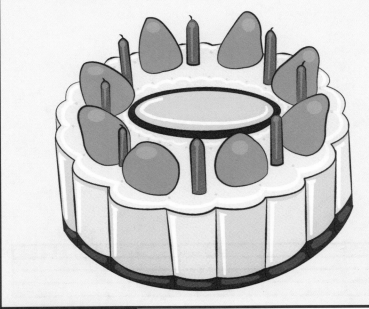

SOLUTION ON PAGE 279

92 LOGICAL THINKING WITH MATCHSTICKS

By removing four matchsticks can you rearrange those left so that the top and bottom lines and the left and right columns all still add up to nine?

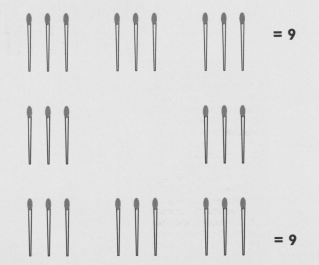

Only the most devious of lateral thinkers will find a second way to do this. Can you?

SOLUTION ON PAGE 279

93   MORE MATCHSTICK TRICKERY!

a) By moving just two matchsticks, can you increase the number of squares by two?
b) By moving one more matchstick, can you increase the square count by another two?

SOLUTION   ON PAGE 279

94   INTERGALACTIC INGENUITY

Five pairs of husband and wife aliens arrive for an intergalactic meeting on Earth. For ease of recognition, the males are known by the letter M followed by an odd number and the females by F and an even number. Each pair has different distinguishing features and has prepared a different subject for discussion. They arrive in different types of spacecraft and dock in a set of five bays. The pairs sit in five double seats in the auditorium.

1. M1 is preparing his speech on time travel and has arrived in a warp distorter.
2. The mind-reading couple who have four arms each have parked their nebula accelerator between the space oscillator and the astro carrier.
3. F6, in the seat next to the left-end pair, says to the alien next to her, "My husband M3 and I have noticed that you have three legs."
4. F4 admires the galaxy freighter owned by the pair who each have three eyes, who are in the next seats.
5. The husband of F8 is turning his papers on time travel with12 fingers.
6. M5, in the middle pair of seats, says to F10 in the next pair of seats, "The pair with webbed feet on your other side have an astro carrier."
7. M7 and F2 are studying their papers on anti-gravity. The husband of F6 is studying his papers on nuclear fission.

Who is the wife of M9 and who is the male speaker on nuclear fission?

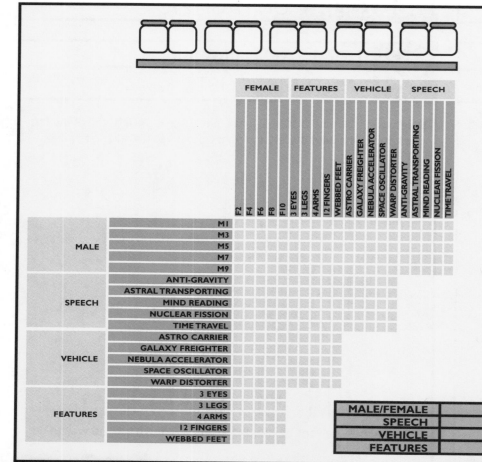

MALE/FEMALE					
SPEECH					
VEHICLE					
FEATURES					

SOLUTION   ON PAGE 279

95 SEARCHING SEGMENTS

Place the 12 segment links below over the triangular grid in such a way that each link symbol on the grid is covered by an identical symbol. The connecting segments must not be rotated. Not all the connecting lines will be covered.

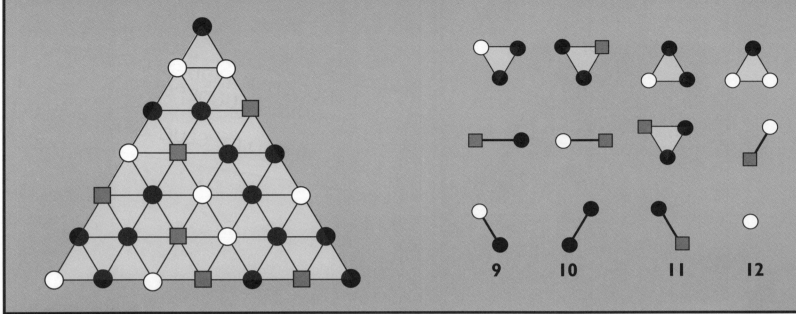

SOLUTION ON PAGE 279

96 SEQUENCE SOLUTION

Which shape comes next in this sequence?

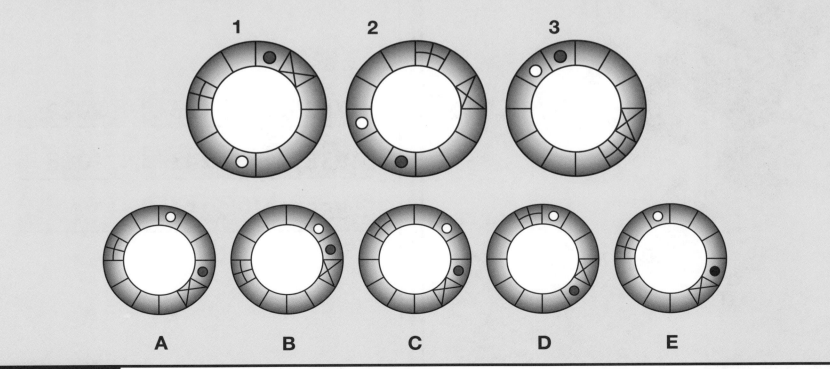

SOLUTION ON PAGE 279

97 NOT SO SCIENTIFIC

What is it that you can see with the naked eye, seems to have no weight and yet the more of them you put into an empty container, the lighter the container becomes? Two answers are possible.

SOLUTION   ON PAGE 279

98 STRANGER DANGER

What word in each list below does not belong?

1. CLANDESTINE HIDDEN DETECTIVE COVERT UNDERCOVER

2. BULLET PELLET SLUG DART SHELL

SOLUTION   ON PAGE 279

99 LINKS

What number should replace the question mark?

7628	5126	3020
9387	6243	1088
8553	2254	?

SOLUTION   ON PAGE 279

100 NUMBER LOGIC

What number should replace the question mark?

A	B	C	D	E
8	2	6	3	4
5	3	4	2	3
9	1	7	3	5
7	6	8	3	?

SOLUTION ON PAGE 279

101 PASSWORD

Below are the names of some CIA agents, and their undercover internet passwords.

What is agent Rickard's password?

NAME	PASSWORDS
Agent Sherman	1.14.19.8.5.18.13
Agent Dawson	15.14.4.1.23.19
Agent Jewkes	5. 9.10.5.23.11
Agent Rickard	?

SOLUTION ON PAGE 279

102 TAKE A TILE

Look at the pattern of tiles. Which of the following tiles replaces the question mark?

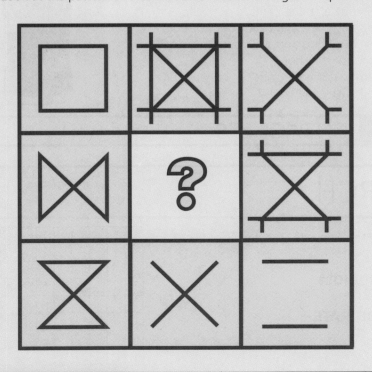

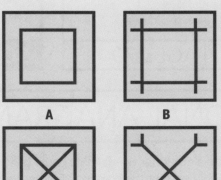

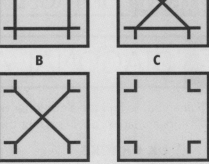

SOLUTION ON PAGE 279

103 FORMULATION

The numbers on the right are formed from the numbers on the left using the same formula in each question. Find the rule and replace the question mark with a number.

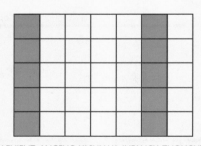

8 ⟶ 23

3 ⟶ 13

11 ⟶ 29

2 ⟶ ?

SOLUTION ON PAGE 279

104 ANTONYMS

Can you find a word beginning with the letter "H", which is opposite in meaning to the following?

1. EXCEPTIONAL
2. DIGNIFY
3. DOCILE
4. DESPAIRING
5. VILLAIN
6. SERIOUS
7. FRIENDLY
8. FREE
9. PROSPERITY
10. SATISFIED

SOLUTION ON PAGE 279

105 COLUMNS

Rearrange the order of the given words and place one word on each row of the grid. If the words are in the correct order, the name of a country can be read down each of the shaded columns. What are the countries?

LENIENT ANGELIC YASHMAK INFANCY THOUGHT

SOLUTION ON PAGE 279

106 JUNK FOOD DILEMMA

In break-time at a shop children can buy chips, candy and soda. Two more children buy candy only than chips only. Thirty-seven children do not buy any candy at all. Two more children buy both chips and soda but no candy than candy only. A total of 60 children buy soda, but only nine of them have soda only. Twelve children buy chips only. One more child buys candy only than candy and soda only, and three more buy both chips and candy but no soda than buy chips and soda but no candy.

1. How many children buy all three items?
2. How many children buy chips and candy but no soda?
3. How many children buy chips and soda but no candy?
4. How many children visit the shop?
5. How many children do not have chips?
6. How many children have candy only?

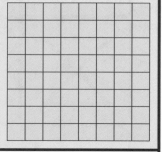

SOLUTION ON PAGE 279

107 DIAGONAL ANAGRAM SEARCH

Solve each anagram to find the eight-letter words that should be written along the line opposite. The names of two animals will appear reading down each of the diagonals (corner to corner).

UK CRACKS   ANGEL TOE   FED IDIOM

REBEL CAR   RAPID SEA   POOR RATE

A NICE SUN   ALL FEWER

SOLUTION ON PAGE 279

108 CELTIC CAPER

SOLUTION ON PAGE 279

109 TEC TOTAL

If a detective had worked the following hours on these days, how many hours had he worked on Wednesday and Thursday?

SUNDAY=7

MONDAY=13

TUESDAY=6

WEDNESDAY=?

THURSDAY=?

SOLUTION ON PAGE 280

110 STONE SOLUTION

You are on a jungle mission when you reach a river. The only way to cross it is by carefully stepping from stone to stone, from one side to the other. Pick the wrong stones and you'll fall in. The river is full of crocodiles.

Starting at A, and stepping on only one stone from each row, which sequence of stones should you choose?

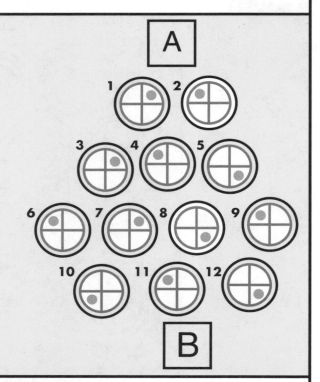

SOLUTION ON PAGE 280

111 DECODER

You have been sent this coded message.

What does it say?

MLWMZYZ VSG MLRHHRN WMZ
MIFGVI LG VHZY.

SOLUTION ON PAGE 280

112 TOXIC TIPPLE

One of the glasses of wine below is the odd one out. It also contains a deadly poison.

Which one should you not drink?

RESSD
1

ACERVOOT
2

STEV
3

TOSRURES
4

CELACKEN
5

SOLUTION ON PAGE 280

113   KERCHING!

In each vertical column the letters add up to 10. What letter must you put in the empty box to make that column equal 10 and open the lock?

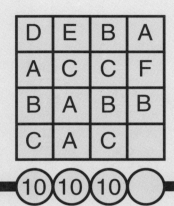

D	E	B	A
A	C	C	F
B	A	B	B
C	A	C	

⑩ ⑩ ⑩ ◯

SOLUTION   ON PAGE 280

114   CODE CONUNDRUM

Each field agent needs a code number to contact the command centre. What is the missing two-digit code number?

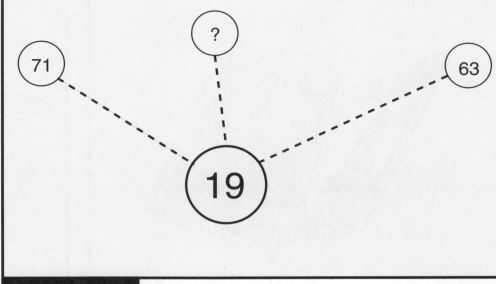

71   ?   63

19

SOLUTION   ON PAGE 280

115   DOG DELIGHT

There is a somewhat confusing situation at the dog show this year. Four brothers – Andy, Bill, Colin and Donald – each enter two dogs, and each has named his dogs after two of his brothers. Consequently, there are two dogs named Andy, two named Bill, two named Colin and two named Donald.

Of the eight dogs, three are corgis, three labradors and two dalmatians. None of the four brothers owns two dogs of the same breed. No two dogs of the same breed have the same name. Neither of Andy's dogs is named Donald and neither of Colin's dogs is named Andy. No corgi is named Andy and no labrador is named Donald. Bill does not own a labrador.

Who are the owners of the dalmatians and what are the dalmatians' names?

SOLUTION   ON PAGE 280

116   TALL STORY

Move from square to square, including diagonally to discover the name of a famous Chicago landmark.

C	R	S	E	R
Y	D	R	A	E
T	S	T	O	W

SOLUTION   ON PAGE 280

117 SPY PUZZLE

At the start of the year, the CIA had a total of 613 field operatives. In January they recruited 30 new officers, in February 15, and in March 23 more. However, during January, 17 moved to other departments, 31 left, and 2 swapped jobs with FBI agents.

How many operatives did the CIA have at the beginning of April?

SOLUTION   ON PAGE 280

118 CHEERS!

One of the glasses of wine below is the odd one out. It also contains a deadly poison.

Which one should you not drink?

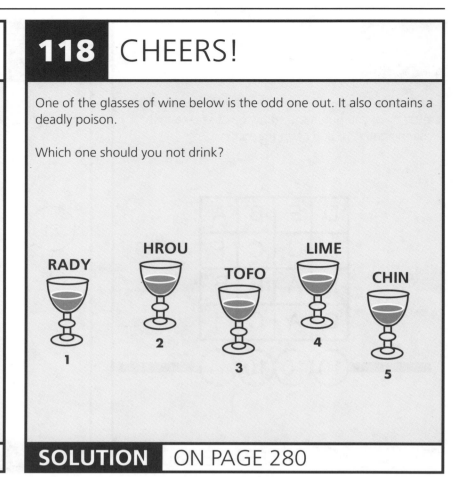

SOLUTION   ON PAGE 280

119 SATELLITE SOLUTION

You are agent F, on a mission. You need to send a message to base S via your laptop computer and a satellite link. However, you need to choose the correct satellite.

Which one do you choose?

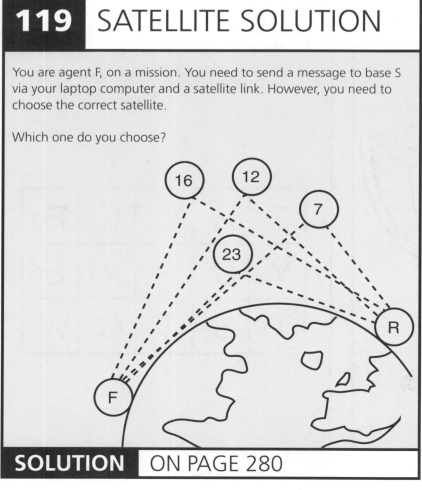

SOLUTION   ON PAGE 280

120 ODD SHAPE

Which symbol does not belong in this sequence?

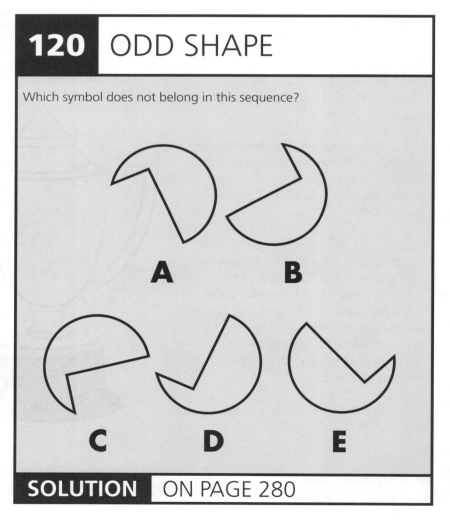

SOLUTION   ON PAGE 280

121 CODE SOLUTION

Complete this code sequence by adding the missing number.

| 3 | 5 | 9 | ? | 33 | 65 |

SOLUTION ON PAGE 280

122 SLUG SOLVER

Which bullet is an exact copy of bullet A?

SOLUTION ON PAGE 280

123 PISTOL POSER

Below is a pistol and five magazines.
Which one fits this pistol?

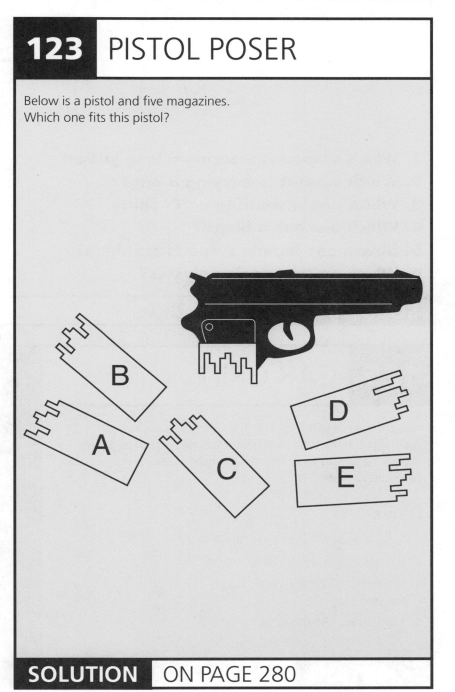

SOLUTION ON PAGE 280

124 IDENTITY PARADE

Spend two minutes looking at this line-up of suspects, then cover up the diagram. Do not refer to it while you answer the questions.

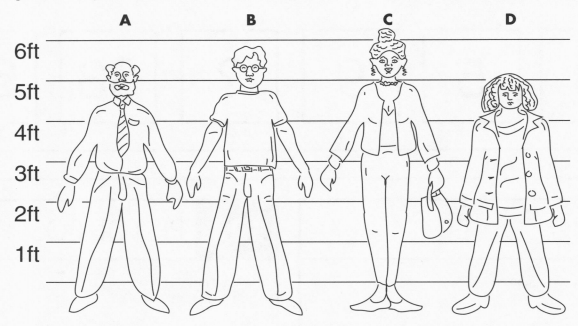

1. **Which suspect is wearing a long jacket?**
2. **Which suspect is carrying a bag?**
3. **Which one is wearing a "T" shirt?**
4. **Which one has a beard?**
5. **How many female suspects are there?**
6. **Which one is wearing glasses?**
7. **Which suspect is wearing a necktie?**
8. **Which suspect is wearing a skirt?**
9. **Who is wearing a belt?**
10. **Who is the tallest?**
11. **Which one is wearing a necklace?**
12. **Which woman is wearing her hair up?**

SOLUTION ON PAGE 280

125 CAR GRID

You are in a car that is parked and facing east on a straight road. You set off in the direction of the facing road and after some time driving you finish up 2.7 miles to the west of where you started. How?

Clues

1. It is not a car with hovering capabilities.

2. It is not on a trailer or being towed.

3. You have not gone around the world.

4. You cannot turn the car around.

SOLUTION ON PAGE 280

126 CONSTELLATIONS

Each clue is the Latin name for a constellation in the night sky. Your task is to enter the English name in the grid provided at the appropriate number.

Across

3 Sextans
5 Sagitta
6 Crater
8 Camelopardis
10 Lupus
11 Vela
13 Gemini
14 Aquila
16 Aries
17 Vulpecula
18 Norma

Down

1 Lepus
2 Draco
3 Dorado
4 Taurus
7 Reticulum
9 Pisces
10 Cetus
12 Cygnus
13 Mensa
15 Leo

SOLUTION ON PAGE 280

127 FRONT FOOT FORWARD

A man's right foot was facing due north and his left foot after one pace was pointing south. How was this possible?

Clues

1. The one pace was taken in the direction of the right foot and he did not turn in mid-stride.

2. His feet both pointed in the same direction.

3. His right foot had not been twisted around when it had been initially planted on the ground.

SOLUTION ON PAGE 280

128 TRIANGLES

Using only seven straight lines, can you draw a shape that includes 11 non-overlapping triangles?

SOLUTION ON PAGE 280

129 LOGICAL DEDUCTIONS OF WHO OR WHAT AM I?

Who am I?

Sometimes I am one before I'm one.
When I'm under one I, and others like me are given the same name. Males and females have different titles.
When I am over one but remain young these names change. Between the ages of one and two males and females can also be given the same name.
When I am fully grown I am called another name.
All through my life people give me a name that is personal to me.
I am eight and male.

SOLUTION ON PAGE 280

130 LOGICAL DEDUCTIONS OF WHO OR WHAT AM I?

Who am I?

I am deceased, but my name and actions are well known.
I was a leader of my people but I never had a crown.
I was often upset with my people and they were sometimes upset by me.
I passed on messages and rules.
I warned people of death and destruction.
My most famous work was in stone.

SOLUTION ON PAGE 280

131 COOL CORPSE

After death, the human body cools at a rate of 1.5 degrees F per hour from the normal 98.4 degrees.

A pathologist took the temperature of a body at a scene of crime and it was 93.9 degrees F.

How long had this person been dead?

SOLUTION ON PAGE 280

132 WORD MATCH

1. PARIS *is to* FRANCE as LONDON *is to*:
   JAPAN   AMERICA   GREECE   ENGLAND

2. NILE *is to* EGYPT as MAIN *is to*:
   AUSTRIA   FRANCE   ENGLAND GERMANY

3. TEN *is to* PENTAGON as EIGHT *is to*:
   HEXAGON   OCTAGON   SQUARE   TRIANGLE

4. FLOOD *is to* RAIN as DULL *is to*:
   SUN   CLOUD   SNOW   ICE

5. HAND *is to* WRIST as FOOT *is to*:
   KNEE   ARM   CALF   ANKLE

6. GREEN *is to* EMERALD as BLUE *is to*:
   DIAMOND   SAPPHIRE   RUBY   GARNET

7. RABBIT *is to* BUCK as TURKEY *is to*:
   STAG   COCK   ROOSTER GANDER

8. IRIS *is to* EYE as CILIA *is to*:
   HAIR   SKIN   BONES   TEETH

9. IO *is to* JUPITER as GANYMEDE *is to*:
   MERCURY   SATURN   VENUS   URANUS

10. CALORIE *is to* ENERGY as LUMEN *is to*:
    ELECTRICITY PRESSURE   LIGHT   HUMIDITY

SOLUTION ON PAGE 280

133 MOUSE MOVES

A square cage consists of 216 open chambers. An electronic robot mouse is placed in the bottom right-hand front chamber.
You are able to operate the mouse by remote control, moving it three chambers to the right or left and two chambers up or down.

Are you able to get the mouse into the central chamber, and if so, what is the minimum number of moves by which this can be achieved?

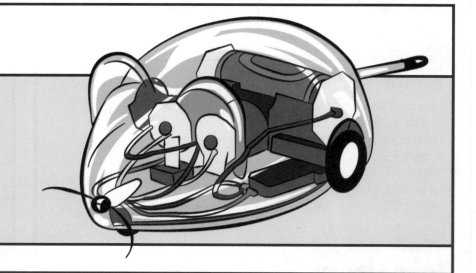

SOLUTION ON PAGE 280

134 NUMBER LOGIC

What numbers should replace the question mark?

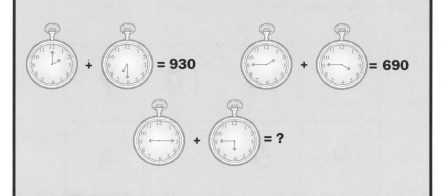

135 HIDDEN WORDS

Read the sentence carefully to discover a series of associated words hidden in it. The connected words will be found by joining the end of one word somewhere in the sentence with the beginning of the next word. What are the connected words?

Please will all staff leave any extra bags in front of the coach as luggage was placed behind it and forgotten last time, and this was not realized until we arrived at Oslo customs.

SOLUTION   ON PAGE 280

136 THREE SQUARES

Look at the group of three squares. They have a certain feature which is shared by only one of the groups of three squares below. What is it, and which group matches?

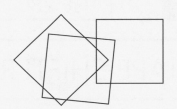

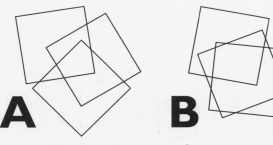

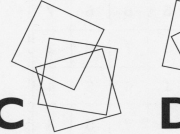

A   **B**

C   **D**

SOLUTION   ON PAGE 280

137 BARRELS OF FUN

A wine merchant has six barrels of wine and beer containing
30 gallons
32 gallons
36 gallons
38 gallons
40 gallons
62 gallons

Five barrels are filled with wine and one with beer. The first customer purchases two barrels of wine; the second customer purchases twice as much wine as the first customer.

Which barrel contains beer?

SOLUTION   ON PAGE 280

SOLUTION   ON PAGE 280

138 HIDDEN CONNECTIONS

The following words have a hidden connection. What is it?

DISPLAYED DRAMATICALLY FULFILMENT SHOWERING

SOLUTION   ON PAGE 280

140 STUDY TIME

Three college students – Anne, Bess and Candice – each study four subjects. Two of them study physics; two study algebra; two study English; two study history; two study French; two study Japanese.

Anne: if she studies algebra then she also takes history;
  if she studies history she does not take English;
  if she studies English she does not take Japanese.

Candice: if she studies French she does not take algebra;
  if she does not study algebra she studies Japanese;
  if she studies Japanese she does not take English.

Bess: if she studies English she also takes Japanese;
  if she studies Japanese she does not take algebra;
  if she studies algebra she does not take French.

What do you know about these three students?

	ANNE	BESS	CANDICE
PHYSICS			
ALGEBRA			
ENGLISH			
HISTORY			
FRENCH			
JAPANESE			

SOLUTION   ON PAGE 280

139 NUMBER PLACEMENT

The numbers 4–16 have already been inserted into the grid, almost – but not quite – at random. Following just two simple rules, where would you place the numbers 1, 2 and 3 in the grid?

	14	10	7
9	6		4
16		13	11
12	8	5	15

SOLUTION   ON PAGE 280

141 SHAPE SHIFTER

Divide these two grids into FOUR identical shapes. The sum of the numbers in each section must give the total shown.

Total 45

3	6	3	4	4	6
4	4	7	2	8	3
5	8	5	5	6	7
6	5	3	7	8	2
8	3	1	6	5	4
2	7	8	7	5	3

SOLUTION   ON PAGE 280

142 WORD STEPPING

Start with a word on the top line, move down, sideways, diagonally, or up to the second word, then tack the next word on the end to form a new or compound word, and so on. Use 16 words to form 15 compound words.

Eg. Whim - Per
Per - Son

Whim	Break	Sup	Penny	Currant
Fast	Per	Piece	Bun	Weight
Net	Son	Time	Meal	Bath
Her	Step	Table	Cock	Pit
Father	Ring	Value	Ball	Boy
Let	Worm	Screw	Cap	Size

SOLUTION ON PAGE 280

143 WORD LOGIC

What word has a similar meaning to the first word and rhymes with the second word?

1.	FRUIT	—	GATE
2.	STOPPER	—	FORK
3.	SPHERE	—	WALL
4.	INSTRUMENT	—	CARP
5.	GROOVE	—	BLOT
6.	PRICE	—	LOST
7.	LEAN	—	SHIN
8.	LINK	—	FOND
9.	FACE	—	TILE
10.	LOAN	—	SEND

SOLUTION ON PAGE 280

144 FORMULATION

The numbers on the right are formed from the numbers on the left using the same formula in each question. Find the rule and replace the question mark with a number.

18 ⟶ 15

20 ⟶ 16

6 ⟶ 9

14 ⟶ ?

SOLUTION ON PAGE 280

145 ANIMAL FARM

A farmer keeps only four types of animals. He has a total of 560 animals. If he had 10 sheep less he would have twice as many sheep as he has cows. If he had 10 cows less he would have three cows for every pig, and he has two and one half pigs to every horse.

1. How many pigs does he have?

2. How many horses does he have?

3. If he swaps 75% of his cows for 7 sheep per cow, how many animals will he have in total?

4. How many sheep will he have after the swap?

SOLUTION ON PAGE 280

146 SYMBOL SOLUTION

What numbers should replace the symbols in this grid if only the numbers 1 to 7 can be used?

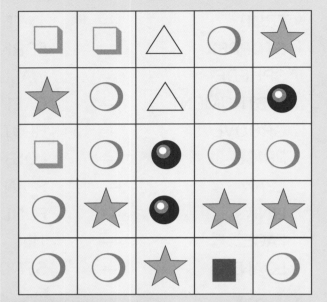

SOLUTION   ON PAGE 280

147 NUMBER LOGIC

What numbers should replace the question marks in the series below?

1.	7	9	16	25	41	?		
2.	4	14	34	74	?			
3.	2	3	5	5	9	7	14	?	?
4.	6	9	15	27	?			
5.	11	7	−1	−17	?			
6.	8	15	26	43	?			
7.	3.5	4	7	14	49	?		

SOLUTION   ON PAGE 280

148 MATHS MYSTERY

What number is missing from this number grid?

A	B	C	D	E
7	5	3	4	8
9	8	8	8	8
6	4	9	3	5
8	3	6	?	9

SOLUTION   ON PAGE 280

149 WATCH IT!

What number should replace the question mark?

 +  = 174

 +  = 993

 −  = ?

SOLUTION   ON PAGE 281

150 DOES IT ADD UP?

Two mothers and two daughters went shopping for new dresses for a wedding celebration. They each returned with a new dress, but they had only bought three dresses. How can this be correct?

SOLUTION ON PAGE 281

151 NUMBER NONSENSE

What number should replace the question mark?

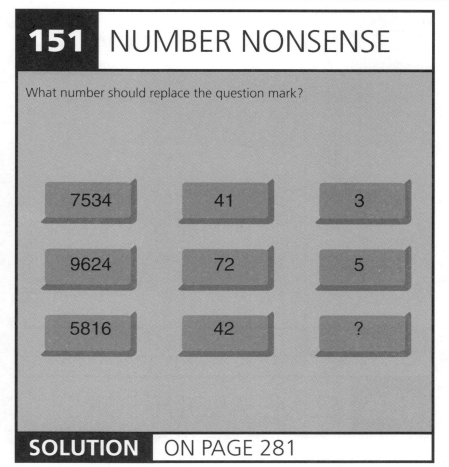

7534	41	3
9624	72	5
5816	42	?

SOLUTION ON PAGE 281

152 SHAPER SHIFTER

Divide this grid into four identical shapes. The sum of the numbers contained within each of the shapes must give a total of 120.

8	7	6	8	7	12	9	1
7	12	7	6	4	3	2	14
8	9	7	8	5	7	11	1
8	8	10	7	6	16	10	1
4	9	13	4	12	2	15	6
8	5	2	2	4	9	8	15
6	9	8	14	14	8	2	1
9	6	10	5	12	1	5	17

SOLUTION ON PAGE 281

153 GRID ENIGMA

The values of grids A and B are given. What is the value of the grid C?

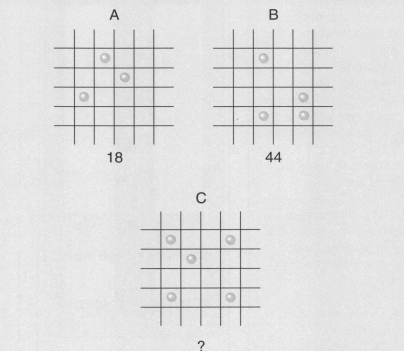

A   B

18   44

C

?

SOLUTION ON PAGE 281

154 MATHS MYSTERY

Can you calculate the number missing in the figure below? Each number is used once only and is not reversed.

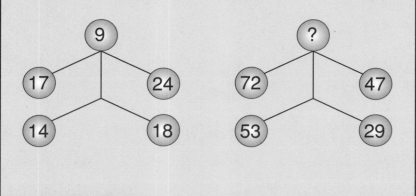

SOLUTION   ON PAGE 281

156 SUMS ABOUT SONS

A woman has two sons, Graham and Frederick. Frederick is three times as old as Graham. If you square Frederick's age you arrive at the same total as when you cube Graham's age. If you subtract Graham's age from Frederick's you arrive at the number of steps in the path to the family's front door. If you add Graham's age to Frederick's you arrive at the number of palisades in the family's fence. If you multiply their ages you arrive at the number of bricks in the family's front wall.

If you add these last three numbers together you have the family's house number, which is 297.

How old are Graham and Frederick?

SOLUTION   ON PAGE 281

155 ROUTE FINDER

Starting at the top number, find a route that goes down one level each time until you reach the bottom number.

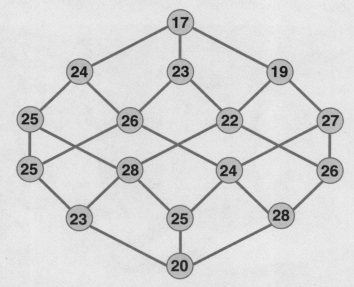

1. Can you find a route where the sum of the numbers is 130?
2. Can you find two separate routes that give a total of 131?
3. What is the highest possible score and what route/s do you follow?
4. What is the lowest possible score and what route/s do you follow?
5. How many ways are there to score 136 and what route/s do you follow?

SOLUTION   ON PAGE 281

157 CIRCULAR LOGIC

What is the value of the last string? Black, white and shaded circles have different values.

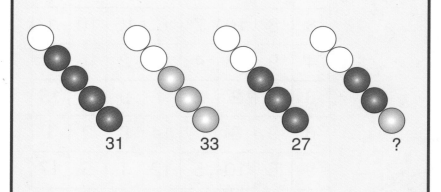

SOLUTION   ON PAGE 281

158 LOGICAL DEDUCTIONS OF WHO OR WHAT AM I?

What am I?

I have been around for over a thousand years, but my appearance and format has changed with time.

I have been mechanical in construction in one form up to the present day and in electromechanical form since the 1930s in my current form.

I have been miniaturized in my current form and I am used by almost all schoolchildren and adults alike.

You have counted on me to help you for years.

SOLUTION ON PAGE 281

159 FUNNY FORMULA

The numbers on the right are formed from the numbers on the left using the same formula in each question. Find the rule and replace the question mark with a number.

10 ⟶ 12

19 ⟶ 30

23 ⟶ 38

14 ⟶ ?

SOLUTION ON PAGE 281

160 MATHS MYSTERY

Start at the top-left circle and move clockwise. Calculate the number that replaces the question mark.

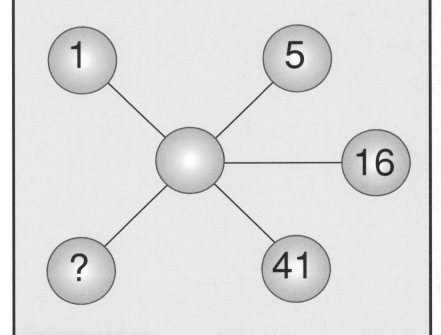

SOLUTION ON PAGE 281

161 THE TRAIN DRIVER

You are driving a train. It stops at Milton Keynes and 25 people board it. It then goes to Leicester where 55 people get on and 43 get off. The next stop is Nottingham where three people get off and only one gets on. The train continues its journey, making Doncaster its next stop, where 19 get on and 13 get off. The next stop is York, which is the final destination. The driver then gets off the train also, and looks in the mirror in the washrooms. What colour eyes does the driver have?

No clues for this one. It should be easy.

SOLUTION ON PAGE 281

162 AMAZING DISCOVERY

SOLUTION ON PAGE 281

163 SPY SOLUTION

Here are four actors who have played James Bond. Which is the odd one out?

DAVID NIVEN

SEAN CONNERY

ROGER MOORE

TIMOTHY DALTON

SOLUTION ON PAGE 281

164 NO BANG

To de-activate this explosive device you must press the correct sequence of exactly five buttons until you reach "PRESS". You must press each button once only. Each button is marked with U for up, D for down, L for left and R for right. The number of moves is also on each button.

Which button is the first one you must press?

SOLUTION ON PAGE 281

165 STIFF ANSWER

Join eight letters together using straight lines, without crossing over a line, to find the name of a cop from a 1960s American TV show.

SOLUTION ON PAGE 281

166 CUBE DIAGONALS

Two diagonals have been drawn on two faces of the cube. Using logical reasoning and lateral thinking, can you work out the angle between the two diagonals AB and AC?

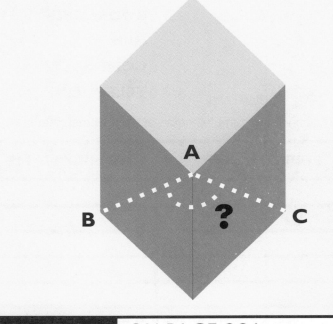

SOLUTION ON PAGE 281

167 HOUSEHOLD ITEMS

Five women each purchase a household item for use in a different room in their house.

1. Mrs Simpson does not keep her item in the bedroom.
2. Amy has a television; Mrs Griggs has a hi-fi.
3. Kylie does not keep her item in the bedroom.
4. Clara does not have a telephone.
5. Mrs Williams does not keep her item in the kitchen.
6. Kylie keeps hers in the conservatory.
7. Michelle has a bookcase; Mrs Dingle has a computer.
8. Michelle does not keep hers in the living room.
9. Mrs Pringle keeps hers in the study; Roxanne keeps hers in the kitchen.

		FAMILY NAME					ITEM					ROOM				
		WILLIAMS	SIMPSON	PRINGLE	DINGLE	GRIGGS	TELEVISION	BOOKCASE	HI-FI	COMPUTER	TELEPHONE	LIVING ROOM	KITCHEN	CONSERVATORY	BEDROOM	STUDY
FIRST NAME	KYLIE															
	AMY															
	CLARA															
	MICHELLE															
	ROXANNE															
ROOM	LIVING ROOM															
	KITCHEN															
	CONSERVATORY															
	BEDROOM															
	STUDY															
ITEM	TELEVISION															
	BOOKCASE															
	HI-FI															
	COMPUTER															
	TELEPHONE															

Can you work out the full name of each woman, her item and where she keeps it?

FIRST NAME	FAMILY NAME	ROOM	ITEM

SOLUTION ON PAGE 281

168 THE GEARBOX

The gearbox below consists of four gearwheels with intermeshing gears and two pulley belts, or drive belts. If the large 48-tooth gearwheel rotates exactly 10 times in a clockwise direction, in what direction will the pointer be facing on the gearwheel at the bottom of the arrangement, and how many times will it rotate?

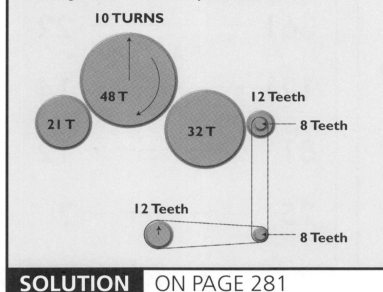

10 TURNS

21 T **48 T** **32 T** **12 Teeth** **8 Teeth**

12 Teeth **8 Teeth**

SOLUTION ON PAGE 281

169 SPOT THE SHAPE

Each of the nine squares in the grid marked 1A to 3C should incorporate all the lines and symbols which are shown in the squares of the same letter and number immediately above and to the left. For example, 2B should incorporate all the lines and symbols that are in 2 and B.

One of the squares is incorrect. Which is it?

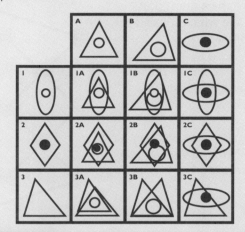

SOLUTION ON PAGE 281

170 FATHERS AND DAUGHTERS

A group of friends get together with their daughters for the evening.

1. John is 52 years old and his daughter is not called Eve.
2. Len has a daughter aged 21 years, and Betty is three years older than Eve.
3. Kevin is 53 years old and Diana is 19 years old.
4. Eve is 18 years old, and Nick has a daughter called Carol.
5. Alison is 20 years old and her father is called John.
6. Kevin has a daughter aged 19 years, and Eve's father is called Malcolm.
7. Malcolm is three years older than Nick.

		FATHER'S AGE					DAUGHTER'S AGE					DAUGHTER				
		50	51	52	53	54	17	18	19	20	21	ALISON	BETTY	CAROL	DIANA	EVE
FATHER	JOHN															
	KEVIN															
	LEN															
	MALCOLM															
	NICK															
DAUGHTER	ALISON															
	BETTY															
	CAROL															
	DIANA															
	EVE															
DAUGHTER'S AGE	17															
	18															
	19															
	20															
	21															

FATHER	DAUGHTER	FATHER'S AGE	DAUGHTER'S AGE

SOLUTION ON PAGE 281

171 ROUTE FINDER

Starting at the top number, find a route that goes down one level each time until you reach the bottom number.

1. Can you find a route where the sum of the numbers is 216?

2. Can you find two separate routes that give a total of 204?

3. What is the highest possible score and what route/s do you follow?

4. What is the lowest possible score and what route/s do you follow?

5. How many ways are there to score 211 and what route/s do you follow?

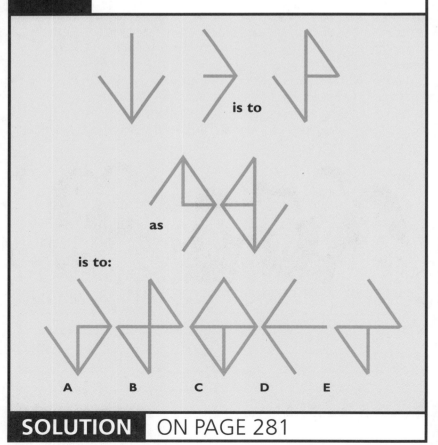

SOLUTION ON PAGE 281

172 FORMULATION

The numbers on the right are formed from the numbers on the left using the same formula in each question. Find the rule and replace the question mark with a number.

361 ⟶ **22**

121 ⟶ **14**

81 ⟶ **12**

25 ⟶ **?**

SOLUTION ON PAGE 281

173 LUCID LINES

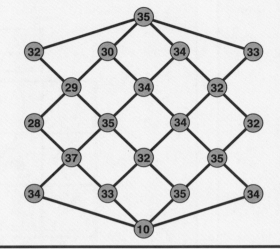

is to

as

is to:

A   B   C   D   E

SOLUTION ON PAGE 281

174 TRYING TRIANGLES

What is the smallest number of segments of equal area and shape that the rectangle can be divided into so that each segment contains the same number of triangles?

SOLUTION ON PAGE 281

175 SUSPICIOUS CIRCLES

Which of these circles is the odd one out?

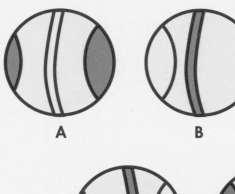

A   B   C

D   E

SOLUTION ON PAGE 281

176 WEIRD WITNESS

Below are two versions of a witness statement. Can you find 10 differences between them?

STATEMENT OF WITNESS

At around eleven thirty I was sitting on a wall by the supermarket in Logan Street. I saw the car slowly pull into the car park and stop over by the fence. Three guys got out. One was a tall black guy in a dark blue suit. The other two were white. One had a beard, and wore a light grey suit, the other wore a brown leather jacket. By the door of the bar they stopped to talk to an older guy with grey hair. He seemed to be in charge. They talked for a few minutes and then they all walked into Garfield Street. I watched them until they turned right into the park.

A

STATEMENT OF WITNESS

At around eleven thirty, I was sitting on a wall by the supermarket in Logan Street. I saw the car slowly pull in to the car park and stop over by the fence. Three guys got out. One was a tall black guy in a dark blue suit. The other two wore white. One had a beard and wore a light gray suit, the other wore a brown leather jacket. By the door of the bar they stopped to talk to an older guy with grey hair. He seemed to be in charge They talked for a few minute and them they all walked into Garfeld Street. I watched them until they tuned right in to the park.

B

SOLUTION ON PAGE 281

177 HOW TO TRICK THE GENIE?

The king had a magic lamp that contained a genie. He also had a beautiful daughter who loved Aladdin, but the king did not like Aladdin and did not wish them to marry. He did not wish to upset his daughter, so one day he rubbed on the lamp and devised a plan with the genie. The king said he would call upon Aladdin and his daughter and seek a test of worthiness from the genie for Aladdin. They would all have to abide by the results. Aladdin was passing by when he heard the king and the genie planning the event. The genie said, "I will produce two envelopes for Aladdin to choose his fate. We will tell him that one contains the words 'Get Married' and the other will contain the words 'Banished Forever.' Aladdin must choose one envelope, but I will make sure that both envelopes have 'Banished Forever' written on them."

How did Aladdin trick the genie and the king?

SOLUTION ON PAGE 281

178 AMAZINGLY COMPLICATED

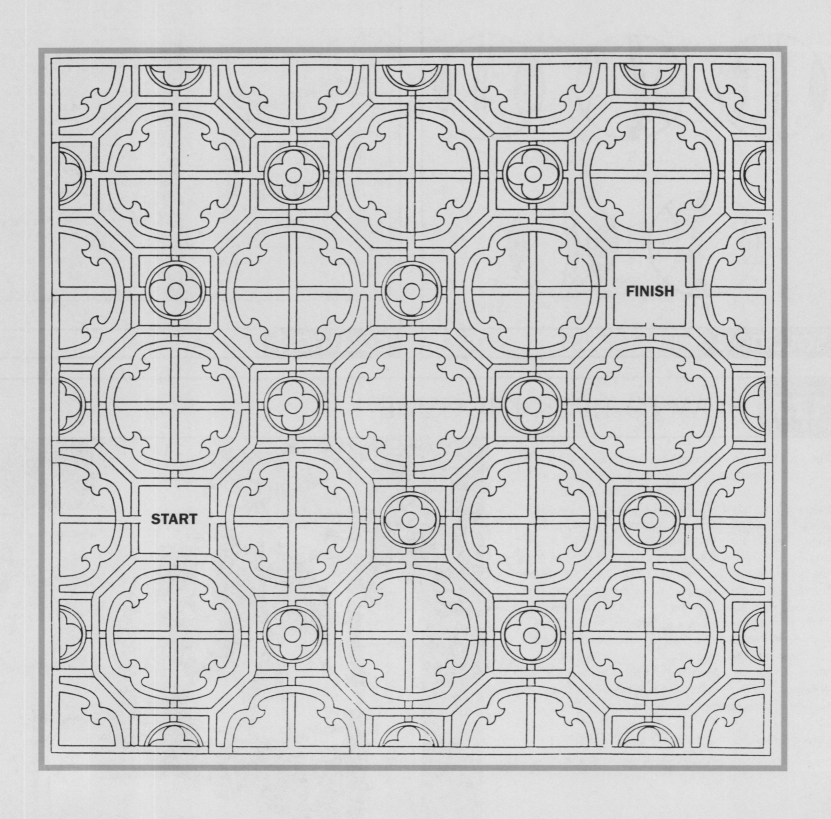

179 I ♥ NEW YORK

In the grid below are, Wall Street, Fourth Ave, Madison Ave and SoHo. The remaining letters spell out a well known New York location.

T	E	E	R	T	S	L	L	A	W	T
M	A	D	I	S	O	N	A	V	E	E
E	Q	A	U	S	M	I	O	H	O	S
R	S	E	V	A	H	T	R	U	O	F

SOLUTION ON PAGE 281

180 TEC TOTALS

Below are some UK cities, with the number of Detective Agencies in each city. How many are there in Edinburgh?

LONDON 10

BIRMINGHAM 9

MANCHESTER 7

NEWCASTLE 9

GLASGOW 6

EDINBURGH ?

SOLUTION ON PAGE 281

181 NO BANG

To de-activate this explosive device you must press the correct sequence of buttons until you reach "PRESS". You must press each button exactly once. Each button is marked with U for up, D for down, L for left and R for right. The number of moves is also on each button.

Which button is the first one you must press?

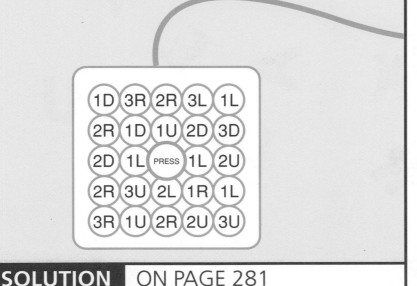

SOLUTION ON PAGE 281

182 MONEY MYSTERY

Recently, detectives discovered the proceeds of a robbery. It was a small bundle of $5 notes numbered from 759385 to 759500. How much money was in the bundle?

A	B	C
$270	$360	$425

D	E	F
$580	$595	$600

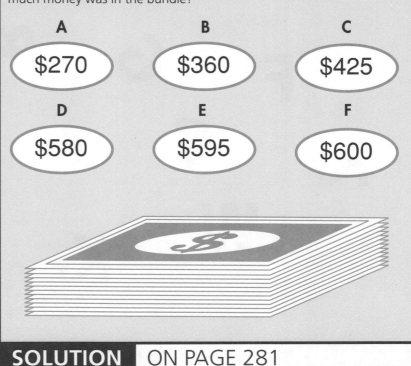

SOLUTION ON PAGE 281

183 SWITCH SOLUTION

Which piece will connect up this circuit?

A   B   C   D

SOLUTION ON PAGE 281

184 DECODE IT

You have been sent this coded message. But is it from a friend, or an enemy agent?

zpvs xifsfbcpvut ibt cffo ejtdpwfsfe. mfbwf uif dpvousz opx jg zpv wbmvf zpvs mjgf.

SOLUTION ON PAGE 281

185 LOST IT!

Below you will find an entire alphabet with some letters missing. Work out which letters are absent and then use them to make a word with psychological connections.

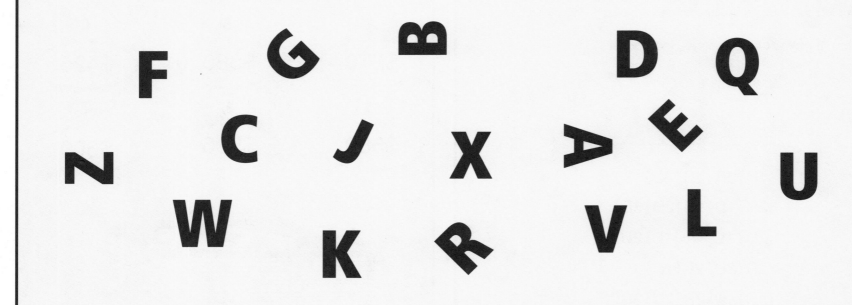

SOLUTION ON PAGE 281

186 LITTLE GREY CELLS

Move from square to square, including diagonally, to discover the name of a famous fictional Belgian detective.

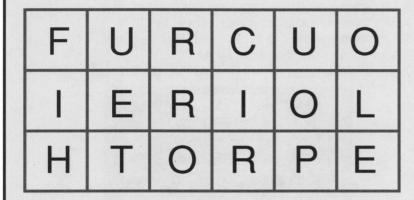

F	U	R	C	U	O
I	E	R	I	O	L
H	T	O	R	P	E

SOLUTION ON PAGE 281

187 MURDER MATHS

If the gun is 7, and the knife 11, What is the value of the rope?

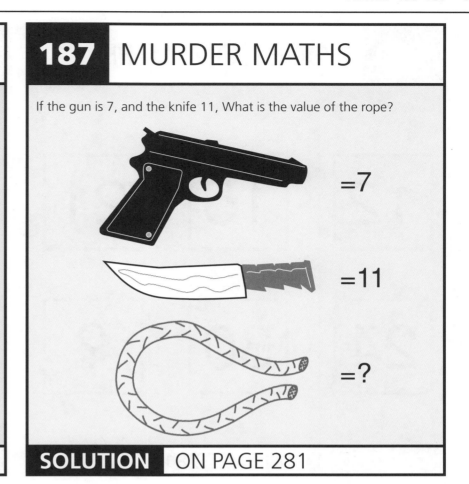

=7

=11

=?

SOLUTION ON PAGE 281

188 FORMULA FRENZY

The numbers on the right are formed from the numbers on the left using the same formula in each question. Find the rule and replace the question mark with a number.

5 ⟶ **65**

2 ⟶ **50**

14 ⟶ **110**

8 ⟶ **?**

SOLUTION ON PAGE 281

189 WHAT'S THE WORD?

Can you fill in the missing word, which means the same as those in the boxes?

CORROBORATOR

TESTIFIER

OBSERVER

SOLUTION ON PAGE 281

190   CODE COMPUTER

Complete this code sequence by adding the next number.

12	15	21
24	30	?

SOLUTION   ON PAGE 281

191   PLAY WATCHING

Four husband and wife couples go to see a play. They all sit in the same row, but no husband sits next to his wife, and a man and a woman are at opposite ends of the row. Their names are Andrews, Barker, Collins and Dunlop.

1. Mrs Dunlop or Mr Andrews is in the end seat.
2. Mr Andrews is mid-way between Mr Collins and Mrs Collins.
3. Mr Collins is two seats from Mrs Dunlop.
4. Mrs Collins is mid-way between Mr and Mrs Barker.
5. Mrs Andrews is next to the end seat.
6. Mr Dunlop is two seats from Mr Andrews.
7. Mrs Collins is closer to the right end than the left end.

Work out the seating arrangements along the row.

SOLUTION   ON PAGE 282

192   SIGN OF GUILT

Which one of these signatures is a forgery?

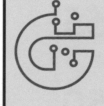

A Mary Carter.   E Mary Carter.

B Mary Carter

D Mary Carter

C Mary Carter

SOLUTION   ON PAGE 282

193   SHORT CIRCUIT

You are attempting to sabotage some electrical circuits. Which one of these is not a mirror image of the circuit below?

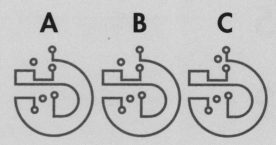

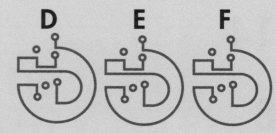

A   B   C

D   E   F

SOLUTION   ON PAGE 282

194 MAP READING & TRACKING

Detective X has been in charge of an operation to track the movements of enemy agents. He has filed his report on their various movements, but has made an error. Unfortunately, all the map co-ordinates are back to front, so where he says, for instance, square Z1 it should really read A28. It is your task to sort this out:

1. Enemy agent Z met enemy agent Q at square K8.
2. Enemy agent Y met enemy agent H at square R20.
3. Enemy agent Z left square K22, went north 4, east 8 and then west 5. What square did he end on?
4. Enemy agent Z left square O19 and went east 5, north 3 and then to 3 south of where he had started. What square did he end on?
5. Enemy agent H left square H4. At the same time agent Y left square X20. H went south 10, then east 10. Y went north 7 and west 6. Which of the 2 ended on the truly northernmost square?
6. Enemy agent Z left square N23 and went 6 east. Agent Y left V15 and went west 13 and then south 8. Z then went west 9. Which square was left between them?

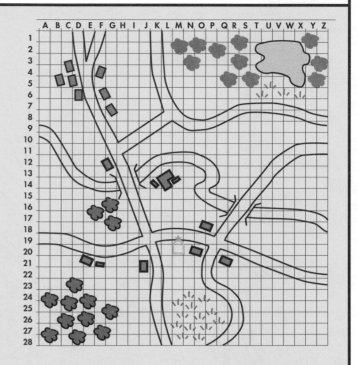

SOLUTION | ON PAGE 282

195 WHAT'S THE WORD?

Can you fill in the missing word, which means the same as those in the boxes?

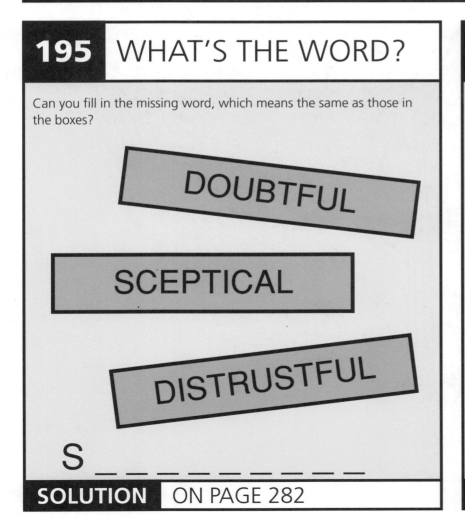

DOUBTFUL

SCEPTICAL

DISTRUSTFUL

S _ _ _ _ _ _ _ _

SOLUTION | ON PAGE 282

196 FIND THE NAME

Hidden in this grid are these names: Cindy, Grace, Lisa, Susan and Teresa. The letters that are left spell out another name.

What is it?

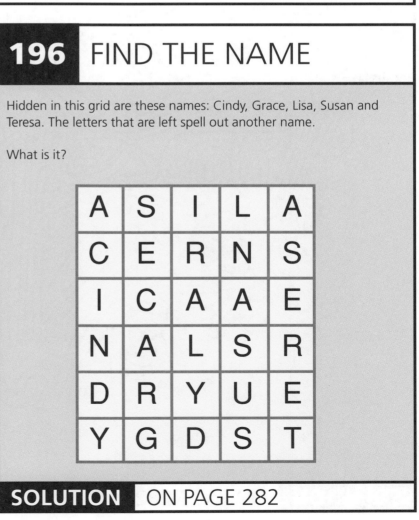

A	S	I	L	A
C	E	R	N	S
I	C	A	A	E
N	A	L	S	R
D	R	Y	U	E
Y	G	D	S	T

SOLUTION | ON PAGE 282

197 CELTIC CONUNDRUM

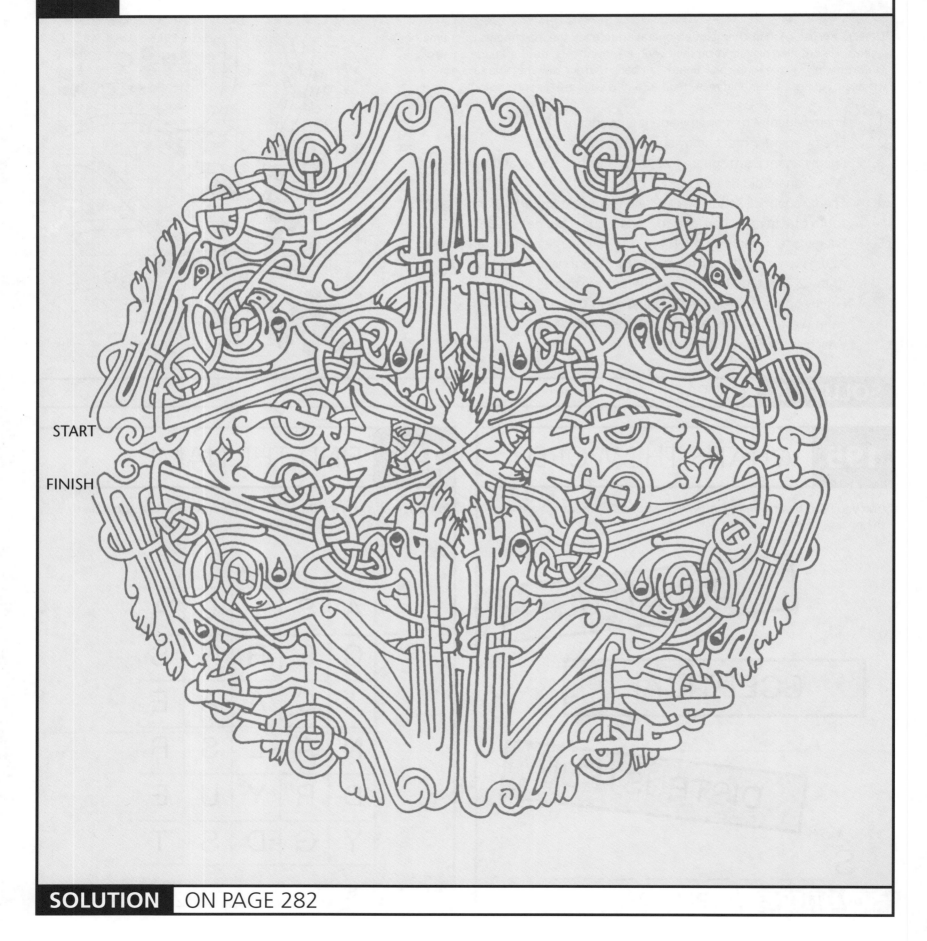

START

FINISH

SOLUTION ON PAGE 282

198 THREE TOO MANY

Delete three of the four given letters in each square to create a crossword of good English words.

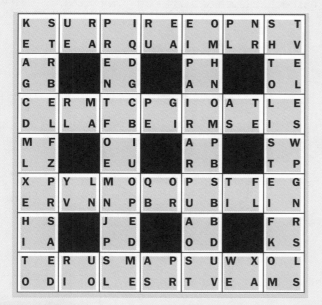

SOLUTION ON PAGE 282

199 THE TWINS CAUSE CONFUSION

A father always wanted four sons. His ancestors had always had large families and so he thought nothing about it. He was, however, upset in later life because he had only produced three sons. His eldest son was now 28 years old and he had given him a quarter of his land as his inheritance already. He had not passed other shares to his other sons before a wonderful event occurred; twins, and both boys! He immediately split the remaining land into four equally shaped parts, which were also equal in area, and gave each remaining child a share. How did he do this, given that he had divided the land awkwardly?

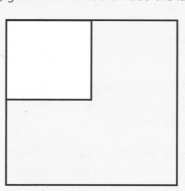

SOLUTION ON PAGE 282

200 CLEANING CONFUSION

At a dry-cleaner's one more customer brings in a jacket only than trousers only. Three times as many people bring in trousers, jacket, and a skirt as bring in a skirt only. One more person brings in a jacket and a skirt but no trousers than a skirt and trousers but no jacket. Nine people bring in trousers only. The same number of customers bring in a jacket only as trousers and a skirt but no jacket. Thirty-two customers do not bring in a skirt and 24 customers do not bring in a jacket.

a) How many customers bring in all three of the items?
b) How many customers bring in only one of the three items?
c) How many customers bring in a jacket only?
d) How many customers bring in two of the three items?
e) What is the total number of customers bringing in any of the three items?

SOLUTION ON PAGE 282

201 TAKE THE TRAIN

Modernization of the transport systems is a continuous process, with the main emphasis on decreasing journey time. Trains are now probably the fastest form of travel for medium-length journeys. On average, trains can now cover the same distance in 3/4 of the original time.
How much faster do trains now travel as a fraction of their original speed?

SOLUTION ON PAGE 282

202 WORD CONNECTION

In the following sentence there are associated words that are hidden. These words can be found by looking at the end of one word somewhere in the sentence and connecting it to the beginning of the next word. What are the connected words?

A. The ballot usually takes no more than half an hour, then the fun begins. The hi-fi attachments are in place for David's party. In the fridge there is a large samosa above the sandwiches and a chocolate gateau diagonally placed on the shelf below to give more space.

B. If anything is wrong with the replica shirts then management must be informed so that they can combat escalating problems.

C. While Grandfather sang an impromptu ballad, the wood on the campfire began to char perfectly and Grandmother joyfully recited age-old rumours.

D. According to forces protocol, Lieutenant Barnabas settles the cashbox error and ensures the young soldiers' faces will be agleam.

E. The cream beret that I managed to drop all through the mud at the Mexico rally has been dry-cleaned and should now appear lovely and clean.

SOLUTION | ON PAGE 282

204 DART DIFFERENCE

You throw three darts at this strange dartboard. How many ways are there to score 50 without a miss and no set of three numbers occurring in a different order?

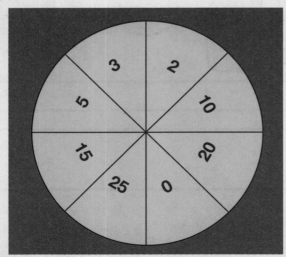

SOLUTION | ON PAGE 282

203 CONFUSING PAPER MODEL

Using a rectangular piece of paper can you make the model shown? You can make three straight-line cuts to the paper and the paper model must not be glued or held together with clips.

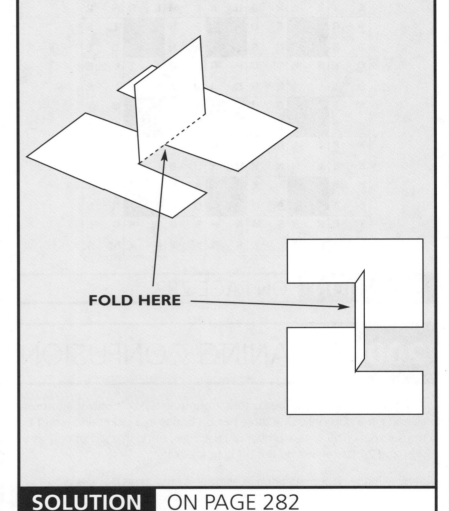

FOLD HERE

SOLUTION | ON PAGE 282

205 RIGHT ROYAL MUDDLE

Which letter do you need to complete the series below?

R A S E A

SOLUTION | ON PAGE 282

206 | PISTOL POSER

The Walther PPK is a favourite of British intelligence agents. Can you spot 10 differences between these two?

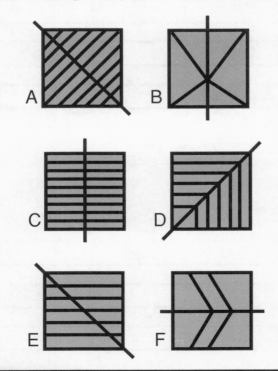

SOLUTION ON PAGE 282

207 | FORMULATION

The numbers on the right are formed from the numbers on the left using the same formula in each question. Find the rule and replace the question mark with a number.

5 ⟶ 38

12 ⟶ 80

23 ⟶ 146

9 ⟶ ?

SOLUTION ON PAGE 282

208 | ODD ONE OUT

Which of the following six shapes is the odd one out?

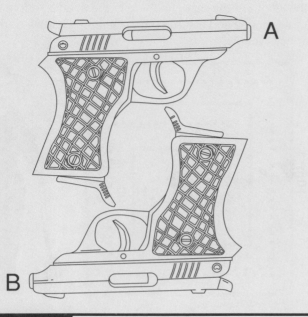

SOLUTION ON PAGE 282

209 | BROADWAY, NY

In Broadway, New York City, a man saw a new type of bus, as shown below. It was stationary and he could not tell which way it was going.

Can you?

SOLUTION ON PAGE 282

210 LOGICAL CLOCKS

These clocks follow a weird kind of logic. What time should the fourth clock show? Choose from the four options provided.

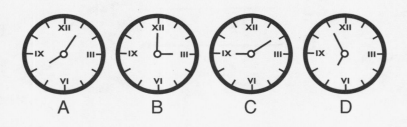

A   B   C   D

SOLUTION ON PAGE 282

211 ROUND AND ROUND THE GARDEN

A woman has a garden path 2m wide, with a hedge on either side. The path spirals into the middle of the garden. One day the woman walks the length of the path, finishing in the middle. Ignore the width of the hedge and assume she walks in the middle of the path. How far does she walk?

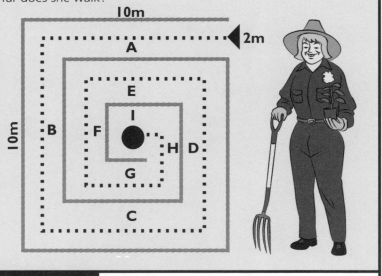

SOLUTION ON PAGE 282

212 RIFLE RANGE

Three soldiers – Colonel Ketchup, Major Mustard and Captain Chutney – have a shooting competition. They each fire six shots, shown below, and each score 71 points. Colonel Ketchup's first two shots score 22; Major Mustard's first shot scores 3.

Who hits the bull's eye?

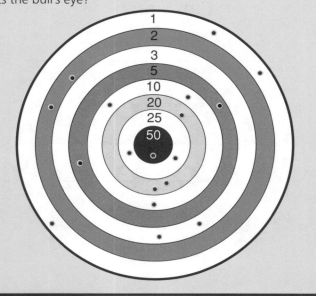

SOLUTION ON PAGE 282

213 MISSING LINK

74882	3584	
29637		192
74826		

Fill in the missing numbers from these bars. Just enough information has been provided to work out the logic. The logic is the same in each line of numbers.

Now try this one:

528	116	
793		335
821		

SOLUTION ON PAGE 282

214 SPY STORY

Merged together in this grid are the names of a famous actor who has played a spy, and a well known spy film. Can you unravel them?

E	M	I	I	D	C	T	H	E	A	L	E	D
												L
												N
												C
			L	E								A
			E									A
			I	N	V	I	E	A				

SOLUTION ON PAGE 282

215 CIRCULAR LOGIC

What is the value of the last string? Black, white and shaded circles have different values.

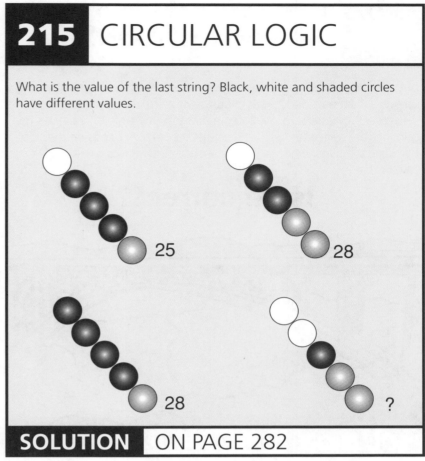

SOLUTION ON PAGE 282

216 TRIANGLES AND TRAPEZIUMS

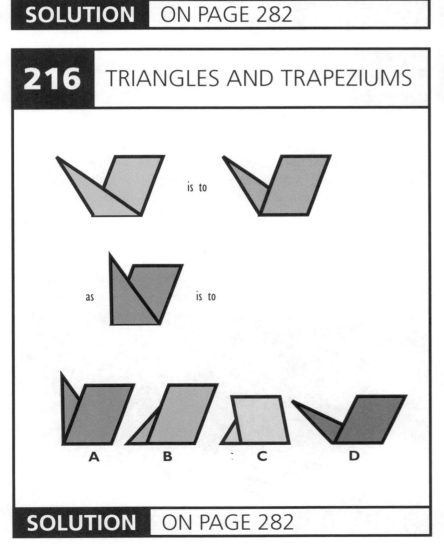

SOLUTION ON PAGE 282

217 CUP AND BALL TRICK

Here are views of six non-standard, six-sided dice. Which of the six dice can not be made up from the flat-plan net at the bottom? .

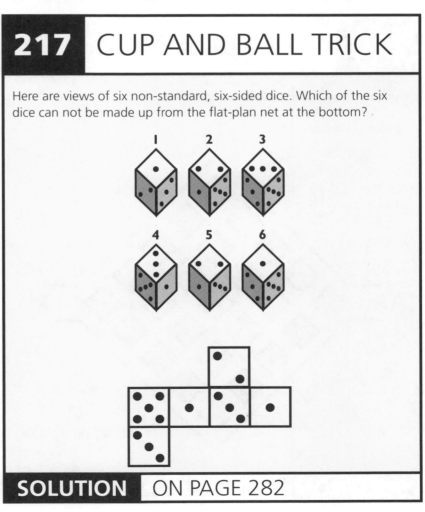

SOLUTION ON PAGE 282

218 CARRIER PIGEONS

A driver approaches a bridge. He notices that the maximum weight allowed is 20 tons and knows that his empty truck weighs 20 tons. However, he has a cargo of 200 pigeons which weigh 1lb each. As the pigeons are asleep on perches he stops the vehicle, bangs on the side to wake the birds, who start flying around, then drives over the bridge.

Is he correct?

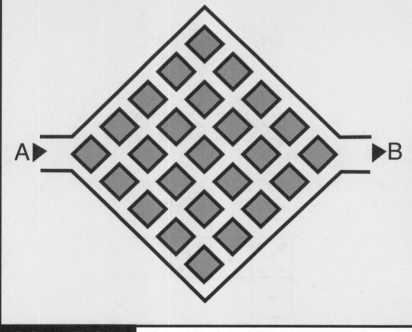

SOLUTION ON PAGE 282

219 CIRCLES AND TRIANGLES

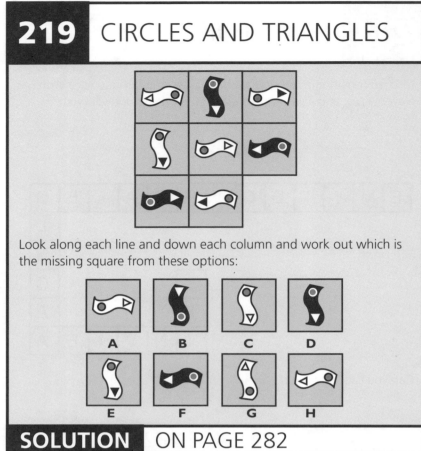

Look along each line and down each column and work out which is the missing square from these options:

SOLUTION ON PAGE 282

220 CITY SLICKER

City blocks have been built between two main roads – A and B – in a grid, like Manhattan, New York. Always moving toward B, how many different routes are there?

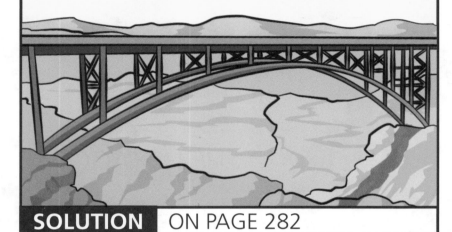

SOLUTION ON PAGE 282

221 EVOLUTION

Three uninhabited islands were within swimming distance from each other but only at certain times of the year. This depended on the strong currents that flowed between them. A group of naturalist explorers put animal x on island A, animal y on island B and animal z on island C. No other animals were on the islands and no animals visited the islands.

When the explorers returned several years later they found island A had no animals on it. Island B had animals x and y plus one new animal on it, and island C had the same type of animals as island B plus z and another new animal. Can you name the five animals?

SOLUTION ON PAGE 282

222 BOND BEVVY

What is this well known line from the Bond films? The vowels are missing and the words are in the wrong order.

NT SHKN MRTN STRRD

SOLUTION   ON PAGE 282

223 COMMON SENSE?

The following word has been constructed according to a simple rule. Could you add an 'S' without breaking the rule?

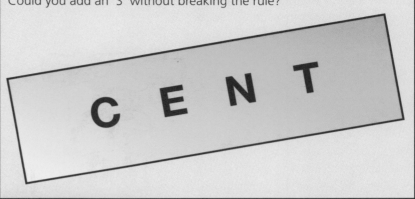

C E N T

SOLUTION   ON PAGE 282

224 NUMBER MYSTERY

Can you calculate the number missing in the figure below? Each number is used once only and is not reversed.

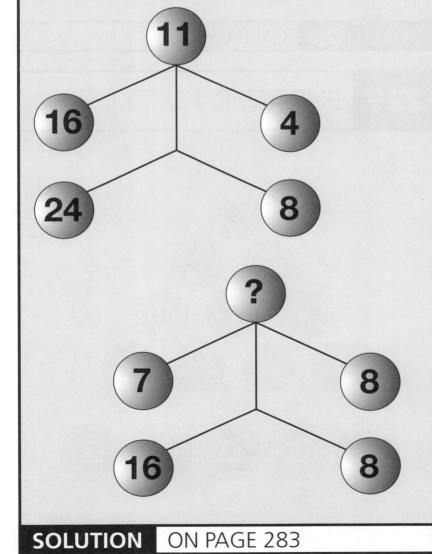

SOLUTION   ON PAGE 283

225 ROUND THE HEXAGONS

Can you work out what should be the contents of the top hexagon?

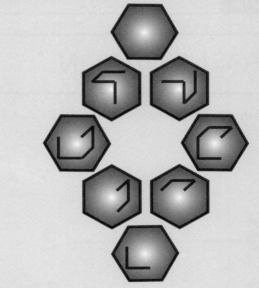

Choose from option

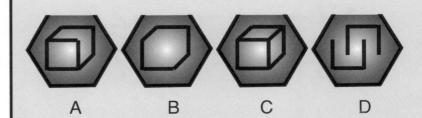

A   B   C   D

SOLUTION   ON PAGE 283

226 WATER DIVING

Two men are arguing about whether a square open-topped water tank is half full or not. How can they decide without removing the water or using any measuring device?

SOLUTION   ON PAGE 283

227 SPY CENTRE

Each field agent needs a code letter and number to contact the command centre.

What are the missing two code numbers?

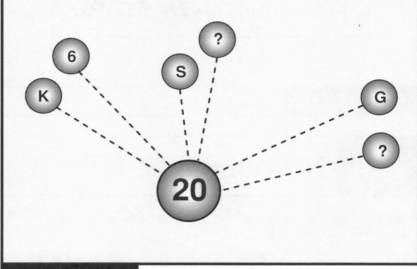

SOLUTION   ON PAGE 283

228 FORMULATION

The numbers on the right are formed from the numbers on the left using the same formula in each question. Find the rule and replace the question mark with a number.

6 ⟶ 2

13 ⟶ 16

17 ⟶ 24

8 ⟶ ?

SOLUTION   ON PAGE 283

229 PYRAMID PUZZLE

Look at the sequence of shapes. Which of the following options carries on the sequence?

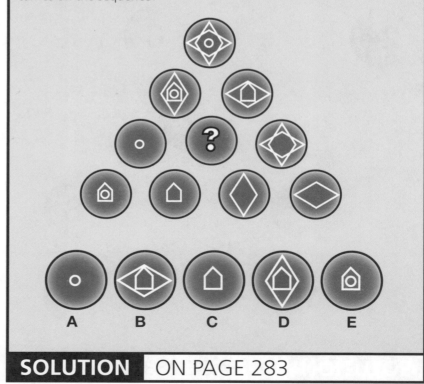

SOLUTION   ON PAGE 283

230 SKI-LIFT

There are ten places to embark and disembark on the ski-lift at the ski resort. It is possible to purchase a single ticket between any two stations.

How many different tickets are needed for skiers to go to every station from every other station?

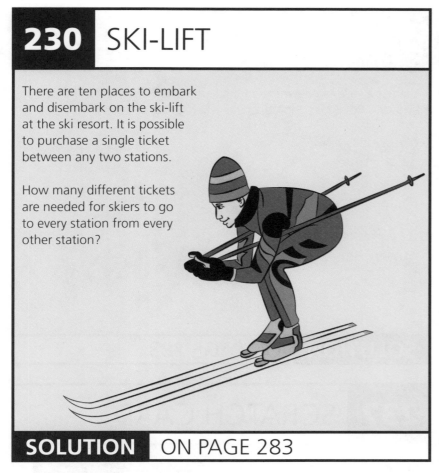

SOLUTION ON PAGE 283

231 ROUND IN CIRCLES

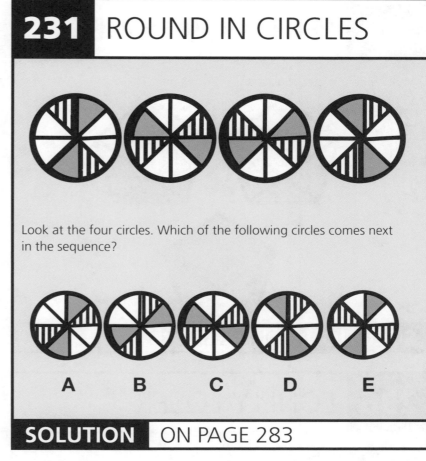

Look at the four circles. Which of the following circles comes next in the sequence?

A   B   C   D   E

SOLUTION ON PAGE 283

232 MAKING MOVES

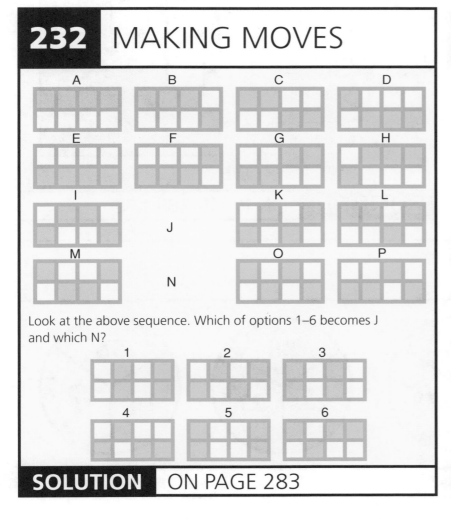

Look at the above sequence. Which of options 1–6 becomes J and which N?

SOLUTION ON PAGE 283

233 PYRAMIDAL LOGIC

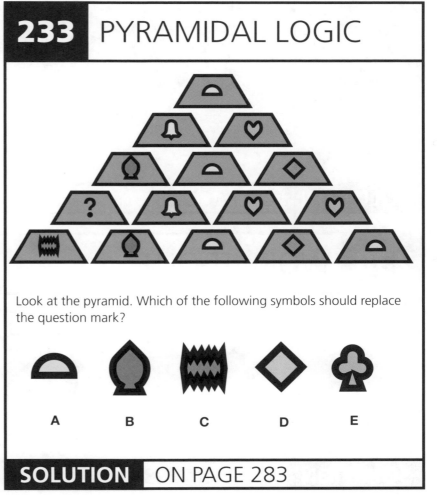

Look at the pyramid. Which of the following symbols should replace the question mark?

A   B   C   D   E

SOLUTION ON PAGE 283

234 PENTAGON FIGURES

What number should replace the question mark?

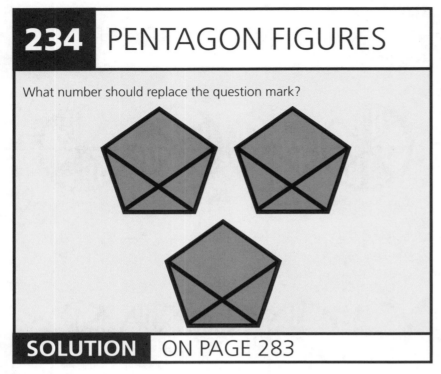

SOLUTION ON PAGE 283

235 SUN SHINE

There is a valley somewhere on the Earth. The Sun is nearer the valley by over 4,800km at noon than it is when it rises or sets.

Where is this valley?

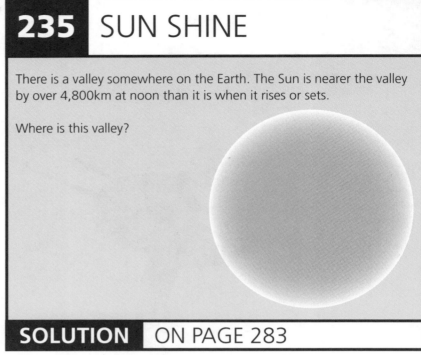

SOLUTION ON PAGE 283

236 LONELY LOSER

Which of the following figures is the odd one out?

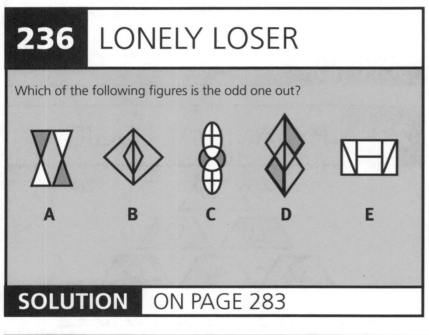

SOLUTION ON PAGE 283

237 SCRATCH CARD

At the fairground there is a competition – you purchase a ticket on which there is a number of scratch-off squares. One square is marked "loser"; two others have identical symbols. If these appear before the loser square appears, you win a prize. The odds against winning are 2:1 against.

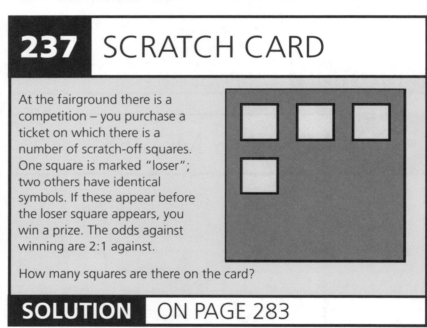

How many squares are there on the card?

SOLUTION ON PAGE 283

238 WORK IT OUT

What number should replace the question mark?

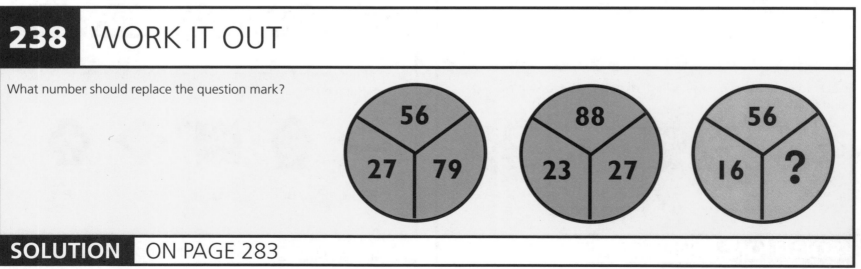

SOLUTION ON PAGE 283

239 MAZE MYSTERY

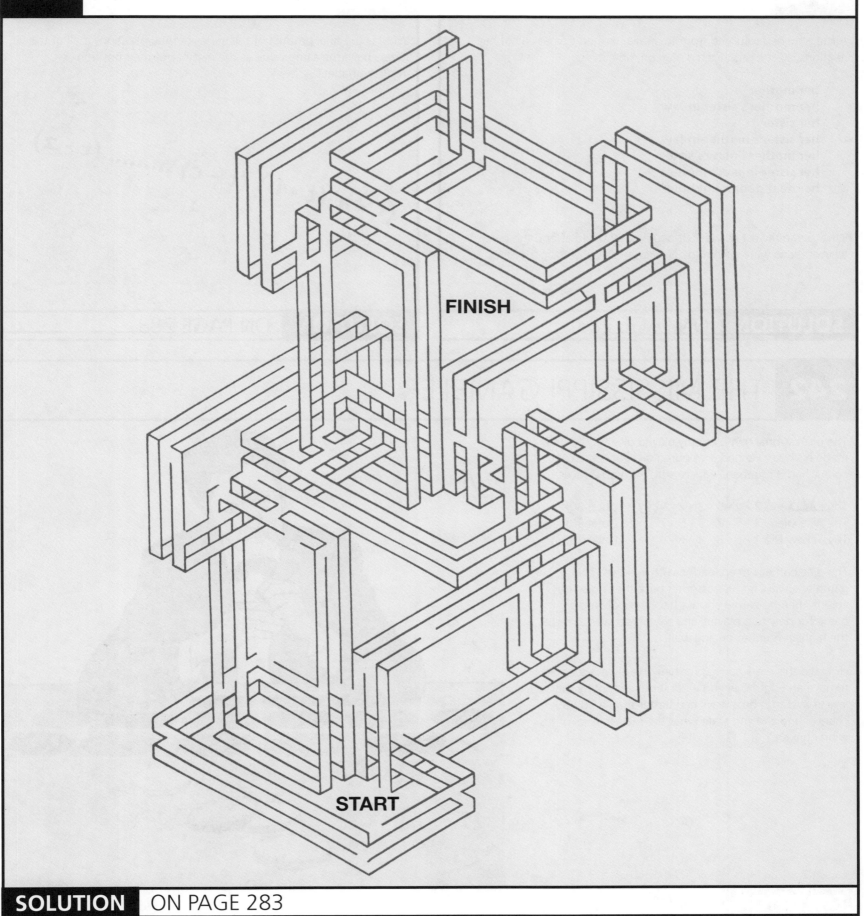

FINISH

START

240 CONFUSING FAMILY RELATIONS

Alice, who had returned from Australia, wished to meet all of her relations, so she organized a reunion. She invited:

her mother
her mother's sister-in-law
her sister
her sister's mother-in-law
her mother-in-law's sister
her sister-in-law's mother
her next door neighbour.

What is the fewest number of people that could attend the party if all invitations were accepted? No illegal relationships permitted.

SOLUTION   ON PAGE 283

241 LOOK FOR THE SIMPLE SOLUTION

What is the final product of this series of multiplications if all of the letters have the same value as the number of their position in the alphabet?

$$(t - a)(t - b)(t - c) \ldots\ldots(t - z)$$

SOLUTION   ON PAGE 283

242 THE MISSISSIPPI GAMBLER

The professional gambler only played dice but he had made his own. He had 3 coloured dice, and each colour had 3 numbers, which were each on 2 faces.

The Red Die: 2 - 4 - 9 - 2 - 4 - 9   (total 30)
The Blue Die: 3 - 5 - 7 - 3 - 5 - 7   (total 30)
The Yellow Die: 1 - 6 - 8 - 1 - 6 - 8   (total 30)

The dice had not been loaded with weights. The gambler always let his customer have the choice of colour, then he would choose his. It was always a game for only two players and the object was to have the highest number on any wall.

How did this work so well for him? He always seemed to have an edge. Can you work it out so that by the law of averages he always had better than a 50 : 50 chance, and can you state what the real chances of his winning were?

SOLUTION   ON PAGE 283

243 | THE FAIRGROUND GAME

At a fairground game, players had three darts each to attempt to win a teddy bear, a board game, or a beer glass. There were four winners of teddy bears and games not but glasses. Two more people won both a glass and a teddy bear but no game than those who won a glass and a game but no teddy bear; 43 of the prize-winners did not win a teddy bear, and 48 of the prize-winners did not win a game. Nine people won both a glass and a teddy but no game, and 31 people did not win a glass; 74 people won at least one prize.

a) How many people won a teddy bear only?
b) How many people won all three prizes?
c) How many people won a glass only?
d) How many people won two prizes only?
e) How many people won a game only?

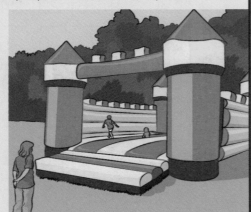

SOLUTION ON PAGE 283

245 | CIRCULAR LOGIC

What is the value of the last string? Black, white and shaded circles have different values.

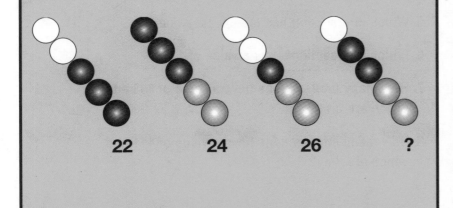

22   24   26   ?

SOLUTION ON PAGE 283

244 | SO YOU THINK YOU'RE GOOD AT MATHS?

Can you rearrange the following addition to make an answer of 100? You can use each number only once but you can add any mathematical symbols you wish.

$$\frac{6\ 1}{1\ 8}$$

SOLUTION ON PAGE 283

246 | NUMBER MYSTERY

Can you calculate the number missing in the figure below? Each number is used once only and is not reversed.

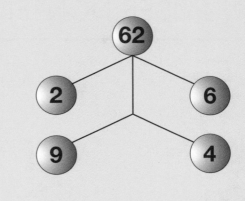

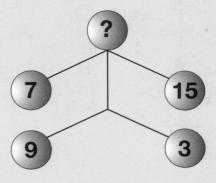

SOLUTION ON PAGE 283

247 | TIE TANGLE

The number in the middle knot of the following bow ties is reached by using all of the outer numbers only once. You cannot reverse the numbers to obtain the answers. Which number should replace the question mark?

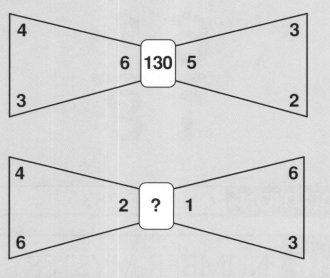

SOLUTION   ON PAGE 283

248 | GRID GAME

In the grid below, the intersections have a value equal to the sum of their four touching numbers.

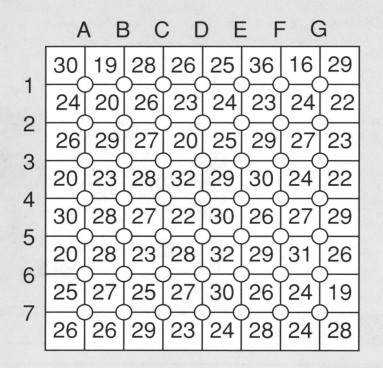

Can you answer the following:

1. **What are the grid references for the three intersection points with a value of 100?**

2. **Which intersection point/s has a value of 92?**

3. **How many intersections have a value of less than 100?**

4. **Which intersection has the highest value?**

5. **Which intersection has the lowest value?**

6. **Which intersection/s has a value of 115?**

7. **How many intersections have a value of 105 and which are they?**

8. **How many intersections have a value of 111 and which are they?**

249 | NUMBER NONSENSE

Can you find the missing value on the roof of the house? Each of the numbers on the windows and door must be used only once and no number can be reversed.

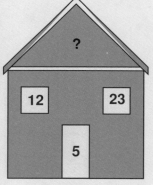

SOLUTION   ON PAGE 283

SOLUTION   ON PAGE 283

250 MATHS MYSTERY

What number is missing from the segment below?

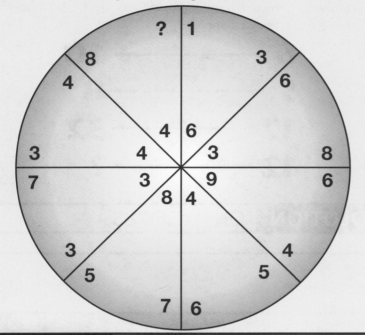

SOLUTION ON PAGE 283

252 NUMBER NONSENSE

Can you determine what number should replace the question marks?

2	6	7	9	1			6	1	4	3	8			4	0	3	3	5	
8	0	2	7	6	D	F	A	9	4	4	2	3	B I H	?	?	?	?	?	G C E
5	3	0	2	4			3	2	6	8	7			1	9	7	8	1	

SOLUTION ON PAGE 283

253 MATHS MYSTERY

Start at the top-left circle and move clockwise. Calculate the number that replaces the question mark.

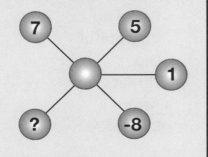

SOLUTION ON PAGE 283

251 CONFUSING FAMILY RELATIONS

A family has five children, of which half are boys. How can this be?

SOLUTION ON PAGE 283

254 FORMULATION

The numbers on the right are formed from the numbers on the left using the same formula in each question. Find the rule and replace the question mark with a number.

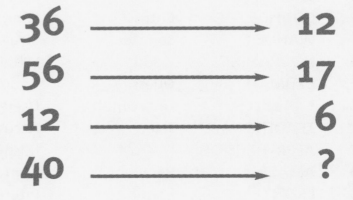

36	→	12
56	→	17
12	→	6
40	→	?

SOLUTION ON PAGE 283

255 MATHS MYSTERY

Can you calculate the number missing in the figure below? Each number is used once only and is not reversed.

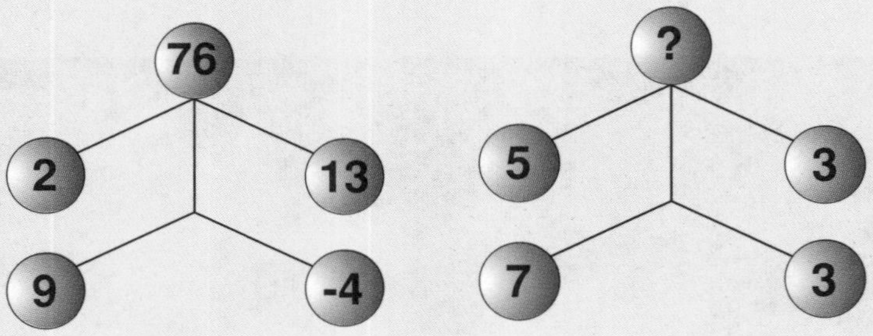

SOLUTION ON PAGE 283

256 FORMULATION

The numbers on the right are formed from the numbers on the left using the same formula in each question. Find the rule and replace the question mark with a number.

$$6 \longrightarrow 10$$
$$5 \longrightarrow 8$$
$$17 \longrightarrow 32$$
$$12 \longrightarrow ?$$

SOLUTION ON PAGE 283

257 WORD MATCH

In each line below match the first given word with the word that is closest in meaning.

		A	B	C	D	E
1.	RESCUE	Retrieve	Liberate	Salvage	Redeem	Help
2.	PROTESTOR	Rebel	Dissenter	Demonstrator	Marcher	Speaker
3.	AGGRAVATE	Anger	Insult	Enrage	Provoke	Instigate
4.	ETIQUETTE	Custom	Courtesies	Example	Manners	Protocol
5.	INVOLVEMENT	Participation	Concern	Responsibility	Implication	Association
6.	HERMIT	Solitaire	Recluse	Monk	Loner	Hoarder
7.	HASSLE	Problem	Nuisance	Worry	Bother	Trouble
8.	FICTIONAL	Legendary	Invention	Informal	Genuine	Imaginary
9.	EQUIVALENT	Alike	Twin	Equal	Even	Similar
10.	FASCINATE	Catch	Charm	Captivate	Occupy	Win
11.	THRIVING	Fit	Strong	Wholesome	Flourishing	Nourishing
12.	CONFIDE	Entrust	Limit	Secret	Disclose	Speak
13.	WANDER	Saunter	Stray	Veer	Drift	Depart
14.	NOURISHING	Good	Wholesome	Healthy	Improving	Worthy
15.	ESTIMATE	Guess	Roughly	Calculate	Close	Nearly
16.	THANKLESS	Unprofitable	Useless	Ungrateful	Worthless	Unsatisfying
17.	TRADITIONAL	Fixed	Accustomed	Old	Usual	Age-long
18.	APPREHENSION	Distrust	Misgiving	Threat	Wariness	Hunch
19.	AMAZE	Bewilder	Confuse	Astonish	Startle	Stagger
20.	PROFIT	Earnings	Interest	Revenue	Gain	Value

SOLUTION ON PAGE 283

258 AMAZINGLY COMPLICATED

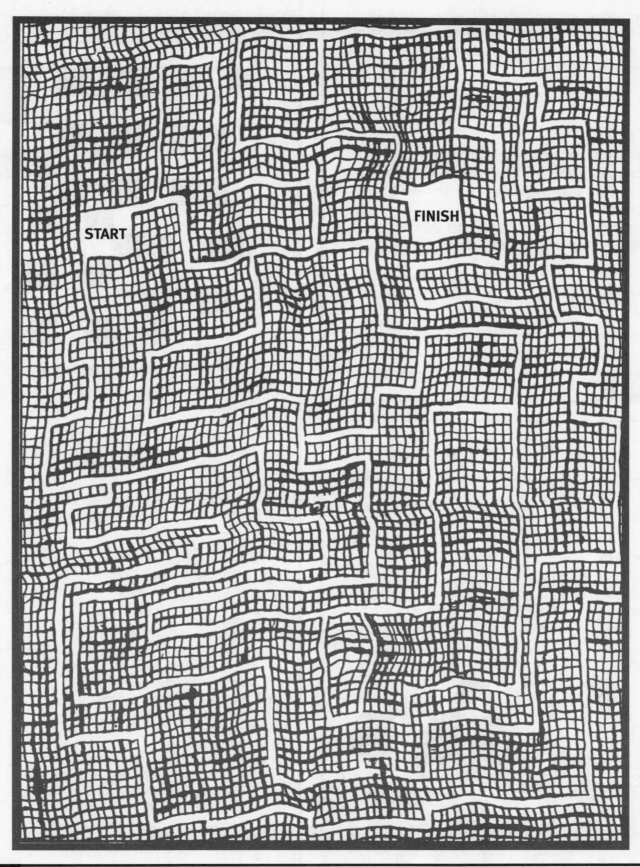

259 IN THE DIRT

Two children were playing in the loft of a barn before it gave way and they fell to the ground below. When they dusted themselves off, the face of one was dirty while the other's was clean. Only the clean-faced boy went off to wash his face. Why?

Clues

1. **Neither of them needed cold water to stop bruising and neither child was hurt.**
2. **Neither child put their dirty hands on their faces.**
3. **It was dusty and they had both sweated.**
4. **Their faces had not touched the ground.**

SOLUTION ON PAGE 284

261 DINNER PARTY

The people in the picture have all ordered different dishes, named below. One of them is in for a nasty surprise. Who is it?

Tom had: **EEMTOTEL**
Lucy had: **LPALAE**
Harry had: **OOITSTR**
Michelle had: **LMNALEASLO**

SOLUTION ON PAGE 284

260 SIMPLEX

To make a change, this is a straightforward crossword.

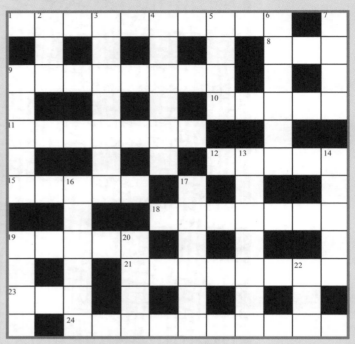

Across

1 Official diplomatic envoy (10)
8 Employment (3)
9 Dig out and remove (8)
10 Doctrine (5)
11 Without foundation in fact (7)
12 Round-up (5)
15 Unfrequented (5)
18 Ingenuous (7)
19 Words of a song (5)
21 Highly regarded (8)
23 Pointed tool for piercing small holes (3)
24 Relating to the simplest principles (10)

Down

2 Coalesce (3)
3 Unyielding (7)
4 Exerting force by weight, but not motion (6)
5 Habitual nourishment (4)
6 Damaged irreparably (6)
7 Relish (4)
9 Banish (5)
13 Wealthy (7)
14 Lubricated (5)
16 Conditional release of a prisoner (6)
17 Rapid succession of clattering sounds (6)
19 Soil mixture of clay, silt, and sand (4)
20 Yield by treaty (4)
22 Make a mistake (3)

SOLUTION ON PAGE 284

262 SQUARE SORT

This grid consists of three squares marked A, B and C, and three squares marked 1, 2 and 3. The nine inner squares should incorporate the lines and symbols of both the letter and the number squares. One of the nine squares is incorrect. Which is it?

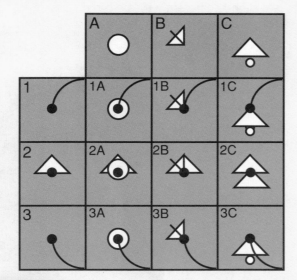

SOLUTION ON PAGE 284

264 FIVE CIRCLES

All five circles have the same diameter. Draw a line moving through point A in such a way that it divides the five circles into two groups with equal areas.

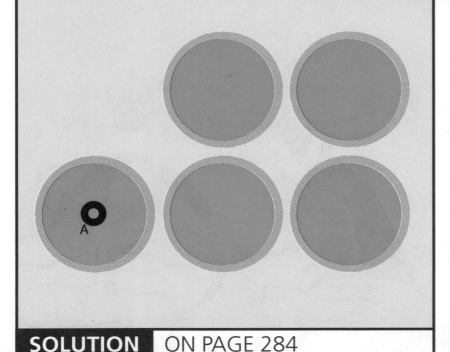

SOLUTION ON PAGE 284

263 GENERATION GAP

I am four times as old as my daughter. In 20 years time I shall be twice as old as her. How old are we now?

SOLUTION ON PAGE 284

265 LATERAL LOGIC

Look at these shapes. Does option A, B, C or D continue the sequence?

SOLUTION ON PAGE 284

266 SHADY SQUARES

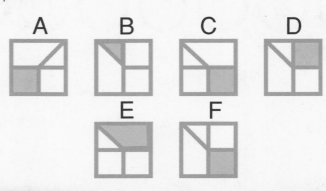

Look at the three squares. Does option A, B, C, D, E or F continue the sequence?

SOLUTION ON PAGE 284

267 FIGURE COLUMNS

Look at the three columns of figures. Which column comes next in the sequence?

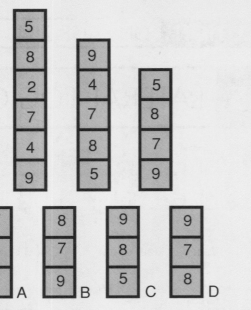

A   B   C   D

SOLUTION   ON PAGE 284

268 EIGHTEEN TREES

A gardener has 18 trees which he wishes to plant in a variety of straight rows of five trees per row. He sets himself the task of planting the 18 trees in such an arrangement that he will obtain the maximum number of rows of five trees per row.
There are two slightly different ways he can do this.
Can you find both ways?

SOLUTION   ON PAGE 284

269 NOTABLE NUMBER

Fill in the missing number. The last number is correctly shown as 7, not 8.

99   45   39   36   28   21

72   27   18   21   ?   13   7

SOLUTION   ON PAGE 284

270 COUNTING CREATURES

At the zoo there are penguins and huskies next to each other.
In all, I can count 72 creatures and 200 legs.

How many penguins are there?

SOLUTION   ON PAGE 284

271 LINE ANALOGY

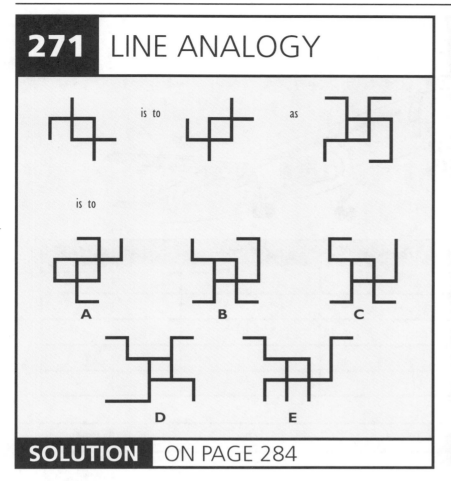

272 CHESS STRATEGY

A master has to win two games of chess in a row in order to win a prize. In total, he has to play only three games, alternating between a strong opponent, whom he can sometimes beat, and a weak opponent, whom he can always beat. Should he play strong, weak, strong; or weak, strong, weak?

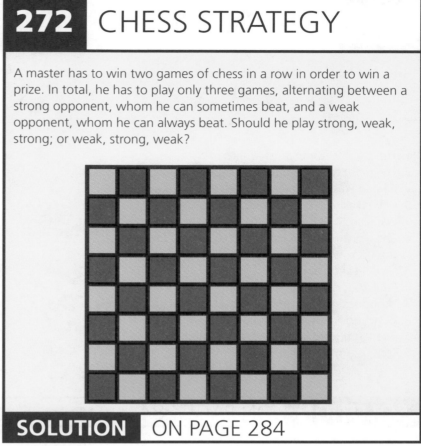

SOLUTION ON PAGE 284

273 CAREFUL CALCULATION

If the upper pair of numbers total 9825, what do the lower pair of numbers total?

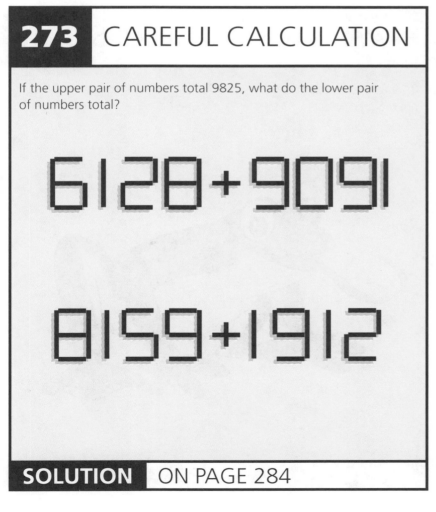

SOLUTION ON PAGE 284

274 NUMBER CRUNCHING

Look at the diagrams. What number should replace the question mark?

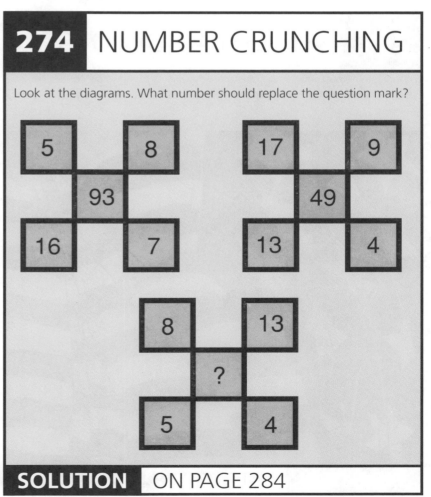

SOLUTION ON PAGE 284

275 | FIVE PILOTS

Five pilots take their flights from five different UK airports to five different countries.

Can you sort them out?

1. The aircraft from Stansted flies to Nice.
2. The flight from Cardiff has a captain named Paul.
3. Mike flies to JFK, New York, but not from Gatwick.
4. The flight from Manchester does not go to the USA.
5. Nick flies to Vancouver.
6. Paul does not fly to Roma.
7. Nick does not fly from Manchester.
8. Robin does not fly from Stansted.
9. The flight from Heathrow, not piloted by Tony, is not for Berlin.

NAME	AIRPORT	DESTINATION

SOLUTION | ON PAGE 284

276 | THE GREAT DIVIDE

If a man lives in San Francisco, why can't he be buried in England?

SOLUTION | ON PAGE 284

277 | FROGS AND FLIES

If 29 frogs catch 29 flies in 29 minutes, how many frogs are required to catch 87 flies in 87 minutes?

SOLUTION | ON PAGE 284

278 ISLAND ACCESS

There is a lake with an island in the middle. On the island is a tree. The lake is deep and is 80 yards in diameter. There is another tree on the mainland. A non-swimmer wishes to get across to the island, but all he has is a length of rope 300 yards long.

How does he get accross?

SOLUTION ON PAGE 284

279 TARGET

Find 12 six-letter words by pairing up the 24 three-letter segments. Each bit is used once only.

INF
FEN
MON
QUE
TER
CAR
DER
TEN
ENS
TEM
DAY
ORM
CEL
ERS
RUL
LAR
DON
SYS
GAR
PAR
JES
DEN
TED
PET

SOLUTION ON PAGE 284

280 ANOTHER MANSION MURDER

The Lord of the Manor has been murdered. The visitors to the manor were Abbie, Bobby and Colin. The murderer was the visitor who arrived at the manor later than at least one of the other two visitors. One of the visitors was a detective who arrived at the manor earlier than at least one of the other two visitors. The detective arrived at midnight. Neither Abbie nor Bobby arrived at the manor after midnight. The earlier arriver of Bobby and Colin was not the detective. The later arriver of Abbie and Colin was not the murderer. Who then was it who committed the murder?

SOLUTION ON PAGE 284

281 GARDEN GAME

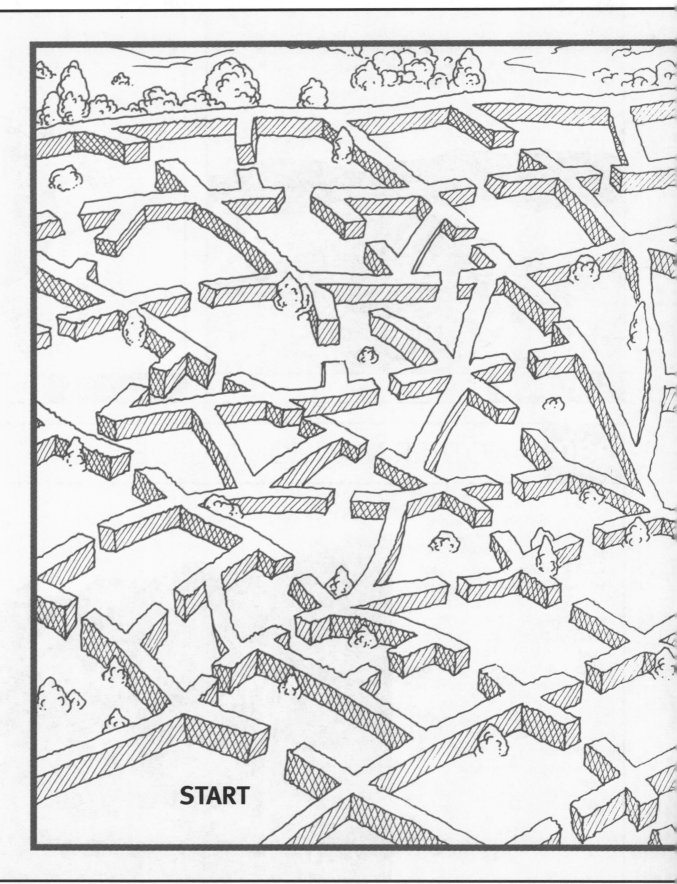

START

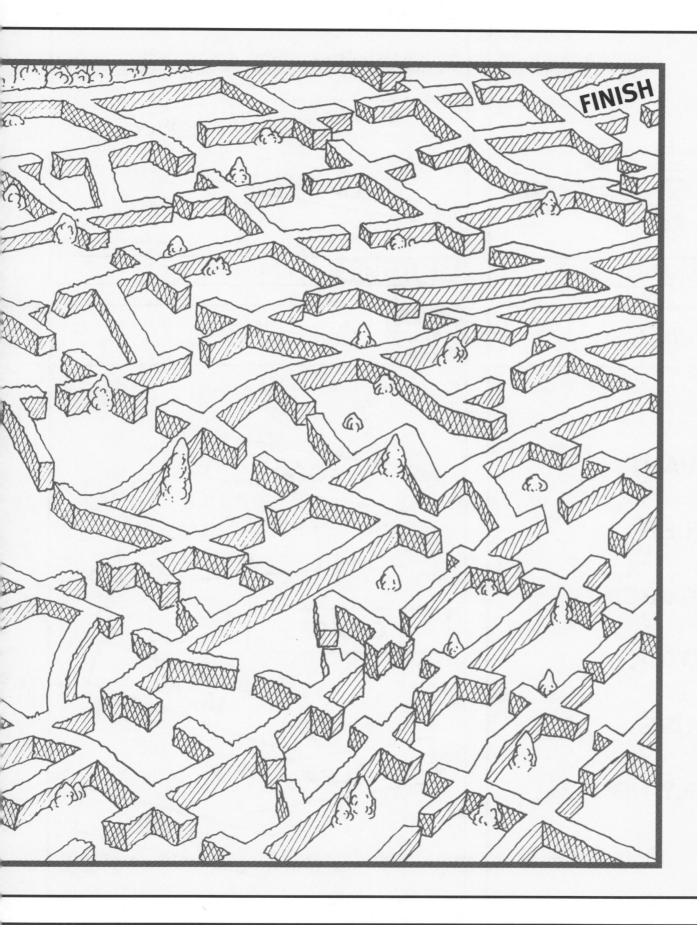

FINISH

282 TOXIC TIPPLE

One of the glasses of wine below is the odd one out. It also contains a deadly poison.

Which one should you not drink?

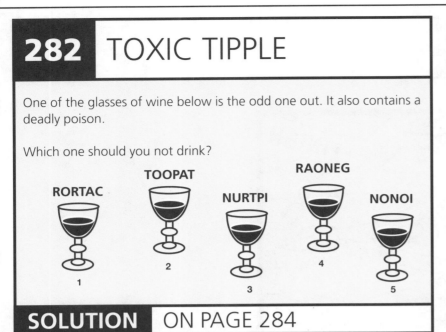

RORTAC — 1
TOOPAT — 2
NURTPI — 3
RAONEG — 4
NONOI — 5

SOLUTION ON PAGE 284

283 SPY STORY

Can you fill in the missing word, which means the same as those in the boxes?

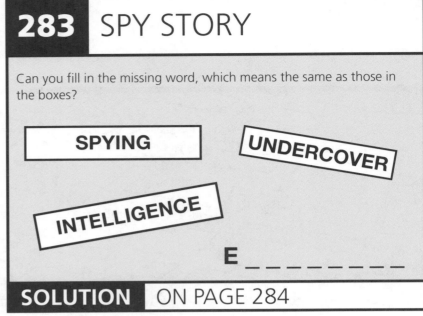

SPYING

UNDERCOVER

INTELLIGENCE

E _ _ _ _ _ _ _ _ _

SOLUTION ON PAGE 284

284 WORD WATCH

If you examine the following words carefully you will discover a connection. Could the word ADORABLE join the list?

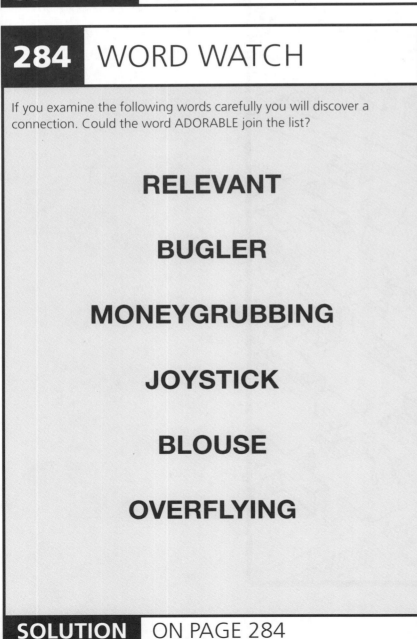

RELEVANT

BUGLER

MONEYGRUBBING

JOYSTICK

BLOUSE

OVERFLYING

SOLUTION ON PAGE 284

285 FOUR-LETTER WORDS

Look carefully at the following groups of four letters. Only one of them can be rearranged to make four four-letter words.

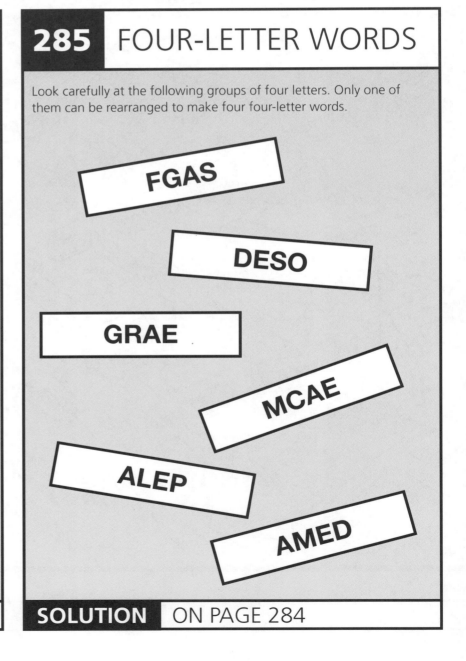

FGAS

DESO

GRAE

MCAE

ALEP

AMED

SOLUTION ON PAGE 284

286 TV TRAUMA

Below are the titles of four TV detective shows. However, the vowels are missing and the letters are all jumbled up. Which are they?

BMLC
DRRM HS TRW
HT FXLS
CHRLS GNSL

SOLUTION ON PAGE 284

287 DEIGHTON DILEMMA

Move from square to square, including diagonals, to discover the name of a movie spy played by Michael Caine.

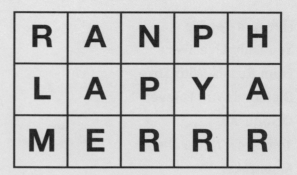

R	A	N	P	H
L	A	P	Y	A
M	E	R	R	R

SOLUTION ON PAGE 285

288 HELLO SAILOR

Five sailors of different rank are at different ports on different ships.

		COMMANDER	CAPTAIN	STEWARD	PURSER	SEAMAN	CRUISER	WARSHIP	FRIGATE	SUBMARINE	AIRCRAFT CARRIER	MALTA	CRETE	FALKLANDS	GIBRALTAR	PORTSMOUTH
NAME	PERKINS															
	WARD															
	MANNING															
	DEWHURST															
	BRAND															
LOCATION	MALTA															
	CRETE															
	FALKLANDS															
	GIBRALTAR															
	PORTSMOUTH															
SHIP	CRUISER															
	WARSHIP															
	FRIGATE															
	SUBMARINE															
	AIRCRAFT CARRIER															

1. Manning is at the Falklands, and the purser is Dewhurst.
2. Brand is on a warship, and the purser is not on the cruiser.
3. Perkins is on the aircraft carrier, and Ward is at Portsmouth.
4. The commander is at the Falklands, and Manning is on a submarine.
5. The warship is at Crete, and Perkins is at Malta.
6. The frigate is at Gibraltar and the steward is at Malta.
7. Brand is a captain and the seaman is not on the frigate.

Work out the details of each sailor.

NAME	RANK	SHIP	LOCATION

SOLUTION ON PAGE 285

289 SHAKEN NOT STIRRED

The titles of 10 James Bond films are hidden in this grid. Can you find them all?

A	X	T	B	N	U	V	T	C	O	D	A	P	K	V	E	I	J	O	O
M	L	O	L	L	A	B	R	E	D	N	U	H	T	G	R	S	F	P	O
F	A	I	E	D	O	A	P	Z	K	X	I	P	O	I	E	Q	R	N	V
W	O	T	V	C	K	N	Z	N	B	N	U	Y	B	P	V	P	O	X	U
K	E	R	V	E	H	N	K	W	W	X	N	P	D	I	E	D	M	U	T
U	C	D	Y	E	A	X	I	P	V	T	M	S	O	S	R	I	R	D	S
G	I	C	X	O	Z	N	Y	S	S	U	P	O	T	C	O	R	U	Y	S
M	W	A	L	T	U	M	D	F	D	H	G	M	A	O	F	G	S	U	D
O	T	S	C	N	A	R	B	L	A	G	M	O	L	L	E	C	S	O	N
L	E	I	Q	O	S	C	E	V	E	M	S	S	A	D	R	B	I	L	R
R	V	N	A	R	F	Q	W	Y	U	T	A	I	E	E	A	S	A	K	U
C	I	O	E	E	N	L	L	N	E	U	D	F	L	R	S	O	W	U	N
F	L	R	U	K	L	L	X	T	U	S	R	I	E	U	D	I	I	L	V
R	Y	O	L	A	A	R	R	B	S	N	O	B	E	N	N	P	T	L	Y
I	L	Y	X	R	S	T	C	B	J	O	O	N	R	A	O	T	H	T	E
G	N	A	V	N	E	R	C	O	Z	I	E	S	L	D	M	N	L	V	X
N	O	L	Y	O	B	T	Q	H	O	C	T	V	Y	Y	A	Y	O	Z	N
K	U	E	T	O	A	S	E	T	Q	I	M	S	O	E	I	L	V	M	K
T	O	T	O	M	O	R	R	O	W	N	E	V	E	R	D	I	E	S	O
V	Y	Y	A	N	D	F	E	B	N	R	Y	J	A	S	T	G	A	E	B

1. **Live and Let Die**
2. **You Only Live Twice**
3. **From Russia With Love**
4. **Diamonds Are Forever**
5. **Octopussy**
6. **Tomorrow Never Dies**
7. **Moonraker**
8. **Casino Royale**
9. **For Your Eyes Only**
10. **Thunderball**

SOLUTION ON PAGE 285

290 FORMULATION

The numbers on the right are formed from the numbers on the left using the same formula in each question. Find the rule and replace the question mark with a number.

31 → 12
15 → 4
13 → 3
41 → ?

SOLUTION ON PAGE 285

291 THE UNKNOWN

Move from square to square, including diagonally, to discover the name of a famous TV detective.

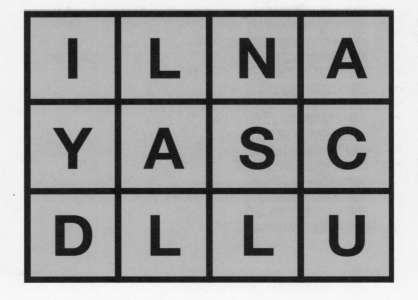

I	L	N	A
Y	A	S	C
D	L	L	U

SOLUTION ON PAGE 285

292 KIDNAPPED

The writer of this note is being held hostage. But why should you not pay the ransom?

Hi,

I don't know where to start. As you know, I have been taken hostage and they have told me to write and tell you what and how to pay.

Don't try anything like going to the police. Leave $100,000 dollars tonight at the map co-ordinates below.

There's no chance of escape, but I'm OK.

Love Sally.

8-2,6-8,5-3,3-7,5-5,7-9,3-5,4-3.

SOLUTION ON PAGE 285

293 CODED

Can you crack this code message?

siettli os on weshongtun steti

SOLUTION ON PAGE 285

294 DOUBLE HELIX

Match this strand of DNA to an identical one in the samples below.

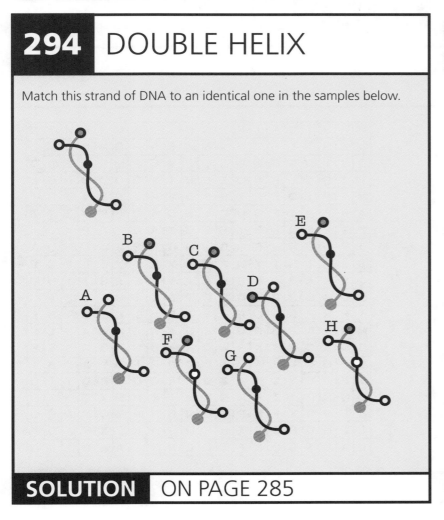

SOLUTION ON PAGE 285

295 PASSAGE POSER

You need to get from side A to side B of this building. Which underground passage do you take?

SOLUTION ON PAGE 285

296 PRESIDENT PROBLEM

If this is CLINTON:

Who are these American Presidents?

SOLUTION ON PAGE 285

297 GUN RUNNING

Bully Bill and Dynamo Dan are cattle ranchers. One day they decide to sell their stock and become sheep farmers. They take the cattle to market and receive for each steer a number of dollars equal to the total number of steer that they sell. With this money they purchase sheep at $10 per head, and with the money left over they purchase a goat.

On the way home they argue and so decide to divide up their stock, but find that they have one sheep over. So Bully Bill keeps the sheep and gives Dynamo Dan the goat.

"But I have less than you," says Dynamo Dan, "because a goat is worth less than a sheep."

"Alright," says Bully Bill, "I will give you my Colt .45 to make up the difference."

What is the value of the Colt.45?

SOLUTION ON PAGE 285

298 MOVIE MAYHEM

There are 10 film titles hidden in this grid. Can you find them all?

1. **Police Academy**
2. **Speed**
3. **Lethal Weapon**
4. **Dirty Harry**
5. **Kindergarten Cop**
6. **Blue Steel**
7. **Naked Gun**
8. **Seven**
9. **L A Confidential**
10. **The Untouchables**

A	R	J	T	C	I	I	K	L	S	O	I	O	A	M	K	R	A	T	O
L	K	N	A	L	E	T	H	A	L	W	E	A	P	O	N	D	O	H	L
D	L	I	D	G	R	X	G	A	C	P	V	C	P	M	L	N	E	E	Q
E	S	D	N	L	B	W	O	L	C	D	I	V	B	O	D	O	N	U	L
M	E	F	I	D	S	F	I	B	K	D	V	P	L	S	E	V	E	N	I
A	H	E	B	T	E	O	O	C	L	R	D	K	U	F	K	N	Z	T	Z
F	I	F	E	O	L	R	I	E	B	G	Y	A	E	K	O	P	V	O	A
J	P	N	O	K	N	P	G	G	I	N	R	Z	S	J	J	O	U	U	A
S	J	D	I	R	T	Y	H	A	R	R	Y	A	T	Y	G	L	V	C	L
J	S	X	A	B	W	E	S	H	R	I	I	L	E	L	B	I	T	H	M
B	D	J	C	R	E	J	C	O	O	T	S	L	E	H	G	C	E	A	U
I	H	K	P	B	W	C	E	J	Y	I	E	L	L	H	X	E	T	B	F
M	N	A	K	E	D	G	U	N	I	Q	I	N	B	H	B	A	S	L	S
D	Q	S	D	A	B	K	H	W	C	R	I	B	C	M	G	C	S	E	E
C	P	O	E	X	F	W	V	I	D	O	D	R	F	O	Y	A	C	S	I
M	E	M	E	N	C	K	A	Z	D	C	E	C	D	I	P	D	Y	I	G
C	Q	S	P	I	Z	E	K	N	H	M	I	Z	H	M	X	E	D	X	D
A	F	P	S	Y	F	H	P	E	G	Q	D	B	P	Z	C	M	A	C	O
E	F	R	Q	C	C	R	X	H	K	N	R	A	K	E	X	Y	F	O	F
D	A	L	A	C	O	N	F	I	D	E	N	T	I	A	L	D	I	J	D

SOLUTION ON PAGE 285

299 FULL OF LEAD

Merged together here are two infamous gangsters. Who are they?

E	B	D	O	Y	N	L	N	C	I	&	E

SOLUTION ON PAGE 295

300 WIRE TAP

You are going to put a tap on a suspect's telephone. Find the wire which goes from the telephone exchange to the suspect's telephone.

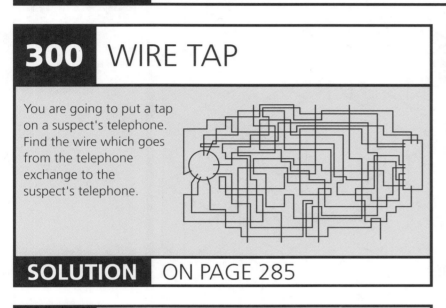

SOLUTION ON PAGE 285

301 MATHS MYSTERY

Can you work out the pattern to fill in the missing number?

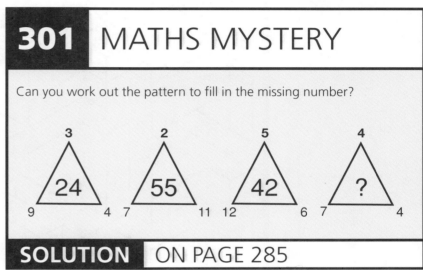

SOLUTION ON PAGE 285

302 GRASS GAME

Below are the current number of police informers in each of these New York districts.

How many in the Wall Street district?

SOLUTION ON PAGE 285

303 PASSWORD POSER

You are attempting to hack into a secret database. To get in you need to key in the correct password. This password is a sequence of 3 x 2 letters.

FBI
Code Red
Authorized Personnel I Only

What are the 6 missing letters to make 2 four letter words on each line?

UN - - VE
IN - - AD
FA - - RO

Enter Password (6 letters)

SOLUTION ON PAGE 285

304 WILD WALLS

START

FINISH

SOLUTION ON PAGE 285

305 THE MILLIONAIRE'S INHERITANCE

A millionaire leaves $14,148,167 to his seven sons and the rest to charity. In his will he makes a proviso that everything must be given to charity if the sons cannot divide the money equally between them. Is there a way in which they can inherit?

SOLUTION ON PAGE 285

307 WORD LOGIC

Rearrange the letters given and make as many words as you can that use all of the letters. At least three words are possible from each group.

1. A E G I L N R Y
2. E N O R S W
3. B D E N O R S U
4. A C D E I L M S
5. A C E E R R S T
6. E E L R S T W
7. A D E E R R S T
8. A D E L P
9. A E E N R S T
10. D E L M O R S

SOLUTION ON PAGE 285

306 HAND IN HAND

Clues 1 down and 12 across (both three words) are not given. These will be discovered by solving the remaining clues.

Across
2 Play a part (3)
4 Court official (5)
5 Female domestic fowl (3)
8 From within (3)
10 Frozen water (3)
13 Expire (3)
14 In favor of (3)
15 The 19th letter of the Greek alphabet (3)
17 Carriage of body (5)
18 Single (3)

Down
2 Type of tree (3)
3 Decimal base (3)
6 The Roman god of love (5)
7 Acid (5)
8 Aged (3)
9 Definite article (3)
10 Little devil (3)
11 The self (3)
15 In addition (3)
16 Employ (3)

SOLUTION ON PAGE 285

308 WORD MATCH

In each of the following groups of words a hidden common connection is present. Can you identify the connection?

1. NARROWLY	TRAILER	GULLIBLE	JAYWALKING
2. MARIGOLDS	JADEDNESS	EPISCOPAL	CHAMBER
3. DISEASE	BETIDE	UNWAVERING	THREEFOLD
4. CHROME	CORNICE	CLIMATE	BONNIEST
5. BARNACLE	CHUTNEY	CRUSHED	CONTENTED
6. COOKING	SHOOTER	MICROWAVE	ACRYLIC
7. NARROWLY	GLANCED	HOAXERS	BURGUNDY
8. ISSUE	SKIMPY	PAMPHLET	BANNER
9. COMBATING	APPROXIMATE	OPERATE	PIGMENT
10. CUSTARD	RISKY	HONEYMOON	MISUNDERSTAND

SOLUTION ON PAGE 285

309 WORD PROBLEM

When each of the following words is rearranged, one group of letters can be used to prefix the others to form longer words. Which word is used as the prefix and what does it become?

	A	B	C	D
1.	RILE	COTS	MUSE	STILE
2.	SHORE	DIE	DUST	TEN
3.	FEATS	LOPE	RYE	BANE
4.	DENT	SON	LYRE	REED
5.	MAD	DEN	SAGE	LESS
6.	TOP	MOOR	EAT	LESS
7.	RED	AND	LEG	RIDE
8.	EMIT	BLEAT	STILE	RILE
9.	SHORE	HOSE	FILES	SHELF
10.	GIN	CEDES	COLA	FILED

SOLUTION ON PAGE 285

310 BALL BAGS

This probability problem can be solved through logical thought.

You have two bags, each one containing eight balls: four white and four black. A ball is drawn out of bag one and another ball out of bag two.

What are the chances that at least one of the balls is black?

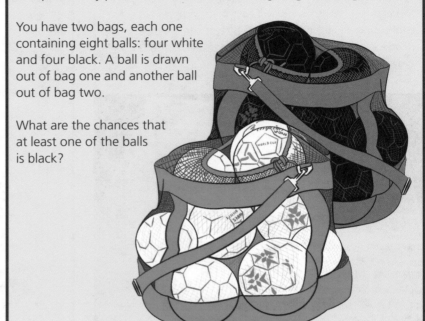

SOLUTION ON PAGE 285

311 GRID GAME

The values of grids A and B are given. What is the value of the grid C?

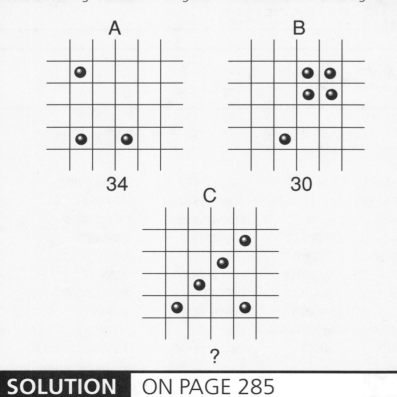

A 34

B 30

C ?

SOLUTION ON PAGE 285

312 SHAPE SHIFTER

Divide this grid into four identical shapes. The sum of the numbers contained within each of the shapes must give the total 134.

5	7	8	15	4	7	5	6
11	6	9	8	16	12	10	10
7	12	10	12	3	11	6	8
6	7	2	5	7	7	15	10
12	15	10	8	5	12	8	7
6	7	11	13	9	6	9	6
9	8	10	6	8	8	1	2
3	6	4	10	10	10	15	15

SOLUTION ON PAGE 285

313 | MISSING NUMBER

What number should replace the question mark?

3569	2307	104
7678	5426	380
9925	4185	?

SOLUTION ON PAGE 285

314 | MATHS IN MOTION

The numbers in box 1 move clockwise to the positions shown in box 2. In which positions should the missing numbers appear?

1

22	15	34
12		14
23	21	19

2

14		12
19		23

SOLUTION ON PAGE 285

315 | GRID GAME

What number is missing from this number grid?

A	B	C	D	E
7	8	7	9	7
5	5	8	5	9
6	3	7	3	9
4	4	8	6	?

SOLUTION ON PAGE 286

316 | TRAIN YOUR MIND

From Ammington to Cadfield is 375 miles by rail. Brotherton is on the line between them and is 150 miles from Ammington.

At 12.00 a train sets out from Ammington and travels to Brotherton, arriving at 13.15. It waits there for 15 minutes and then travels on to Cadfield, arriving at 15.00.

Another train leaves Cadfield at 12.30 and travels non-stop to Ammington at an average speed of 100 miles per hour.

How far from Brotherton do the two trains pass each other and at what time?

SOLUTION ON PAGE 286

317 SHEPHERD'S STORY

A shepherd is planning to build a rectangular enclosure for his sheep, using an existing wall for one side of it. He uses pieces of pre-made fencing, each 2m in length, and will not allow any overlap of the sections. The width of the enclosure must be greater than 20m and the length greater than 40m. He has only 45 sections of fence. What size should he build the structure to enclose the greatest possible area?

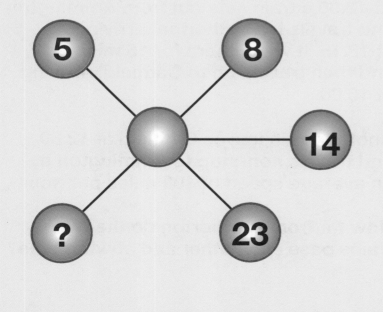

SOLUTION   ON PAGE 286

318 CIRCULAR LOGIC

What is the value of the last string? Black, white and shaded circles have different values.

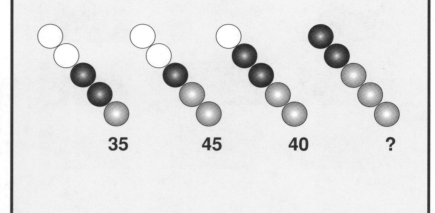

35   45   40   ?

SOLUTION   ON PAGE 286

319 MATHS MYSTERY

Start at the top-left circle and move clockwise. Calculate the number that replaces the question mark.

SOLUTION   ON PAGE 286

320 TIE TANGLE

The number in the middle knot of the following bow ties is reached by using all of the outer numbers only once. You cannot reverse the numbers to obtain the answers. Which numbers should replace the question marks?

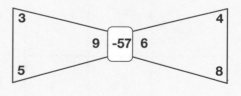

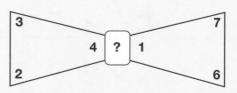

SOLUTION   ON PAGE 286

321 GRID GAME

In the grid below, the intersections have a value equal to the sum of their four touching numbers.

Can you answer the following:

1. What are the grid references for the three intersection points with a value of 100?
2. Which intersection point/s has a value of 92?
3. How many intersections have a value of less than 100?
4. Which intersection has the highest value?
5. Which intersection has the lowest value?
6. Which intersection/s has a value of 115?
7. How many intersections have a value of 105 and which are they?
8. How many intersections have a value of 111 and which are they?

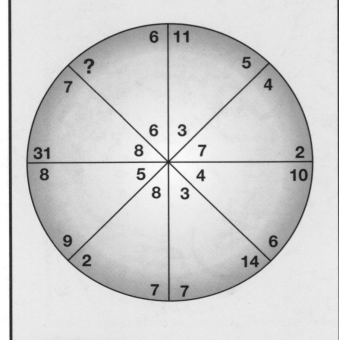

	A	B	C	D	E	F	G
1	30	19	28	26	25	36	16	29
2	24	20	26	23	24	23	24	22
3	26	29	27	20	25	29	27	23
4	20	23	28	32	29	30	24	22
5	30	28	27	22	30	26	27	29
6	20	28	23	28	32	29	31	26
7	25	27	25	27	30	26	24	19
	26	26	29	23	24	28	24	28

SOLUTION ON PAGE 286

322 HOUSE HORROR

Can you find the missing values on the roof of the house below? Each of the numbers on the windows and door must be used only once and no number can be reversed.

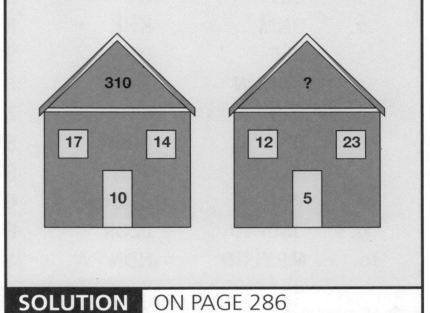

SOLUTION ON PAGE 286

323 MATHS MYSTERY

What number is missing from the segment below?

SOLUTION ON PAGE 286

324 WORD MATCH

Rearrange the following to form five connected words or names. What are they?

1. TOUGHDUN	FACETIKUR	BRAGGRINDEE	CAJPALKF	CRANOOMA
2. HETCS	RESSERD	STEETE	BALET	DAWBRORE
3. DIALDOFF	PRONDOWS	FUNERSLOW	CHISUFA	GONEIBA
4. OCAIR	ELOUS	HTAENS	HAGABDD	GANKKOB
5. TREAKA	FOLG	BYGUR	DUOJ	TINDBONAM
6. WOIBE	SORS	SCONKAJ	STRANDISE	PLESREY
7. NARI	LICHE	RUGAPAYA	LISARE	HOLDALN
8. PORIPNEPE	SORTITO	ZAPIZ	MAISAL	PATAS
9. GUTTSTART	MORDDNUT	BRINLE	NOBN	GRELEBIDEH
10. CREMRUIT	NINACNOM	NACEYEN	MUNCI	GRONEAO

SOLUTION ON PAGE 286

325 VOWEL INVESTIGATION

Add the vowels in the following groups of letters to form five words, one of which does not belong with the others. Which word is the odd one out?

1.	GLV	HT	SCRF	SHWL	BRCLT
2.	DNM	KHK	NYLN	SLK	WL
3.	PLT	DSH	SCR	CHN	BKR
4.	BNGLW	FLT	HS	GRDN	MSNTT
5.	QRTT	GTR	ZTHR	TRMBN	PN
6.	DNCR	GRCR	SLR	DRVR	STDNT
7.	BLTMR	RZN	PHNX	CHCG	HSTN
8.	VDK	BRBN	GRVY	DVCT	BRNDY
9.	DMNND	LLGR	FRTSSM	HRPSCHRD	CRSCND
10.	MRYLND	NDN	NVD	GRG	BSTN

SOLUTION ON PAGE 286

326 LOVELY LABYRINTH

SOLUTION ON PAGE 286

327 HONEY COMB

Find 14 minerals in the honey comb. The letters can go in any direction, but must be adjacent. Letters can be used more than once in a word.

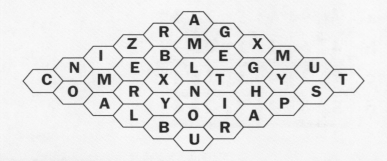

328 THE CHEETAH AND THE HYENA

The cheetah tells lies on Mondays, Tuesdays and Wednesdays, and tells the truth on each of the other days of the week. The hyena lies on Thursdays, Fridays and Saturdays, but tells the truth on each of the other days.

One day the lion heard them talking. The cheetah said, "Yesterday I lied all day," to which the hyena responded with exactly the same words. What day was it?

SOLUTION | ON PAGE 286

329 FORMULATION

The numbers on the right are formed from the numbers on the left using the same formula in each question. Find the rule and replace the question mark with a number.

21 ⟶ 436
15 ⟶ 220
8 ⟶ 59
3 ⟶ ?

SOLUTION | ON PAGE 286

330 THE CAR PROBLEM

When you are moving forward in your car are there parts of the car that appear to be going backward while being attached to the car?

SOLUTION | ON PAGE 286

331 COCKTAIL STICKS

By moving only three of the cocktail sticks in the shape below, can you make four equal triangles? All of the cocktail sticks must be used.

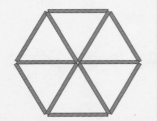

SOLUTION | ON PAGE 286

332 COCKTAIL STICKS

By moving two cocktail sticks can you rearrange the shape below so that you will be left with eight squares of the original size?

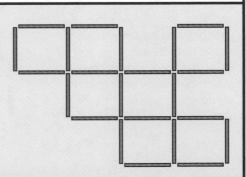

SOLUTION | ON PAGE 286

333 ROTATIONS

Using the logic of the first grid, complete the incomplete grid.

10	18	3
7		9
2	4	11

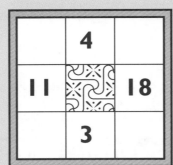

	4	
11		18
	3	

SOLUTION   ON PAGE 286

334 COMPLEX NUMBERS AND LETTER GRID

Using the logic of the first grid, complete the incomplete grid.

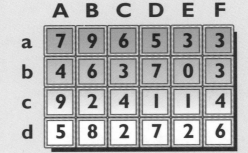

	A	B	C	D	E	F
a	7	9	6	5	3	3
b	4	6	3	7	0	3
c	9	2	4	1	1	4
d	5	8	2	7	2	6

7	7	5	6	1	9
4	9	6	6	0	0
3	5	1	9	0	6
8	9	4	6	?	?

SOLUTION   ON PAGE 286

335 DOZY POLICEMAN

A small boy was riding his bicycle around the housing estate where he lived. He went up and down roads that had no outlets, in and out of trees, up and down the curbs. Unfortunately, he took a sharp turn and the front wheel of his bicycle hit a curb. The small boy fell from his bicycle and was knocked unconscious. Fortunately, there was a policeman at the scene of the accident, You would have thought that an ambulance might have been called, and all details of the accident and statements from anyone who witnessed the accident taken. Why was this not done?

SOLUTION   ON PAGE 286

336 CHANGING WORDS

Changing only one letter and making a new word each time, can you find the shortest routes between the two given words to change the first word into the second word? The order of letters may not change.

A)	SEAT	–	TRAM	(3 letter changes)
B)	HEAD	–	TAIL	(4 letter changes only)
C)	STONE	–	BRICK	(7 letter changes)
D)	WHITE	–	BLACK	(7 letter changes)
E)	HERE	–	JUNK	(5 letter changes)
F)	FAIR	–	RIDE	(6 letter changes)
G)	WRITE	–	CARDS	(5 letter changes)
H)	BROWN	–	TREES	(4 letter changes)
I)	GLASS	–	CHINA	(6 letter changes)
J)	GREEN	–	BLACK	(6 letter changes)

SOLUTION   ON PAGE 286

337 COMPLEX NUMBERS AND LETTER GRID

Using the logic of the first grid, complete the incomplete grid.

	A	B	C	D	E	F
a	7	8	3	5	7	9
b	3	7	4	5	2	9
c	2	2	1	2	2	2
d	4	2	7	5	0	8
e	6	5	9	8	6	4
f	8	2	1	7	5	6

9	1	6	8	4	5
8	3	2	8	8	2
3	0	?	3	1	1
0	9	?	4	9	9
6	4	9	9	1	5
7	1	4	9	6	7

SOLUTION ON PAGE 286

338 DECIMATED

In Roman times, soldiers who were to be punished were forced to form a line, and every tenth one was executed. This is the origin of the word "decimate". If you were one of 1000 soldiers lined up in a circle, with every second soldier being executed until only one remained, in which position would you want to be in order to survive?

SOLUTION ON PAGE 286

339 LOGICAL DEDUCTIONS OF WHO OR WHAT AM I?

What am I?

I give birth, but I am the male of the species.
I am covered by consecutive rings of body armour.
I have a long tubular snout and live in warm waters.
My eyes can work independently of one another.
I am not a mammal.

SOLUTION ON PAGE 286

340 THE RECTOR TOTAL

If each letter is substituted for a number in this addition, can you determine what the value of each letter should be?

```
  C E L L A R
  C O R P S E
  C O L L A R
    C L O S E
     C A S E
+    C O P S
-------------
  R E C T O R
```

SOLUTION ON PAGE 286

341 THE RABBIT FAMILY

How many male and female rabbits are there in a family if each male has one fewer female relative than he has male relatives, and each female has two males fewer than twice the number of female relatives she has?

SOLUTION ON PAGE 286

342 ROTATIONS

Using the logic of the first grid, complete the incomplete grid.

SOLUTION   ON PAGE 286

344 MAGIC SQUARES

Can you complete these two magic squares so that each of the following items total 34? You must use each of the numbers 1–16 once only.

The rows across   = 34
The columns down   = 34
The cross diagonals   = 34
The centre 4 numbers   = 34
Each corner block of
4 numbers   = 34

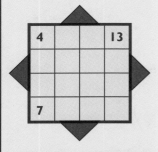

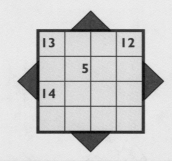

SOLUTION   ON PAGE 286

346 EXTINCT? I DON'T THINK SO

Can you think of an animal, which, if made extinct and all of the seeds from that animal were also destroyed, could repopulate the world in under two years?

SOLUTION   ON PAGE 287

343 COMPLEX NUMBERS AND LETTER GRIDS

Using the logic of the first grid, complete the incomplete grid.

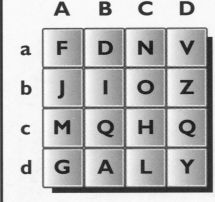

SOLUTION   ON PAGE 286

345 FORMULATIONS

The numbers on the right are formed from the numbers on the left using the same formula in each question. Find the rule and replace the question mark with a number.

9 ⟶ 85
6 ⟶ 40
13 ⟶ 173
4 ⟶ ?

SOLUTION   ON PAGE 286

347 THE FIRE STATION LOCATION

The drawing below represents the time it takes to go between towns for the fire engine. You have to locate a fire station that minimizes the travel times to each location. Where would you locate the station to minimize the longest journey?

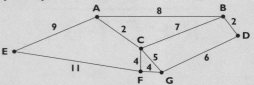

SOLUTION   ON PAGE 287

348 COCKTAIL STICKS

Moving only three of the cocktail sticks in the shape below, can you make seven triangles and three diamond shapes?

SOLUTION ON 287

349 STRANGE BUT TRUE!

Two famous people once challenged each other to a duel. Seconds were selected and weapons were chosen. Pistols were suggested, but one of them objected saying that this was most unfair to him. One of the duellists was much taller and was therefore a larger target, whereas the other was a smaller target. How was this resolved?

CLUES
1. The suggestion came from the shorter man and his seconds.
2. They could still fire at the same time and in the traditional way.
3. They were both given only one shot.

SOLUTION ON PAGE 287

350 CELL STRUCTURE

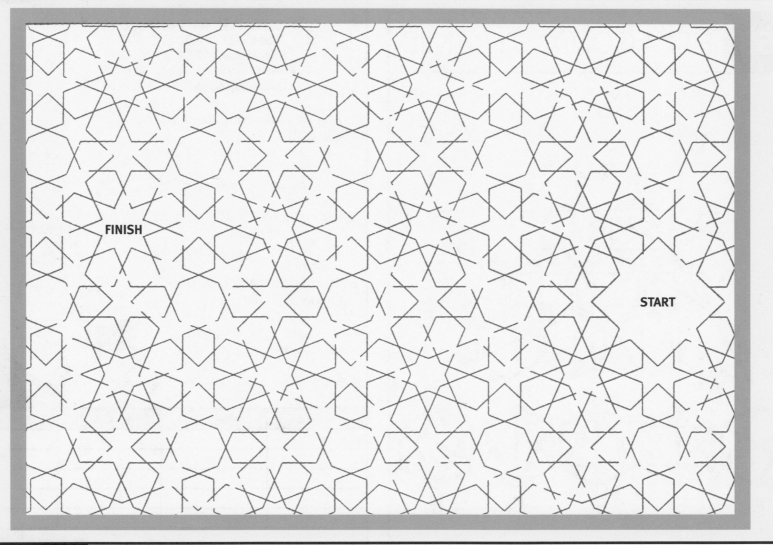

SOLUTION ON PAGE 287

351 THE MEETING

The man from Nepal came by plane to visit the man from China who wore a chain around his neck. What was the weather like when the man from Iran joined them?

SOLUTION ON PAGE 287

353 HEXAGONAL PYRAMID

Look at the pyramid. From the following options, choose the contents of the top hexagon.

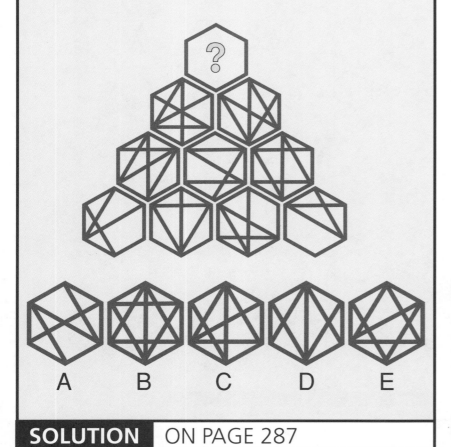

A   B   C   D   E

SOLUTION ON PAGE 287

352 FAIRGROUND FIESTA

At the carnival five boys of different ages eat different foods and take different rides.

		AGE					RIDE					FOOD				
		11	12	13	14	15	BIG DIPPER	DODGEMS	MOUNTAIN	WHIRLIGIG	CROCODILE	ICE CREAM	HOT DOG	CANDY FLOSS	FRIES	GUM
NAME	SAM															
	JOE															
	DON															
	LEN															
	RON															
FOOD	ICE CREAM															
	HOT DOG															
	CANDY FLOSS															
	FRIES															
	GUM															
RIDE	BIG DIPPER															
	DODGEMS															
	MOUNTAIN															
	WHIRLIGIG															
	CROCODILE															

1. Ron eats ice cream, Joe does not chew gum.
2. Sam, who is 14 years old, is not on the mountain.
3. The boy on the crocodile is 15 years old.
4. Len is not on the dodgems; Don is on the whirligig.
5. The boy eating ice cream is 13 years old.
6. The boy on the dodgems is eating a hot dog.
7. Joe eats fries on the big dipper.
8. Don, who is 12, is eating candy floss.

Work out the details of each boy.

NAME	AGE	RIDE	FOOD

SOLUTION ON PAGE 287

354 LOGIC CIRCLES

Look at the four circles. Should A, B, C, D or E continue the sequence?

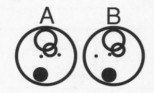

SOLUTION ON PAGE 287

355 STRANGE SERIES

What is the next figure in this series?

SOLUTION ON PAGE 287

356 SUSPICIOUS SHAPE

What is the next figure in this series?

SOLUTION ON PAGE 287

357 SEQUENCE SEARCH

Look at the four circles. Which of the following options comes next in this sequence?

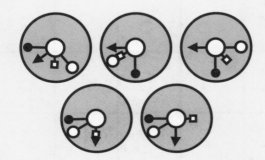

SOLUTION ON PAGE 287

358 SYMBOL SEARCH

Each line and symbol which appears in the four outer circles is transferred to the middle circle according to a few rules. If a line or symbol occurs in the outer circles:
once, it is transferred;
twice, it is possibly transferred;
three times, it is transferred;
four times, it is not transferred.

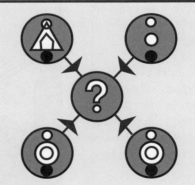

Which of the following circles should appear at the centre of the diagram?

SOLUTION ON PAGE 287

359 BIRD FANCIERS

Five men from different countries each like a different bird. Each bird has a different collective noun.

		COUNTRY					BIRD					COLLECTIVE NOUN				
		GERMANY	BELGIUM	FRANCE	ENGLAND	SCOTLAND	OWLS	PLOVERS	STARLINGS	CROWS	RAVENS	MURMURATION	WING	UNKINDNESS	MURDER	PARLIAMENT
NAME	ALBERT															
	ROGER															
	HAROLD															
	CAMERON															
	EDWARD															
COLLECTIVE NOUN	MURMURATION															
	WING															
	UNKINDNESS															
	MURDER															
	PARLIAMENT															
BIRD	OWLS															
	PLOVERS															
	STARLINGS															
	CROWS															
	RAVENS															

1. Roger does not like plovers, which are not called a parliament.
2. The man who likes crows comes from France. This is not Edward, who is not from Scotland.
3. Albert likes owls; a group of starlings is called a murmuration.
4. Harold comes from Germany and likes ravens.
5. The man from England likes starlings.
6. Edward does not like the group called an unkindness of ravens.
7. The man who likes the group called murder comes from France.
8. Cameron is not from Belgium; Albert is not from Scotland.
9. The man who likes the group called wing is not from Germany.

Work out the details for each man.

NAME	COUNTRY	BIRD	COLLECTIVE NOUN

SOLUTION   ON PAGE 287

360 WORD MATCH

Join the letters of the given words to form a single word using all of the letters.

1.	PEER	+	DAMP
2	MEAL	+	DIVE
3.	HALL	+	SEES
4.	RATE	+	RUSE
5.	WALL	+	FREE

SOLUTION   ON PAGE 287

361 FOMULATION

What is the next figure in this series?

31 ———→ 12
15 ———→ 4
13 ———→ 3
41 ———→ ?

SOLUTION   ON PAGE 287

362 GRID GAME

What number is missing from this number grid?

	A	B	C	D	E
	3	5	4	6	3
	4	8	5	9	7
	6	1	5	4	6
	2	2	?	1	4

SOLUTION   ON PAGE 287

363 MOVING MYSTERY

The numbers in box 1 move clockwise to the positions shown in box 2. In which positions should the missing numbers appear?

1

3	5	8
1		6
17	7	9

2

	1	
5		8
	7	

SOLUTION ON PAGE 287

364 NUMBER NONSENSE

What number should replace the question mark?

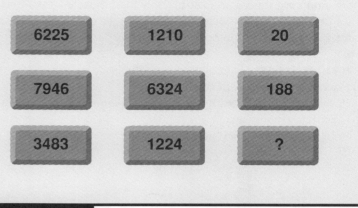

6225	1210	20
7946	6324	188
3483	1224	?

SOLUTION ON PAGE 287

365 GRID GAME

A triangle denotes the grid value and a circle denotes twice the grid value. The values of grids A and B are given. What is the value of the grid C?

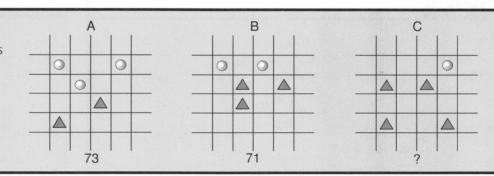

A: 73 B: 71 C: ?

SOLUTION ON PAGE 287

366 MATHS MYSTERY

Can you calculate the number missing in the figure below? Each number is used once only and is not reversed.

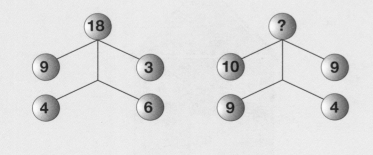

18 9 3 4 6

? 10 9 9 4

SOLUTION ON PAGE 287

367 CIRCULAR LOGIC

What is the value of the last string? Black, white and shaded circles have different values.

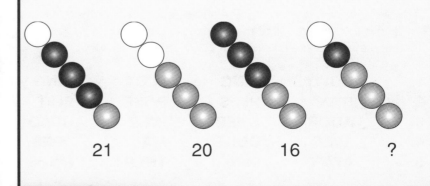

21   20   16   ?

SOLUTION ON PAGE 287

368 A WAITER'S LOT IS NOT A HAPPY ONE

A waiter is serving vegetables to 51 diners in a hotel. There are peas, carrots, and cauliflower. Two more diners want peas and carrots only than those who wanted just peas. Twice as many people want peas only as cauliflower only. Twenty-five diners do not want cauliflower, 18 diners do not want carrots, and 13 diners do not want peas. Six diners want cauliflower and peas but no carrots.

a) How many diners want all three vegetables?
b) How many diners want cauliflower only?
c) How many diners want two of the three vegetables?
d) How many diners want carrots only?
e) How many diners want peas only?

SOLUTION ON PAGE 287

369 TIE TANGLE

The number in the middle knot of the following bow ties is reached by using all of the outer numbers only once. You cannot reverse the numbers to obtain the answers. Which number should replace the question mark?

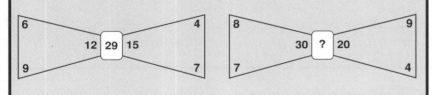

SOLUTION ON PAGE 287

371 PREFIX POSER

Each of the following words has the prefix missing. The prefix on each question is the same for all of the words in that question. Can you find the prefixes for the following?

1. _ _ _ DOWY   _ _ _ KING   _ _ _ LLOT   _ _ _ RING
2. _ _ _ ITAN   _ _ _ PLES   _ _ _ POSE   _ _ _ SUIT
3. _ _ _ ADOR   _ _ _ CHED   _ _ _ INEE   _ _ _ URED
4. _ _ _ EVER   _ _ _ DDLE   _ _ _ MACE   _ _ _ PPER
5. _ _ _ AWAY   _ _ _ MING   _ _ _ THER   _ _ _ MERS

SOLUTION ON PAGE 287

370 HOUSE HORROR

Can you find the missing value on the roof of the house below? Each of the numbers on the windows and door must be used only once and no number can be reversed.

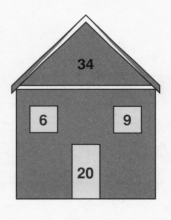

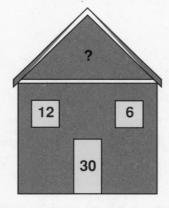

SOLUTION ON PAGE 287

372 SYNONYMS

For each word shown write another word with the same meaning beginning with the letter "C".

1. PSYCHIC
2. ACCURATE
3. INFORMAL
4. SLINGSHOT
5. ANGEL

6. ATROCITY
7. OPPOSE
8. PUNISH
9. INEXPENSIVE
10. INFANT

SOLUTION ON PAGE 287

374 FORMULATION

The numbers on the right are formed from the numbers on the left using the same formula in each question. Find the rule and replace the question mark with a number.

7 ⟶ 15
16 ⟶ 51
4 ⟶ 3
21 ⟶ ?

SOLUTION ON PAGE 287

376 NUMBER NONSENSE

Can you calculate the number missing in the figure below? Each number is used once only and is not reversed.

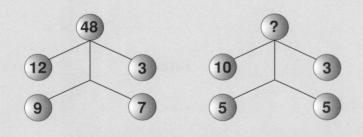

SOLUTION ON PAGE 287

373 MATHS MYSTERY

What number is missing from the segment below?

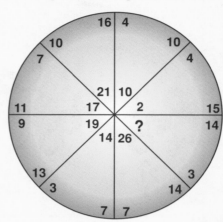

SOLUTION ON PAGE 287

375 STUDENT STORY

At a college teaching crafts, sciences and humanities, the new intake of students can study a maximum of two of the three subjects. One more student is studying a craft and a humanities than a craft only. Two more are studying both a science and a humanities than are studying both a craft and a science. Half as many are studying both a craft and a humanities as are studying both a craft and a science. Twenty-one students are not doing a craft subject. Three students are studying a humanities subject only and six are studying a science only.

1. How many students are not studying a science?
2. How many students are studying both a science and humanities?
3. How many students are studying two subjects?
4. How many students are studying only one subject?
5. How many students are not doing a humanities subject?
6. How many students are studying a craft only?

SOLUTION ON PAGE 287

377 CIRCULAR LOGIC

What is the value of the last string? Black, white and shaded circles have different values.

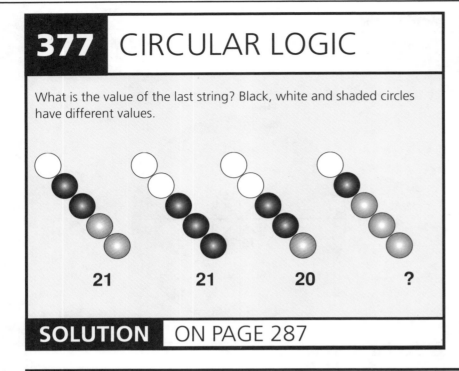

378 NUMBER NONSENSE

Start at the top-left circle and move clockwise. Calculate the number that replaces the question mark.

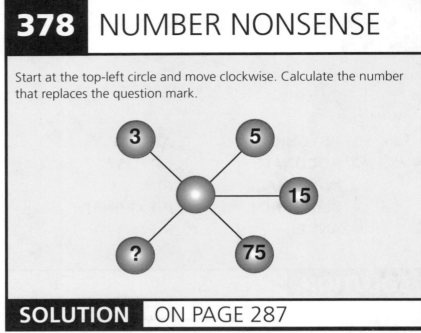

SOLUTION   ON PAGE 287

SOLUTION   ON PAGE 287

379 CELL STRUCTURE

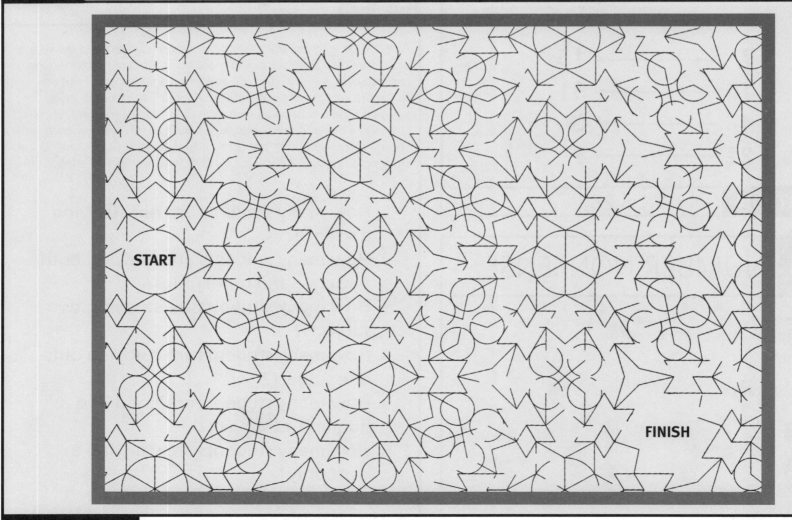

SOLUTION   ON PAGE 287

380 THE GRAVEL QUARRY

Big Al and Little Joe had just robbed a jeweller's but the police were not far behind them. Their escape route went near an abandoned gravel quarry where Little Joe worked when the quarry was open. They stopped and dropped the bag containing the jewels over the edge of the rim and saw where it landed. Just to make sure it was well hidden, they threw some dry sand over the bag where it had landed. After 20 seconds they looked over the edge and they could not see the bag, and the sand blended with the damp sandy surface below. Two miles further on the police arrested the men and later had to release them for lack of evidence. Big Al killed Little Joe the next day and got away with the murder.
What were the circumstances?

CLUES

1. Neither of them had told the police where to find the jewels.
2. No animal, bird or person moved the jewels.
3. The jewels had gone from the spot where they were stacked.
4. Big Al did not take the jewels in the night and he did not suspect Little Joe of taking the jewels. Little Joe did not suspect Big Al of removing the jewels.
5. They remembered the correct spot exactly.
6. A warning sign had been placed so that it could not be seen from above.

SOLUTION ON PAGE 287

381 FORMULATION

The numbers on the right are formed from the numbers on the left using the same formula in each question. Find the rule and replace the question mark with a number.

21 ⟶ 436
15 ⟶ 220
8 ⟶ 59
3 ⟶ ?

SOLUTION ON PAGE 287

383 EASY EQUATION

Correct this equation so that it makes sense by freely moving the given four digits but without introducing any additional mathematical symbols.

$$76 = 24$$

SOLUTION ON PAGE 287

382 WORD SEARCH

Find at least 18 living or extinct creatures in the grid. Words may run in any direction but only in a straight line and without any gaps.

T	C	R	O	B	I	N	M
H	R	I	P	A	K	O	Y
R	A	E	U	T	S	C	C
U	N	E	P	Q	B	H	O
S	E	T	U	U	I	O	K
H	I	I	C	C	O	W	C
T	T	K	K	O	O	R	E
O	W	L	I	B	R	E	G

SOLUTION ON PAGE 287

384 TRYING TROMINOES

Consider the three trominoes. Now choose one of the following to accompany them.

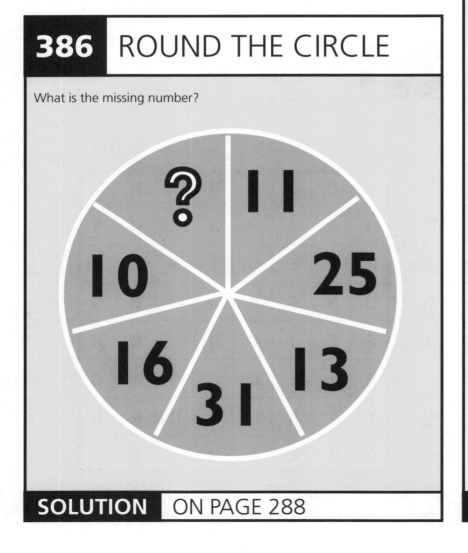

SOLUTION   ON PAGE 287

385 UNWANTED GUEST

Which is the odd one out?

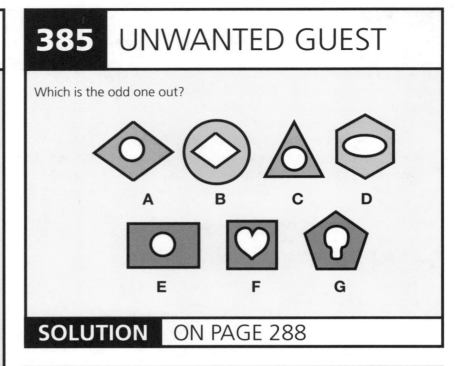

SOLUTION   ON PAGE 288

386 ROUND THE CIRCLE

What is the missing number?

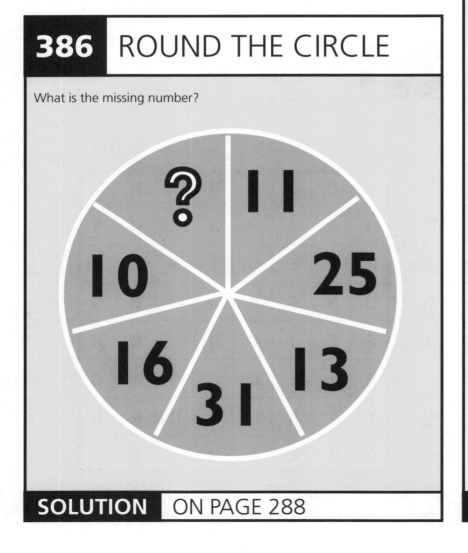

SOLUTION   ON PAGE 288

387 FOLLOWING FUN

Look at the sequence. Which of the following options comes next?

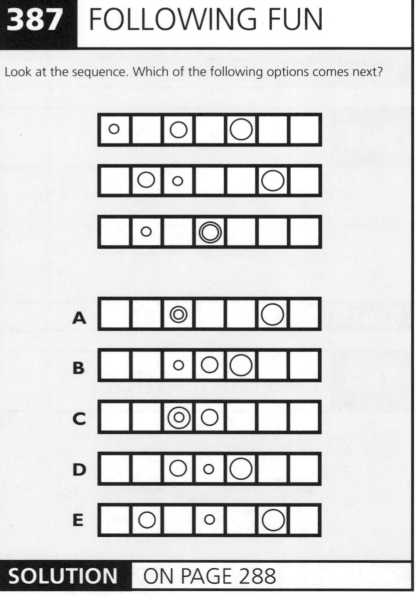

SOLUTION   ON PAGE 288

388 TRIANGLE TEASER

Work out the three missing numbers in the third triangle.

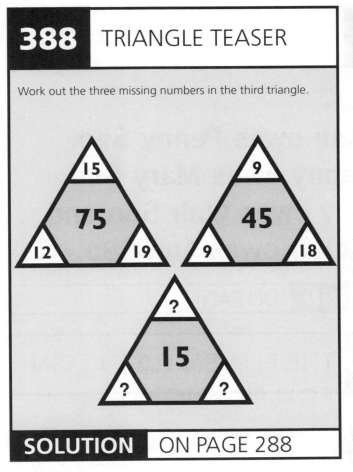

SOLUTION ON PAGE 288

389 CHANGING TRAINS

A woman usually leaves work at 5.30pm, calls at the supermarket, then catches the 6pm train, which arrives at the station in her home town at 6.30pm. Her husband leaves home each day, drives to the station and picks her up at 6.30pm, just as she gets off the train.

Today the woman finishes work about five minutes earlier than usual, decides to go straight to the station instead of calling at the supermarket, and manages to catch the 5.30pm train, which arrives at her home station at 6pm. Since her husband is not there to pick her up she begins to walk home. Her husband leaves home at the usual time, sees his wife walking, turns around, picks her up and drives home, arriving there 10 minutes earlier than usual.

Assume that all the trains arrive precisely on time. For how long does the woman walk before her husband picks her up?

SOLUTION ON PAGE 288

390 LINKS?

What number should replace the question mark?

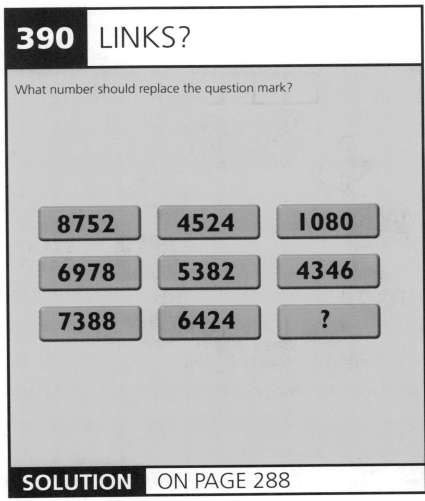

8752	4524	1080
6978	5382	4346
7388	6424	?

SOLUTION ON PAGE 288

391 EQUAL SEGMENTS

Divide this grid into four identical shapes so that the sum of the numbers in each section is as given below.

TOTAL 50

8	8	3	6	5	5
8	4	4	7	7	4
5	5	5	8	3	5
9	8	3	4	7	3
7	5	9	3	5	8
6	4	4	8	3	4

SOLUTION ON PAGE 288

392 | CLASSIC CAR

An Englishman who was a collector of classic cars was invited to display one of them at a rally in the USA. He noticed that he was not getting the mileage per gallon of fuel in America that he got in England. Why?

CLUES

1. The fuel was the same octane from the same oil company.
2. He had tested it on long and short distances.
3. It was not due to hills.
4. It had nothing to do with humidity.

SOLUTION | ON PAGE 288

393 | TIME TO SETTLE UP

What is the smallest number of cheques needed to settle the following debts, if all debts are paid by cheque?

Ann owes Penny $20. Penny owes Mary $40. Mary owes Clair $60 and Clair owes Ann $80.

SOLUTION | ON PAGE 288

394 | NUMERICAL LINKS

The two words in the puzzle below have a connection with the numbers. Can you identify the missing numbers?

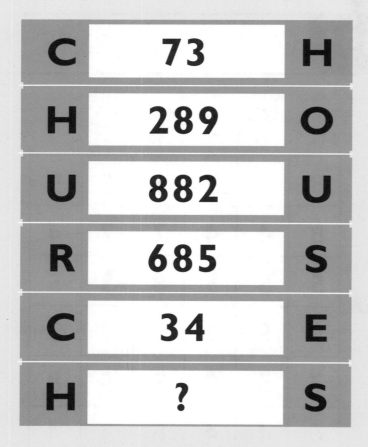

C	73	H
H	289	O
U	882	U
R	685	S
C	34	E
H	?	S

SOLUTION | ON PAGE 288

395 | THE ELEVEN-CARD CON

The object of the game is to lift the last card. Two players can take either one or two adjoining cards each time. Player 1 starts from the centre. If Player 1 removes one card, then you remove two cards from the opposite side of the circle of cards so that the cards are split into two groups of four cards each. If Player 1 removes two cards on the first move, you only remove one card but split the cards into two groups of four. What strategy does the second player now need to adopt to win virtually every game? Remember, two cards can only be lifted if they are next to each other.

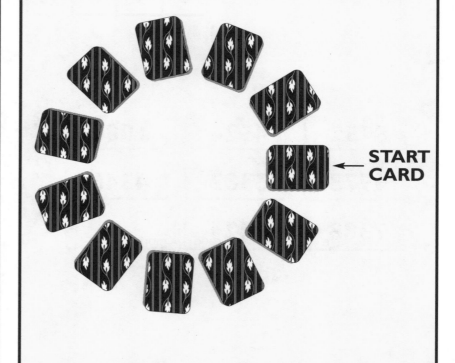

← **START CARD**

SOLUTION | ON PAGE 288

396 | DUNGEON DILEMMA

You are trapped in an underground dungeon. You manage to open the air conditioning vent and crawl into the system. Which route do you take to get to the outside?

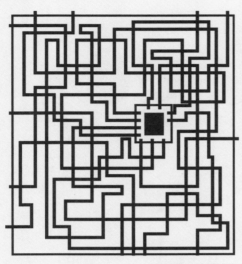

SOLUTION   ON PAGE 288

397 | DOOR NUMBER PUZZLE

Two workmen are putting the finishing touches to a new door they have fitted to house number 4761. All that is left to do is to screw the four metal digits to the door. Being a Mensa member, Patrick could not resist challenging Bruce by asking him if he could screw the digits onto the door to give a four-figure number which could not be divided exactly by 9. When they had resolved that puzzle Bruce then asked Patrick if he could screw the same digits onto the door to give a four-figure number which could not be divided exactly by 3.

What are the answers to the two puzzles? Can either of them be done?

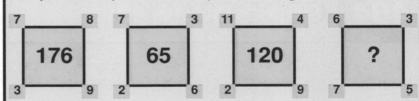

SOLUTION   ON PAGE 288

398 | CHRISTIE CRIME

Move from square to square, including diagonally, to discover the name of a famous TV detective.

J	I	S	A
E	M	S	M
L	P	R	A

SOLUTION   ON PAGE 288

399 | MATHS MYSTERY

Can you find the pattern and discover the missing number?

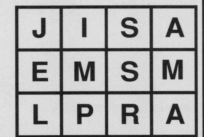

7   8   7   3   11   4   6   3

176   **65**   **120**   **?**

3   9   2   6   2   9   7   5

SOLUTION   ON PAGE 288

400 | CHIVS IN CHICAGO

These crimes were committed in Chicago this month. How many stabbings?

Poisonings	Stabbings	Shootings
100	**?**	**81**

SOLUTION   ON PAGE 288

401 | CODE NAME

Two famous fictional detectives are merged together here.

Who are they?

SOLUTION   ON PAGE 288

402 RUN OUT OF STEAM

Mr Smith's place of employment is nine miles from his home. One day he decides to jog to work in order to increase his fitness. He estimates the journey time to be a little over 1 hour and 45 minutes. As he sets off the village clock strikes 7 a.m.

At first he feels fine, but before long his energy begins to fade and he realizes he will not be able to run the whole distance. A passing taxi is the answer to his prayer. Mr Smith hails the cab and completes his journey, arriving at work 1 hour and 10 minutes earlier than he had anticipated.

Assuming Mr Smith could run at 1/6 the speed of the cab, how far did he run before he hailed the taxi?

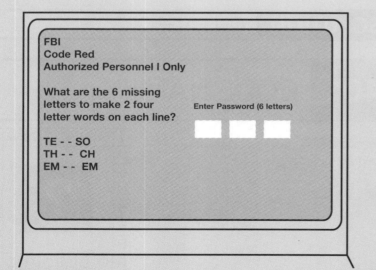

SOLUTION ON PAGE 288

404 CODE CRACKER

You are attempting to hack into a secret database. To get in you need to key in the correct password. This password is a sequence of 3 x 2 letters.

FBI
Code Red
Authorized Personnel I Only

What are the 6 missing letters to make 2 four letter words on each line?

Enter Password (6 letters)

TE - - SO
TH - - CH
EM - - EM

SOLUTION ON PAGE 288

403 OBSERVATION

Observation skills are crucial in detective work.
Spend 2 minutes looking at this page then answer the questions without referring to the diagram.

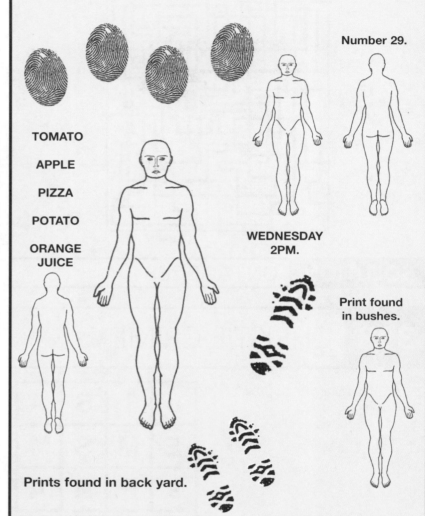

TOMATO

APPLE

PIZZA

POTATO

ORANGE JUICE

Number 29.

WEDNESDAY 2PM.

Print found in bushes.

Prints found in back yard.

1. How many bodies are there?

2. How many of them are facing the front?

3. What drink is mentioned?

4. What 4 foods are mentioned?

5. How many small shoe prints?

6. What day is mentioned?

7. How many fingerprints are there?

8. What time is mentioned?

9. What number is mentioned?

10. Where was the large shoe print found?

SOLUTION ON PAGE 288

405 CODED CITIES

If this is New York:

What are these American Cities?

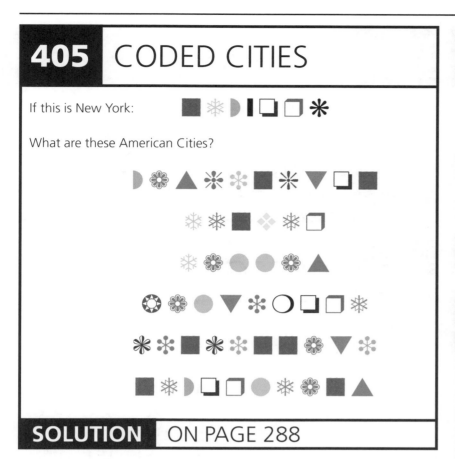

SOLUTION ON PAGE 288

408 WINE WORD

Hidden in this grid are Pasta Sauce, Tomato, Cheese and Pepper. The remaining words spell out the name of a famous Italian wine.

What is it?

E	C	U	A	S
A	P	H	E	T
T	E	A	S	O
S	P	I	E	M
A	P	I	E	A
P	E	T	H	T
C	R	N	C	O

SOLUTION ON PAGE 288

410 CODE BREAKER

What does this code message say?

ba in tha truen ti balgruda ut feva

SOLUTION ON PAGE 288

406 WORD WATCH

Can you fill in the missing word, which means the same as those in the boxes?

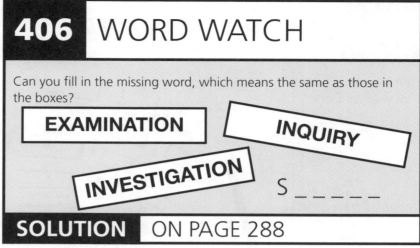

EXAMINATION

INQUIRY

INVESTIGATION

S _ _ _ _ _ _

SOLUTION ON PAGE 288

407 SCENE OF CRIME

You are a Scene of Crime officer. You have just arrived at a homicide and have to cordon off the area. This is shown here.

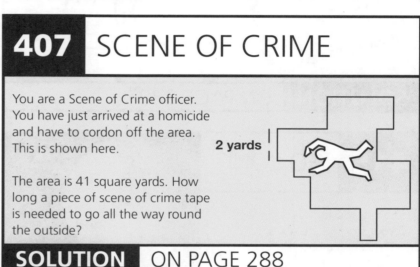

2 yards

The area is 41 square yards. How long a piece of scene of crime tape is needed to go all the way round the outside?

SOLUTION ON PAGE 288

409 MIXED MESSAGE

Can you read this message?

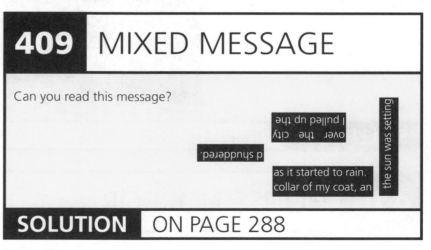

SOLUTION ON PAGE 288

411 TRICKY TAKEAWAY

From which number can you take away half and leave nothing?

SOLUTION ON PAGE 288

412   WHERE TO WAIT?

Where should you wait for your contact?

SHOPPING LIST

A packet of tea.
1 half pound of herrings.
A tub of ice cream.
2 pounds of raisins.
6 donuts.
1 quarter pound of anchovies.
1 pound of veal.
6 eggs.

SOLUTION   ON PAGE 288

415   GO LONG

How can you throw a ball with all your strength, and make it stop and come back to you, without it hitting a wall or any other obstruction, and without anything being attached to it?

SOLUTION   ON PAGE 288

416   HOUSE HORROR

Can you find the missing value on the roof of the second house? Each of the numbers on the windows and door must be used only once and no number can be reversed.

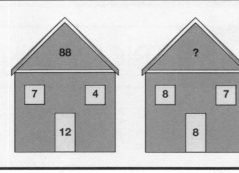

SOLUTION   ON PAGE 288

413   LOSE A LETTER

Which of the following letters does not belong in this sequence?

based

SOLUTION   ON PAGE 288

414   LOST BOND

Join the letters together using straight lines, and without crossing over a line, to find the name of a former James Bond actor.

S	Y	P	S
T	B	E	G
R	N	O	R
Z	E	G	O
A	L	E	M

SOLUTION   ON PAGE 288

417   WORD MATCH

In each line can you underline the two words that are nearest in meaning?

A	**B**	**C**	**D**	**E**
Encourage	Indicate	Assure	Suggest	Promise
Assembly	Direction	Presentation	Construction	Preparation
Early	Instant	Alert	Immediate	Efficient
Prospect	Verification	Proof	Trial	Demonstration
Skill	Professional	Cleverness	Readiness	Talent

SOLUTION   ON PAGE 288

418   SHAPE SORTER

Which of the following is the odd one out?

SOLUTION   ON PAGE 288

419 BOX BUNGLE

Which of these boxes can be made from the template? No sign is repeated on more than one side of the box.

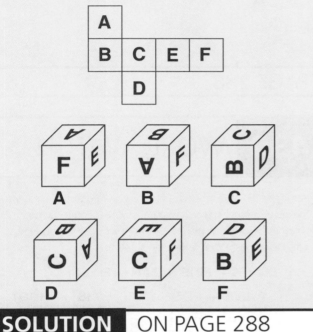

SOLUTION ON PAGE 288

420 BOXES

Which of these boxes can be made from the template? No sign is repeated on more than one side of the box.

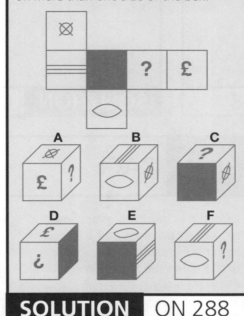

SOLUTION ON 288

421 SKYSCRAPER SIZZLER

A woman lives in a skyscraper 36 floors high and served by several elevators, which stop at each floor going up and down. Each morning she leaves her apartment on one of the floors and goes to one of the elevators. Whichever one she takes is three times more likely to be going up than down.

Why is this?

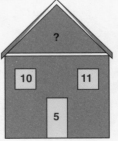

SOLUTION ON 288

422 MATHS MYSTERY

Start at the top-left circle and move clockwise. Calculate the number that replaces the question mark in the following:

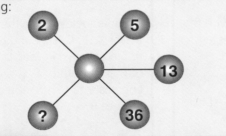

SOLUTION ON PAGE 288

423 TIES

The number in the middle knot of the following bow ties is reached by using all of the outer numbers only once. You cannot reverse the numbers to obtain the answers. Which number should replace the question mark?

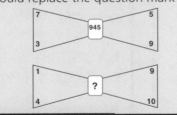

SOLUTION ON 288

424 HOUSES

Can you find the missing value on the roof of the second house? Each of the numbers on the windows and door must be used only once and no number can be reversed.

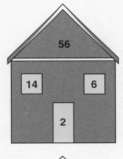

SOLUTION ON 288

425 SHAPE SHIFTER

Which of the following is the odd one out?

A   B   C   D   E

SOLUTION ON PAGE 288

426 ZOO QUEST

Take one letter from each of the following words and form the name of another animal:

**CHEETAH
PANDA
MOUSE
ZEBRA
LION**

SOLUTION ON PAGE 288

427 BOX PROBLEM

Which of these boxes can be made from the template? No sign is repeated on more than one side of the box.

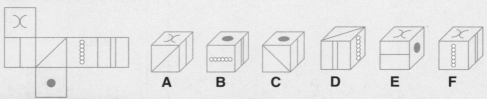

A   B   C   D   E   F

SOLUTION ON PAGE 288

428 Q HERE

Six people, A, B, C, D, E and F, are in a supermarket queue. F is not at the end of the queue, and he has two people between him and the end of the queue who is not E. A has at least four in front of him but is not at the end either. D is not first and has at least two behind him, and C is neither first nor last.
List the order of people from the front.

SOLUTION ON 288

429 RACE

From the information given, find the names and positions of the first eight to finish the marathon:
Sean finishes the marathon in fourth place. He finishes after John but before Sandra. Sandra finishes before Robert but after Liam. John finishes after Rick but before Alex. Anne finishes two places after Alex. Liam is sixth to finish the race.

SOLUTION ON 288

430 WORD WATCH

Remove one letter from the first given word and place it into the second word to form two new words. You must not change the order of the letters in the words and you may not use plurals. What letter needs to move?

e.g. LEARN — FINE   (LEAN — FINER)

1. WAIVE — NOSE
2. HONEY — EAST
3. OLIVE — CAST
4. RIFLE — LAKE
5. WAIST — HOOT
6. PAINT — BLOT
7. TRUST — DEER
8. VITAL — ABLE

SOLUTION ON PAGE 288

431 MATHS MYSTERY

1. How many numbers 1–15 appear in their own triangle?
2. Of the numbers 1–15, which numbers are missing?
3. Which number/s is/are in all three shapes?
4. From the sum of the numbers appearing in only two shapes, deduct the sum of the numbers appearing in only one shape.
5. If each numbered shape is separated from the whole, how many numbers will not be in a square, rectangle, or triangle?

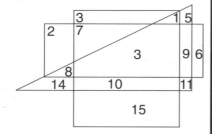

SOLUTION ON PAGE 288

432 WORDS

Match the word groups below with the given word. Which group completes each line? Answer A, B, C, D or E.

1. YOGHURT, 2. TREACHEROUS
3. LIZARD, 4. BERNE, 5. SCALES

A	B	C
Anaconda	Butter	Toaster
Alligator	Milk	Colander
Terrapin	Cheese	Skillet

D	E
Dangerous	Cairo
Threatening	Paris
Hazardous	Athens

SOLUTION ON 289

433 COMPASS

The map below gives the location of 6 towns A, B, C, D, E and F, but they are not in any given order. D is south-west of B and south of E. C is northeast of A and east of F. E is southeast of F and west of B.

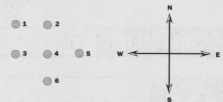

1. Which town is at point 2?
2. Which town is furthest south?
3. Which town is northwest of E?
4. Which town is at point 3?
5. Which town is furthest east?
6. Which town is due south of B?

SOLUTION ON 289

434 FIND THE LETTERS

The following words are lacking the same three letters. If you can discover what they are you will be able to form four five-letter words.

P _ R _

R _ _ P _

_ P _ R _

_ P _ _ R

SOLUTION ON 289

435 BLANKET

A man walked to the top of a hill carrying a blanket. Over 100 people died because of this. Why?

Clues

1. People did not die of suffocation.
2. The blanket was clean to start with but became very dirty.
3. Neither the blanket nor the man carried any diseases.
4. It was warm work.

SOLUTION ON 289

436 THE RAIL WORKERS

Two rail workers were repairing a line when an express train came thundering toward them at speed. The train driver was not aware that they were working on the line so he did not have the chance to slow down. The two workers ran straight toward the express train between the lines that the express was using. Why?

Clues

1. They had not gone mad and did not wish to die.
2. They had forgotten the express was due.
3. They would have been killed if they ran the other way.

SOLUTION ON PAGE 289

437 THE DETECTIVE BOOKING CLERK

The policeman and his wife went to a ski resort in Colorado. The policeman's wife was found dead at the foot of a large drop at the edge of a cliff. The booking clerk who had organized the holiday contacted the local police and the husband was arrested for murder. How did the clerk know it was foul play?

Clues

1. The clerk had never met the policeman or his wife.
2. The local police would not have arrested the policeman without the clerk's information.
3. The ski tracks did not show any foul play.
4. She died from the fall.
5. She was good on skis.

SOLUTION ON PAGE 289

438 THE BOOKS

A lady walked up to the counter with two books and the assistant said, "That will be $6.95, please." The woman handed over the money and walked away without the books. Why was that?

SOLUTION ON PAGE 289

439 LOST TIME

A clock on the wall falls to the floor and the face breaks into three pieces. The digits on each piece of clock add up to the same total. What are the digits on each piece?

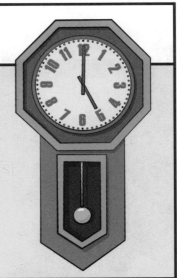

SOLUTION ON PAGE 289

440 STICKY BUSINESS

A stick breaks into three pieces. Without measuring the pieces or trying to construct a triangle, how can you quickly determine whether the pieces will form a triangle?

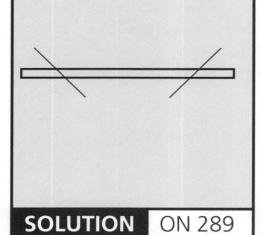

SOLUTION ON 289

441 LITTLE AND LARGE

Which is the odd one out?

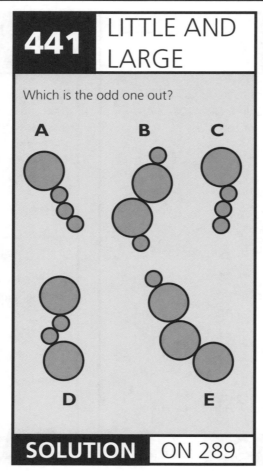

A **B** **C**

D **E**

SOLUTION ON 289

442 PYRAMID PLOT

Consider the pyramid. Which of the following five options replaces the question mark?

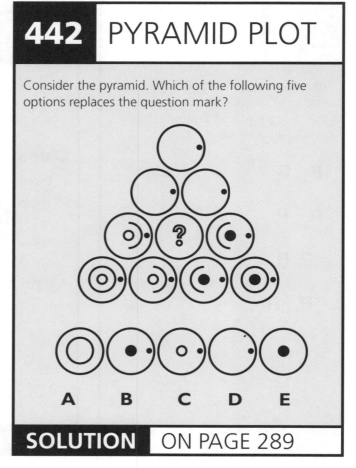

A **B** **C** **D** **E**

SOLUTION ON PAGE 289

443 ON VACATION

Mr Allen always goes to the same place for his vacation. This year, money is a little tight, so he takes with him only $420 to cover his hotel bill and spending money. He budgets his expenditure very carefully and tries to make the vacation last for as long as possible. As the money runs out and the vacation inevitably draws to a close, Mr Allen recalculates his finances. He finds that if he had spent $7 a day less he could have extended his vacation for another five days.

How long a vacation did he have?

SOLUTION ON PAGE 289

444 OLD FRIENDS

A woman was walking down the street when she ran into an old friend whom she hadn't seen since school.

"Hello, I haven't seen you for twenty years," she said. "How are you?"

"Well, I got married ten years ago, and this is our son," was the response.

"Hello," said the woman to the boy, "and what is your name?"

"It's the same as Daddy's."

"Ah, then it's Michael," said the woman.

How could she have known this when the boy's name had not been mentioned?

SOLUTION ON PAGE 289

445 AMAZING PROBLEM

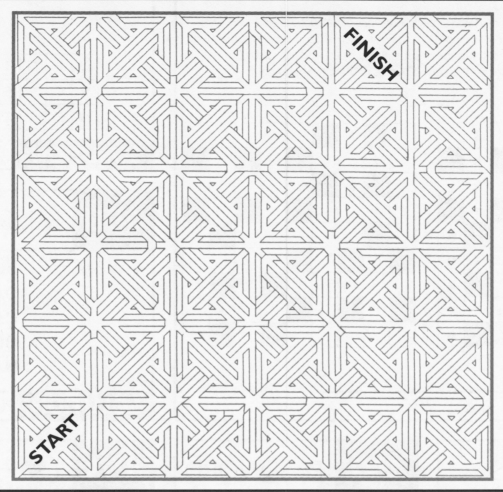

SOLUTION ON PAGE 289

446 CLUELESS CROSSWORD

In each square are four letters. Your task is to cross out three, leaving one letter in each square, so that the crossword is made up in the usual way with good English words.

S Q	T I	I T	U R	L E	I F	S E
M T	C U	A N	D E	A T	E O	N T
W K		O B		E A		E C
E C		A M		N R		A I
E A	N O	A E	B A	R E	K E	M E
L M	E X	I B	G N	J L	C A	A G
O N		L T		G A		H P
L I		M J		N E		L E
T E	A E	A E	O P	J C	M N	G K
L G	O L	S N	M A	D E	D O	E T

SOLUTION ON PAGE 289

447 BLANK OUT

Place the 20 words in the crossword, some horizontally and some vertically, so that each horizontal and vertical line forms a word. There are no blanks.

caves   coned
dates   hexed
honed   lover
manor   mar
mated   motor

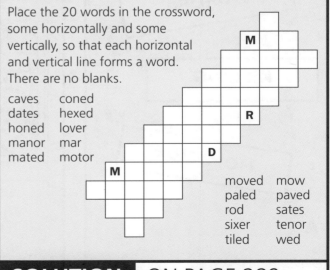

moved   mow
paled   paved
rod   sates
sixer   tenor
tiled   wed

SOLUTION ON PAGE 289

448 CRYPTOCROSS

A cryptogram is a coded message in which each letter has been substituted by another. This is what has happened in the crossword to the right. Each letter has been substituted for another, for example, all the As have been substituted by Es, and the Cs by Ps. Can you decode the crossword and enter the correct words in the right-hand grid?

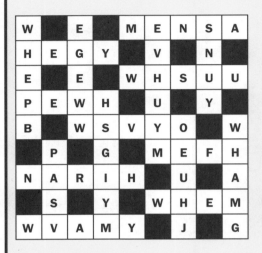

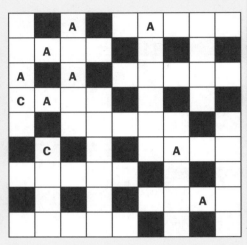

SOLUTION ON PAGE 289

449 SUBWAY

Find Dr Watson and Poirot in this grid. The remaining letters make up a word that means working in disguise.

U	P	O	I	R	O	T	N
V	C	E	E	O	D	R	R
N	O	S	T	A	W	R	D

SOLUTION ON PAGE 289

450 MISSING PERSON

What three letters can you put on the end of these, to make five six-letter words?

JUM
DAM
CAM
BUM
HAM

?

SOLUTION ON PAGE 289

451 CRIMES

Can you fill in the missing word, which means the same as those in the boxes?

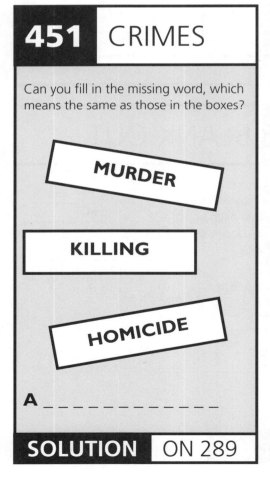

MURDER

KILLING

HOMICIDE

A _ _ _ _ _ _ _ _ _ _ _ _ _ _

SOLUTION ON 289

452 PASSWORD

You are attempting to hack into a secret database. To get in you need to key in the correct password. This password is a sequence of 3 x 2 letters.

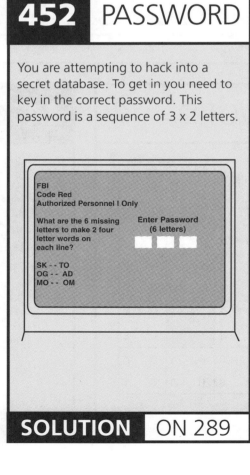

FBI
Code Red
Authorized Personnel l Only

What are the 6 missing letters to make 2 four letter words on each line?

Enter Password
(6 letters)

SK - - TO
OG - - AD
MO - - OM

SOLUTION ON 289

453 I ♥ NEW YORK

Hidden in this square are: Harlem, SoHo, Lexington and Times Square. The remaining letters spell out a famous New York landmark.

O	O	H	O	S	M	E	L	R	A	H
N	O	L	E	X	I	N	G	T	O	N
B	I	B	K	R	L	R	D	E	Y	G
T	I	M	E	S	S	Q	U	A	R	E

SOLUTION ON PAGE 289

454 PLEASED PUPILS

There are five pupils, each in a different class. Each pupil takes a subject and sport which she enjoys.

			CLASS					SUBJECT					SPORT				
		2	3	4	5	6	HISTORY	ALGEBRA	CHEMISTRY	GEOGRAPHY	BIOLOGY	TENNIS	SQUASH	SWIMMING	RUNNING	BASKETBALL
NAME	ALICE															
	BETT															
	CLARA															
	DORIS															
	ELIZABETH															
SPORT	TENNIS															
	SQUASH															
	SWIMMING															
	RUNNING															
	BASKETBALL															
SUBJECT	HISTORY															
	ALGEBRA															
	CHEMISTRY															
	GEOGRAPHY															
	BIOLOGY															

1. The girl who plays squash likes algebra and is not in class 5.

2. Doris is in class 3 and Betty likes running.

3. The girl who likes running is in class 2.

4. The girl in class 4 likes swimming, and Elizabeth likes chemistry.

5. Alice is in class 6 and likes squash but not geography.

6. The girl who likes chemistry also enjoys basketball.

7. The girl who likes biology also likes running.

8. Clara likes history but not tennis.

Work out the class, subject and sport of each girl.

NAME	CLASS	SUBJECT	SPORT

SOLUTION ON PAGE 289

455 MAP MEETING

An agent has sent you this message in code. Work out where you are supposed to meet her.

> NVVG NV MVZI GSV LOW YIRWTV ZG MRMV.

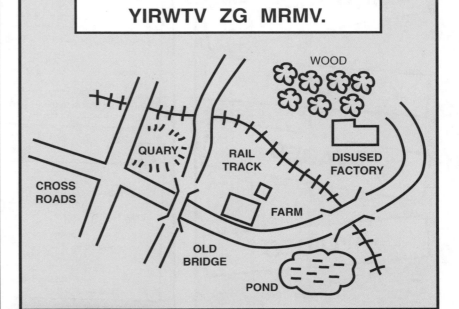

SOLUTION ON PAGE 289

456 TROUBLE

What three letters can you put on the end of these, to make five six-letter words?

BAR

CAR

BAN

MIS

WIN

?

SOLUTION ON 289

457 HACKER

You are attempting to hack into a secret database. To get in you need to key in the correct password. This password is a sequence of 3 x 2 letters.

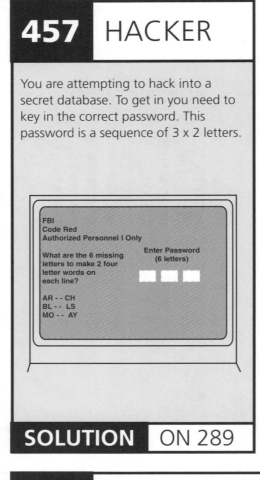

FBI
Code Red
Authorized Personnel I Only

What are the 6 missing letters to make 2 four letter words on each line?

Enter Password
(6 letters)

AR - - CH
BL - - LS
MO - - AY

SOLUTION ON 289

458 CODE BREAKER

You are agent J, on a mission. You need to send a message to base P via your laptop computer and a satellite link. However, you need to choose the correct satellite.

Which one do you choose?

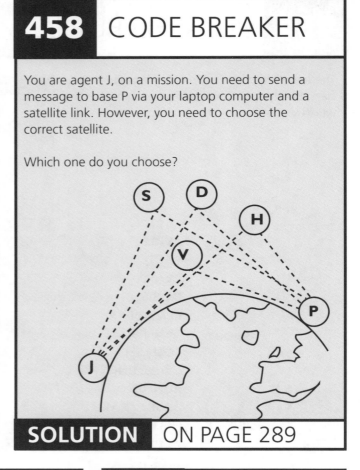

SOLUTION ON PAGE 289

459 ANTONYM

Which word means the opposite of those in the boxes?

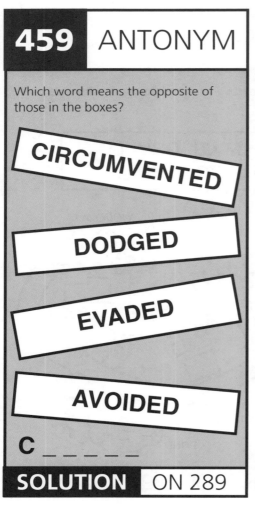

CIRCUMVENTED

DODGED

EVADED

AVOIDED

C _ _ _ _ _ _

SOLUTION ON 289

460 RELIABLE WITNESS

Below are two versions of a witness statement. Can you find 10 differences between them?

A

STATEMENT OF WITNESS

It was Wednesday late afternoon, and I was on my way home from work. I turned right out of Baker Street and into Market Street, I suppose this was about 5.30 pm.

I was walking down the left side, towards Douglas Road, when a tall man rushed out of a shop doorway, and grabbed the woman's bag. He pushed past me, knocking me into a wall, and ran into Baker Street. It all happened very quickly. I remember that he was tall, had close cropped hair and was wearing sunglasses. He also wore a long grey coat.

B

STATEMENT OF WITNESS

It was wednesday late afternoon, and I was on my way home from work. I turned right out of Baker Street and into Market Street, I suppose this was about 5.33 pm.

I was walking down the left side, toward Douglas Road, where a tall man rushed out of a shop doorway, and grabbed the womans' bag. He rushed past me, knocked me into a wall, and ran into Baker Street. It happened very quickly. I remember that he was tall had close cropped hair and was wearing glasses. He also wore a long grey coat.

SOLUTION ON PAGE 289

461 CODED

Here are some agent code letters. What is the code letter of the command centre?

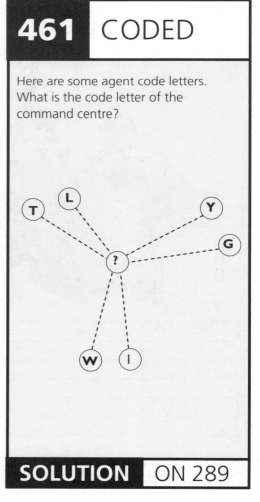

SOLUTION ON 289

462 SCENE OF CRIME

The length of crime scene tape needed to go all the way round this area is 24 yards. How many square yards is the area?

SOLUTION ON 289

463 AGENT SEARCH

What have each of the following FBI agents got in common with the place where they each live?

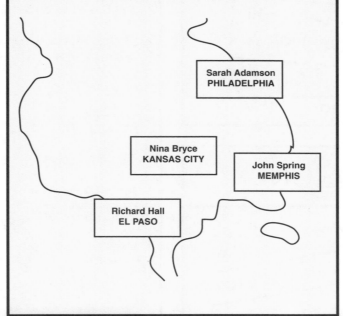

Sarah Adamson
PHILADELPHIA

Nina Bryce
KANSAS CITY

John Spring
MEMPHIS

Richard Hall
EL PASO

SOLUTION ON PAGE 289

464 NY TECS

The 250 detectives in the New York 13th Precinct are trained in a variety of skills. 70% are trained in unarmed combat, and 20% of these are also trained in hostage negotiation. This is 400% more than the total number who are at the rank of sergeant.

1. How many officers are trained in unarmed combat?
2. How many of the officers who are trained in unarmed combat are not skilled in hostage negotiation?
3. How many sergeants are there?

SOLUTION ON 289

465 SHOE-IN

These two prints were found at a crime scene. Can you spot eight differences between them?

SOLUTION ON 289

466 WINNING WAGER

Bill says to Jim, "Let's have a wager on each frame. We will play for half of the money in your wallet on each frame, and we will have 10 frames. Since you have $8 in your wallet, we will play for $4 on the first frame. I will give you $4 if you win and you will give me $4 if I win. When we start the second frame you will have either $12 or $4, so we will play for $6 or $2, etc."

They play 10 frames. Bill wins four and loses six frames but Jim finds that he has only $5.70 left and so has lost $2.30. How is this possible?

SOLUTION ON PAGE 289

467 SWITCH

Which piece will connect up this circuit?

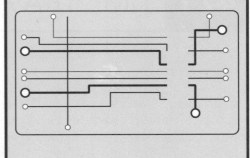

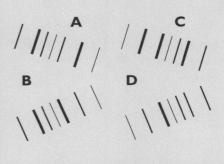

A   C

B   D

SOLUTION ON 289

468 EMAIL AGENT

You have received this e-mail from agent G. It is in code, so what does it say?

> **c qcff ullcpy nigilliq. wbywe hi
> ihy cm qunwbcha nby biomy.**

SOLUTION ON PAGE 289

470 CAR CONFUSION

Which of these car number plates is the odd one out?

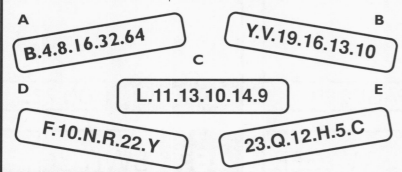

A B.4.8.16.32.64

B Y.V.19.16.13.10

C L.11.13.10.14.9

D F.10.N.R.22.Y

E 23.Q.12.H.5.C

SOLUTION ON PAGE 289

471 TIME TRAVEL

New York is five hours behind London, and London is two hours behind Athens.

A CIA agent is going to meet a contact two hours' drive from Athens in Greece. He is booked on the 9am flight from New York to London which will take seven hours. In London he will have to wait one hour for the connecting flight to Athens. This flight will take three and a half hours.

What time should he arrange to meet his contact?

SOLUTION ON PAGE 289

469 BLOCKED

The grid below represents apartment blocks in a city. Each block has a letter. They are arranged like this: D is just below T, L comes just after K, and Q is between B and M.

Your task is to follow the witness statements below to discover finally where the burglar is hiding.

1. I live in the block just behind the one in front of T. He ran past me in there!

2. I saw him in the one that is just below that. He ran into the one that is two in front of that one.

3. I saw him go into the one that is between that one and Q.

4. I saw him later. He was in the one just after the one that is just below the one that is just in front of that one.

WHICH APARTMENT BLOCK IS HE IN?

R	T	Y	U	O
S	D	F	G	H
K	L	Z	X	C
B	Q	M	W	A
E	N	P	J	V

SOLUTION ON PAGE 289

472 CELTIC CROSS

SOLUTION ON PAGE 289

473 COMBINATION TEASER

A certain room is steel-lined and has no entrances or exits other than a single, solid door which fits flush in the jamb when closed. There is only one key to the room and it belongs to Ed. Ed locked Fred in the room and went away for an hour with the key in his pocket; when he came back the door was open and Fred had escaped. Fred had not picked the lock, since there is no keyhole on the inside of the door; and nothing in the room was damaged or disturbed. How did Fred get out?

SOLUTION ON PAGE 289

475 CARRY ON THE PATTERN

Which circle fits into the blank space to carry on the pattern?

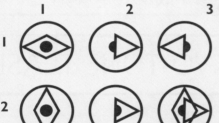

SOLUTION ON PAGE 290

474 JOLLY RANCHER

Lucky Mr Thrifty, from Ohio, inherited a sheep ranch in Australia. The documents sent to him by the local attorney described the land as a triangular section, bounded by straight lines joining three small towns. Town B was directly west of Town A, while town C lay somewhere between the two, but several miles to the north. The distance between A and B was 12 miles, between A and C 17 miles and between B and C 14 miles.

Not wanting to emigrate to Australia Mr Thrifty instructed the solicitor to sell the land at a price of $1,000 per square mile.

How much money can he expect to receive from the sale of the land?

SOLUTION ON PAGE 289

476 GRITTY GRID

Each of the nine squares in the grid marked 1A to 3C should incorporate all the lines and symbols shown in the squares of the same letter and number. For example, 3C should incorporate the shapes in 3 and C.

One of the squares is incorrect. Which is it?

SOLUTION ON PAGE 290

477 FANCY FIGURES

Find a logical reason for arranging these numbers into four groups of three numbers each:

106 168 181 217 218 251 349
375 433 457 532 713

GROUP 1	GROUP 2	GROUP 3	GROUP 4

SOLUTION ON PAGE 290

478 CHANGING SHAPE

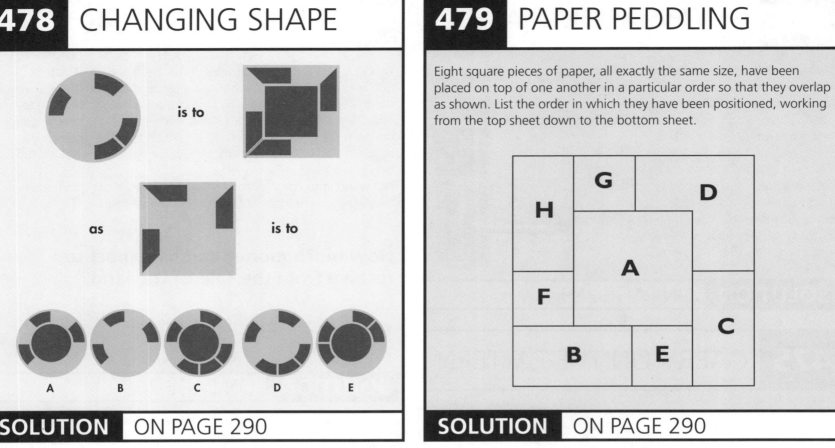

SOLUTION ON PAGE 290

479 PAPER PEDDLING

Eight square pieces of paper, all exactly the same size, have been placed on top of one another in a particular order so that they overlap as shown. List the order in which they have been positioned, working from the top sheet down to the bottom sheet.

SOLUTION ON PAGE 290

480 SHAPELY SEQUENCES

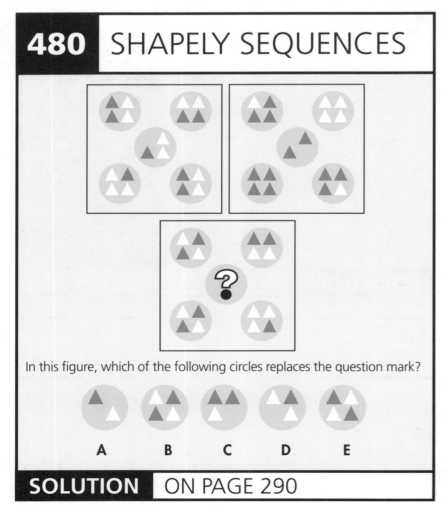

In this figure, which of the following circles replaces the question mark?

SOLUTION ON PAGE 290

481 TWO-TONE TEASER

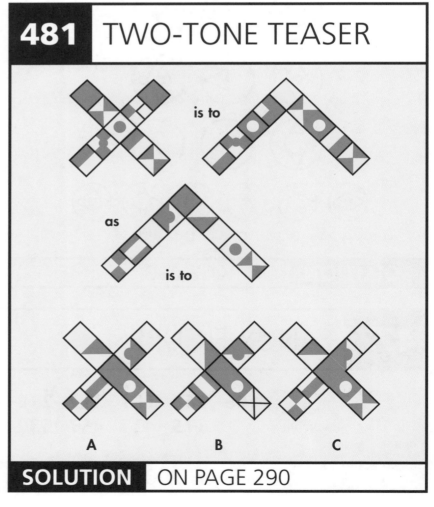

SOLUTION ON PAGE 290

482 CREATURE COMFORTS

In the North live different creatures, each of which has its own particular characteristics and its own particular treasure.

		COUNTRY					APPEARANCE					TREASURE				
		NORWAY	IRELAND	SCOTLAND	ENGLAND	WALES	REPULSIVE	UGLY	MISCHIEVOUS	OBNOXIOUS	MALEVOLENT	GOLD	DIAMONDS	RUBIES	EMERALDS	SILVER
CREATURE	ELF															
	GOBLIN															
	LEPRECHAUN															
	TROLL															
	IMP															
TREASURE	GOLD															
	DIAMONDS															
	RUBIES															
	EMERALDS															
	SILVER															
APPEARANCE	REPULSIVE															
	UGLY															
	MISCHIEVOUS															
	OBNOXIOUS															
	MALEVOLENT															

1. Leprechauns are mischievous, rubies come from Scotland.

2. Imps have silver, elves come from Norway.

3. Scotland has trolls, goblins have gold.

4. Elves are malevolent, Scotland has obnoxious creatures.

5. Goblins are repulsive, imps come from England.

6. Goblins are not ugly, Wales has no mischievous creatures.

7. Ireland has no diamonds.

Work out the creature, characteristics and treasure of each country.

CREATURE	COUNTRY	APPEARANCE	TREASURE

483 BOXING CLEVER

To which of the five boxes below can a dot be added so that both dots then meet the same conditions as the box above?

A B C

D E

484 STOCKING SEARCH

A woman has 43 stockings in her drawer: 21 blue, 8 black and 14 striped. She has fused the lights and cannot see into the drawer.

How many stockings must she take out to make certain that she has a pair of each?

SOLUTION ON 290

485 DECORATIVE CARDS

There are four cards on a table. Each one has either black or white on one side, and a star or a triangle on the other.

1    2

3   4

How many cards – and which ones – must you turn over in order to work out whether every black card has a triangle on its other side?

SOLUTION ON PAGE 290

486 CASINO CHIPS

A casino uses only $5 and $8 chips on its standard roulette wheel.

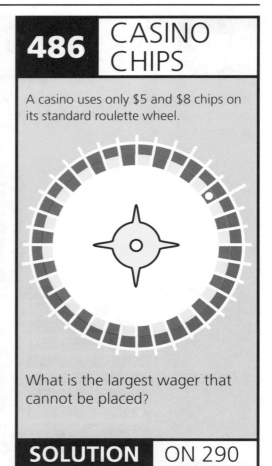

What is the largest wager that cannot be placed?

SOLUTION ON 290

487 CIRCLE SEQUENCE

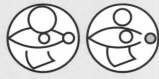

Look at these circles. Which of the following options comes next in the sequence?

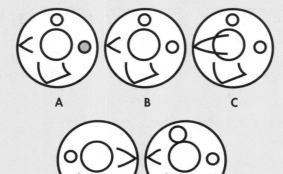

A   B   C

D   E

SOLUTION ON PAGE 290

488 DIAMOND DIVISION

Divide the diamond into four equal shapes, each containing one of each of the following five symbols:

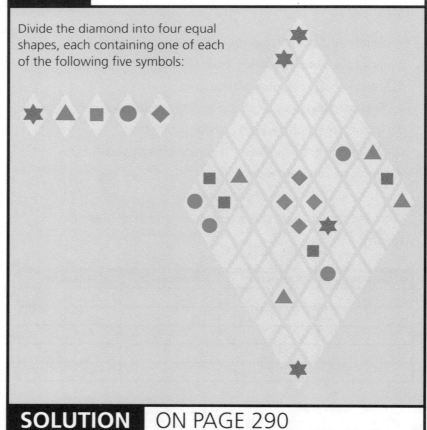

SOLUTION ON PAGE 290

489 FABULOUS FOOTBALL

Five players each play for a different team in a different position, and each wears a different shirt.

		TEAM					POSITION					SHIRT				
		CAROLINA PANTHERS	DALLAS COWBOYS	GREEN BAY PACKERS	OAKLAND RAIDERS	CLEVELAND BROWNS	RUNNING BACK	TACKLE	QUARTERBACK	KICKER	CORNERBACK	BLACK	YELLOW	RED	BLUE	PURPLE
NAME	DAVID															
	CLAUDE															
	VICTOR															
	SAMUEL															
	BILL															
SHIRT	BLACK															
	YELLOW															
	RED															
	BLUE															
	PURPLE															
POSITION	RUNNING BACK															
	TACKLE															
	QUARTERBACK															
	KICKER															
	CORNERBACK															

1. The Carolina Panthers player wears a purple shirt.

2. Samuel is not a running back; the tackle plays for the Dallas Cowboys.

3. The quarterback wears yellow; Claude plays for the Dallas Cowboys.

4. The kicker does not play for the Green Bay Packers.

5. David does not play for the Oakland Raiders; Samuel wears black.

6. The cornerback is at the Oakland Raiders; David plays in yellow.

7. Victor is in the Cleveland Browns and does not wear blue.

8. Bill is the kicker, and the Cleveland Browns player wears red.

Can you work out the details?

NAME	TEAM	POSITION	SHIRT

SOLUTION ON PAGE 290

490 RELATIVE RESIDENCES

1. Mrs Rivers' name is not Tracy, and her front door is not red.
2. Mrs Manby's name is Cheryl and she does not live at The White House.
3. Chez Nous does not have a black door, and neither does Mrs Hill's house.
4. Peggy's house has a green door and is not Rose Cottage.
5. Cheryl's house does not have a red door, but Hill House does.
6. Mabel's house has a blue door, but her name is not Mrs Sullivan.
7. Tracy's house is named Riverside.
8. Mrs Stevens' house is called Rose Cottage.
9. Grace's front door is not orange.
10. Dorothy does not live at Valley View, which does not have a green door.
11. Mrs Sullivan lives at Valley View and does not have a black door.
12. Mrs Peters does not have a white door.

Work out each woman's full name, the name of her house and the shade of its front door.

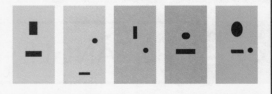

FIRST NAME	SURNAME	HOUSE NAME	FRONT DOOR

SOLUTION ON PAGE 290

491 MURDER MYSTERY

Five murder suspects, including the guilty party, are being interrogated by the police at the scene of a brutal murder. Of the five statements made, just three are the truth.

Who committed the murder?

ALF WHITE	"David Dark is the murderer"
BARRY GLOOMY	"I am innocent"
CYRIL SHADY	"It wasn't Ernie Black"
DAVID DARK	"Alf White is lying"
ERNIE BLACK	"Barry Gloomy is telling the truth"

SOLUTION ON PAGE 290

492 SHAPES

Which of the following is the odd one out?

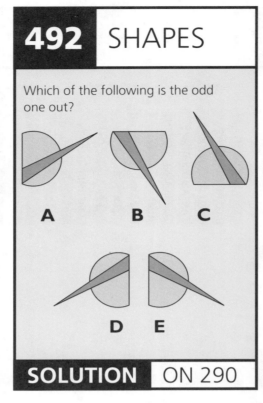

A   B   C

D   E

SOLUTION ON 290

493 SWITCHES

Which of the following is the odd one out?

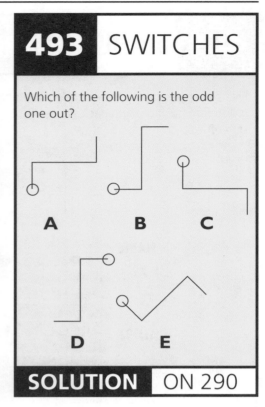

A   B   C

D   E

SOLUTION ON 290

494 HOUSE HORROR

Can you find the missing value on the roof of the second house? Each of the numbers on the windows and door must be used only once and no number can be reversed.

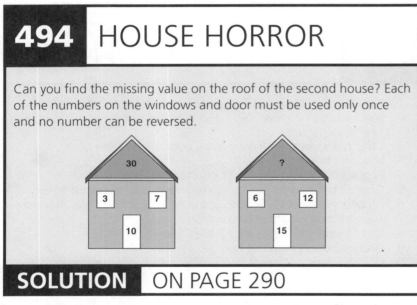

SOLUTION ON PAGE 290

495 MATHS MYSTERY

Start at the top-left circle and move clockwise. Calculate the number that replaces the question marks in the following:

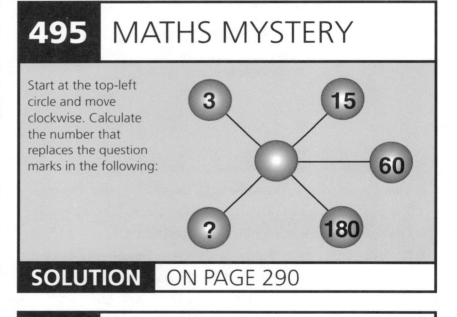

SOLUTION ON PAGE 290

496 TIE TANGLE

The number in the middle knot of the following bow ties is reached by using all of the outer numbers only once. You cannot reverse the numbers to obtain the answers. Which number should replace the question mark?

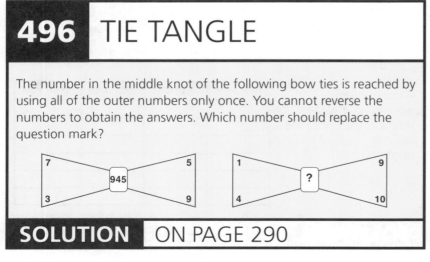

SOLUTION ON PAGE 290

497 FORMULATION

The numbers on the right are formed from the numbers on the left using the same formula in each question. Find the rule and replace the question mark with a number.

25 ⟶ 72   16 ⟶ 18

31 ⟶ 108   19 ⟶ ?

SOLUTION ON PAGE 290

498 RACE RIDDLE

On sports day the fastest runners are taking part in the sprint, the hurdles and the relay. One more person takes part in the hurdles only than the sprint only. The same number take part in the sprint and the hurdles as take part in the relay and the hurdles. Eleven of the athletes taking some part in these three races do not do the relay. Five people take part in the sprint and the relay and three enter all three races. There are four teams of four runners in the relay. One more person is running in both the relay and the sprint than in the hurdles only.

1. How many people are taking some part in any of the three races?

2. How many people are taking part in the relay only?

3. How many people do not take part in the hurdles?

4. How many people do not take part in the sprint?

5. How many people take part in both the hurdles and relay but not the sprint?

6. How many people take part in two races only?

SOLUTION ON PAGE 290

499 DOG DILEMMA

At a kennel there are Labradors, Alsatians and Greyhounds and also crosses of these breeds. There are two more true Labradors than true Alsatians. Six dogs are Alsatian and Labrador crosses. Ten dogs have no Labrador or Alsatian in them. Only one dog is a mixture of all three breeds. There are twice as many Labrador and Alsatian crosses than Labrador and Greyhound crosses. There is one more Alsatian and Greyhound cross than Labrador and Greyhound cross. Twenty-two dogs do not have any Alsatian in them. There are 40 dogs in total in the kennels.

1. How many true Labradors are there?
2. How many true Alsatians are there?
3. How many true Greyhounds are there?
4. How many Labrador and Greyhound crosses are there?
5. How many Alsatian and Greyhound crosses are there?
6. How many dogs do not have any Labrador in them?

SOLUTION ON PAGE 290

500 MAZE MUDDLE

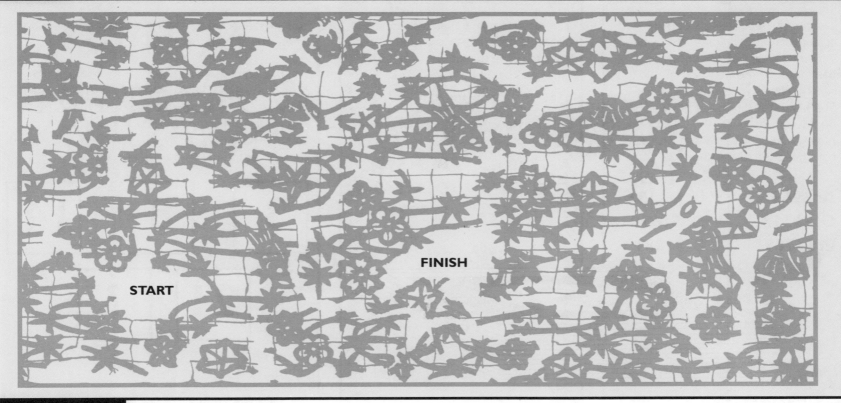

SOLUTION ON PAGE 290

501 TARGET

Find 12 six-letter words by pairing up the 24 three-letter segments. Each sector is used once only.

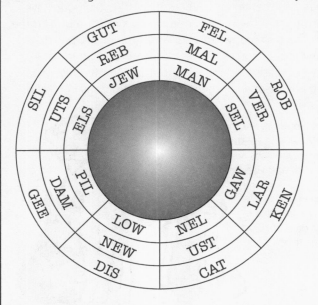

SOLUTION | ON PAGE 290

502 MAGIC SQUARE

The phrase below is an anagram of five words, which, when placed correctly in the grid, will form a Magic Square where all five words can be read horizontally and vertically.

GENERAL GREEN REVEALED ERROR

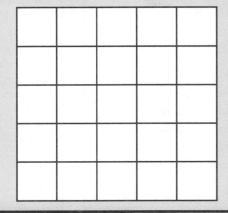

SOLUTION | ON 290

503 EDUCATING ERIC

Eric goes to school every morning but he rarely does homework and never achieves high marks in tests. There are 30 children in his class and 29 of them are good students. Eric is not related to anyone at the school and is not a special student. Why does he never get into trouble?

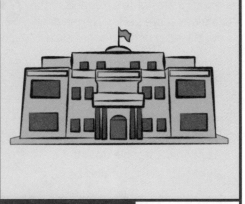

SOLUTION | ON 290

504 FORGERY FRACAS

Last month, a boat was stopped by customs in the San Francisco bay area. On board were bundles of forged banknotes. There were $5 notes with serial numbers ranging from 20361 to 20584, and $10 notes with serial numbers from 17888 to 17940. If the money had been real, what would have been the total value?

A: $942   B: $1135
C: $1513   D: $1650
E: $1789   F: $1881

SOLUTION | ON 290

505 TRIAL TROUBLE

At a recent criminal trial, two bundles of forged banknotes were presented as evidence. One bundle contained $1 notes numbered from 207663 to 208001, and another contained $20 notes numbered from 655517 to 655579. How much money was there?

A: $886   B: $1599
C: $1677   D: $1940
E: $2106   F: $2220

SOLUTION | ON 290

506 CUTTING CONUNDRUM

You are manacled to a table as a deadly laser cutter creeps towards your body...

You manage to free your left hand and reach the control panel, but you need to key in the last number of the sequence to stop the laser and free yourself.

You only have one minute to solve the code before you are cut to ribbons!

| 3 | 8 | 14 |

| 21 | ? |

SOLUTION | ON PAGE 290

507 RAPID EXIT

You must disarm a missile which is programmed to launch in 60 seconds. Its target is New York.

There are three wires leading from the control panel to the missile, but which one do you cut? Only one is connected to the flashing LED. Cut that wire and you win. Cut the wrong one and ...

Is it A, B, or C?

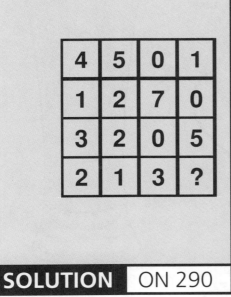

SOLUTION ON 290

508 DOOR DILEMMA

You reach an electronic door, but to activate the lock you must key in the missing letter.

SOLUTION ON 290

509 PATH PROBLEM

Get off the beach and head for the safety of the cave. Make sure you take the right path. Pick either of the others, and you're shark food!

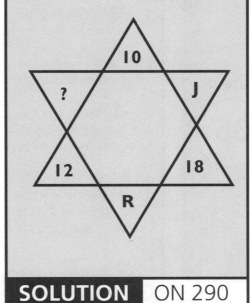

SOLUTION ON PAGE 290

510 CAVE CONUNDRUM

Find the missing number...

SOLUTION ON 290

511 DROP DILEMMA

You're on top of a cliff. There are three winding paths, but only one will take you to the boat at the bottom. The other two lead to certain death on the treacherous rocks below.

Is it path A, B or C?

SOLUTION ON PAGE 291

512 BOAT BOTHER

What is the missing number in the combination?

2	3	5
9	17	?

SOLUTION ON 291

513 ROCKY PROBLEM

As you head out to sea you are faced with five possible routes through the rocks. Choose correctly and you've made it, choose a wrong route, and it's certain doom!

To discover the route, find the odd one out ...

ROUTE A
23

ROUTE B
44

ROUTE C
71

ROUTE D
35

ROUTE E
62

SOLUTION   ON PAGE 291

514 GRID GAME

The grid below represents apartment blocks in a city. Each block has a letter. They are arranged like this: D is just below T, L comes just after K, and Q is between B and M. Your task is to follow the witness statements below to discover finally where the burglar is hiding.

1. I saw him go into the apartment just above M.

2. I saw him go into the one just before the one above that.

3. Well, I saw him in the apartment that is just in front of the one that is two below that.

4. I thought I saw him leave the apartment below that, but I was mistaken. I'm certain that I saw him later; he was in the one that is just behind the one that I just said I thought he was in.

Which apartment block is he in?

R	T	Y	U	O
S	D	F	G	H
K	L	Z	X	C
B	Q	M	W	A
E	N	P	J	V

SOLUTION   ON PAGE 291

515 CANDLE CONUNDRUM

If the gun = 81, and the knife = 2 what is the numerical value of the candlestick?

$$\text{candlestick} + \text{gun} \div \text{knife} = 199$$

SOLUTION   ON 291

516 NO BANG

To de-activate this explosive device you must press the correct sequence of 8 buttons until you reach "PRESS". You must press each button once only. Each button is marked with U for up, D for down, L for left and R for right. The number of moves is also on each button.

Which button is the first one you must press?

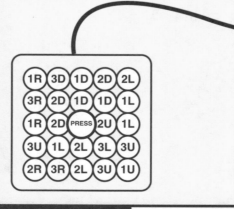

1R	3D	1D	2D	2L
3R	2D	1D	1D	1L
1R	2D	PRESS	2U	1L
3U	1L	2L	3L	3U
2R	3R	2L	3U	1U

SOLUTION   ON 291

517 BEST BEER

A man can drink a barrel of beer in 27 days. A woman can drink a barrel of beer in 54 days.

If they both drink out of the same barrel at their respective rates, how long will it take for the barrel to be emptied?

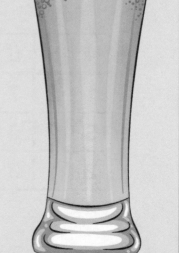

SOLUTION   ON PAGE 291

518 SPEEDY SOLUTION

These detectives in the Washington Police Department are trained in various skills. How many are trained in speed driving?

SPEED DRIVING ?

MARKSMANSHIP 9

SELF DEFENSE 7

NEGOTIATION 5

SOLUTION ON 291

519 CHICAGO PUZZLE

You have arranged to meet "M" in Chicago. But where?

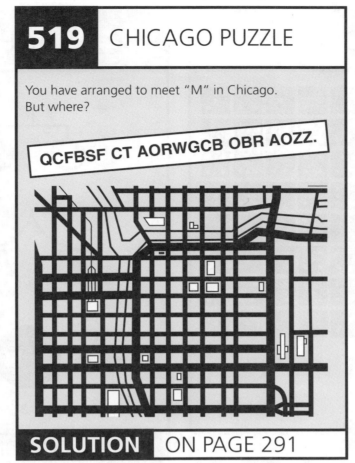

QCFBSF CT AORWGCB OBR AOZZ.

SOLUTION ON PAGE 291

520 DRINK DILEMMA

One of the glasses of wine below is the odd one out.

Which one is it?

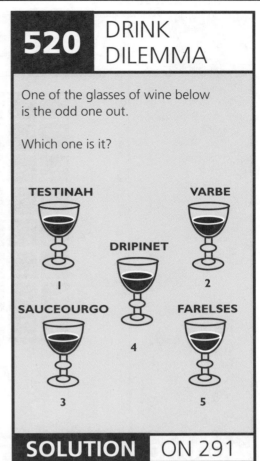

TESTINAH

VARBE

DRIPINET

1

2

SAUCEOURGO

FARELSES

3

4

5

SOLUTION ON 291

521 WRITE ANSWER?

Below are five crime writers. Which is the odd one out?

P.D. James

Jonathan Gash

Dick Francis

Ed McBain

Barbara Vine

SOLUTION ON 291

522 AMAZINGLY EASY

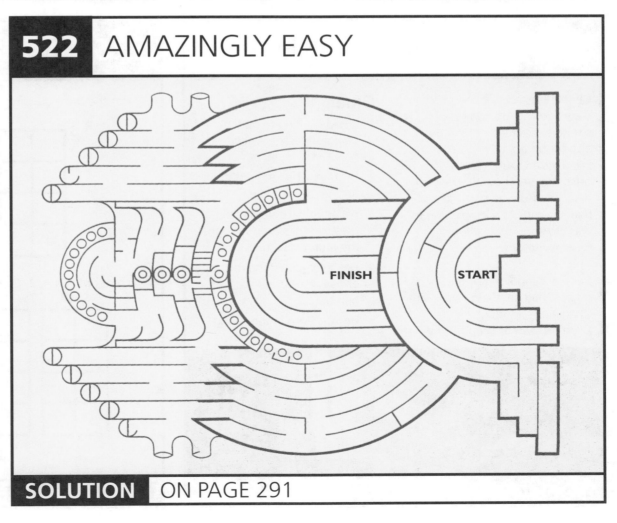

FINISH   START

SOLUTION ON PAGE 291

523 DRAWING DOMINOES

Draw lines in this box to reveal 28 dominoes, as follows:

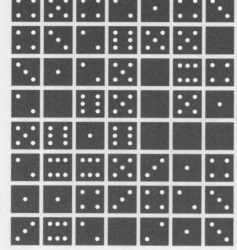

0–0
0–1   1–1
0–2   1–2   2–2
0–3   1–3   2–3   3–3
0–4   1–4   2–4   3–4   4–4
0–5   1–5   2–5   3–5   4–5   5–5
0–6   1–6   2–6   3–6   4–6   5–6   6–6

SOLUTION ON PAGE 291

524 SHAPELY SEARCH

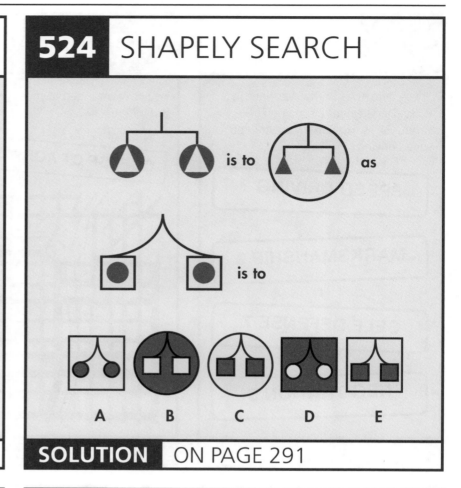

is to ... as

... is to

A   B   C   D   E

SOLUTION ON PAGE 291

525 THE ABANDONED

Charlie was abandoned at an early age and life had been a struggle, not just for him, but also for his adoptive parents. He killed his adoptive parents' offspring, yet they still worked hard to ensure he survived and had a home. As soon as Charlie was old enough he left his parents, never to return.

Neither the police nor the social services had anything to do with Charlie, even though he also killed his own offspring. Why?

Clues

1. It had nothing to do with being underage when he killed.

2. His family had a reputation for punctuality.

3. His adoptive parents did not press charges even though the murders were brutal.

4. He never joined the military or had a social service number.

5. He was born in the spring.

SOLUTION ON PAGE 291

526 SWEET SEQUENCE

Look at the three drawings.

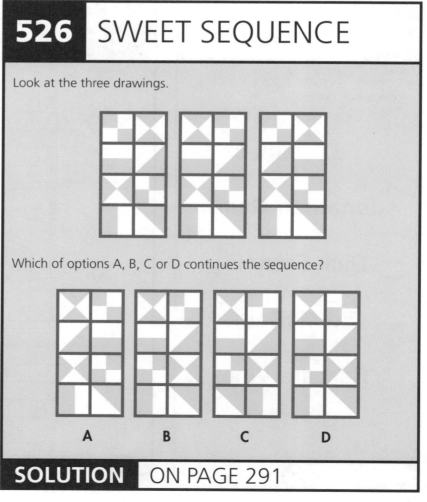

Which of options A, B, C or D continues the sequence?

A   B   C   D

SOLUTION ON PAGE 291

527 PROBABILITY PARADOX

This puzzle requires no prior knowledge about the rules of probability and can be solved by logical reasoning.

Four balls are placed in a bag. One is black, one white and the other two red. The bag is shaken and someone draws two balls from the bag. He looks at the two balls and announces that one of them is red.

What are the chances that the other ball he has drawn out is also red?

SOLUTION   ON PAGE 291

528 SKYSCRAPER

A window cleaner was cleaning windows on the fifteenth floor of a skyscraper when he slipped and fell. He suffered only minor bruising. How was this possible when he did not have his safety harness on and nothing slowed his fall?

SOLUTION   ON PAGE 291

529 NOT REALLY A PREMONITION

A farmer went into a field and into a very large barn-like structure on the edge of the field. Later he came out, and as he was approaching the middle of the field he knew that when he reached it he would be dead. How did he know that?

Clues

1.   It was not the farmer's field.
2.   He had been to the same field on numerous occasions.
3.   He did not do any work on the field.

SOLUTION   ON PAGE 291

530 PAULINE'S PENS

Pauline Jones, the schoolteacher, had an obsession for fine ball-point pens. She had many in her collection, but she only used four of them for work. Each of these pens contained a different coloured ink. Sometimes she only took one pen to work, sometimes two, sometimes three and occasionally all four. She tried to take a different combination of pens to school with her each day.

For how many consecutive days can she take a different selection of pens to work?

SOLUTION   ON PAGE 291

531 ON THE FARM

A group of children visited a farm and saw:

a)   **One animal with half as many letters as its plural**

b)   **One animal with half as many letters as its young**

c)   **One animal with the same number of letters as its plural**

When the group moved further on they saw the same again but each animal was different. Can you work out what the animals were?

SOLUTION   ON PAGE 291

532 SQUARE GRIDS

How many squares can you see in this drawing?

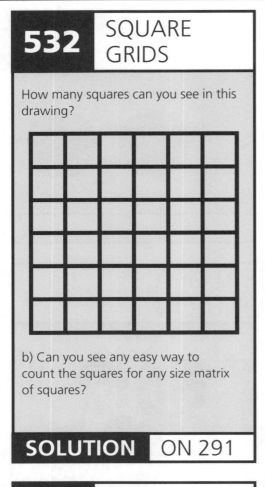

b) Can you see any easy way to count the squares for any size matrix of squares?

SOLUTION ON 291

533 SEQUENCE SOLVER

What comes next in this series?

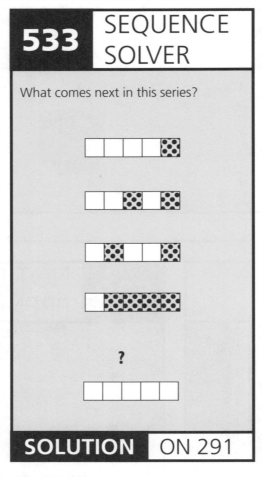

?

SOLUTION ON 291

534 EQUAL SHAPES

Can you divide this matrix along the lines into four parts that contain both a triangle and a star? Each part must be exactly the same shape and size, but the triangle and star positions will vary.

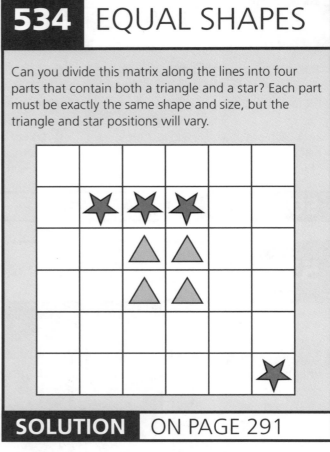

SOLUTION ON PAGE 291

535 DOUBLE SQUARE

If you make two straight cuts on a piece of paper shaped as a cross (see below), can you rearrange the cut cross to form two squares?

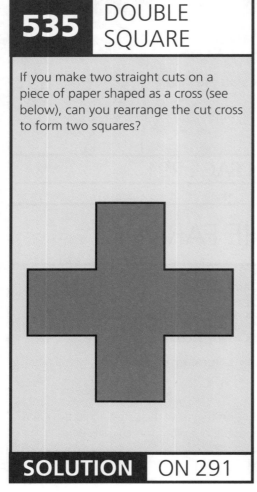

SOLUTION ON 291

536 TRIANGLES

Which triangle has the larger area?

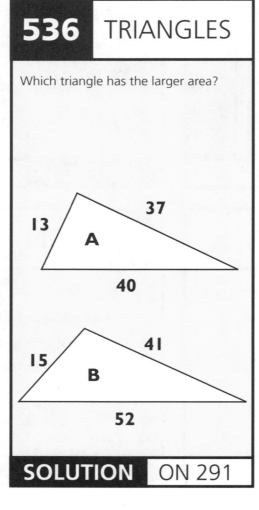

SOLUTION ON 291

537 FRUIT FLY

An insect makes a beeline for, and attaches itself to, a fruit. What was the fruit if the combination of the two has become a widely used tool for builders and decorators?

SOLUTION ON PAGE 291

538 POISONOUS INSECT

A lady saw a poisonous insect crawl into a hole in the wall behind her television set. Fearing for the safety of her children she wished to rid her family of this danger to them. It was late in the evening and she did not have any chemicals that would kill the bug since she hated to kill any living being. She did not wish to damage the house by digging into the wall. How did she get the bug without killing it?

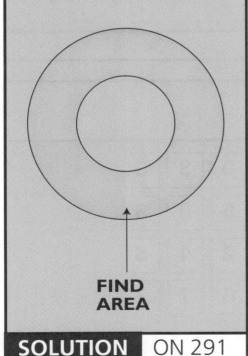

SOLUTION   ON 291

539 MISS PUNCTUAL

Miss Punctual was, as her name suggested, always on time. She would always get up in the mornings at the same time, get herself prepared for work, leave the house on time, get to work on time; in fact she worked to the clock and you could tell the time by what she was doing. One morning, however, she was awakened by her alarm clock buzzer and she felt that her biological clock was out of phase with the world. She got herself ready and went to work, but arrived over 30 minutes late. She apologized, and said that she now felt well. What went wrong?

Clues

1. She was not ill.
2. She had not set the clock differently.
3. As soon as she got to work she felt fine.
4. Each of the things she had to do took the same time as normal

SOLUTION   ON PAGE 291

540 HOLES IN PAPER

If you fold a piece of paper in half and cut a hole along the fold you will have one hole in the paper when it is unfolded. If you fold the paper in half, then half again at right angles and repeat so that you have made six folds, and then cut a hole in the last folded side, how many holes will you have in the paper when you unfold it? Try it in your head before reaching for the scissors.

SOLUTION   ON 291

541 WASHERS

How can you, by making only one single measurement, calculate the shaded area of a circular washer?

FIND AREA

SOLUTION   ON 291

542 HIDDEN WORDS

Read the sentence carefully to discover a series of associated words hidden in it. The connected words will be found by joining the end of one word somewhere in the sentence with the beginning of the next word. What are the connected words?

A large wooden spoon to stir is so important; in the non-stick saucepan syrup will scorch identically to other sugary substances and will taste as terrible as you can imagine.

SOLUTION   ON PAGE 291

543 CONNECT

The following words have a hidden connection. What is it?

BEAUTIES

SHOESTRING

WHATEVER

BELTING

SOLUTION   ON 291

544 MORE LOGICAL DEDUCTION

What number should replace the question mark?

Baltic   **= 34**
Arctic   **= 34**
Ionian   **= 38**
Caspian   **= ?**

SOLUTION ON 291

545 TARGET PRACTICE

You have a maximum of six bullets but you are required to score exactly 100. Can you do it on this unusual target?

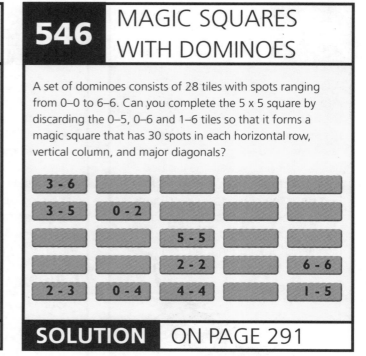

SOLUTION ON 291

546 MAGIC SQUARES WITH DOMINOES

A set of dominoes consists of 28 tiles with spots ranging from 0–0 to 6–6. Can you complete the 5 x 5 square by discarding the 0–5, 0–6 and 1–6 tiles so that it forms a magic square that has 30 spots in each horizontal row, vertical column, and major diagonals?

3 - 6				
3 - 5	0 - 2			
		5 - 5		
		2 - 2		6 - 6
2 - 3	0 - 4	4 - 4		1 - 5

SOLUTION ON PAGE 291

547 HAM IT UP

There is a choice of cheese, ham, or salad, or any combination of the 3, for sandwich fillings. The same number of people have ham only as have all 3 of the fillings. Twice as many have both ham and salad but no cheese as have all 3 fillings; 14 people do not have cheese. Three more people have cheese only as salad only; 8 people have both ham and salad but no cheese; 12 people do not have salad; and 14 people do not have ham.

a)   How many people have all three fillings?
b)   How many people have cheese only?
c)   How many people have both cheese and salad but no ham?
d)   How many people have only one filling?
e)   How many people have only two fillings?

SOLUTION ON 291

548 DIVIDED SQUARE

This field measures 177m x 176m. It has been split up into 11 squares that exactly equal the total area. The squares are only roughly drawn to scale. All new squares are in whole metres. Can you calculate the size of each square?

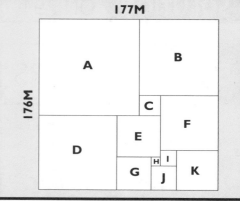

SOLUTION ON PAGE 291

549 FIGURE FRENZY

Work out how the numbers relate to each other and you will be able to replace the question mark with a number.

1	7	0	3	5
4	6	5	0	5
3	8	2	4	5
8	9	6	7	?

SOLUTION ON PAGE 291

550 SPIDER'S LOGIC

What is the value of the end web?

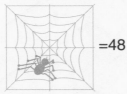 =48

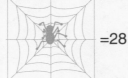 =28

 =?

SOLUTION   ON PAGE 291

551 GRID CODES

The word-frame below, when filled with the correct letters, will create the name of a planet. The letters are arranged in the coded square below. There are two alternatives to fill each square of the word-frame, one correct the other incorrect. What is the planet?

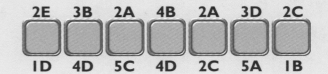

	A	B	C	D	E
1	B	Y	X	S	C
2	T	W	R	X	J
3	H	A	G	M	Q
4	V	I	G	U	F
5	E	O	P	D	Z

SOLUTION   ON PAGE 292

552 BLOW UP

A family planning a party had inflated a number of balloons with air and tied the ends so that they would not deflate. They left the balloons on the floor of their front room while they went shopping. When they came back, all the balloons were two inches above the floor. Why was this? The room and balloons were at the same temperature; the doors were firmly closed and had draft excluders fitted; there were no air currents involved; and the balloons did not contain any lighter-than-air gases.

SOLUTION   ON PAGE 292

553 FIVERS

Place the 36 five-letter words in the grid to complete the crossword.

ALIVE	ALTER
ASTER	ASTIR
DARTS	DENIM
EATER	EDICT
ELOPE	EMITS
ENTER	EXUDE
FEAST	FREED
GAPES	GELID
GRATE	GULCH
HAREM	IRATE
ISSUE	LEVER
LINEN	LINER
LOPES	NICER
POINT	POLES
RISEN	SCOUT
SEDAN	STEER
STRIP	TARNS
TOTAL	VALID

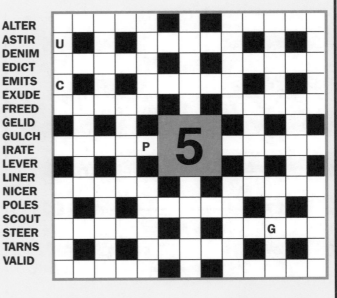

SOLUTION   ON PAGE 292

554 THE NEWS VENDOR

This puzzle involves newspapers. A newsagent sells 70 copies of the *Echo*, 60 of the *Moon* and 50 of the *Advertizer*.

17 customers buy both the *Echo* and the *Moon*, 15 buy both the *Moon* and the *Advertizer* and 16 buy both the *Echo* and the *Advertizer*. Three customers buy all three papers.

How many customers does the vendor have?

SOLUTION   ON PAGE 292

555 FORMULATION

The numbers on the right are formed from the numbers on the left using the same formula in each question. Find the rule and replace the question mark with a number.

8 ──────────→ **100**

13 ─────────→ **225**

31 ─────────→ **1089**

17 ─────────→ **?**

SOLUTION   ON PAGE 292

556 TV TROUBLE

A survey has been carried out on TV viewing. The survey shows the percentages of people who watch soaps, documentaries and movies. 26% of people watch all three. 39% of people do not watch documentaries. The percentage of people watching soaps only plus the percentage of people watching movies only is the same as the number who watch both movies and documentaries. 27% of people do not watch movies, 14% watch both soaps and documentaries and 3% watch documentaries only.

1. What percentage of people watch both soaps and movies but no documentaries?
2. What percentage watch soaps only?
3. What percentage watch movies and documentaries but not soaps?
4. What percentage watch movies only?
5. What percentage watch only two out of the three types of show?
6. What percentage watch only one type of show?

SOLUTION   ON PAGE 292

557 MATHS MYSTERY

Can you calculate the number missing in the figure below? Each number is used once only and is not reversed.

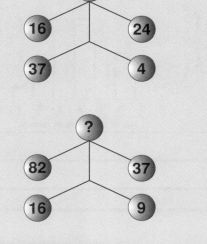

SOLUTION ON 292

558 TIE TANGLE

The number in the middle knot of the following bow ties is reached by using all of the outer numbers only once. You cannot reverse the numbers to obtain the answers. Which number should replace the question mark?

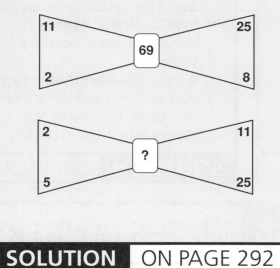

SOLUTION ON PAGE 292

559 HOUSES

Can you find the missing value on the roofs of the second house? Each of the numbers on the windows and door must be used only once and no number can be reversed.

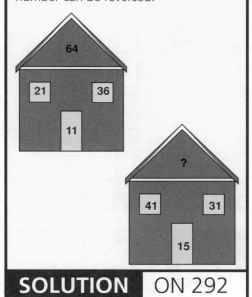

SOLUTION ON 292

560 SERIES SEARCH

Can you discover the next letter in this series?

O O T T F E

SOLUTION ON PAGE 292

561 LETTER LOGIC

The letters follow a certain logic. Find out what it is and replace the question mark with a letter.

R	V	T	Y
Q	O	M	G
H	J	F	?

SOLUTION ON PAGE 292

562 DICE DILEMMA

Six children invent a game with dice, where the winner is the person with the highest score. The only rules are that if the same score is obtained by any other person in the round, both their round scores are doubled. Anyone rolling a double has their round score deducted.

Rolling a double and having the same rolled total as another player will give you a minus total that is double the rolled value. A thrown double is denoted by an *.

When the scores are adjusted for the children's rules, which player:

1. Came third?
2. Won?
3. Came last?
4. Was winning after round three?
5. Had an even score?
6. Had a score divisible by 5 (with no remainder)?

Player	round 1	round 2	round 3	round 4	round 5
A	7	7	4*	9	10
B	5	8	9	6*	9
C	9	11	5	8*	6
D	8	8*	6	4	11
E	10	9	7	5	6
F	6	4	5	11	8

SOLUTION ON PAGE 292

563 WORD WONDER

Which of these words will produce the most anagrams? All the anagrams must be proper English words, though some of them may be quite obscure.

TARSE
TALON
TANGS
TEEMS
THROW

SOLUTION ON PAGE 292

564 EXASPERATING EXAMS

The graph below shows the examination results of students taking their school leaving exams. 30 children took tests.

1. **What was the average number of exam passes per student?**
2. **If the top five students were not in this class, what would have been the average number of exam passes per student?**
3. **If 10% took eight tests, 70% took six tests and 20% took four tests, how many test papers had a fail mark?**

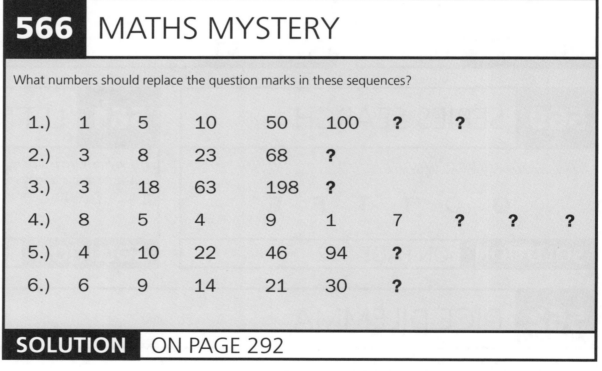

SOLUTION ON PAGE 292

565 MISSING NUMBER

What number should replace the question mark and what are the values of the symbols?

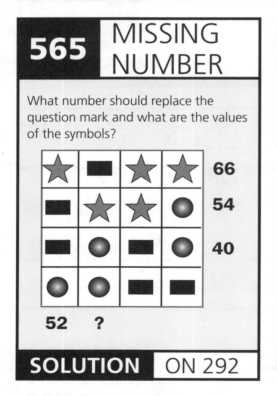

SOLUTION ON 292

566 MATHS MYSTERY

What numbers should replace the question marks in these sequences?

1.)	1	5	10	50	100	?	?
2.)	3	8	23	68	?		
3.)	3	18	63	198	?		
4.)	8	5	4	9	1	7	?	?	?
5.)	4	10	22	46	94	?		
6.)	6	9	14	21	30	?		

SOLUTION ON PAGE 292

567 FIND THE NUMBER

What number should replace the question mark?

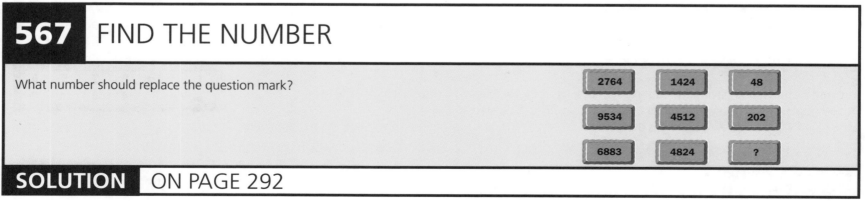

SOLUTION ON PAGE 292

568 GONE FISHING

Five men staying at the coastal hotel decide to go fishing on the pier. They sit next to each other, using different bait, and catch different numbers of fish.

Work out where each man lives, his occupation, the bait he is using, and how many fish he catches.

1. The plumber, called Henry, catches one fish fewer than Dick.
2. The electrician is next to the banker and uses bread for his bait.
3. The man at the north end of the pier is the banker, who is sitting next to Fred.
4. The salesman catches only one fish, and is sitting at the south end of the pier.
5. Meal is the bait used by Malcolm, and the man from Orlando catches 15 fish.
6. The man from New York uses shrimps for bait and is sitting next to the man who catches one fish.
7. Joe is from Los Angeles and uses worms as his bait.
8. The man in the middle is from Tucson and uses a bait of maggots.
9. The banker catches six fish.

10. Dick, who is the middle fisherman, is two seats away from the man from St Louis.
11. The man who is sitting next to the man from New York catches 10 fish and is a professor.
12. Henry did not sit next to Joe.

	NORTH ← PIER → SOUTH				
NAME					
OCCUPATION					
TOWN					
BAIT					
CATCH					

SOLUTION ON PAGE 292

569 FIGURE IT OUT

Can you calculate the number missing in the figure below? Each number is used once only and is not reversed.

216
9   12
6   3

?
12   20
8   2

SOLUTION 292

570 STAR SOLUTION

FINISH

START

SOLUTION ON PAGE 292

571 MYSTERY NUMBER

Start at the top-left circle and move clockwise. Calculate the number that replaces the question mark.

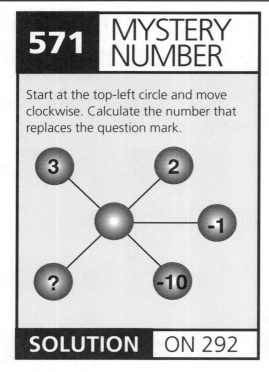

572 TIE TANGLE

The number in the middle knot of the following bow ties is reached by using all of the outer numbers only once. You cannot reverse the numbers to obtain the answers. Which number should replace the question mark?

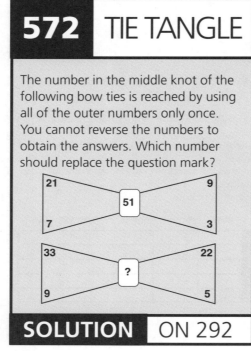

573 SHAPE SHIFTER

The shapes and names are connected. Which list should Robert join?

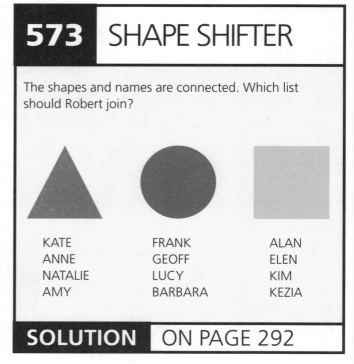

KATE	FRANK	ALAN
ANNE	GEOFF	ELEN
NATALIE	LUCY	KIM
AMY	BARBARA	KEZIA

SOLUTION ON 292

SOLUTION ON 292

SOLUTION ON PAGE 292

574 ODD ONE OUT

Which of the following is the odd one out?

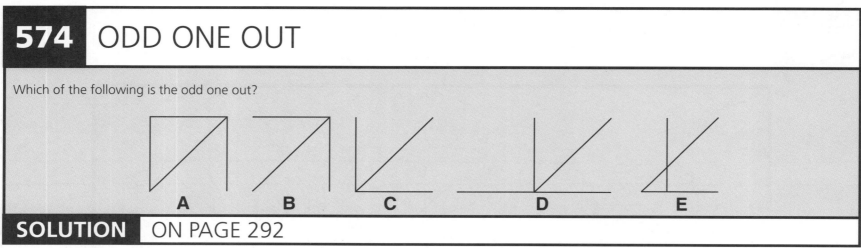

A   B   C   D   E

SOLUTION ON PAGE 292

575 MISSING NUMBER

What number should replace the question mark?

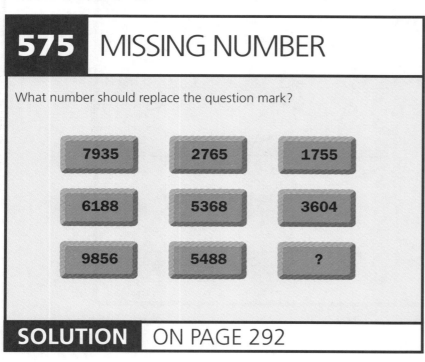

7935	2765	1755
6188	5368	3604
9856	5488	?

SOLUTION ON PAGE 292

576 COTTON CONUNDRUM

A reel of cotton is 1.1 inches in diameter. The cotton is one-hundredth of an inch (0.01 inch) in thickness, and it is wound to a depth of 0.4 inches around the central spindle. What is the simplest way of determining the total length of cotton wound on the reel?

SOLUTION ON PAGE 292

577 WEATHER CHANGES

When we look back at the summers of our childhood we only remember the good days and forget the dull, dismal, rainy days when we sat in our rooms, bored out of our minds, and stared endlessly out of the rain-splattered window. We probably remember only half a dozen days from each summer, which merge together to form one long, hot, sunny memory.

I have recently collected data on the changes in the weather where I live, and have arrived at the following possibilities for the month of June. If it is fine today, the probability is that it will be fine tomorrow is 3/4. If it is wet today, the probability that it will be fine tomorrow is 1/3. Today is Thursday, and the weather is warm and sunny. I plan to go walking on Sunday. What is the probability that Sunday will be a fine day?

SOLUTION ON PAGE 292

578 WORD CROSS PUZZLE

In 1913 a new type of puzzle was devised by Liverpool-born Arthur Wynne. It was the first crossword puzzle to be published and appeared on Sunday December 21, 1913, in the New York World, and was called a Word Cross Puzzle. Our puzzle here reproduces Arthur Wynne's original grid, but has an entirely different set of clues and answers.

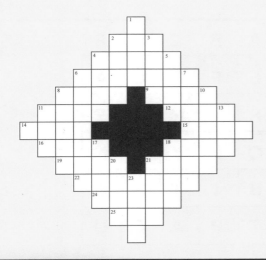

Across

2 Twenty-four hours (3)
4 Hairs (5)
6 Kind of raisin (7)
8 Heap (4)
9 Thick cord (4)
11 Of sound mind (4)
12 Unit of speech (4)
14 Heroic story (4)
15 Machine for weaving (4)
16 Afresh (4)
18 Knot or knob (4)
19 Stumble (4)
21 Fury (4)
22 Frugal use (7)
24 Rogue (5)
25 Numbered cube (3)

Down

1 Gasp for breath (4)
2 Valley (4)
3 Time taken for the Earth to revolve around the Sun (4)
4 Cross between horse and ass (4)
5 Frozen flakes of vapour (4)
6 Genuine (7)
7 Expression of regret (7)
8 Tinting matter (5)
10 Wear away (5)
11 Medicinal spring (3)
13 Female deer (3)
17 Thread through core of a candle (4)
18 Word by which thing or person is known (4)
20 Small body of water (4)
21 Wander (4)
23 Small metal spike (4)

SOLUTION ON PAGE 292

579 HIDDEN WORDS

Read the sentence carefully to discover a series of associated words hidden in it.

The connected words will be found by joining the end of one word somewhere in the sentence with the beginning of the next word. What are the connected words?

For those in even the slightest doubt whether honesty is the best policy, remember the trouble near the beacon goalposts by the gang escalates into something we are unable to control.

SOLUTION   ON PAGE 292

582 CARD SHARP

In a card shop five times as many people buy a card only as wrapping paper only. One more person buys both a card and a bow but no wrapping paper as a bow only. Twice as many people buy both a bow and wrapping paper but no card as buy all three. Twelve people do not buy a card and 18 do not buy wrapping paper; 15 people buy a card only and four people buy all three, and 30 people do not buy a bow.

a) How many people buy one of the items only?
b) How many people buy two of the items only?
c) How many people buy wrapping paper only?
d) How many customers are there in total?
e) How many people buy a bow, wrapping paper, but no card?

SOLUTION   ON PAGE 292

580 HIDDEN CONNECTIONS

The following words have a hidden connection. What is it?

DECODING ZEROES SPIKED SHAKER

SOLUTION   ON PAGE 292

581 PERPLEXING PROBLEM

All these words have something in common. Discover what it is – can BORN join the list?

SOLO	ROCK
PAIRS	SABLE
ANISE	DEANS
MISER	

SOLUTION   ON PAGE 292

583 GREAT GOLFERS

Mr Peters, Mr Edwards and Mr Roberts are playing a round of golf together. Half-way through the game Mr Peters remarks that he has just noticed that their first names are Peter, Edward and Robert. "Yes," says one of the others, "I'd noticed that too, but none of us has the same surname as our own first name. For example, my first name is Robert."

What are the full names of the three golfers?

SOLUTION   ON PAGE 292

584 GRID CODES

The word-frame below, when filled with the correct letters, will create the name of a state of the US. The letters are arranged in the coded square right. There are two alternatives to fill each square of the word-frame, one correct, the other incorrect. What is the state of the U.S.?

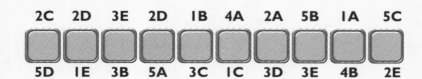

	A	B	C	D	E
1	E	F	O	G	A
2	R	V	M	I	S
3	Q	L	Y	K	N
4	B	I	T	H	D
5	T	P	A	C	U

SOLUTION   ON PAGE 292

585 EMPTY SQUARES

Should A, B, C, or D replace the empty squares in the grid?

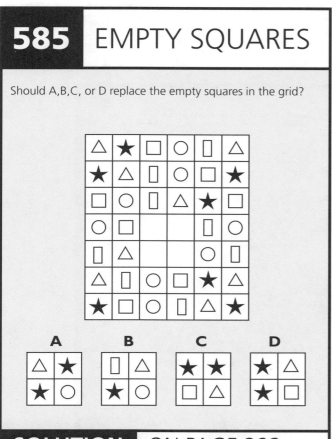

A   **B**   **C**   **D**

SOLUTION ON PAGE 292

586 EMPTY SQUARES

What number should replace the question marks?

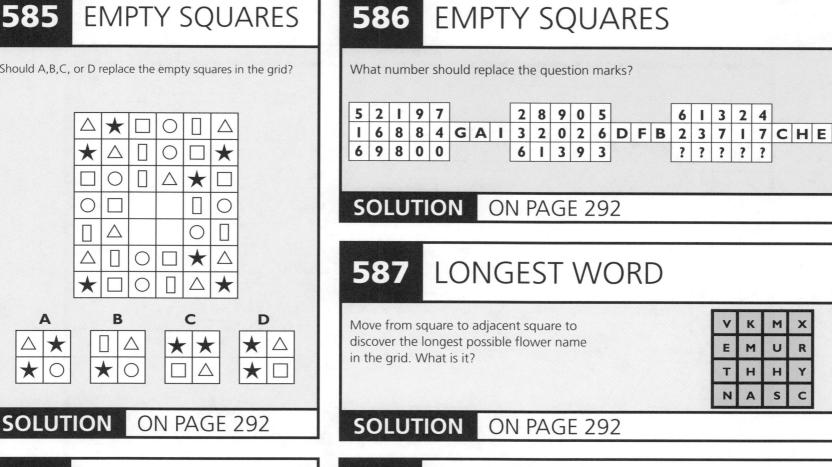

SOLUTION ON PAGE 292

587 LONGEST WORD

Move from square to adjacent square to discover the longest possible flower name in the grid. What is it?

V	K	M	X
E	M	U	R
T	H	H	Y
N	A	S	C

SOLUTION ON PAGE 292

588 NUMBER LINKS

Rearrange the tiles and place them touching one another in a 3 x 3 square, so that all adjacent letters are the same. If placed correctly, a type of dinosaur will be read around the outer rim. What is it?

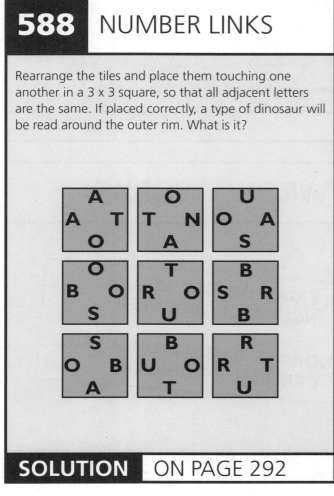

SOLUTION ON PAGE 292

589 UNUSUAL SAFES

Here is an unusual safe. Each button must be pressed once only in the correct order to reach OPEN. The number of moves and the direction is marked on each button (1S would mean move one space south, etc.). Which button is the first you must press?

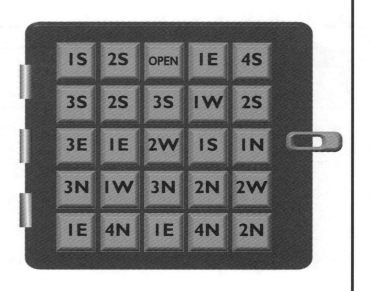

SOLUTION ON PAGE 293

590 MIRACLE MAZE

SOLUTION ON PAGE 293

591 ALPHABET CROSSWORDS

Using all 26 letters of the alphabet complete the grid. Six letters have been placed.

SOLUTION ON PAGE 293

592 WRONG WORDS

What word in each list below does not belong?

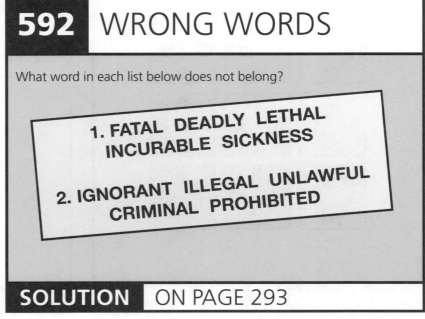

1. FATAL DEADLY LETHAL INCURABLE SICKNESS

2. IGNORANT ILLEGAL UNLAWFUL CRIMINAL PROHIBITED

SOLUTION ON PAGE 293

593 CODEBREAKER

Crack the code to discover the names of 5 crime writers.

QBUSJDJB DPSOXFMM

FE NDCBJO

FMNPSF MFPOBSE

KPIO HSJTIBN

DBSPM PDPOOFMM

SOLUTION ON 293

594 LOCK BREAKER

In each vertical column the letters add up to either 4 or 5. What letter could you put in the empty box to make that column equal 5 and open the lock?

U	R	V	S	X
S	F	P	N	L
Q	T	I	D	?
Z	R	J	M	H

5 4 5 4 5

SOLUTION ON PAGE 293

595 FLIGHT

The girl named below can fly without the aid of an aeroplane. How does she do it? A close look at her name should tell you.

GEORGINA ALLEN

SOLUTION ON 293

596 HIDDEN WORDS

Read the sentence carefully to discover a series of associated words hidden in it. The connected words will be found by joining the end of one word somewhere in the sentence with the beginning of the next word. What are the connected words?

It took much effort of mine radically jumping into the cold river to rejoin eradicating the myth that I could not do it.

SOLUTION ON PAGE 293

597 SIMPLE SOLUTION

Rearrange the letters below to make just one word:

O S N D J W U
O T E R

SOLUTION ON PAGE 293

598 STRANGE SAYING

The rebus below represents a well-known proverb. Can you work out what it is?

A TISTITCHME RESCUES IX

SOLUTION ON PAGE 293

599 EMPTY SQUARES

Should A, B, C, or D replace the empty squares in the grid?

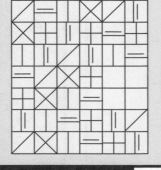

A   B   C   D

SOLUTION ON PAGE 293

600 EMPTY SQUARES

What number should replace the question marks?

```
4 2 5 3 1       7 0 1 3 6       1 9 9 0 8
3 8 2 8 7 F D A 2 2 1 4 5 H I E 5 7 4 6 7 G B C
8 0 1 7 7       9 1 3 8 6       ? ? ? ? ?
```

SOLUTION ON PAGE 293

---

601 LONGEST WORD

Move from square to touching square to discover the name of a famous musical. Use as many of the letters as possible. What is it?

R	A	T	F	P
E	H	O	H	Q
P	E	M	N	A
O	S	O	T	J

SOLUTION ON 293

---

602 NUMBER LINKS

Rearrange the tiles and place them touching one another in a 3 x 3 square, so that all adjacent letters are alphabetically consecutive. If placed correctly, the name of a city in the USA will be read. What is it?

SOLUTION ON PAGE 293

---

603 COCKTAIL STICKS

By moving two cocktail sticks in this arrangement, can you form 15 squares?

SOLUTION ON 293

---

606 PROVERB

The words below form a rebus that refers to a well-known saying. Can you work out what it is?

ONE	ANOTHER
ONE	ANOTHER
ONE	ANOTHER
ONE	ANOTHER
ONE	ANOTHER
ONE	ANOTHER

SOLUTION ON 293

---

604 NUMBER GRID

Find the number to replace the question mark.

A	20	14	8	12
B	3	4	16	4
C	6	7	?	6
D	10	8	4	8

SOLUTION ON PAGE 293

---

605 EQUAL SEGMENTS

Divide this grid into four identical shapes so that the sum of the numbers in each section is as given below.

TOTAL 60

9	6	8	8	2	5
7	4	5	8	6	9
8	8	7	7	6	9
9	6	8	9	6	8
6	4	6	8	5	4
7	7	5	8	7	5

SOLUTION ON 293

607 SALARY INCREASE

A company gives a choice of two plans to the union negotiator for an increase in salary. The first option is an initial salary of $20,000 to be increased after each 12 months by $500. The second option is a half-yearly initial salary of $10,000 to be increased after each six months by $125. This half-yearly salary is to be calculated and paid over six months.

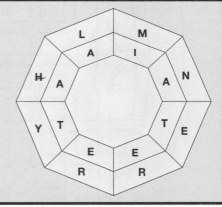

Can you advise the union negotiator which is the plan he should recommend to his members?

SOLUTION   ON PAGE 293

608 WORD MATCH

What do the following words have in common?
DISMAY ENSUED AKIMBO DISGRACEFUL ANGINA

SOLUTION   ON PAGE 293

609 FUNNY FISH

One of these fish has stolen something from someone. name the object stolen and the gender of the victim.

**SHARK   SALMON
HERRING   HADDOCK
PLAICE**

SOLUTION   ON PAGE 293

610 UNUSUAL SAFES

Here is an unusual safe. Every single button must be pressed once only in the correct order to reach OPEN. The number of moves and the direction is marked on each button (3C would mean three moves clockwise, and 1A would mean one move anti-clockwise). Which button is the first you must press?

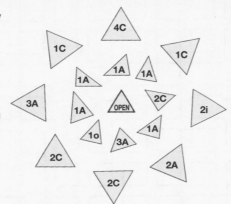

SOLUTION   ON PAGE 293

611 ADD ONE

Place a letter in the middle of the diagram so that a word can be read along each straight line. What are the four words?

SOLUTION   ON PAGE 293

612 BLANK TO BLANK

Can you fill in the blanks in these sentences? The second blank is an anagram of the first.

1. Lucy made a note in her ———— of the day she visited the ————.

2. At the fruit shop the lady picked up a ———— which was very ————.

3. The father told his son a ————, but his mother said it was too ———— at night.

4. The chef turned the heat on the cooker down to ———— the ———— boiling over.

5. The woman asked her husband what he wanted to ———— with his cup of ————.

SOLUTION   ON PAGE 293

613 CODE WHEEL

Place each of the letters in the middle of this circle in a box around the edge. If correctly placed, the letters will be the first letter of one word and the last of another, and eight six-letter words will be read. What are they?

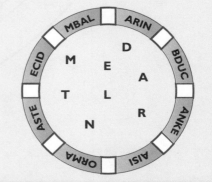

SOLUTION   ON PAGE 293

614 CHINESE CHASE

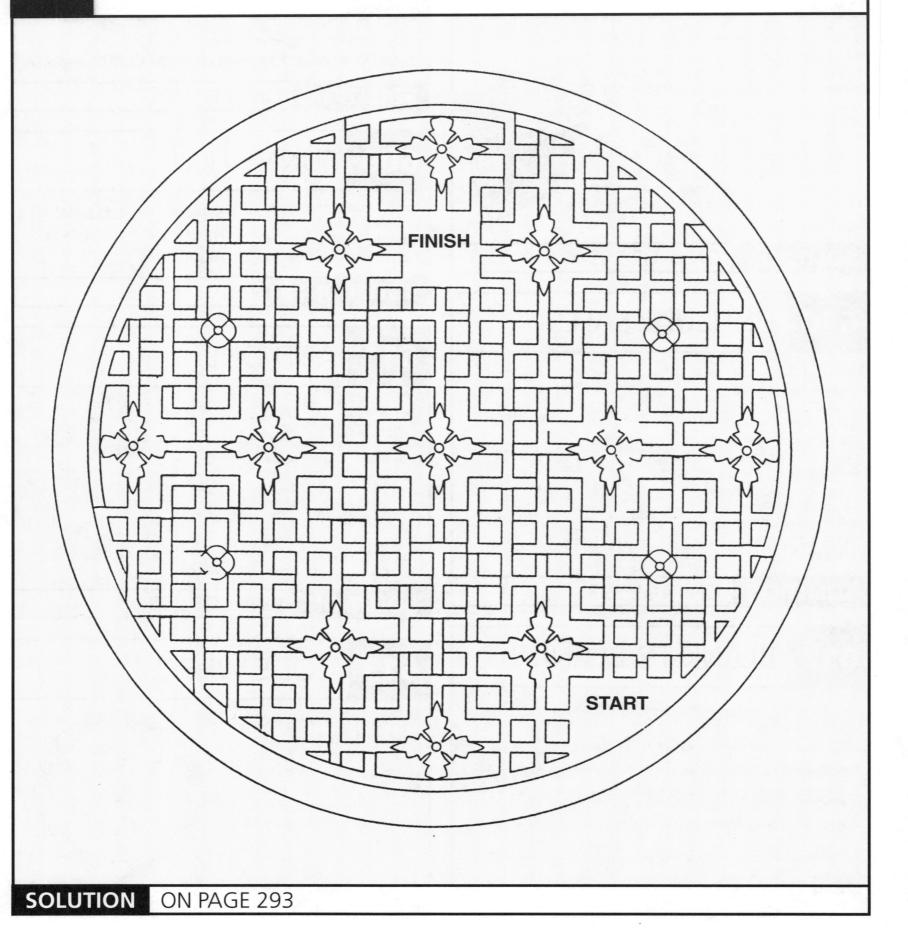

SOLUTION ON PAGE 293

615 SECURITY LAPSE

A nightwatchman once requested an urgent meeting with his company's CEO. The CEO was a busy man and was about to fly to a conference in Paris, but gave the employee five minutes of his time. The man nervously explained that he had woken after a terrible dream the previous night. He dreamed that the CEO's plane flying to France had crashed and everyone on board had been killed. He begged the CEO not to take the flight. The CEO thanked the employee for his concern but flew to the conference anyway. The plane did not crash and the conference was uneventful, but as soon as the CEO got back to the office he fired the nightwatchman. Why?

SOLUTION ON PAGE 293

617 RUM RHYME

Here is a well-known nursery rhyme to which something strange has been done. Can you spot what it is?

**Mary had a tiny lamb,
Its wool was pallid as snow,
And any spot that Mary did walk,
This lamb would always go.
This lamb did follow Mary to school,
Although against the law,
How girls and boys did laugh and play,
This lamb in class all saw.**

SOLUTION ON PAGE 293

619 SCENE OF CRIME

The normal body temperature is 98.4 degrees F. But when dead, the body cools at 1.5 degrees F per hour for the first five hours. After that it cools at one fifth of this.
At a recent scene of crime the temperature of the body was found to be 90 degrees F.

How long had the victim been dead?

SOLUTION ON PAGE 293

616 DOUBLE JIG WORD

Place the words listed below into one of the two crosswords grids. Each word is used once only.

AIM	AIRMAN	ATTITUDE	APOLOGETIC	ARCTIC
BABE	BLEAT	COMPROMISE	CONTRADICT	COPY
CORDIAL	CORONA	CYCLE	DECLARED	DISMISs
DOC	DUODENAL	EARN	ELAPSE	ENDEAR
EON	ESCARPMENT	GENTLEMAN	HOEDOWN	IMPLY
INCREASE	IRATE	ITEM	LEA	LIMITED
MAINE	MAPLE	NEST	OBLONG	ODIOUS
ONAGER	OWN	PARTNER	PHI	PIONEER
ROWEL	SCRAPE	SIGN	SOUTH POLE	SUM
TASTE	TORSO	UNI	VICTOR	YEARN

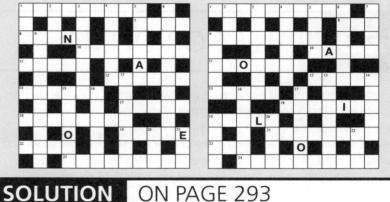

SOLUTION ON PAGE 293

618 LOCK BREAKER

What letter and number have to be added to the grid to open the lock?

I	O	V
E	R	E
N	U	I
N	?	F

9 ? 5

SOLUTION ON PAGE 293

620 AGENT ANSWER

Below are the names of some CIA agents, each with their service number.

What is Robert Sinclair's service number?

NAME	NUMBER
Agent Ryan Brookes	15
Agent Peter O'Neill	16
Agent Susan Mitchell	17
Agent Robert Sinclair	?

SOLUTION ON PAGE 293

621 ANIMAL MAGIC

Take five and put it infront of nine, then add two-thirds of ten so that you end up with a female animal.

5 IX 10

SOLUTION ON PAGE 293

622 FIND THE LINK

Four of the words in the diagram are linked by a common factor. What is it?

TRAP	–	SHOUT
FRIEND	–	LIVED
BOOK	–	REGAL
BATS	–	PIG

SOLUTION ON PAGE 293

623 BALLET OR OPERA

A survey discovers that eight more people like opera only than ballet only. One more person likes the theatre only than the opera only; 44 people taking part in the survey do not like opera at all; 67 people do not like ballet; nine more people like theatre only than ballet only; 14 people like both ballet and opera but not theatre, and 26 like both opera and theatre but not ballet; 78 people like the opera.

a)	How many people like opera only?
b)	How many people like ballet only?
c)	How many people like theatre only?
d)	How many people like all three?
e)	How many people took part in the survey?

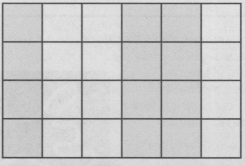

SOLUTION ON PAGE 293

624 PENTAGONS

Write each of the following five-letter words clockwise around a pentagon. Where two pentagons join, the two facing segments must contain the same letter. Some letters are given for you. How should the completed diagram look?

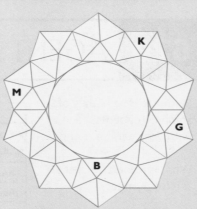

OCCUR, KNACK, AGREE, ODOUR, IGLOO, CHINA, SKATE, BUILD, STAMP, TASTE.

SOLUTION ON PAGE 293

625 COLUMNS

Rearrange the order of the given words and place one word on each row of the grid. If the words are in the correct order, the name of a fruit can be read down each of the shaded columns. What are the three fruits?

AUTUMN PEOPLE RHYMES EYELID

SOLUTION ON PAGE 293

626 LETTER GRID

Use the letters given to complete the square so that four other words can be read down and across. What are the words?

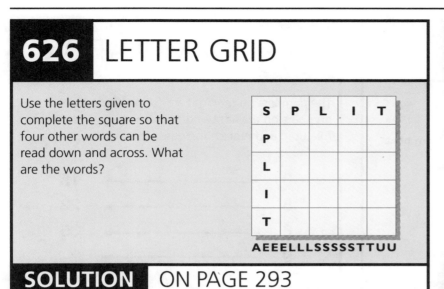

S	P	L	I	T
P				
L				
I				
T				

AEEELLLSSSSSTTUU

SOLUTION ON PAGE 293

627 FORMULATION

The numbers on the right are formed from the numbers on the left using the same formula in each question. Find the rule and replace the question mark with a number.

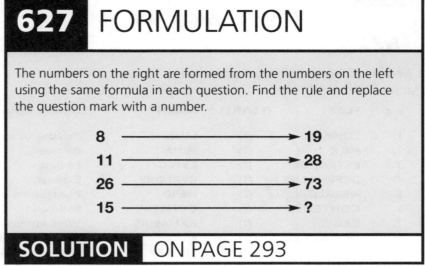

8 ⟶ 19
11 ⟶ 28
26 ⟶ 73
15 ⟶ ?

SOLUTION ON PAGE 293

628 MATHS MYSTERY

Start at the top-left circle and move clockwise. Calculate the number that replaces the question marks.

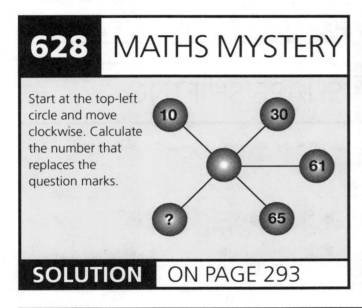

10   30
61
?   65

SOLUTION ON PAGE 293

629 COMPLETE THE SEQUENCE

Which arrangement is missing from the sequence?

A   B   C   D   E

SOLUTION ON PAGE 293

630 MISSING SHAPE

Which arrangement is missing from the sequence?

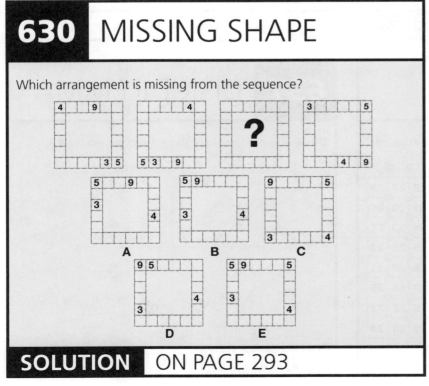

A   B   C

D   E

SOLUTION ON PAGE 293

631 EXAM ENIGMA

A, B, C, and D take part in school examinations. Only one sits French and that is neither B nor C. B is the only one sitting three tests. A sits Maths and one other exam. D takes Maths and English only. C sits Geography only.

1. Which exam does B not take?

2. Which person sits French?

3. Who takes Maths but not English?

4. How many sit two exams?

5. Who sits English but not Geography?

SOLUTION ON PAGE 293

632 WORD WONDER

What word, which is alphabetically between the two given words, answers the clues?

	e.g.	**FLAP**	**(FLARE)**	**FLASH**	**Distress signal from boat**
I.		**LUMP**	(?)	**LUNCH**	**Relating to moon**
2.		**MILK**	(?)	**MIME**	**Birdseed**
3.		**ESTRANGE**	(?)	**ETHIC**	**Endless**
4.		**DEPENDENT**	(?)	**DEPLORE**	**Exhaust**
5.		**HERALD**	(?)	**HERD**	**Plant-eating animal**
6.		**CONTEMPT**	(?)	**CONTEST**	**Satisfied**
7.		**BAGEL**	(?)	**BAHAMAS**	**Wind instrument**
8.		**NUISANCE**	(?)	**NUMB**	**To render void**
9.		**SECTOR**	(?)	**SEDATE**	**Free from danger**
10.		**MAGIC**	(?)	**MAGNOLIA**	**Industrialist**

SOLUTION ON PAGE 294

633 FORMULATION

The numbers on the right are formed from the numbers on the left using the same rules. Discover the rule used and replace the question mark.

3 ⟶ 15
5 ⟶ 23
8 ⟶ 35
9 ⟶ ?

SOLUTION ON PAGE 294

634 FIGURE IT OUT

The numbers in the left-hand box move clockwise around the square to the positions shown in the box on the right. In which positions should the missing numbers appear?

SOLUTION ON PAGE 294

635 SHAPE SHIFTNG

The values of grids A and B are given. What is the value of the symbols in the C grid?

A	B	C
10	9	?

SOLUTION ON PAGE 294

636 NUMBER SQUARE

In the grid below the intersections have a value equal to the sum of the four adjacent numbers.

1. Can you find two of the four intersections that have values of 100?
2. Which intersections have the lowest value?
3. What is the highest intersection value?
4. What is the highest intersection value on row 7?
5. What is the lowest intersection value on column B?
6. Which row or column has the most intersection values at 100 or more?
7. Which row or column of intersections has the lowest total value?

	A	B	C	D	E	F	G
1	17	34	20	23	21	19	27	25
2	21	23	22	24	21	32	26	24
3	18	27	19	27	30	26	19	17
4	26	35	19	21	25	18	26	22
5	19	21	24	19	16	28	28	21
6	24	27	17	29	17	29	18	26
7	23	25	22	32	20	26	27	22
	27	18	20	23	24	29	20	22

SOLUTION ON PAGE 294

637 DISK DILEMMA

What number should replace the question mark?

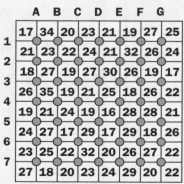

SOLUTION ON PAGE 294

638 MAZE MYSTERY

START

FINISH

SOLUTION ON PAGE 294

639 SHOE SOLUTION

If rubber shoes are used in tennis, cleats in baseball, and spikes in running, in what sport are the shoes made entirely of metal?

SOLUTION ON PAGE 294

640 DEMON CROSSWORD

In this crossword puzzle, all of the blanks have been replaced by spurious letters. You have to find and fill the blanks to produce the puzzle, which is symmetrical, and then add the answer numbers.

M	A	L	L	E	T	I	S	A	B	R	E	S
A	P	I	T	C	H	E	A	R	S	E	X	E
S	A	M	P	L	E	D	B	A	N	G	E	R
T	W	I	R	L	S	E	L	P	O	A	R	V
E	S	T	E	G	E	N	E	S	B	R	T	E
R	I	S	E	R	S	A	V	O	L	D	E	R
S	Y	L	V	A	N	V	I	L	E	A	D	S
C	A	S	E	S	H	A	L	V	A	L	V	E
L	N	A	N	S	A	L	V	E	D	O	R	L
I	G	N	T	E	L	L	E	R	S	C	A	D
M	E	D	I	A	L	O	S	C	R	A	P	E
B	L	A	N	D	O	W	T	A	L	L	E	R
S	A	L	L	O	W	E	S	T	E	E	D	S

SOLUTION ON PAGE 294

641 MAGIC SQUARES

Here are five interlocking Magic Squares. Each square consists of five five-letter words, which can be read both horizontally and vertically. Clues are given below for each Magic Square, but in no particular order.

CLUES 1–5

Abrupt
Apparatus for cooking
Defeated person
50/50 wager
Small island

CLUES 6–10

Cut on slant
Dwelling
Egg-shaped
Older and learned person
To remove frozen water (2-3)

CLUES 11–15

Adversary
Julius Caesar, for example
Rub out
Sufficient
US town associated with witchcraft

CLUES 16–20

After now
Dinner platter
Essence of roses
To rag
Went wrong

CLUES 21–25

International telegraph service using teleprinters
Military blockade
Prankish spirit in Shakespeare's *The Tempest*
Substance used to raise bread
Weird

SOLUTION ON PAGE 294

---

642 ODD JOB?

Move from square to square, including diagonals, to discover the name of a character from the film "Goldfinger".

E	R	N	U	S
R	A	P	S	Y
S	O	L	A	G

SOLUTION ON 294

---

643 AGENT ANSWER

On a recent undercover operation, there were a number of male and female FBI agents. Each male agent had twice as many female colleagues as male ones, but each female agent had the same number of male and female colleagues.

Why was this?

SOLUTION ON 294

---

644 BARTENDER'S BEER

A man goes into a bar in New York. "Glass of beer please," he says to the bartender. "Light or special?" asks the bartender. "What's the difference?" asks the man. "Light is 90 cents, special is $1," replies the bartender. "I'll have the special," says the man, placing $1 on the counter.

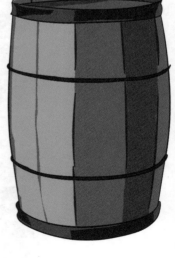

Another man comes into the bar. "Glass of beer please," he says, placing $1 on the counter. The bartender gives him the special.

Why would he do that?

SOLUTION ON PAGE 294

645 POLICE PERSONS

The Chicago Police Department has 431 female officers. They recently launched a TV campaign to recruit another 15, which was successful. A few weeks later, five more joined the force, but this was offset by 18 leaving.

How many female officers are there now?

SOLUTION ON PAGE 294

647 SYMBOL SEQUENCE

Which is the missing symbol in this sequence?

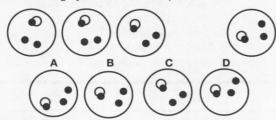

A   B   C   D

SOLUTION ON PAGE 294

649 STREET SOLUTION

You are in Washington DC to meet a contact. The following coded e-mail message tells you where and when.

Noo nyadrut aslairom. Emnlocni. Leht.

SOLUTION ON PAGE 294

646 ODD ONE OUT

You have been given what you believe is a secret formula, however there is one number too many. Which is the odd one out?

| 14 | 29 | 78 | 51 | 46 | 12 |

SOLUTION ON PAGE 294

648 MYSTERY MISSION

You are agent K, on a mission. You need to send a message to base K via your laptop computer and a satellite link. However, you need to choose the correct satellite.

Which one do you choose?

SOLUTION ON PAGE 294

650 MUSICAL MADNESS

One of the following musical terms is unlike the others. Which is it?

**RHYME
RHYTHM
TEMPO
BEAT
HARMONY**

SOLUTION ON PAGE 294

651 WRONG WORD

What word does not belong in each list?

1. GUN ARROW BULLET KNIFE CLUB

2. ANGRY FURIOUS ENRAGED
DISTRESSED ANNOYED

SOLUTION ON PAGE 294

652 OBSERVATION

Observation skills are crucial in detective work.

Here is a map showing where a recent homicide took place. It details the scene of crime location, layout of the area, and shows where various witnesses were at the time.

Spend two minutes looking at the map, then cover the image and answer the questions.

1. On which street is the crime scene?
2. Which street crosses that one?
3. On the corner of which 2 streets is the car parts shop?
4. How many empty shops are there?
5. Behind which shop is the small patch of waste land?
6. Which witness lives in South Street?
7. Which witness was standing at the bus stop on Loftus Road?
8. How many cars were parked in the car lot?
9. What type of church is on the corner of South Street?
10. Which witness lives at house number 75?
11. What is the house number of the crime scene?
12. If you were to go down the alley in South Street, in which street would you come out?

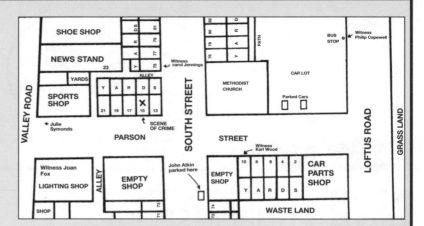

13. Where does the witness Karl Wood live?
14. Who lives in the Lighting Shop?
15. Whose car was parked next to the empty shop?
16. What type of shop is next to the Newsstand?
17. What road is the Newsstand on?
18. Where was Julie Symonds standing?
19. How many bus stops are there?
20. How many parked cars are there in total?

SOLUTION | ON PAGE 294

653 MAZE MYSTERY

SOLUTION | ON PAGE 294

654 GOOD EGGS

My uncle eats two eggs for breakfast every morning, but he neither begs, borrows, steals, finds nor buys the eggs. He doesn't keep chickens, and the eggs are not given to him; nor does he trade them for other goods. No hen comes into his garden and lays the eggs. How does my uncle get the eggs?

SOLUTION ON PAGE 294

655 HOUSE HORROR

What number should replace the question mark?

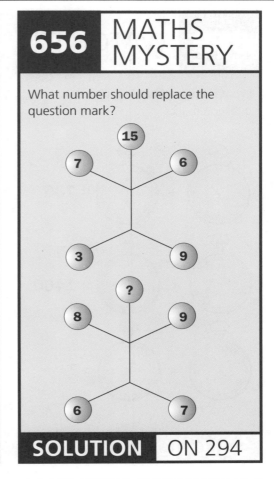

SOLUTION ON 294

656 MATHS MYSTERY

What number should replace the question mark?

15
7   6
3   9
?
8   9
6   7

SOLUTION ON 294

657 CIRCLE CONUNDRUM

Using all of the outer circled numbers once only, can you find the missing numbers in the following circles?

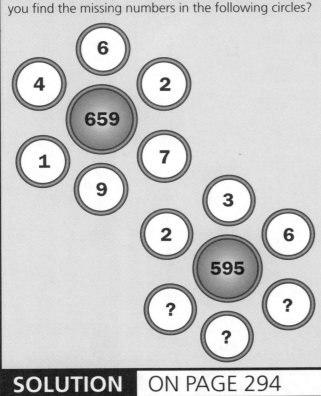

SOLUTION ON PAGE 294

658 WORD MATCH

Which word is closest in meaning to the given word? Is it A, B, C, D, or E?

		A	B	C	D	E
1.	FLAIR	Fashionable	Talent	Style	Able	Quality
2.	BONA-FIDE	Correct	Factual	Genuine	Real	Precise
3.	ARID	Cold	Desolate	Deserted	Dry	Burnt
4.	BOISTEROUS	Carefree	Excessive	Unruly	Evil	Devilish
5.	ENDOW	Testament	Probate	Bequeath	Payment	Insurance
6.	PUNY	Petite	Minute	Weak	Soft	Simple
7.	DEMEAN	Arguable	Cheat	Defraud	Degrade	Libel
8.	ATTEST	Protect	Save	Vouch	Warrant	Defend
9.	MEDITATE	Wonder	Consult	Ruminate	Trance	Rest
10.	FLABBY	Soft	Elastic	Unctuous	Waxy	Flaccid
11.	WILD	Feral	Fierce	Violent	Temperamental	Rural
12.	ACRID	Sharp	Nasty	Tart	Bad-tempered	Pungent
13.	MERGE	Coalition	Fusion	Union	Combine	Incorporate
14.	STABLE	Constant	Durable	Permanent	Static	Unalterable
15.	RAPID	Brisk	Fast	Flying	Hasty	Prompt
16.	GOODWILL	Benevolent	Kindliness	Generous	Zealous	Virtue
17.	IMPLORE	Ask	Begged	Plead	Force	Solicit
18.	DORMANT	Asleep	Comatose	Hibernating	Inactive	Latent
19.	OPACITY	Cloudiness	Dullness	Obscurity	Transparent	Unclear
20.	UPKEEP	Aid	Maintenance	Preserve	Conserve	Promote

SOLUTION ON PAGE 294

659 WATCH IT!

What number should replace the question mark?

+ = 735

+ = 1460

+ = ?

SOLUTION ON 294

660 PICKING PROFESSIONS

Mr Carter, Mr Butler, Mr Drover and Mr Hunter are employed as a carter, a butler, a drover and a hunter. None of them has a name identifying their profession, though. They made four statements:

1. Mr Carter is the hunter.
2. Mr Drover is the carter.
3. Mr Butler is not the hunter.
4. Mr Hunter is not the butler.

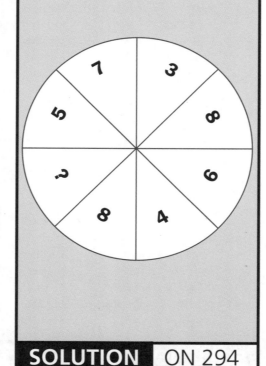

According to those statements, the butler must be Mr Butler, but this cannot be correct. Three of the four statements are untrue. Who is the drover?

SOLUTION ON 294

661 SHAPE SHIFTER

The values of grids A and B are given. What is the value of the C grid?

A   B   C

25   20   ?

SOLUTION ON PAGE 294

662 LETTER LOGIC

The expression below can, if you think about it carefully, be transformed into the name of a country. Beware – the letters are mixed up!

E
0
10
1000
I
100

SOLUTION ON 294

663 MISSING NUMBER

What number should replace the question mark?

7 3
5   8
?   6
8 4

SOLUTION ON 294

664 MATHS MYSTERY

What numbers should replace the question marks?

51
11   8
6   9
?
12   4
20   7

SOLUTION ON PAGE 294

665 DISK DILEMMA

Using all of the outer circled numbers once only, can you find the missing number in the following circle?

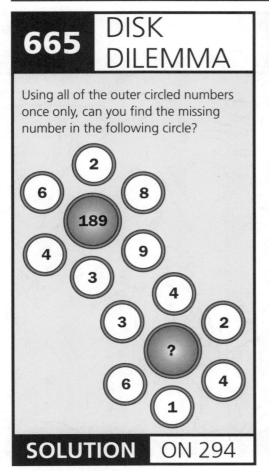

SOLUTION ON 294

666 SHAPE SORTER

Which arrangement is missing from this sequence?

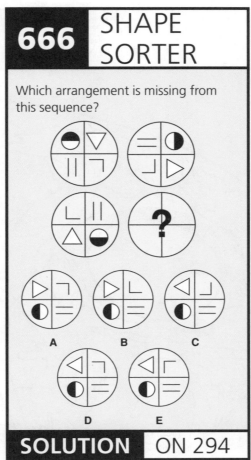

SOLUTION ON 294

667 CONSEQUENCES

Which arrangement is missing from this sequence?

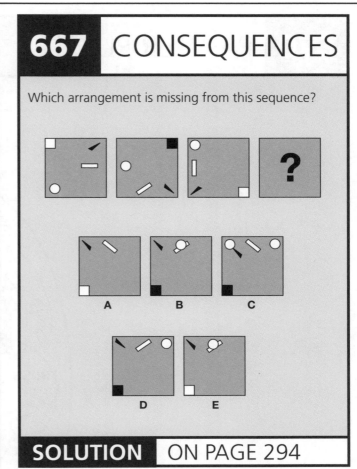

SOLUTION ON PAGE 294

668 TIME TROUBLE

What number should replace the question mark?

X = 105

X = 108

X = ?

SOLUTION ON PAGE 294

669 NUMBER NONSENSE

Divide these two grids into SIX identical shapes. The sum of the numbers in each section must give the total shown.

Total 100

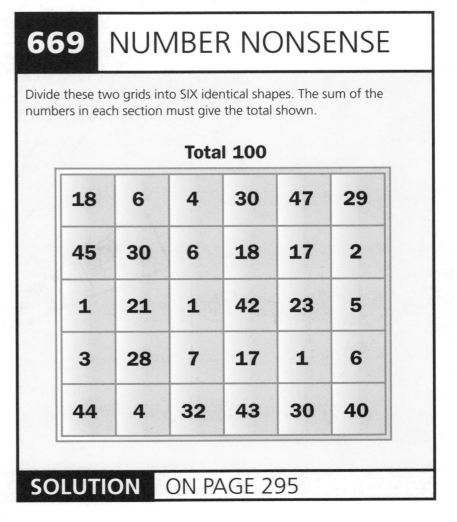

18	6	4	30	47	29
45	30	6	18	17	2
1	21	1	42	23	5
3	28	7	17	1	6
44	4	32	43	30	40

SOLUTION ON PAGE 295

670 | PAINTER PUZZLE

FINISH

START

671 ALPHABET CROSSWORD

Using all 26 letters of the alphabet, once only, fill in the blanks to complete the crossword with good English words.

A   B   C   D
E   F   G   H
I   J   K   L
M   N   O   P
Q   R   S   T
U   V   W   X
Y   Z

K		L		S		U		T
		O	K					
						I	S	E	R
		O	R		E			D
E					T		F	
	J				E	A		E
J	A			S				S
			L		E	S	T
S			I		L		

SOLUTION   ON PAGE 295

672 TIGHT FIT

Insert all the words listed below into the grid. Each word must travel in a straight line in the direction of one of the compass points and start and finish in a shaded square.

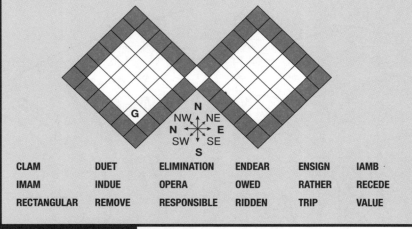

CLAM	DUET	ELIMINATION	ENDEAR	ENSIGN	IAMB
IMAM	INDUE	OPERA	OWED	RATHER	RECEDE
RECTANGULAR	REMOVE	RESPONSIBLE	RIDDEN	TRIP	VALUE

SOLUTION   ON PAGE 295

673 KILLER

The housekeeper was distraught after she found Fred and Ginger lying dead on the floor. There was some broken glass near their bodies, and the carpet was damp. Neither of them was wearing any clothes.

Who had killed Fred and Ginger?

SOLUTION   ON PAGE 295

674 PRISON PROBLEM

Below are the names of some new inmates at the city jail, each with their prison number. What is the number of the last prisoner?

NAME	NUMBER
MIKE JACKS	22.16.11.14
ERIC STONE	23.12.39.29
DAVE WOLFE	05.27.38.18
JOHN BLAKE	?

SOLUTION   ON PAGE 295

675 SPARK SOLUTION

Which piece will connect up this circuit?

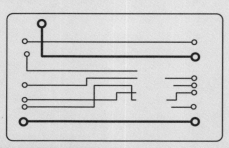

A

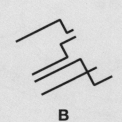

B

C

D

SOLUTION   ON PAGE 295

676 BLOOD BOTHER

Is the missing bloodgroup A, B or O?

NAME	BLOOD GROUP
Bill Davies	A
Paul Freeman	O
Catrina Smith	B
Patricia Jones	?

SOLUTION ON PAGE 295

677 BLOOD BROTHERS?

Sarah's blood group is O-negative. Simon's is A, Jonathon's is A-negative, and David's is O. What blood group does Martin have?

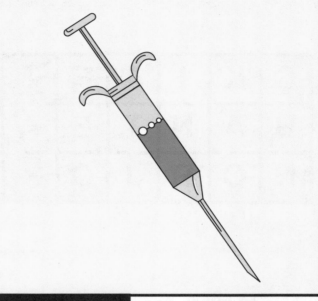

SOLUTION ON PAGE 295

678 CIRCUIT CONUNDRUM

To complete your mission, you need to discover which one of these is not a mirror image of the circuit below.

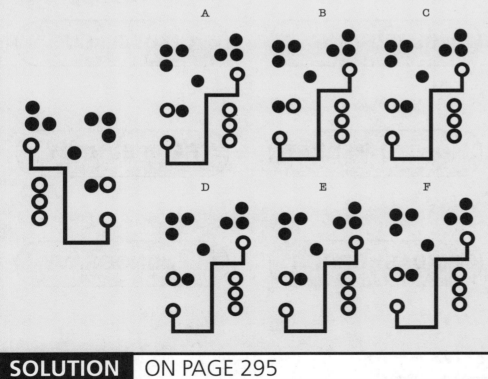

SOLUTION ON PAGE 295

679 SCENE OF CRIME

You are a Scene of Crime officer. You have just arrived at a homicide and have to cordon off the area. This area is shown below.

How many square yards is the area?

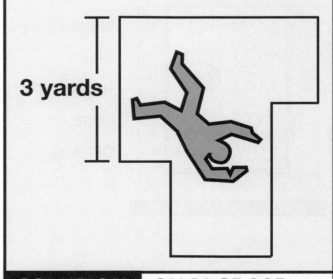

3 yards

SOLUTION ON PAGE 295

680   TAKE OFF

Find Jet, Car and Train in this grid. The remaining letters make up an exotic eastern destination.

C	K	I	A	R	T
B	A	N	T	E	A
N	O	R	J	G	K

SOLUTION   ON PAGE 295

681   LOCK BREAKER

In each vertical column the letters add up to a number.
What letter must you put in the empty box to make that column equal that number and open the lock?

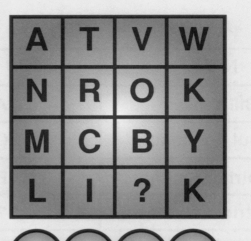

A	T	V	W
N	R	O	K
M	C	B	Y
L	I	?	K

8 10 11 14

SOLUTION   ON PAGE 295

682   SAFE BREAKER

Find the two missing numbers to crack the safe.

A (14)
B (?)
C (6)
D (?)
E (13)

PADLOCK 14
DIAL ?
HANDLE 6
CODE ?
OPEN 13

SOLUTION   ON PAGE 295

683   COP CAPER

Who are these male actors who have appeared in Cop movies?

SLIMEBONG

CRIBWILLSUE

NOSETOWILDCAT

HERIPEMUDDY

FINDASHORROR

LENDNOGRAVY

SOLUTION   ON PAGE 295

684 MAZE MUDDLE

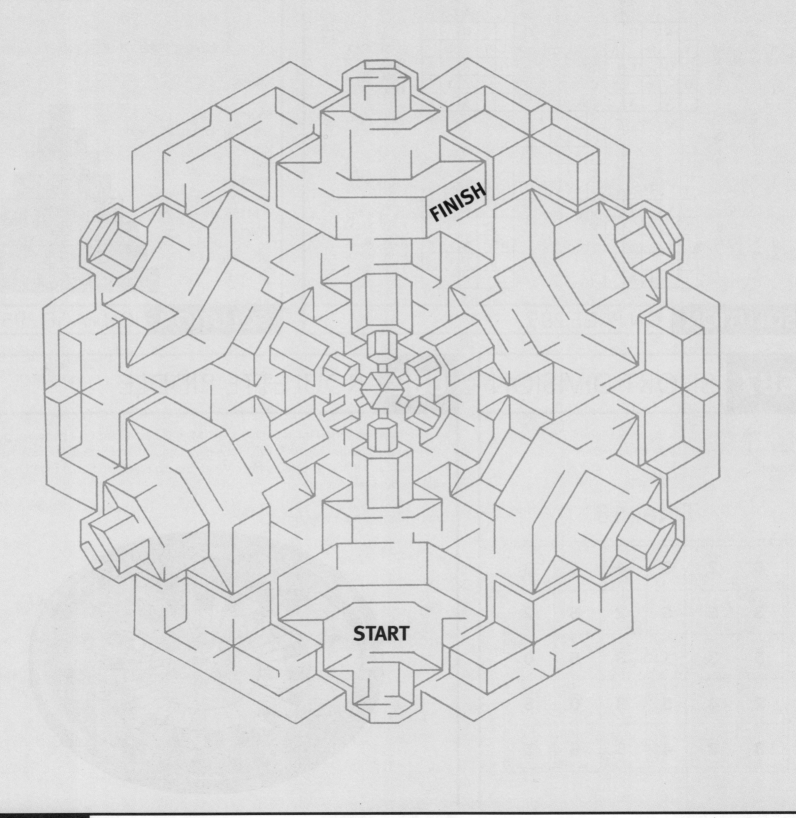

FINISH

START

685 FIVE-PIECE MAGIC SQUARE

The vowels have been positioned in the five grids. Place the consonants to produce five Magic Squares. The words read the same across and down.

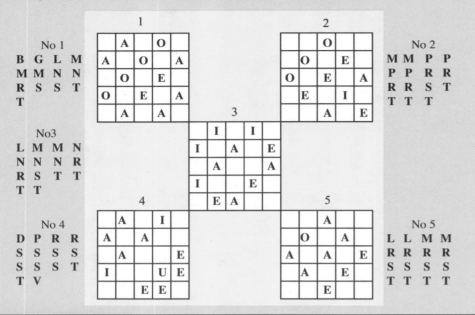

No 1
B G L M
M M N N
R S S T
T

No 2
M M P P
P P R R
R R S T
T T T

No3
L M M N
N M N R
R S T T
R T

No 4
D P R R
S S R S
S S S T
T V

No 5
L L M M
R R M R
R S S R
T T T T

686 PYRAMID

Using all 36 letters of the quotation by Oliver Hereford, below, complete the pyramid with words reading across. Clues are given, but in no particular order.

"I" IS THE MOST POPULAR LETTER IN THE ALPHABET

Clues

Edge
Exclusive right to an invention
Ling
Raise aloft
Raw hide
Roman numeral for 50
3.14159 etc
Unconditional

687 SHORT DIVISION

Divide this grid into SIX identical shapes. The sum of the numbers in each section must give the total shown.

Total 18

6	2	3	4	4	3
3	5	5	2	6	2
5	3	1	3	5	0
2	4	5	3	0	5
3	3	4	6	6	5

688 ROULETTE RIDDLE

A roulette wheel shows the numbers 1–36. My ball has landed on a particular number that I bet on. It is divisible by 3. When the digits are added together, the total lies between 4 and 8. It is an odd number. When the digits are multiplied together the total lies between 4 and 8.

Which number have I bet on?

SOLUTION ON PAGE 295

689 MATHS MYSTERY

Start at the top-left circle and move clockwise. Calculate the number that replaces the question mark in the following:

SOLUTION ON PAGE 295

690 SHAPE SORTER

Which arrangement is missing from this sequence?

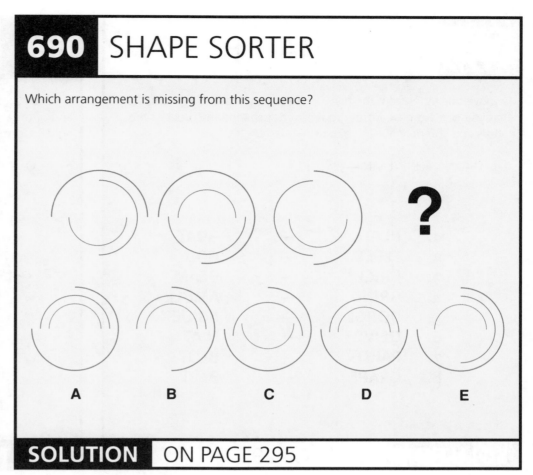

A   B   C   D   E

SOLUTION ON PAGE 295

691 LETTER LOGIC

Which arrangement is missing from this sequence?

A F H I ?

E K M V T

A   B   C   D   E

SOLUTION ON PAGE 295

692 WATCH WORD

Which letter occurs once in each of the first two words but not at all in the last two words?

1.	HARMONIOUS	LIBERATE	but not in	MELANCHOLY	LIKE
2.	RESPECTABLE	PADDOCK	but not in	WATER	PRINT
3.	QUADRUPLE	PLASTIC	but not in	STOP	START
4.	CONVERSE	SKATEBOARD	but not in	INTERACT	SANDWICH
5.	DANGEROUS	HIGHLAND	but not in	CINDER	PARTICLE
6.	CHEMICAL	AMBASSADOR	but not in	DANCE	WEEKEND
7.	FIREFIGHTER	MUSHROOM	but not in	LENDING	REALITY
8.	GLADIATOR	DATABASE	but not in	FORAGE	MEDAL
9.	OCCUPATION	EXCHANGE	but not in	CHART	PARCEL
10.	MULBERRY	PENGUIN	but not in	MERCENARY	OPENING

SOLUTION ON PAGE 295

693 WORD MATCH

Remove one letter from the first word and put it into the second so that you get two new words. You must not change the order of the letters and you may not use plurals.

e.g. LEARN — FINE (LEAN — FINER)

1.	PLATE	—	GOAT
2.	FLEET	—	GOD
3.	PRICE	—	BEAM
4.	GRIND	—	AMBLE
5.	DODGE	—	ABIDE
6.	OLIVE	—	FLAT
7.	PAINT	—	BLOT
8.	GRAPE	—	BEET

SOLUTION ON PAGE 295

694 LETTER LOGIC

On each line, place a letter in the brackets that can be attached to the end of the word to the left and to the beginning of the word to the right to form another word in each case. No plurals are allowed.

e.g. COME (T) OWN

1.	RUIN	( )	RANT
2.	BOOT	( )	EEL
3.	TAN	( )	NOT
4.	LEAN	( )	HIGH
5.	THEM	( )	VERY
6.	SEE	( )	RAFT
7.	PAW	( )	EVER
8.	EVEN	( )	EACH
9.	LUNG	( )	LAND
10.	CAME	( )	PEN

SOLUTION ON PAGE 295

695 FORMULATION

The numbers on the right are formed from the numbers on the left using the same rules. Discover the rule used and replace the question mark.

3 ⟶ 2

9 ⟶ 6

18 ⟶ 12

24 ⟶ ?

SOLUTION ON PAGE 295

696 ANGLE AGONY

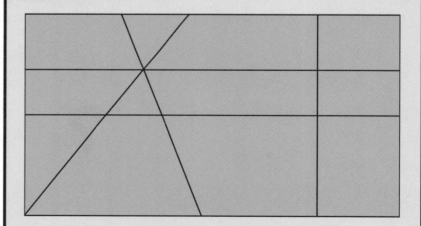

Answer the following questions on the above figure.

1. How many triangles are contained in the drawing?
2. How many right angles can be seen in the drawing?
3. How many sets of parallel lines are there going from side to side or top to bottom?
4. How many different sections are there?
5. How many squares or rectangles are there?

SOLUTION ON PAGE 295

697 MEDAL MYSTERY

The table below shows the numbers of medals won by different regions at a sports meeting. Assume every event had a gold, silver, and bronze medal-winner with no tied results.

	GOLD	SILVER	BRONZE
REGION A	33	21	63
REGION B	72	8	20
REGION C	27	60	36

1. Which region won half the number of bronze medals as Region B won in gold medals?

2. Which region won three times as many bronze medals as Region A won in silver medals?

3. Which region won one-fifth of its total in bronze medals?

4. The sum of which two regions' gold medals matched the silver medals won by Region C?

5. If there were two other regions competing and they won only 12 gold medals between them, how many silver medals and bronze medals did they get between them?

SOLUTION ON PAGE 295

698 FIND THE "R"

Find a word that begins with the letter R that is opposite in meaning to the given word.

1. **FORGETFUL**

2. **ORDERED**

3. **OCCASIONAL**

4. **UNPREPARED**

5. **CAPTURE**

SOLUTION ON PAGE 295

699 HANDKERCHIEF CHALLENGE

Charlie throws out a challenge to Ben in the local bar: "I'll put this ordinary pocket handkerchief on the floor. You stand facing me on one corner and I'll stand on the other corner. Without either of us tearing, cutting, stretching or altering it in any way, I bet you won't be able to touch me."

How can this be done?

SOLUTION ON PAGE 295

700 MISSING NUMBER

What number should replace the question mark?

7935	2765	1755
6188	5368	3604
9856	5488	?

SOLUTION ON PAGE 295

701 LOST NUMBER

What number should replace the question mark?

A	B	C	D	E
3	1	4	7	9
7	0	2	8	6
6	5	1	3	7
2	2	3	9	?

SOLUTION ON PAGE 295

702 LETTER LOGIC

Look at the table. Your task is to rearrange the letters so that no two consecutive letters are adjacent to each other (not even diagonally).

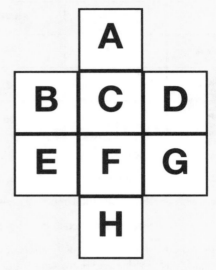

SOLUTION ON PAGE 295

703 SHORT DIVISION

Divide this grid into FOUR identical shapes. The sum of the numbers in each section must give the total of 55.

3	6	4	4	8	6
9	6	6	7	9	2
5	6	5	6	2	7
7	6	7	5	9	3
8	9	4	8	9	7
4	9	6	8	4	6

SOLUTION ON PAGE 295

704 SHAPE SORTER

The values of grids A and B are given. What is the value of C grid?

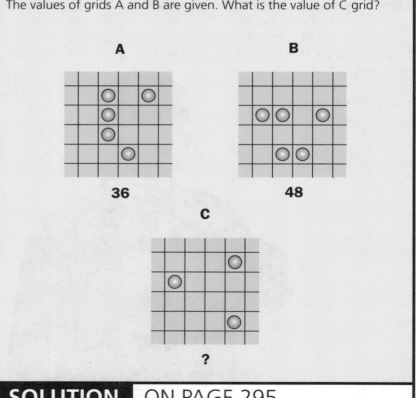

A
36

B
48

C
?

SOLUTION ON PAGE 295

705 MIGHTY MAZE

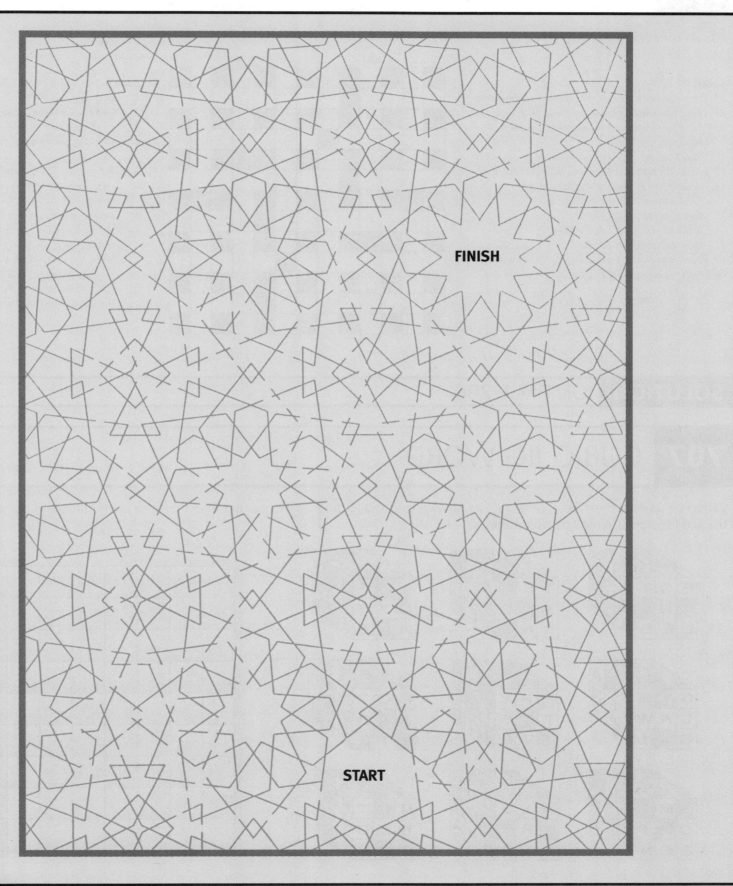

FINISH

START

706 CRYPTIC CLUE CROSSWORD

A brain-bending cryptic crossword.

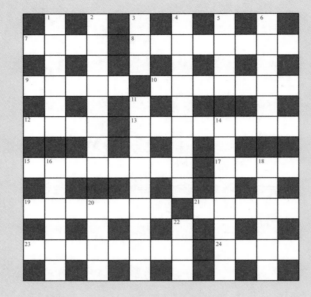

Across

7   There are such gardens that give rise to cheers (4)
8   Fear duet will become well defined (8)
9   Gave three rings and five pounds for a piece of moulding (5)
10 You'll get the garment if you tear old to pieces (7)
12 Knew the part backwards but didn't fall into it (4)
13 Assist a friend? No, just the reverse! (8)
15 Get here late and find it's heavenly (8)
17 Not quite quite. I go! (4)
19 Buy a three-pound song for baby (7)
21 How the gardener feels (5)
23 Sped with rain falling causing a wrenched ankle (8)
24 I get mixed up in T.N.T., which gives me a hue (4)

Down

1   Busy dam-builder (6)
2   Give pal a rose and cause to slip out of place (8)
3   Is this the lizard you see again? (3)
4   Rate willy correctly and discover species of nuphar (5,4)
5   Not the way you'd want a business to go (4)
6   I find two right feet entwined as narrow silk ribbon (6)
11 Helps one keep smiling! (9)
14 Met quote correctly and purchased furnishing material (8)
16 Heavy blows are made as M.P.s hide in hut (6)
18 A halogen element I start with nothing (6)
20 Looks as though the lake has sprung one! (4)
22 Get put together by Dad (3)

SOLUTION ON PAGE 296

707 CUBIC JIG WORD

Each cube contains three faces. Only one face on each cube will fit correctly into the grid. Select the nine correct faces and fit them correctly into the grid to form a symmetrical crossword.

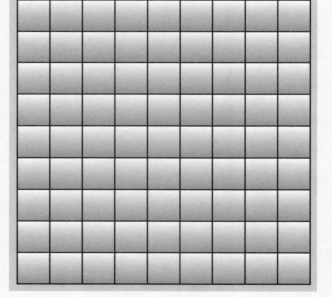

SOLUTION ON PAGE 296

708 CROWD

A man charged through a crowd, ripped open a lady's blouse, punched her in the chest and carried her away with him. However nobody, including two policemen who were nearby, tried to stop him. Why? The man was unarmed and was not a particularly imposing figure physically.

SOLUTION ON PAGE 296

710 HIDDEN CONNECTION

The following words have a hidden connection. What is it?

MALARKEY CROOKED GROWLING TRAILERS

SOLUTION ON PAGE 296

709 HIDDEN WORDS

Read the sentence carefully to discover a series of associated words hidden in it. The connected words will be found by joining the end of one word somewhere in the sentence with the beginning of the next word. What are the connected words?

At speed the little cherub ran off landing headfirst in the bathtub under all the soapy water but jumped out completely unaffected to astound everybody.

SOLUTION ON PAGE 296

711 MORE LOGICAL DEDUCTION

What number should replace the question mark?

Chocolate = 250
Biscuit = 102
Cake = 100
Muffin = ?

SOLUTION ON PAGE 296

712 DEVIOUS CLUES

Two couples were in a jeweller's choosing a ring. If Derek and Janice chose a jade ring, what type of ring did Alan and Ophelia choose?

SOLUTION ON PAGE 296

713 GRID CODES

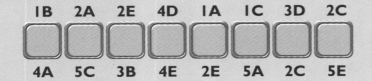

	1B	2A	2E	4D	1A	1C	3D	2C
4A	5C	3B	4E	2E	5A	2C	5E	

The word-frame above, when filled with the correct letters, will create the name of a mountain range. The letters are arranged in the coded square below. There are two alternatives to fill each square of the word frame (one correct, the other incorrect). What is the mountain range?

	A	B	C	D	E
1	I	P	R	F	S
2	Y	W	E	Q	N
3	M	R	J	C	T
4	D	F	L	E	D
5	E	H	A	G	S

SOLUTION ON PAGE 296

714 NUMBER CRUNCH

Take the following digits and rearrange them in such a way that they add up to 99,999.

1 2 3
4 5 6
7 8 9

SOLUTION ON PAGE 296

715 NUMBERS

This is a dreadful puzzle. It is so easy that a young child could understand it, yet people who think they are good at math are regularly flummoxed by it. How do you complete the bottom line?

```
1
1 1
2 1
1 2 1 1
1 1 1 2 2 1
3 1 2 2 1 1
1 3 1 1 2 2 2 1
1 1 1 3 2 1 3 2 1 1
```

SOLUTION ON PAGE 296

716 PENTAGONS

Write each of the following five-letter words clockwise around a pentagon. Where two pentagons join, the two facing segments must contain the same letter. Some letters are given for you. How should the completed diagram look?

ALERT, EBONY, USHER, ALTAR, ANGLE, ACUTE, START, BEACH, EAGER, GRILL.

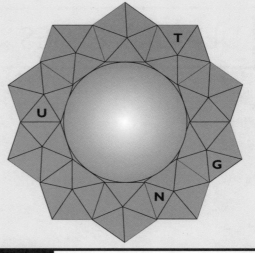

SOLUTION ON PAGE 296

717 SNOW SCENE

In a picture showing a winter scene there are people wearing hats, scarves and gloves. The same number can be seen wearing a hat only as wearing a scarf and gloves only. There are only four people who are not wearing a hat. Five people are wearing a hat and a scarf but no gloves. Twice as many people are wearing a hat only as a scarf only. Eight people are not wearing gloves and seven are not wearing a scarf. One more person can be seen wearing all three than wearing a hat only.

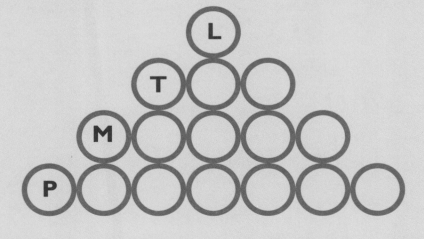

1. How many people are wearing hat, scarf and gloves?
2. How many people are wearing gloves only?
3. How many people are wearing a scarf only?
4. How many people are wearing a hat and gloves but no scarf?
5. How many people are wearing gloves?
6. How many people can be seen in the picture?

SOLUTION | ON PAGE 296

718 LETTER GRID

Use the letters given to complete the square so that four other words can be read down and across. What are the words?

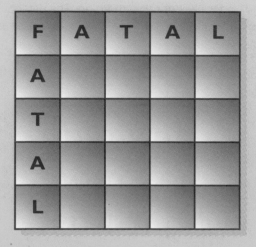

AAAADEEMMOORRYYZ

SOLUTION | ON PAGE 296

719 PYRAMID LETTERS

Use the letters given to complete the pyramid so that words can be read down and across. Across there will be one seven-letter word, one five-letter word, and one three-letter word. Running down will be one four-letter word and two three-letter words. What are they?

A E G I N N N O O R U Y

SOLUTION | ON PAGE 296

720 PRESSING PROBLEM

To de-activate this explosive device you must press the correct sequence of five buttons until you reach "PRESS". You must press each button once only. Each button is marked with U for up, D for down, L for left and R for right. The number of moves is also on each button.
Which button is the first one you must press?

SOLUTION | ON PAGE 296

721 MEAN STREETS

A woman recently engaged the services of a private detective. She was being blackmailed by someone who lived in her apartment block. She had received a number of scrawled notes; the most recent had been pushed under her door that morning. The detective looked at the note for a few moments, and then asked the woman for a pencil...

Five minutes later he went to apprehend the blackmailer.

How did he know who it was?

SOLUTION ON PAGE 296

722 WRITE ANSWER?

Below are the names of five famous crime writers. Unfortunately, the vowels are missing, and the letters are all mixed up.

Can you discover who they are?

1. **THG STRCH**

2. **RLLY NQ**

3. **TRH DNRLL**

4. **RTRH NNC LYD**

5. **DNMYR HNRDLC**

SOLUTION ON PAGE 296

723 LETTER LOGIC

In the grid below are Telephone, Postcard, and Letter. Try to find two more methods of communication.

T	E	L	E	P	H	O	N	E
D	R	A	C	T	S	O	P	L
E	T	T	R	E	I	N	N	M
R	E	T	T	E	L	I	E	A

SOLUTION ON PAGE 296

724 COMPLAINT CONUNDRUM

This letter was recently written to the manager of a store. Is Mrs Lucas really making a complaint?

Dear Sir,

I am writing to complain about our recent bad experience.

I can tell you, We'll never shop in your store again! We were kept waiting over an hour while the assistant chatted with her friend!

I'll tell you what you should Do. Fire The sales assistant. People like that don't know how to do a Job properly.

Later Tonight, when I get in from work, I'm going to write to your head office too. If you don't Leave enough people to serve customers, you're bound to have problems! I think the Key to good store management is in hiring the right staff.

Finally, I'd like to know what you're going to do about this. I hope you will not just leave this letter lying In your Desk.

Mrs Irma Lucas.

SOLUTION ON PAGE 296

725 TREE TEASER

Don and Spencer are engaged by the local council to prune trees on either side of a tree-lined avenue. There is an equal number of trees on either side of the road. Don arrives first and has pruned three trees on the right-hand side when Spencer arrives and points out that Don should be pruning the trees on the left-hand side. So Don starts afresh on the left-hand side and Spencer continues on the right. When Spencer has finished his side he goes across the avenue and prunes six trees for Don, which finishes the job.

Who prunes the most trees and by how many?

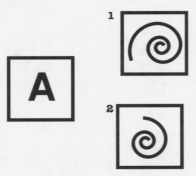

SOLUTION ON PAGE 296

726 TORN IT!

Can you work out what this message says?

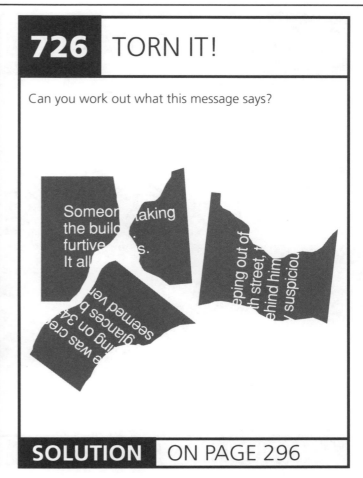

SOLUTION ON PAGE 296

727 JUNGLE GYM

You are on a jungle mission when you reach a river. The only way to cross it is by carefully stepping from stone to stone, from one side to the other. Pick the wrong stones and you'll fall in. The river is full of crocodiles.

Starting at A, and stepping on only one stone from each row, which sequence of stones should you choose?

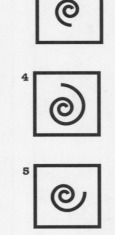
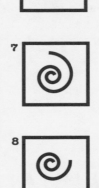

SOLUTION ON PAGE 296

728 AGENT LOCATION

What is the connection between each of these agents and the place where they are based?

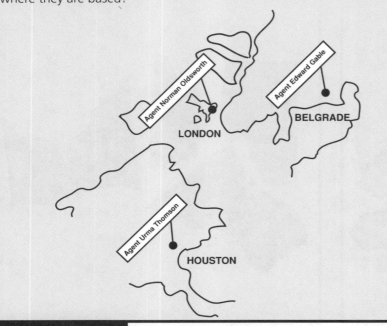

Agent Norman Oldsworth
Agent Edward Gable
BELGRADE
LONDON
Agent Urma Thomson
HOUSTON

SOLUTION ON PAGE 296

729 TEC TROUBLE

Can you fill in the missing word, which means the same as those in the boxes?

INQUIRER

DETECTIVE

INVESTIGATOR

S _ _ _ _ _ _

SOLUTION ON PAGE 296

730 SHELLING OUT?

The Chief of the Chicago Police Department is worried about his budget. He is being forced to cut equipment costs to a minimum. At a recent shoot-out, officers used up: 33 shotgun cartridges, 482 pistol bullets and 269 rifle bullets. This was worrying because the cost of a clip of six pistol bullets has just gone up to 72 cents, with shotgun cartridges 25% more expensive than pistol bullets.
Rifle bullets are, however, 20% cheaper than shotgun cartridges.

How much did this ammunition cost the department?

SOLUTION ON PAGE 296

731 ODD FEET

Here are some footprints found at a scene of crime. Which is the odd one out?

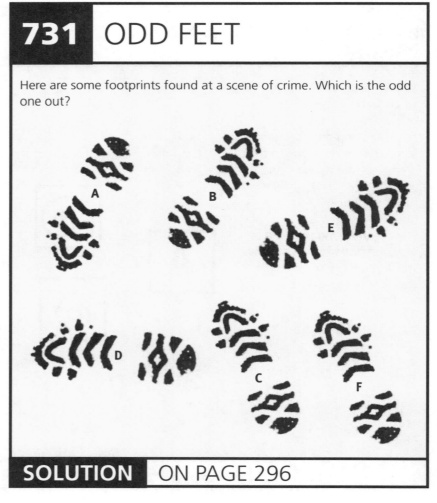

SOLUTION ON PAGE 296

732 DOC DILEMMA

You have found a fragment of a coded message...
If GRFWRU is "DOCTOR" work out what the
message says...

QHZ   BRUN   LV   PB

IDYRULWH   FLWB.

SOLUTION | ON PAGE 296

733 COVERT CONUNDRUM

Can you fill in the missing word, which means the same as those in
the boxes?

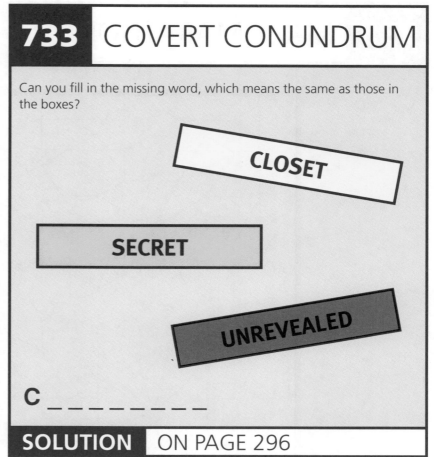

CLOSET

SECRET

UNREVEALED

C _ _ _ _ _ _ _ _ _

SOLUTION | ON PAGE 296

734 STATE SECRETS

If this is KENTUCKY:

What are these American States?

SOLUTION | ON PAGE 296

735 MAZE MARATHON

SOLUTION ON PAGE 296

736 WORDS IN CIRCULATION

The answer to each clue is a six-letter word, which circulates either clockwise or anti- (counter) clockwise around its corresponding number in the grid. Each word can start at any one of the six circles surrounding its number. Adjacent words share letters.

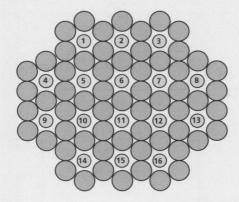

Clues

1. A bow
2. The Clergy
3. Curved
4. Get by threats
5. Secret
6. Mean dwellings
7. Splinter
8. Come back to subject
9. In the direction of
10. Was inclined
11. Seller
12. Winner
13. Subdivision of a circle
14. Sketcher's tool
15. Container
16. Sluggish state

SOLUTION ON PAGE 296

738 CRASH

A father and son were in a dreadful car accident. The father was killed and the son terribly injured. The son was rushed to hospital and straight into the operating theatre. On catching sight of the patient's face, the surgeon recoiled in shock, saying: "I can't possibly operate on this patient – he is my son!" How can this be?

SOLUTION ON PAGE 296

737 CROSSWORD

This puzzle has two identical grids and two sets of clues. The problem is that for each clue there are two options, and you have to work out which answer goes in which grid. The answers to 1 across have already been filled in.

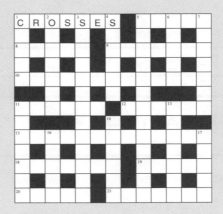

Across

1 Zeros (7)
1 Latin, Celtic, and Maltese, for example (7)
5 Supple (5)
5 Disorder (5)
8 Immerse in water (5)
8 Something given as a basis for reasoning (5)
9 Dispossess (7)
9 Refined (7)
10 Vacillate (4,3,6)
10 Argumentative (13)
11 Consecrate with oil (6)
11 Old U.S. pioneer trail to the Pacific (6)
12 Austere (6)
12 Pep (6)
15 Place for a gamble in the casino (8,5)
15 Means of recording sound (5,8)
18 Occurring at the beginning (7)
18 Influence by money payment (7)
19 Tied (5)
19 Remove from premises (5)
20 Period of darkness (5)
20 Stealing (5)
21 Feared (7)
21 Hide (7)

Down

1 In the form of a square box (5)
1 The lowest point (5)
2 Result (7)
2 Having a fast-moving beat (2,5)
3 Cave explorer (13)
3 Story that arouses concerns about people (5,8)
4 Very fast (6)
4 Calm (6)
5 Country between Switzerland and Austria (13)
5 Prime site to dine on board ship (8,5)
6 Passenger vehicle (5)
6 Excuse for being elsewhere (5)
7 Outermost (7)
7 Natural features of a district (7)
11 Speech (7)
11 Circus performer (7)
13 Tangle (7)
13 Bounce back (7)
14 Remained (6)
14 Plant used in cooking and seasoning (6)
16 Bring together (5)
16 Performing a task or action (5)
17 Praise highly (5)
17 Finished (5)

SOLUTION ON PAGE 296

739 SHAPE SHIFTER

Which arrangement is missing from this sequence?

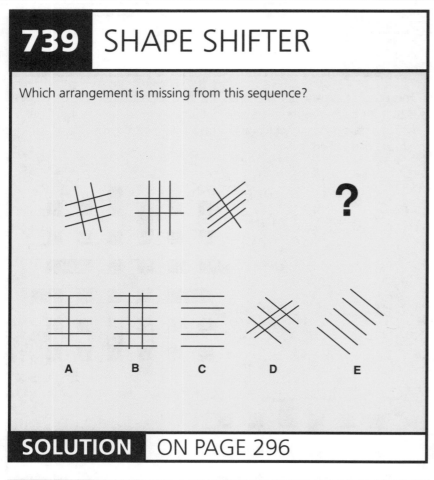

740 CONSEQUENCES

Which arrangement is missing from this sequence?

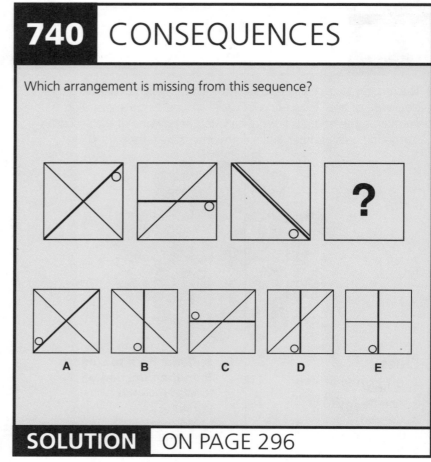

SOLUTION ON PAGE 296

SOLUTION ON PAGE 296

741 WORD MATCH

Which three letters can be added to the front of each word to make new words?

FACE
MISS
PAY
HEAT
SAGE
SENT

742 LOST LETTER

Which arrangement is missing from this sequence?

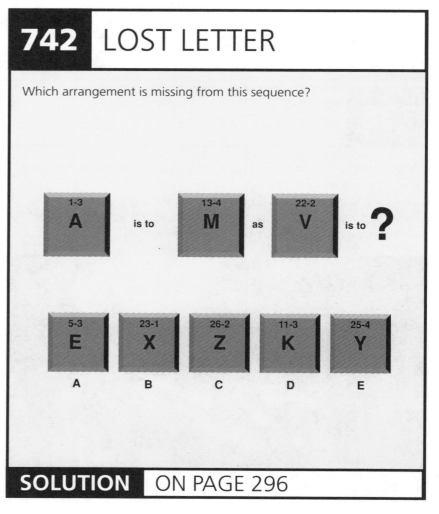

SOLUTION ON PAGE 296

SOLUTION ON PAGE 296

743 WORD MATCH

Match the word groups below with the given word. Which group completes each line? Answer A, B, C, D or E.

1. **REGAL**
2. **CROWD**
3. **PYRENEES**
4. **MISSISSIPPI**
5. **ORANGE**

A	B	C	D	E
Nile	Elegant	Flock	Rockies	Lime
Amazon	Stately	Litter	Alps	Grapefruit
Rhine	Majestic	Gaggle	Pennines	Lemon

SOLUTION ON PAGE 297

744 CAR CONUNDRUM

Three neighbours, Harry, Fred, and Paul, each have three cars, one two-door, one four-door, and one five-door. They each own a Buick, a Ford, and a Toyota. None of the same make of cars has the same number of doors. Harry's Buick has the same number of doors as Fred's Ford. Paul's Buick has the same number of doors as Harry's Ford. Harry's Toyota is a two-door and Fred's Toyota is a four-door.

1. **Who has a five-door Toyota?**
2. **Who has a five-door Ford?**
3. **Who has a two-door Ford?**
4. **Who has a four-door Buick?**
5. **Who has a five-door Buick?**
6. **Who has a two-door Buick?**

SOLUTION ON PAGE 297

745 FORMULATION

The numbers on the right are formed from the numbers on the left using the same rules. Discover the rule used and replace the question marks.

3 → 8

9 → 10

15 → 12

24 → ?

SOLUTION ON PAGE 297

746 LOST NUMBER

What number should replace the question mark?

6459	5204	200
7288	5166	360
9768	7422	?

SOLUTION ON PAGE 297

747 CLUB CONUNDRUM

There are 189 members of the tennis club: eight have been at the club less than three years; 11 are under 20 years of age; 70 wear spectacles; 140 are men.

What is the smallest number of players who had been members for three years or more, were at least 20 years of age, wore glasses and were men?

SOLUTION ON PAGE 297

748 WHICH WATCH

What number should replace the question mark?

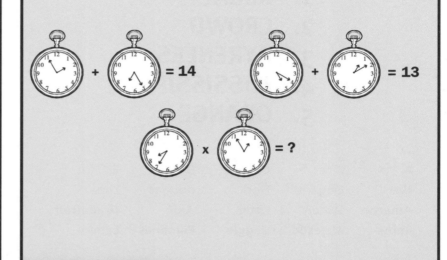

SOLUTION ON PAGE 297

749 DISK DILEMMA

Using all of the outer circled numbers once only, can you find the missing number in the following circle?

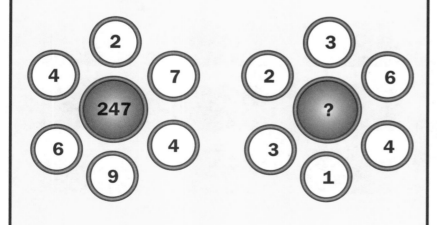

SOLUTION ON PAGE 297

750 LETTER LOGIC

Rearrange each group of letters to form three words using all of the letters.

1.)	D	E	E	I	R	S	V
2.)	E	I	L	M	S		
3.)	A	D	E	L	S	T	
4.)	A	B	E	D	R	S	
5.)	E	O	R	R	S	T	
6.)	A	D	E	G	N	R	
7.)	A	C	E	P	R	R	S
8.)	A	C	E	N	R	T	
9.)	A	C	G	I	N	O	S	T
10.)	A	G	I	N	P	R	R	S
11.)	A	C	E	L	R	T	
12.)	A	C	G	I	N	R	

SOLUTION ON PAGE 297

751 MAZE MUDDLE

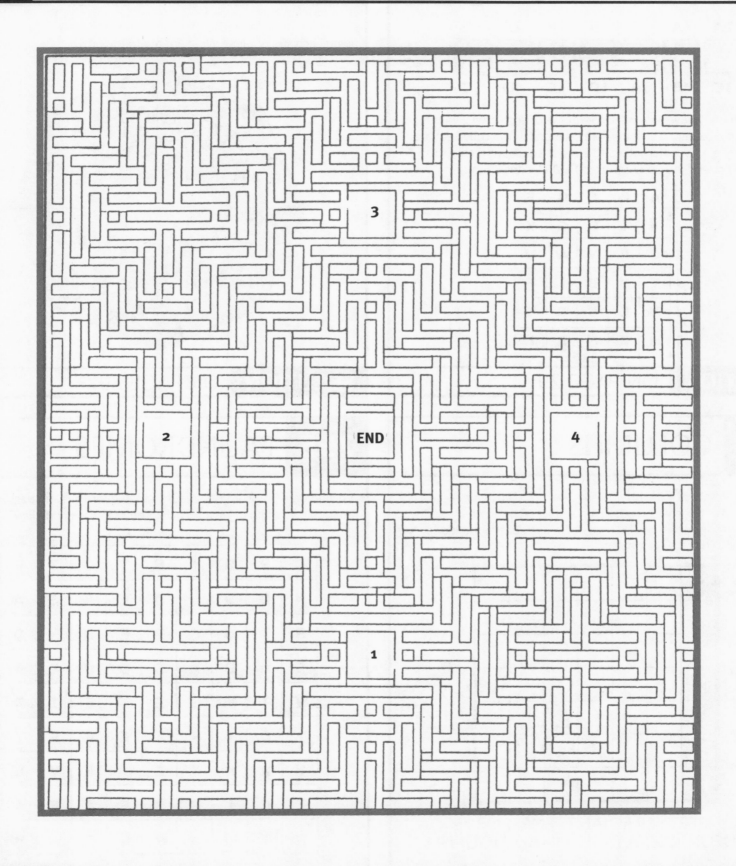

752 GRID CODES

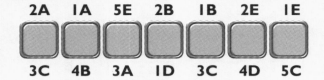

2A	1A	5E	2B	1B	2E	1E

| 3C | 4B | 3A | 1D | 3C | 4D | 5C |

The word-frame above, when filled with the correct letters, will create the name of a country. The letters are arranged in the coded square below. There are two alternatives to fill each square of the word-frame (one correct, the other incorrect). What is the country?

	A	B	C	D	E
1	A	I	D	G	K
2	C	R	V	W	U
3	T	Y	B	J	F
4	N	E	S	O	T
5	H	Z	M	P	L

SOLUTION | ON PAGE 297

753 MISSING LETTER

Place a letter in the middle of the diagram so that a word can be read along each straight line. What are the four words?

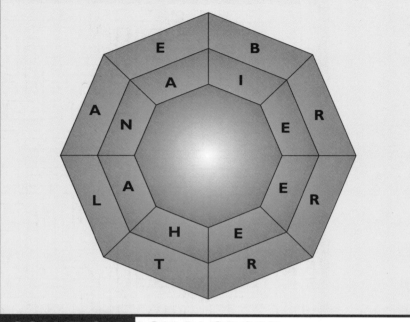

SOLUTION | ON PAGE 297

754 COLUMNS

Rearrange the order of the given words and place one word on each row of the grid. If the words are in the correct order, the name of a Formula 1 racing team can be read down each of the shaded columns. What are the two teams?

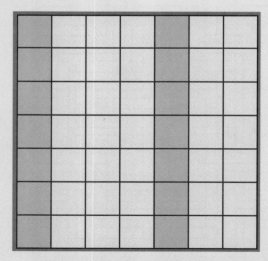

LIBERTY RADIANT EMPEROR
MINDFUL CLOSEST ADMIRAL NOURISH

SOLUTION | ON PAGE 297

755 PALINDROMES

A palindrome is a word that reads the same forward and back, e.g. radar. Can you find at least 25 palindromes in the grid below?

C	R	B	I	B	T	O	T	R
N	O	O	N	O	E	V	E	A
R	T	O	G	B	E	D	N	D
E	A	B	A	S	D	U	E	A
V	T	M	G	E	N	E	T	R
I	O	I	R	X	E	K	E	Y
V	R	N	T	E	M	F	Y	D
E	G	I	G	S	E	A	E	A
R	T	M	A	R	R	A	M	D

SOLUTION | ON PAGE 297

756 PYRAMID LETTERS

Use the letters given to complete the pyramid. Words can be read down and across. Running down will be two words of three letters and one word of four letters. Across there is one word of three letters and one of five letters. What are the words?

S N O W M A N

A A E H K L O T T

SOLUTION ON PAGE 297

757 MERGED WORDS

The names of three birds are merged together here. What are they?

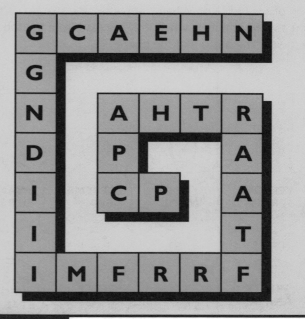

SOLUTION ON PAGE 297

758 THE DINERS

Mr and Mrs A invited three couples around for dinner. They were Mr and Mrs B, Mr and Mrs C, and Mr and Mrs D. The seating arrangements were such that one couple sat apart. Can you figure out which couple this was given the following:

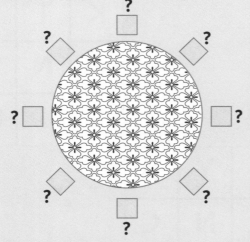

- The person opposite Mrs A was the man who sat on Mr B's left.
- The person to the left of Mrs C was a woman who sat opposite Mr D.
- The person to the right of Mr D was the woman who sat opposite the woman two seats to the left of Mr A.

SOLUTION ON PAGE 297

759 WORD SQUARES

Insert the given letters in the blank spaces so that the same words are read horizontally and vertically.

V	A	L	E	T
A				
L				
E				
T				

BBEEEEENOOSSTTVVY

SOLUTION ON PAGE 297

760 CIRCULAR CROSSWORD

Answer the clues given in the main circles and enter the letters of your answer in the six outer circles. Start at the pointer and move in the direction of the indicator. When completed, the shaded circles will give you a word or phrase when they are read from the top of the puzzle toward the bottom of the puzzle.

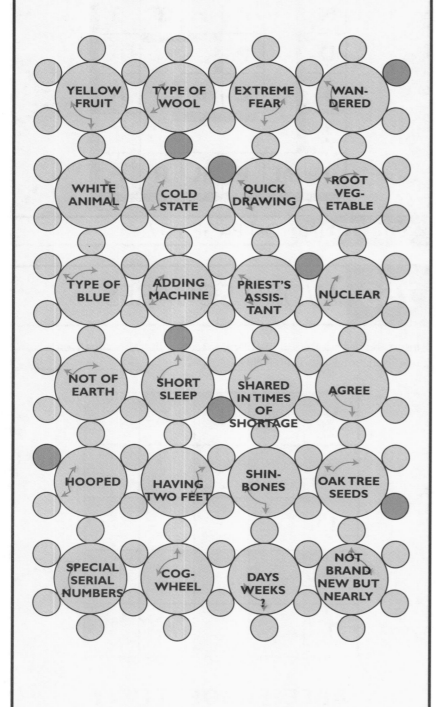

YELLOW FRUIT

TYPE OF WOOL

EXTREME FEAR

WANDERED

WHITE ANIMAL

COLD STATE

QUICK DRAWING

ROOT VEGETABLE

TYPE OF BLUE

ADDING MACHINE

PRIEST'S ASSISTANT

NUCLEAR

NOT OF EARTH

SHORT SLEEP

SHARED IN TIMES OF SHORTAGE

AGREE

HOOPED

HAVING TWO FEET

SHINBONES

OAK TREE SEEDS

SPECIAL SERIAL NUMBERS

COGWHEEL

DAYS WEEKS ?

NOT BRAND NEW BUT NEARLY

SOLUTION ON PAGE 297

761 SQUARE SEARCH

Take one word from each box to make a five-letter word. Repeat until you have nine such words.

D	R	L
I	O	R
T	M	S

E	I	E
A	R	T
O	Y	A

G	R	C
S	C	S
O	N	X

K	T	H
I	N	I
S	I	M

E	Y	E
A	N	C
Y	S	Y

SOLUTION ON PAGE 297

762 TREASURED TREES

Local sports clubs take turns to plant a tree each year in the town's main street. A bird has established a nest in each tree.

1. The crow lives in the beech tree.
2. The lime was planted two years after the tree planted by the golf club.
3. The robin is in the tree planted by the bowling club, which is next to the tree planted by the soccer club.
4. Jim planted his tree in 1971.
5. The starling is in the poplar tree planted by Desmond in 1974.
6. The robin lives in the tree planted by the bowling club, which is next to the tree planted by the soccer club.
7. Tony planted the middle tree – a beech.
8. Bill has an owl in his tree, which is next to the ash.
9. The tree at the right-hand end was planted in 1974 by the soccer club.
10. The elm was planted in 1970.
11. The tennis club planted in 1972.
12. The squash club planted in 1970.
13. Sylvester planted his tree in 1973 and it has a robin in it.
14. The blackbird is in the tree planted by Jim.

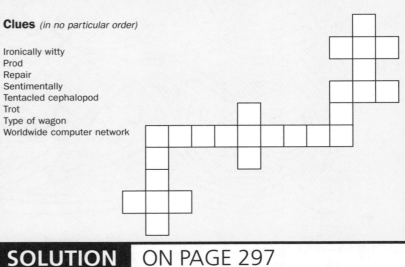

TREE					
PERSON					
CLUB					
BIRD					
YEAR					

Work out which tree was planted by which member of each club and in which year.

SOLUTION ON PAGE 297

764 DEVIOUS CLUES

Kathy works in a BANK, and enjoys OPERA and SPORT. Katy is TWENTY years of age. Katy's partner's hobbies are ROWING and DRAMA, he is a BAKER by trade, and is THIRTY years old.
What is his name?

SOLUTION ON PAGE 297

763 MORE LOGICAL DEDUCTION

Look carefully at the letters in each of the words and work out the connection with the values given. What number should replace the question mark ?

Tagliatelli	=	**40**
Pizza	=	**16**
Macaroni	=	**32**
Spaghetti	=	**?**

SOLUTION ON PAGE 297

765 FIND THE LINK

Does the word WOLF belong on the left or right side of this grid?

BEST	–	**PLEA**
DENS	–	**SODA**
NOSY	–	**LIFE**
FIST	–	**POLE**

SOLUTION ON PAGE 297

766 CROSS ALPHABET

Insert the 26 letters of the alphabet, once only, to complete the crossword. Clues are given but in no particular order.

Clues *(in no particular order)*

Ironically witty
Prod
Repair
Sentimentally
Tentacled cephalopod
Trot
Type of wagon
Worldwide computer network

SOLUTION ON PAGE 297

767 GRID CODES

1D	3D	4D	3B	2C	3A	5E		5E	2C	5B	3E

| 5A | 1B | 4C | 1C | 2A | 5B | 2D | | 3E | 1D | 2A | 4A |

The word-frame above, when filled with the correct letters, will create the name of a film star. The letters are arranged in the coded square below. There are two alternatives to fill each square of the word-frame (one correct, the other incorrect). Who is the film star?

	A	B	C	D	E
1	F	A	S	R	H
2	A	K	E	L	V
3	L	H	X	I	G
4	E	N	C	M	T
5	T	R	B	O	D

SOLUTION   ON PAGE 297

768 COLUMNS

Rearrange the order of the given words and place one word on each row of the grid. If the words are in the correct order, the name of a sweet food can be read down each of the shaded columns. What are the two foods?

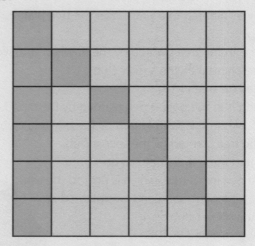

EMPIRE   ROBUST   FULFIL   LADDER   TALENT   INFORM

SOLUTION   ON PAGE 297

769 CELTIC CONUNDRUM

START→

FINISH

SOLUTION   ON PAGE 297

770 | MERGED WORDS

The names of three animals are merged together here. What are they?

M	O	I	P	U	G
O					I
R		L	K		N
U			E		Q
S	R	N	E		H
					O
		S	M	C	

SOLUTION ON PAGE 297

771 | WORD SQUARES

Insert the given letters in the blank spaces so that the same words are read horizontally and vertically.

C	H	E	S	T
H				
E				
S				
T				

DEEELLLLOOOORRSSV

SOLUTION ON PAGE 297

772 | LINK WORD

What word links the words on the left with the words on the right?

clothes   box

hobby   hair

war   play

work   race

SOLUTION ON PAGE 297

773 | MORE CODE WHEELS

In this system of intermeshing wheels, the large wheel rotates clockwise and drives the other wheels. The number of teeth for each wheel is given, and each tooth is represented by a letter. Can you calculate what words, or letters, will be at the indicator positions if:

a)   The large wheel rotates through 2 revolutions?
b)   The large wheel rotates through 5 revolutions?
c)   The large wheel rotates through 7 revolutions?
d)   The large wheel rotates through 4.5 revolutions?

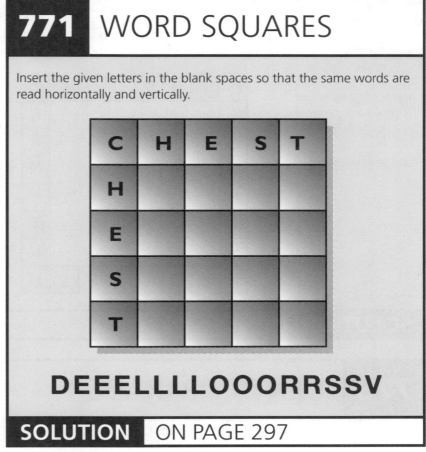

16T   12T   10T   6T

SOLUTION ON PAGE 297

774 | ACTING STRANGE

Merged together in this grid are the names of two actresses who have starred in a major detective movie.

Can you find them?

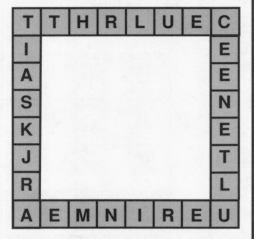

T	T	H	R	L	U	E	C
I							E
A							E
S							N
K							E
J							T
R							L
A	E	M	N	I	R	E	U

SOLUTION | ON PAGE 297

775 | BROKEN EGG

While standing on a hard wooden floor, it is possible to drop an egg three feet without breaking the shell. Nothing can be used to break the fall. How is it done?

SOLUTION | ON PAGE 297

776 | IDENTITY PARADE

Spend two minutes looking at this line up of suspects, then cover the illustration and answer the questions.

1. Which suspect is the tallest?
2. Which one is wearing a suit?
3. Which one is wearing a baseball cap?
4. Which one is wearing glasses?
5. Who is wearing a skirt?
6. Who is wearing shorts?
7. Who is wearing check trousers?
8. Which suspect is wearing a denim jacket?
9. Which one is wearing a belt?
10. Which one is wearing sunglasses?

11. Which one has a shaved head?
12. Who is wearing a check shirt?
13. Who has curly hair?
14. Who has a moustache but no beard?
15. Which one is wearing a sweater?
16. Which one is wearing a necktie?
17. How many have their hands in their pockets?
18. Which suspect has a beard?
19. Which one has an earring?
20. Who is wearing a watch?

SOLUTION | ON PAGE 297

777 MISSION IMPOSSIBLE?

Below are the names of some FBI agents, and the number of missions they have completed.

How many missions has agent Jobson completed?

NAME	MISSION
Agent Nugent	2
Agent Heinemann	1
Agent Golding	3
Agent Jobson	?

SOLUTION ON PAGE 297

778 DABS DILEMMA

Which fingerprint is the odd one out?

SOLUTION ON PAGE 297

779 SOLE SOLUTION

This footprint was found in the back yard at a recent murder scene where the occupant of the house had been killed by a blow to the head.

Police were absolutely certain that the print came from the killer.

How could they be so sure?

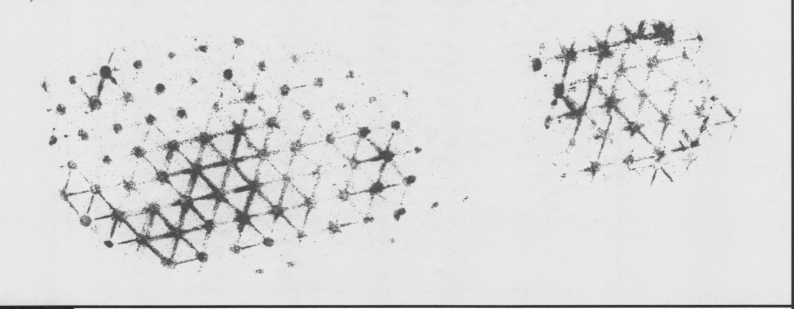

SOLUTION ON PAGE 297

780 JAPANESE JAPE

SOLUTION   ON PAGE 298

781 MUDDLED MESSAGE

What does the message say?

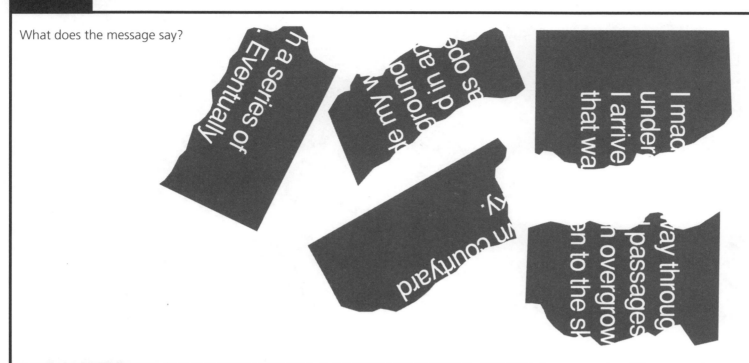

SOLUTION ON PAGE 298

782 TEC TROUBLE

Two detectives were both injured in a shoot-out in New York. One was the other's son, but the other was not the other one's father. Can you explain this?

SOLUTION ON PAGE 298

783 PRECINCT PROBLEM

These are the number of detectives currently working. How many in the twelfth Precinct?

Seventh Precinct
14

Third Precinct
3

Twelfth Precinct
?

SOLUTION ON PAGE 298

784 DABS DILEMMA

This fingerprint was found at a scene of crime. Can you match it to one of these obtained from the FBI database?

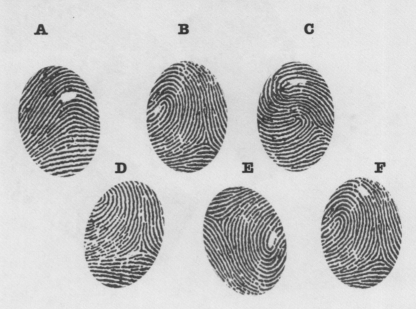

A   B   C

D   E   F

SOLUTION ON PAGE 298

785 GIRL TALK

A census-taker calls at a house. He asks the woman living there the ages of her three daughters.

The woman says, "If you multiply their ages the total is 72; if you add together their ages the total is the same as the number on my front door, which you can see."

The census-taker says, "That is not enough information for me to calculate their ages."

The woman says, "Well, my eldest daughter has a cat with a wooden leg."

The census-taker replies, "Ah! Now I know their ages."

What are the ages of the three girls?

SOLUTION ON PAGE 298

786 CITY SLICKER

If this is ATHENS,

ατηενσ

What are these Capital Cities?

λονδον

παρισ

αμστερδαμ

ωασηινγτον

ηονγ κονγ

χαιρο

SOLUTION ON PAGE 298

787 FLIGHT OF FANCY

A light aircraft took off from London, England at 1am. Its destination was Berlin, 592 miles away. Its purpose was to pick up an MI5 agent who had just emerged from a secret operation. The plane holds twelve gallons of fuel when full, and flies at 90 miles per hour, doing 60 mpg.

Unfortunately, the pilot forgot to refuel in London, and ran out of fuel 202 miles short of Berlin.

How much fuel had the plane on board when it left London?

BERLIN

SOLUTION ON PAGE 298

788 DALLAS DILEMMA

Below are the number of FBI departments in each of these cities.

How many are there in Dallas?

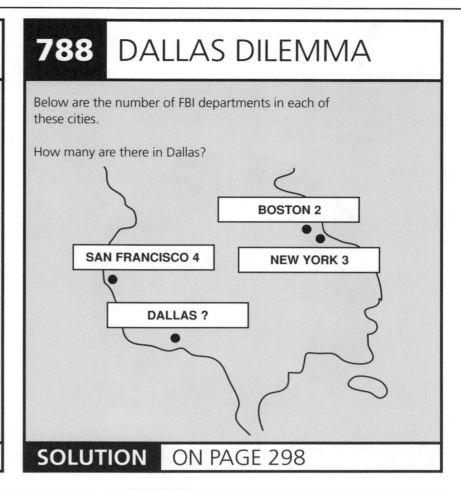

BOSTON 2

SAN FRANCISCO 4

NEW YORK 3

DALLAS ?

SOLUTION ON PAGE 298

789 CONSEQUENCES

What comes next in this sequence?

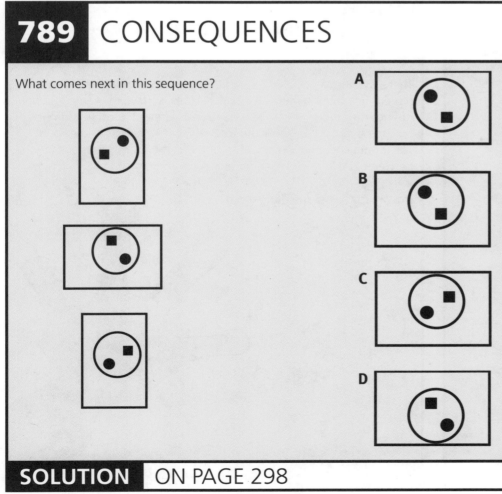

SOLUTION ON PAGE 298

790 PRINT PROBLEM

FINGERPRINT ANALYSIS

There are eight differences between these two fingerprints. Can you find them all?

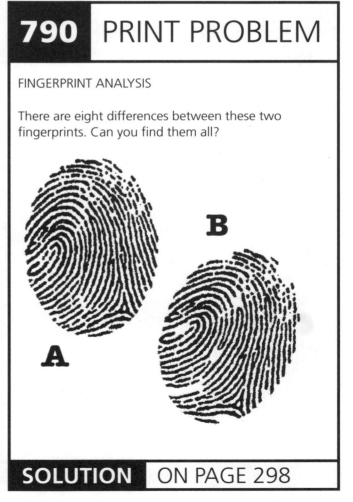

SOLUTION ON PAGE 298

791 PENTAGRAM

The five five-letter fruits have been jumbled. Solve these five anagrams and then transfer the arrowed letters to the key anagram to find a sixth. Words start at the dots.

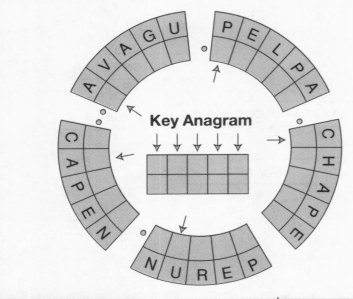

SOLUTION ON PAGE 298

792 KEY CONUNDRUM

Which key fits the tumblers in this lock?

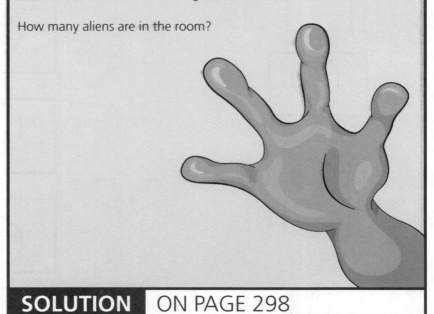

SOLUTION ON PAGE 298

793 SHAPE SHIFTER

Which arrangement is missing from this sequence?

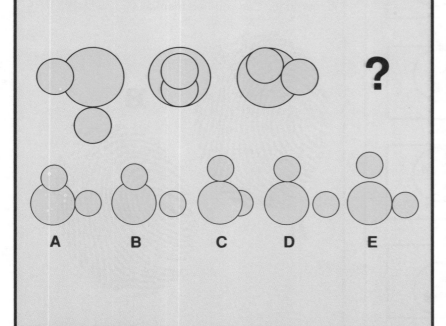

SOLUTION ON PAGE 298

794 FUNNY FINGERS

There is a number of aliens in a room, more than one. Each alien has more than one finger on each hand. All aliens have the same number of fingers as each other. All aliens have a different number of fingers on each hand. If you knew the total number of fingers in the room you would know how many aliens were in the room. There are between 200 and 300 alien fingers in the room.

How many aliens are in the room?

SOLUTION ON PAGE 298

795 CONSEQUENCES

Which arrangement is missing?

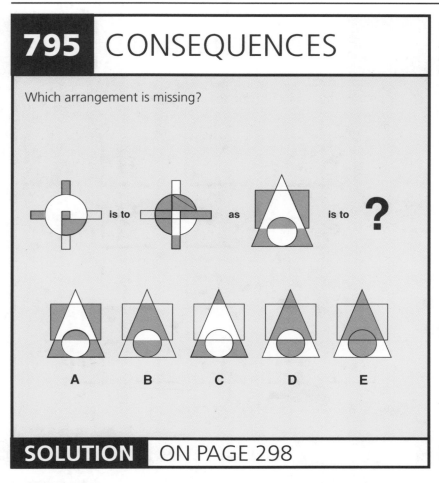

796 SWITCH SOLUTIONS

Which arrangement is missing?

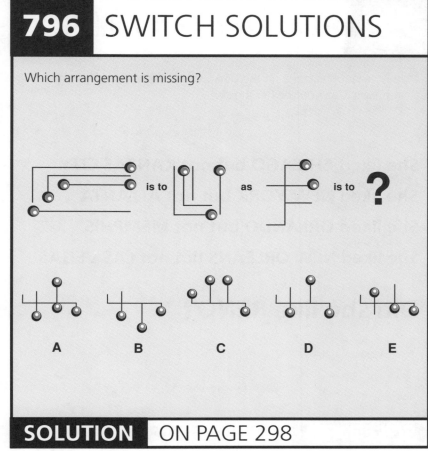

SOLUTION ON PAGE 298

SOLUTION ON PAGE 298

797 BOX BOTHER

Which of these boxes can be made from the template? No sign is repeated on more than one side of the box.

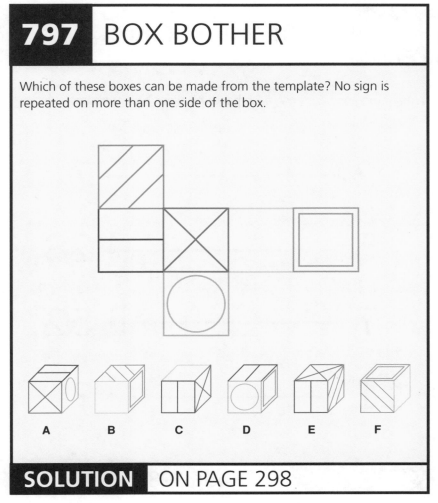

798 SHAPE SORTER

Can you determine which shape has not been used in this diagram?

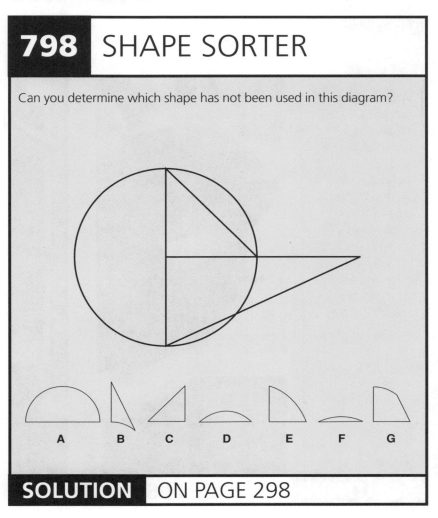

SOLUTION ON PAGE 298

SOLUTION ON PAGE 298

799 | TOUCHY TRAVELLER

Mandy went on vacation in the USA. She liked some places better than others. Can you see her logic?

She liked CHICAGO but not KANSAS CITY

She liked NEW YORK but not ATLANTA

She liked ORLANDO but not MEMPHIS

She liked NEW ORLEANS but not LAS VEGAS

Did she like RENO?

SOLUTION | ON PAGE 298

800 | STAR SOLUTION

In the puzzle below, which shape should replace the question mark?

A   B   C   D   E

SOLUTION | ON PAGE 298

801 | WINDOW

A policewoman stood and watched as a man tried to pick a lock to enter her house. He failed to do so, so he broke a window and gained access that way. The policewoman did not report the incident. Why?

SOLUTION | ON PAGE 298

802 | FORMULATION

The numbers on the right are formed from the numbers on the left using the same rules. Discover the rule used and replace the question marks.

2 $\longrightarrow$ 7

5 $\longrightarrow$ 28

7 $\longrightarrow$ 52

11 $\longrightarrow$?

SOLUTION | ON PAGE 298

803 MISSING NUMBER

What numbers should replace the question marks in these boxes?

	A	B	C	D	E
	1	5	6	2	7
	4	1	5	8	9
	7	3	2	6	9
	6	2	?	4	?

SOLUTION ON PAGE 298

804 WHICH NUMBER?

What number should replace the question mark in this grid?

6	4	6	5	8
2	9	8	2	1
5	0	3	4	7
3	2	1	3	1
4	7	?	4	3

SOLUTION ON PAGE 298

805 WILD GARDEN

SOLUTION ON PAGE 298

806 GRID GAME

Now try this more difficult grid. Can you calculate the values of the symbols?

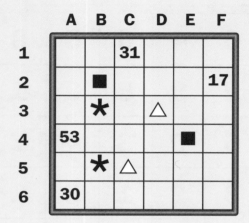

	A	B	C	D	E	F
1			31			
2		■				17
3		✳		△		
4	53			■		
5		✳	△			
6	30					

1. What is the value of square C2?
2. What is the value of square D4?
3. What is the value of square B6?
4. What is the value of the highest square?
5. What is the sum of the boxes in row 1 and column A combined? Count box A1 only once.

SOLUTION   ON PAGE 298

807 CIRCLE CONUNDRUM

Using all of the outer circled numbers once only, can you find the missing numbers in the following circle?

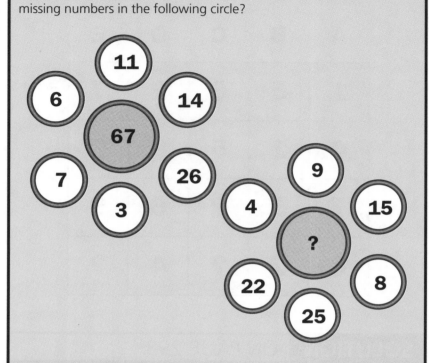

SOLUTION   ON PAGE 298

808 SECRET MESSAGES

A journalist had been recruited by a foreign power to find out the chemicals being used in a top secret project. He was not given any contact name to pass the information on to. He was told to disguise the chemicals within a note in the personal column in the newspaper on April 1st and they would crack his code and obtain the knowledge. Only the journalist knew how he would transmit the message and the code he would use, but the foreign power knew that the message contained the name of 1 gas and 6 other elements or chemicals. The message was contained in the following text:

> **Jacob – Alter Augusts trip to Germany to the unfair one on the Nile.**

Can you find the hidden information?

SOLUTION   ON PAGE 298

809 WORD MATCH

In each of the following groups of words there is a hidden common connection. Can you identify the connection?

1.	IMPORTED	COLANDER	FORSAKE	ANTEATER
2.	MINUTES	SELFISHNESS	TRIBUNAL	SHOWPIECE
3.	EXPANSE	RADISH	MUTINY	DEPOT
4.	ENTWINE	MASSAGE	CRUSTATION	KEROSENE
5.	ROMANTIC	GRUFFLY	MOTHER	BEEFBURGER
6.	TRACTOR	DOVETAIL	CRISPY	STATUTORY
7.	BRANCH	UNICORN	WAISTCOATS	AVARICE
8.	ACCENT	DIMENSION	BRANDISH	HYENA
9.	CLIMATE	BARITONE	NICEST	CORKAGE
10.	TUSSOCK	ADDRESS	SHATTERED	COATING

SOLUTION   ON PAGE 298

810 RIDDLE

What, or where am I?

My first is in FIRE but not in GRATE

My second is in EARLY but not in LATE

My third is in MUSIC and also in TUNE

My fourth is in DISTINCT but not in SOON

My last is in FROST and also in SLEET

When ripe, I am juicy and sweet.

What am I?

SOLUTION ON PAGE 298

811 PREFIX PROBLEM

When each of the following words is rearranged, one group of letters can be used as a prefix for the others to form longer words. Which is the prefix and what does it become?

	A	B	C	D	E
1.	LET	BUS	MILE	RUB	DENT
2.	CHAR	MATS	DIES	NIPS	OPT
3.	SHINES	HIRE	DIE	TIP	SON
4.	EAT	SET	LAP	TAPE	TAME
5.	NIP	LIES	ANT	NOD	NET
6.	TESS	SHIN	LAID	NOTE	ROC
7.	STEM	SINES	RAW	SEND	MITE
8.	BALE	DICE	NIGH	TON	RAY
9.	LEST	SUB	TIES	GINS	DIE
10.	HAS	NET	TOP	OAT	GATE

SOLUTION ON PAGE 298

812 WORD MATCH

In each of the questions below, 3 pairs of words are given. Match the pair to form three longer words.

1.	MAIDEN	VENDOR	HAND	MASTER	NEWS	SHIP
2.	MAN	PAWN	MASTER	LIVERY	PAY	BROKER
3.	SHOOTER	HOUSE	WRITER	SHARP	MASTER	SIGN
4.	PLAY	REEL	NEWS	SCREEN	LIGHT	FOOT
5.	EVER	DAY	DOMES	WHEN	TAIL	WHITE
6.	SPUR	DROP	LILY	LARK	WATER	SNOW
7.	LESS	EARTH	LIST	SACK	QUAKE	RAN
8.	RAM	PEACE	WORD	PART	PASS	ABLE
9.	CRACK	AGE	FOR	BLOCK	WISE	WARD
10.	NAP	HOOD	KID	SOME	FALSE	TROUBLE
11.	MAKER	BOY	LOCK	FRIEND	PEACE	DEAD
12.	TOP	SET	FREE	CARE	MOST	BACK
13.	WHOLE	WIRE	HAY	BAT	SALE	TEN
14.	NECK	ABLE	EYE	BOTTLE	BREAK	SORE
15.	LOVED	GOOD	WILD	BE	LIFE	WILL
16.	SOME	HARDY	FOOL	RAGE	HAND	BAR
17.	ION	AND	LEDGE	REFLECT	KNOW	BRIG
18.	CON	WORK	SIGN	GUESS	POST	TRIBUTE
19.	AGE	HOD	BOND	MAN	SHOW	SLIPS
20.	OUR	FALL	TEN	ROT	RUM	WIND

SOLUTION ON PAGE 298

813 | SHAPE SORTER

Which arrangement is missing from this sequence?

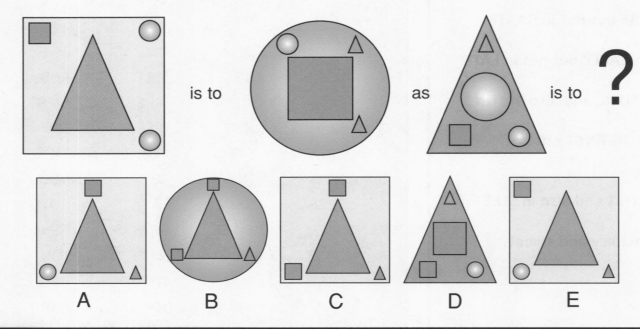

is to ... as ... is to **?**

A   B   C   D   E

SOLUTION | ON PAGE 299

814 | MULTIPLICITY

See if you can work out which letter should replace the question mark.

S	A	N	D
T	H	O	U
D	R	E	D
E	H	U	N
T	H	R	?

SOLUTION | ON PAGE 299

815 | DOT DILEMMA

Which of the shapes – A, B, C, D or E – cannot be made from the dots if a line is drawn through all of the dots at least once?

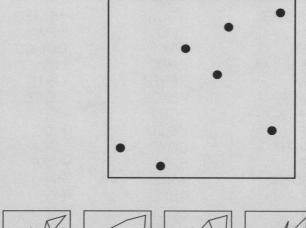

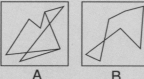

A   B   C   D   E

SOLUTION | ON PAGE 299

816 CIRCUIT CONUNDRUM

To complete your mission, you need to discover which one of these is not a mirror image of the circuit below?

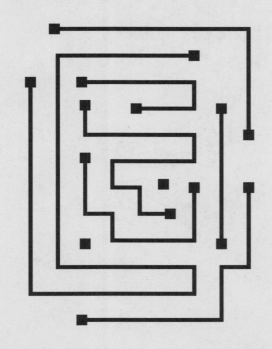

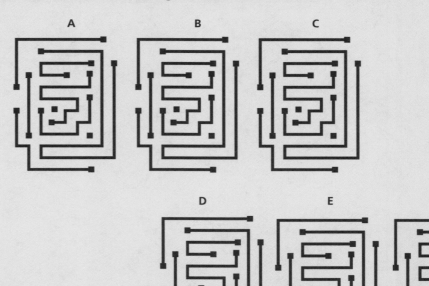

SOLUTION ON PAGE 299

817 SPY COSTS

The FBI is sending secret surveillance equipment to Moscow. In order to keep it secret and not draw any attention, they are sending the shipment as standard air freight. The airline company charges 17 cents per mile, with a surcharge of 5 cents per pound on the weight of the package. This surcharge is added to the final cost.

The package weighs 185 pounds and the distance to Moscow is 4646 miles.

What will be the total cost of sending this package?

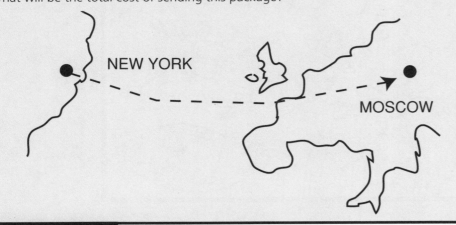

SOLUTION ON PAGE 299

818 THINK OF A NUMBER

Anastasia has thought of a number between 99 and 999. Belinda asks whether the number is below 500; Anastasia answers yes. Belinda asks whether the number is a square number; Anastasia answers yes. Belinda asks whether the number is a cube number; Anastasia answers yes.

However, Anastasia has told the truth to only two of the three questions. Anastasia then tells Belinda truthfully that both the first and the last digit are 5, 7 or 9.

What is the number?

SOLUTION ON PAGE 299

819 MAZE MUDDLE

START

FINISH

820 MISSING LETTER

What is the missing letter in this grid?

F	D	J
G	M	T
H	K	S
I	Q	?

SOLUTION ON PAGE 299

821 MURDER MYSTERY

If the knife has a value of 3 and the rope 12, what is the value of the candlestick?

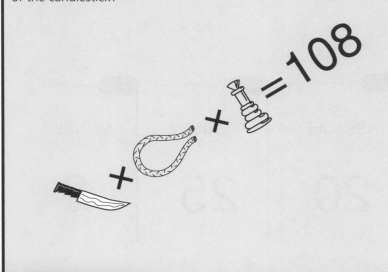

SOLUTION ON PAGE 299

822 NO PI?

Have you ever wondered if the advancement of knowledge would ever have been inhibited if Pi (3.142), the ratio of the circumference of a circle to its diameter, had never been discovered? Would we still be able to find the area of a circle without it? To this end, I offer you this challenge:

Imagine, if you will, that you are a native villager, living in the remotest region on earth. You have had no contact with civilization, but you have developed basic arithmetic skills. You also have a crude measuring stick, but the value of Pi or even its existence is unknown to you. You need, for whatever reason, to find the area of a wheel on the ground in front of you. You can measure quite accurately the diameter of the wheel. You can even find its circumference by rolling it one complete revolution and measuring the distance travelled, but can you calculate the area of the wheel?

SOLUTION ON PAGE 299

823 WORD MATCH

What are these five words associated with police investigations?

SINFORCE

HIMICODE

DEERRATS

DECEITVET

VISIONTARGET

SOLUTION ON PAGE 299

824   HOW MANY MURDERS?

In New York this month the following crimes have been committed. How many murders?

ASSAULT	ROBBERY	MURDER
20	**25**	**?**

SOLUTION   ON PAGE 299

825   MYSTERY MESSAGE

One of your field agents has sent you a message in code. If YKIXKZ GMKTZ is "SECRET AGENT" work out what the message says…

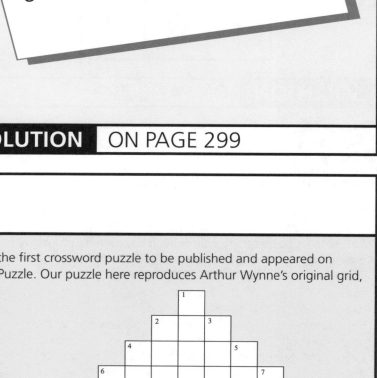

ORR HK GZ ZNK
URJ SORR GZ SOJTOMNZ.

SOLUTION   ON PAGE 299

826   WORD CROSS PUZZLE

In 1913 a new type of puzzle was devised by Liverpool-born Arthur Wynne. It was the first crossword puzzle to be published and appeared on Sunday December 21, 1913, in the New York World, and was called a Word Cross Puzzle. Our puzzle here reproduces Arthur Wynne's original grid, but has an entirely different set of clues and answers.

Across

2   Spasmodic twitch (3)
4   Cut grass (5)
6   Remainder (7)
8   Planet (4)
9   Jane Austen novel (4)
11 Enclosure with bars (4)
12 Flat-bottomed boat (4)
14 Delicate skill in dealing with people (4)
15 Machine for weaving (4)
16 Enticement to capture (4)
18 Grow dim (4)
19 Leave out (4)
21 Degree of speed (4)
22 Teach (7)
24 Rub out (5)
25 Pinch (3)

Down

1   New Zealander (4)
2   Hurl (4)
3   Yield (4)
4   Lake (4)
5   Rubbish heap (4)
6   Syncopated music (7)
7   Strive to equal (7)
8   Portuguese overseas territory (5)
10 Point of entry of current (5)
11 Taxi (3)
13 Part of foot (3)
17 Flow of current (3)
18 Destiny (4)
20 Change direction (4)
21 Harsh grating noise (4)
23 Brother of Abel (4)

SOLUTION   ON PAGE 299

827 ACTING STRANGE

Two famous actors who have played cops in hit films are merged together here. Who are they?

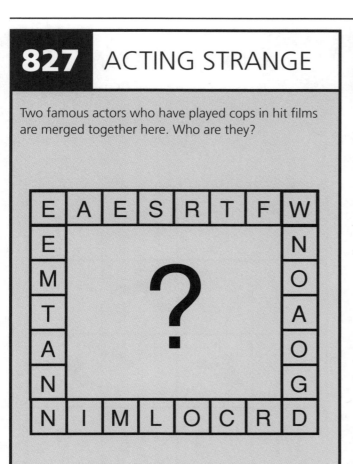

E	A	E	S	R	T	F	W
E							N
M							O
T		**?**					A
A							O
N							G
N	I	M	L	O	C	R	D

SOLUTION ON PAGE 299

828 MURDER MYSTERY

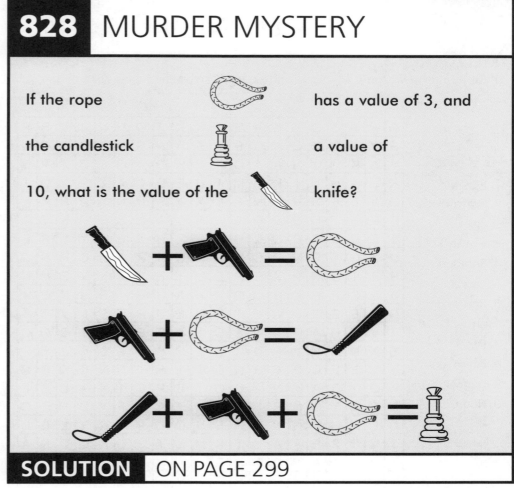

If the rope has a value of 3, and the candlestick a value of 10, what is the value of the knife?

SOLUTION ON PAGE 299

829 LA STORY

You are in Los Angeles to brief an agent. You have arranged to meet in the centre but where? Maybe this list of contact addresses can help you.

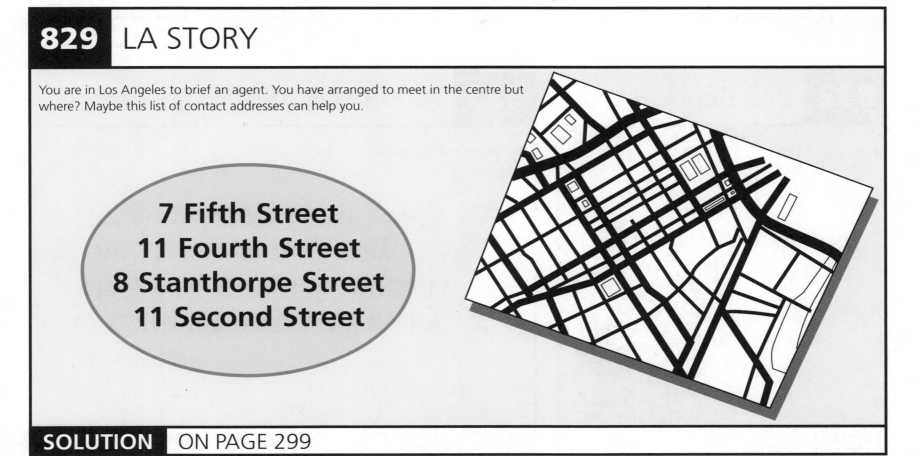

7 Fifth Street
11 Fourth Street
8 Stanthorpe Street
11 Second Street

SOLUTION ON PAGE 299

830 CONCEALED WEAPONS

These 10 murder weapons are hidden in this grid. Can you find them all?

1. Revolver
2. Switchblade knife
3. Gravity knife
4. Shotgun
5. Iron bar
6. Bow and arrow
7. Pistol
8. Poison dart
9. Dagger
10. Noose

Q	W	S	O	O	E	N	A	E	J	X	K	J	O	H	U	J	Z	R	S
E	Y	Y	S	K	O	H	C	E	J	S	R	A	B	N	O	R	I	G	N
V	W	K	M	W	N	A	A	C	B	F	H	O	P	G	F	R	Z	V	G
K	J	A	H	L	I	K	F	M	I	B	E	D	L	A	Z	D	L	D	I
O	J	E	E	U	H	T	N	F	I	X	A	S	P	N	Y	B	R	K	F
R	V	B	T	H	L	B	C	A	W	N	D	A	G	G	E	R	K	T	T
I	S	R	D	F	D	Q	N	H	J	F	Z	H	X	R	M	Y	L	S	E
O	J	G	T	P	M	D	C	N	B	N	U	P	P	A	B	C	R	N	O
R	Z	I	D	H	R	X	E	P	B	L	I	E	J	V	X	Y	Z	U	N
A	E	C	E	P	E	S	O	O	N	H	A	U	H	I	R	J	R	G	I
G	Z	E	B	Z	F	W	E	I	B	U	E	D	R	T	S	L	Y	T	I
I	V	E	H	A	O	A	N	S	O	T	A	P	E	Y	Z	I	D	O	O
S	X	N	N	M	V	R	D	O	Z	S	P	P	J	K	D	R	J	H	I
C	V	L	P	C	G	F	S	N	D	G	I	F	T	N	N	C	Q	S	M
K	O	Y	D	A	M	N	W	D	O	T	S	P	C	I	X	I	E	Z	L
T	S	A	Y	M	N	R	L	A	T	K	T	A	R	F	Y	D	F	Z	G
C	L	N	Q	D	C	N	P	R	E	V	O	L	V	E	R	Y	L	E	U
I	M	O	P	E	A	A	L	T	K	M	L	T	J	O	K	Q	C	N	A
T	B	O	W	A	N	D	A	R	R	O	W	S	I	N	R	J	Q	N	R
M	O	Q	J	X	E	C	I	V	O	L	V	J	D	B	I	A	T	K	K

SOLUTION ON PAGE 299

831 MISSING NUMBER

Fill in the missing number.

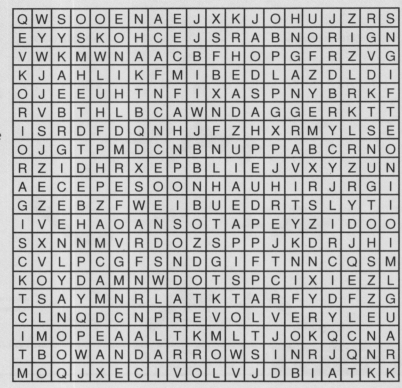

| 11 | 19 | 21 | ? |

SOLUTION ON PAGE 299

832 BIG BEN

How many hands does Big Ben – the famous one in London – have?

SOLUTION ON PAGE 299

833 MIXED MESSAGE

Can you read this message?

THE ENORMOUS SIGNIFICANCE OF FINGERPRINTS IN ESTABLISHING PERSONAL IDENTITY HAS BEEN RECOGNISED FOR MORE THAN A CENTURY.

SOLUTION ON PAGE 299

834 SPOT THE BLOTS

Can you find 10 differences?

SOLUTION   ON PAGE 299

835 BLOTTO

Which blot is different to the others?

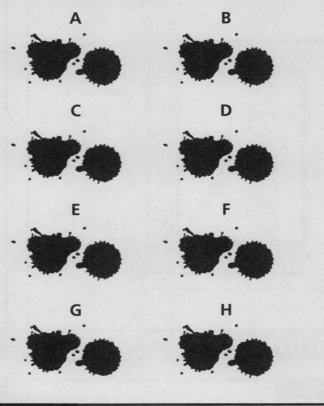

SOLUTION   ON PAGE 299

836 TAKE A SECOND LOOK

This is a series of letters in common use. Can you determine the next in the sequence?

N, W, H, O, I, I, ?

SOLUTION   ON PAGE 299

837 POLICE PROBLEM

At a scene of crime, these police officers were involved in these various activities:

Officer Graham – Photographs

Officer Vincent – Interviewing

Officer Harris – Searching

Which one of these officers took the fingerprints?

Richards, Singer, Thompson or Mitchell?

SOLUTION   ON PAGE 299

838 SAFE SITUATION

Find the two missing numbers to crack the safe.

 9
 4
 8
 ?
 ?

ROUBLE 11

DINAR 4

GUILDER 10

FRANC ?

POUND ?

SOLUTION ON PAGE 299

839 "E" FRAME

In this grid all the consonants are shown, in random order, but the vowels – all of them "E"s – are missing. The number of consonants and "E"s are given as a two-digit code either to the right of each column or at the bottom of each row, with the consonants first. Every consonant is used only once. What are the 16 words?

Across

1 In the middle
2 Peaceful
3 Insect
4 Plan
5 Stay in comfort
6 Stagger
7 Topic
8 Wasted

Down

1 Basic parts
2 Vegetable
3 Covered
4 Measurement of distance
5 Applause
6 Dispatchers
7 Accounts books
8 Milk products

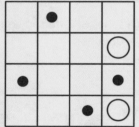

	1	2	3	4	5	6	7	8	
1	W	L	B	G	T	S	S	N	43
2	S	N	D	T	S	S	R	S	33
3	N	R	T	B	R	R	R	L	33
4	S	M	H	H	H	H	C	S	42
5	T	T	T	S	C	S	D	L	42
6	T	Y	S	N	T	N	R	H	33
7	L	C	T	T	M	H	G	C	32
8	M	S	N	L	P	D	L	T	41
	53	42	43	51	42	52	52	43	

SOLUTION ON PAGE 299

840 SPY SOLVER

Join the letters together using straight lines, and without crossing over a line, to find the name of a famous spy.

G M T U

A F E F

J K T I

A E K R

J H A B

SOLUTION ON PAGE 299

841 SHAPE SHIFTER

Which one comes next in this sequence?

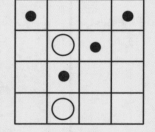 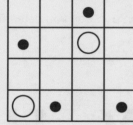 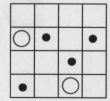

A   **B**   **C**   **D**

SOLUTION ON PAGE 299

842 CODE BREAKER

Can you crack this code?

w-h.y-d.z-f.y-f.t-k.s-o.r-m.v-d.

SOLUTION ON PAGE 299

843 CELTIC CONUNDRUM

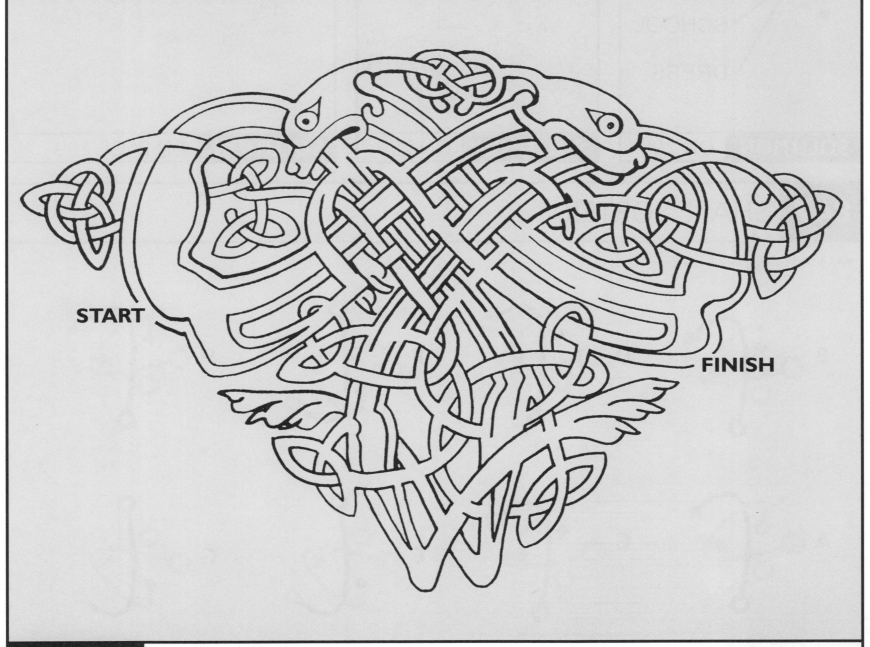

START

FINISH

SOLUTION ON PAGE 299

844 PREFIX PROBLEM

What word can you put in front of these to make five longer words?

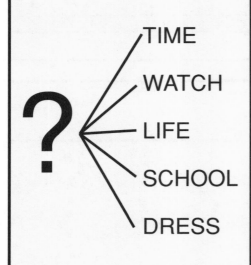

? TIME

WATCH

LIFE

SCHOOL

DRESS

SOLUTION ON 299

845 AGENT PUZZLE

You are agent 17, on a mission. You need to send a message to base 89 via your laptop computer and a satellite link. However, you need to choose the correct satellite.

Which one do you choose?

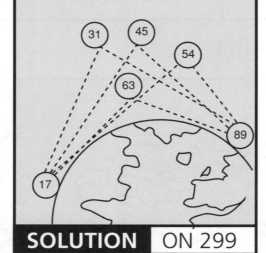

SOLUTION ON 299

846 JOB JUMBLE

Can you find out Joe Smith's profession from this code?

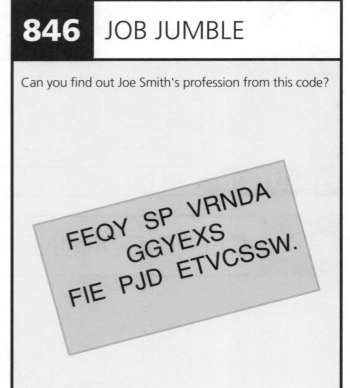

FEQY SP VRNDA GGYEXS FIE PJD ETVCSSW.

SOLUTION ON PAGE 299

847 SHAPE SORTER

Which 2 DNA samples are exact mirror images?

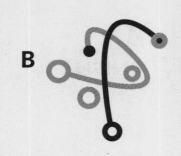
B

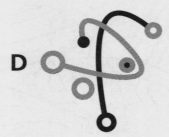
D

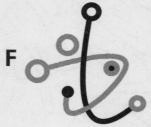
F

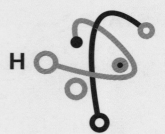
H

A

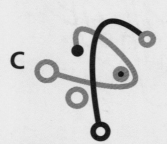
C

E

G

SOLUTION ON PAGE 299

848 CONSEQUENCES

Which of the letters below should be next in this sequence?

L X V ?

P T A G

SOLUTION ON PAGE 299

849 CODE CONUNDRUM

Each field agent needs two code numbers to contact the command centre.

What is the number of the command centre?

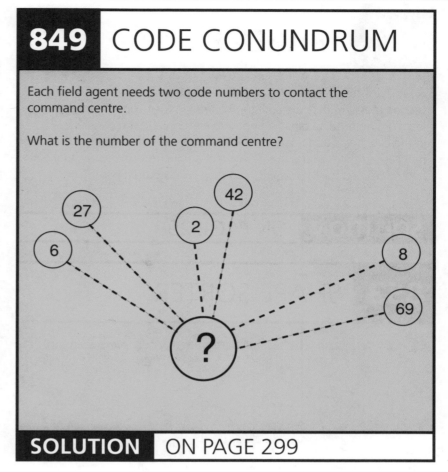

SOLUTION ON PAGE 299

850 JUNGLE JAPE

You are on a jungle mission when you reach a river. The only way to cross it is by carefully stepping from stone to stone, from one side to the other. Pick the wrong stones and you'll fall in. The river is full of crocodiles.

Starting at A, and stepping on only one stone from each row, which sequence of stones should you choose?

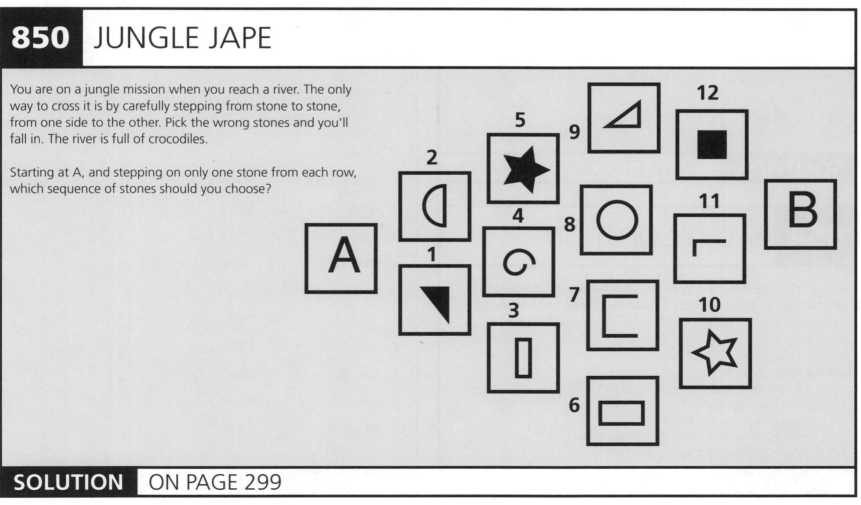

SOLUTION ON PAGE 299

851 TRAGEDY

A family of four were going on a mountaineering trip. Sadly, on the second morning they were all found dead in their cabin, having died from drowning. The taps had not been left on and the water system in the cabin was undamaged. There was no sign of foul play. What had caused them to drown? They were a mile from the nearest lake, it had not rained for two weeks, and there was no dam nearby.

SOLUTION ON PAGE 299

853 SHAPE SORTER

Can you determine which shape has not been used in this diagram?

A   B   C   D   E   F

SOLUTION ON PAGE 300

854 SPORT SOLUTION

A, B, C, D, and E take part in soccer, baseball, tennis, and swimming, of which soccer is the most popular. More choose tennis than baseball. E only plays one sport. B is the only one to take part in swimming. A and one other of the five play baseball. C does not play soccer. D plays two sports but baseball is not one of them. C plays baseball and tennis.

1.   Which sport does A not take part in?
2.   Who plays baseball?
3.   How many play soccer?
4.   Which sport do three of the five take part in?
5.   How many play two of the sports only?

SOLUTION ON PAGE 300

852 SHAPE SHIFTER

Can you determine which shape has not been used in this diagram?

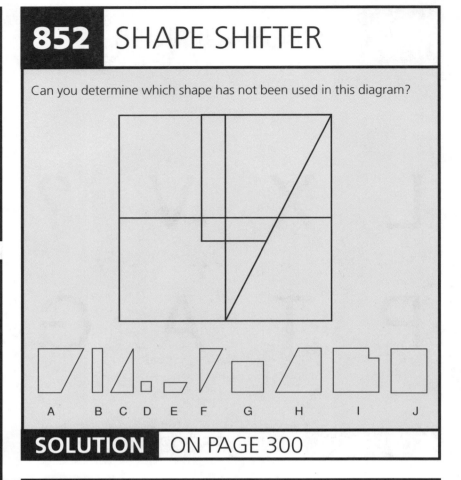

A   B C D E F   G   H   I   J

SOLUTION ON PAGE 300

855 WORD MATCH

What word has a similar meaning to the first word and rhymes with the second one?

eg.	AEROPLANE	—	MET	= JET
1.	COIN FACTORY	—	HINT	=
2.	HOME	—	BEST	=
3.	FOG	—	LIST	=
4.	BARGAIN	—	MEAL	=
5.	GRAIN	—	HORN	=
6.	PARTY	—	TALL	=
7.	BRAWL	—	HEIGHT	=
8.	RULER	—	SING	=
9.	LANTERN	—	RAMP	=
10.	BROAD	—	HIDE	=

SOLUTION ON PAGE 300

856 WORD MATCH

Match the word groups below with the given word. Which group completes each line? Answer A, B, C, D or E.

1. TEAM
2. OREGANO
3. BUTTERFLY
4. MUSSEL
5. DALMATIAN

A	**B**	**C**	**D**	**E**
Lobster	Poodle	Cayenne	Earwig	Pack
Prawn	Whippet	Caraway	Ant	Crew
Crab	Doberman	Garlic	Wasp	Herd

SOLUTION ON PAGE 300

857 FORMULATION

The numbers on the right are formed from the numbers on the left using the same rules. Discover the rule used and replace the question mark.

2 ⟶ 4

4 ⟶ 32

5 ⟶ 62½

7 ⟶ ?

SOLUTION ON PAGE 300

858 MISSING NUMBER

What number should replace the question mark?

SOLUTION ON PAGE 300

859 FIND THE NUMBER

Using all of the outer circled numbers once only, can you find the missing number in the following circle?

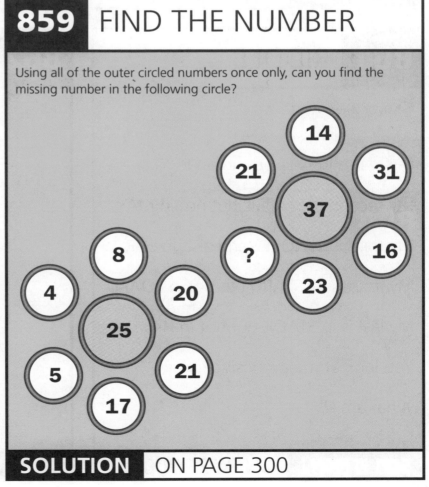

SOLUTION ON PAGE 300

860 TRAIN THE TRAIN DRIVER

A rail depot had an oval track with two branch lines. This was used to train drivers in unusual conditions. The teacher gave them the following problem on the blackboard:

"Move load A to position B and load B to position A without the load going through the tunnel, and return the engine to its starting position."

How did the trainee drivers do this?

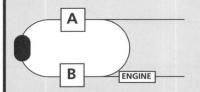

SOLUTION ON PAGE 300

861 RIDDLE

What, or where am I?

My first is in ACT but not in PLAY

My second is in APRIL but not in MAY

My third is in NOBLE and also in LORD

My fourth is in CARD but not in BOARD

My last is in STACK but not in HAY

You look at me every single day.

What am I?

SOLUTION ON PAGE 300

862 WORD MATCH

The words below are all connected, but how?

FRAMER

TERRACE

CREDITOR

HECTARE

RESIGNED

FERRARI

SOLUTION ON PAGE 300

863 STAR SEARCH

There are a number of film stars hidden in this grid. Can you find them all? The names can change direction at any point.

A	Z	T	T	I	P	D	A	R	B
I	O	S	J	B	D	F	R	A	S
D	L	N	O	G	O	F	E	E	T
N	S	I	D	H	I	A	H	C	B
O	O	W	I	N	U	S	C	D	V
R	N	T	E	F	O	S	T	E	R
E	C	H	L	K	M	V	A	W	B
M	A	S	B	E	C	R	E	I	P
A	P	A	R	O	S	N	A	N	N
C	R	B	A	L	Y	S	V	R	O

SOLUTION ON PAGE 300

864 DESCRIPTIONS

What do the following represent?

1. E   art   H

2. _____
   FEET FEET FEET FEET FEET FEET

3. **B   E   D**

4. **O   E   R   T   O**

5. **BUSINES**

6. **PRO – MI – SES**

SOLUTION ON PAGE 300

865 WORD CROSS PUZZLE

In 1913 a new type of puzzle was devised by Liverpool-born Arthur Wynne. It was the first crossword puzzle to be published and appeared on Sunday December 21, 1913, in the New York World, and was called a Word Cross Puzzle. Our puzzle here reproduces Arthur Wynne's original grid, but has an entirely different set of clues and answers. And, for added variety, all the clues – with one exception – are anagrams of the answers.

Across

2	EST	15	AGNT
4	AILNS	16	ACKP
6	EILMMRS	18	BNOS
8	EPST	19	DINR
9	EESW	20	EERS
11	DEPS	22	ADEHLOT
12	DDEI	24	DEIRT
14	EIMN	25	DET

Down

1	AEMS	10	ENORS
2	INPS	11	IPS
3	EIMT	13	ABD
4	DELS	17	KNOT
5	DELW	18	DEES
6	CEILNST	20	ADRT
7	DEEGINR	21	DEHS
8	AEPRS	23	EIRT

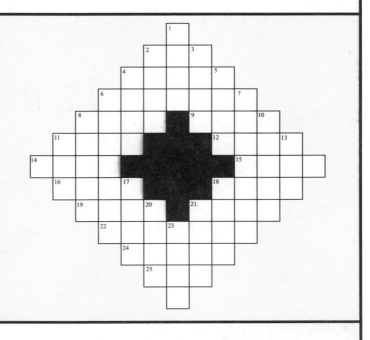

SOLUTION ON PAGE 300

866 ODD ONE OUT

Which of the following is the odd one out?

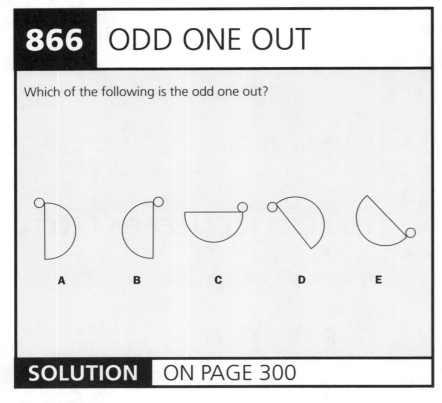

867 SHAPE SORTER

Which of the following is the odd one out?

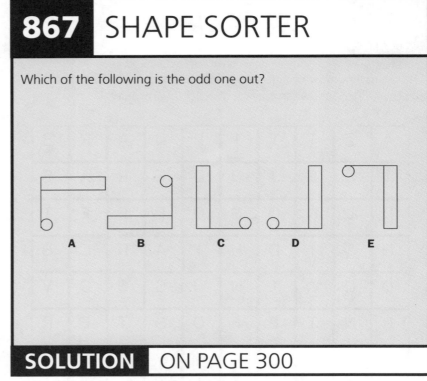

SOLUTION ON PAGE 300

SOLUTION ON PAGE 300

868 FIND THE SHAPE

Should A, B, C, or D fill the empty circle?

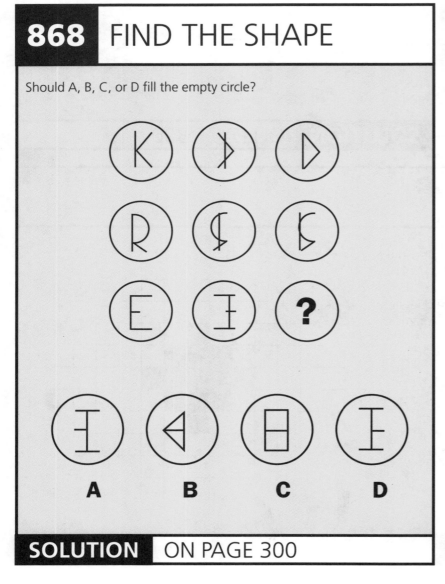

869 LOST LETTER

Should A, B, C, or D fill the empty circle?

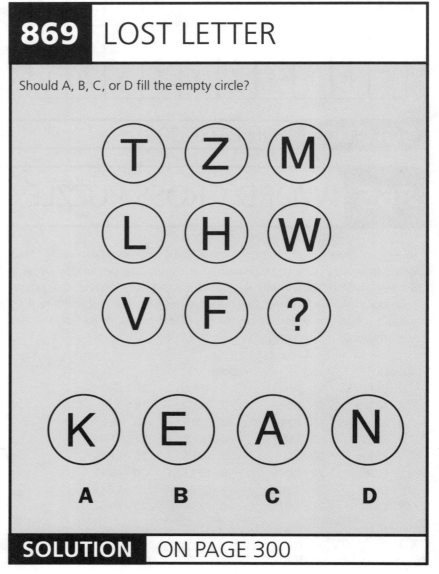

SOLUTION ON PAGE 300

SOLUTION ON PAGE 300

870 GONE FISHING

START

FINISH

SOLUTION ON PAGE 300

871 SHAPE SORTER

Should A, B, C, or D come next in this series?

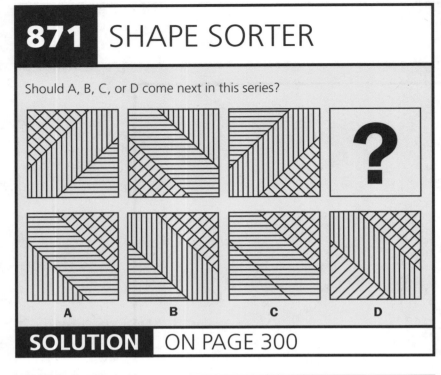

A   **B**   **C**   **D**

SOLUTION ON PAGE 300

873 ANTONYMS

Which word means the opposite of those in the boxes?

CENSURABLE   **CULPABLE**

REPREHENSIBLE   **B** _ _ _ _ _ _ _ _

SOLUTION ON PAGE 300

875 GUN GAME

British MI5 agents prefer to use different makes of handguns. Below are some makes, and the number of agents who use them.

How many prefer a Browning?

WALTHER 1   **SMITH & WESSON 9**

COLT 15   **BROWNING ?**

SOLUTION ON PAGE 300

872 PEN PROBLEM

Three children, Joanna, Richard and Thomas, have a pen, a crayon and a pencil-case on their desks. Each has one cat, one elephant and one rabbit design on their item but none has the same item in the same design as the others. Joanna's pencil-case is the same design as Thomas's pen and Richard's pen is the same design as Joanna's crayon. Richard has a cat on his pencil-case and Thomas has an elephant on his pen.

1. Who has a cat on their pen?
2. What design is Richard's crayon?
3. Who has a rabbit on their pencil-case?
4. What design is Thomas's pencil-case?
5. Who has a rabbit on their crayon?

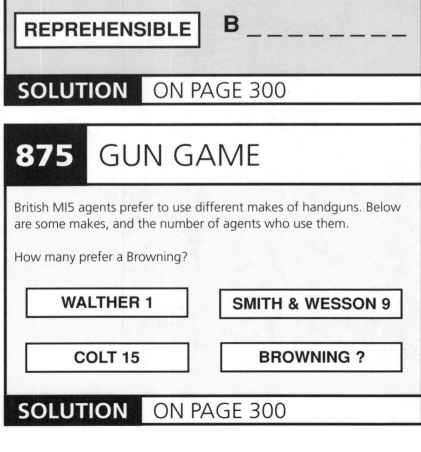

SOLUTION ON PAGE 300

874 SCENE OF CRIME

The length of crime scene tape needed to go all the way round this area is 30 yards. How many square yards is the area?

SOLUTION ON PAGE 300

876 MAP READING & TRACKING

Detective X has been in charge of an operation to track the movements of enemy agents. He has filed his report on their various movements, but has made an error. Unfortunately, all the map co-ordinates are back to front, so where he says, for instance, square X1 it should really read C28. it is your task to sort this out:

1. Enemy agents Z and Q started at square O10, went west for 9, and then split up. Z went north 2, east 5 and then south 4. Q went south 6, west 3 and then north 4. What square was left between them at the end?

2. Enemy agent Y left square G11, went east 6, but doubled back 2, south 4 and then west 2. What square did he end on?

3. Enemy agent H left square I21, went north 1, west 1, south 7 and east 1. What square did he end on?

4. Enemy agent Q started on square R7 and went south 10 then west 5. Enemy agent Z started at F23 and went north 6 and east 5.

What square was between them at the end?

5. Enemy agent Z started at J26. Q started at I 26 and H started at P4. H went south 11, east 3 and south 4. Z went north 9, east 5 and south 2 and Q went east 8 and north 5.

What was the square in the middle, between them?

6. Enemy agents Z and H met up with Y on square G24. They all went north 4 and then split up. Z went north 6 more squares, then 4 more, east 2 and south 7. H and Y went together east 8 where H went 2 north. Y went back 5 and north 2, and then H went 2 east, 2 north and 7 west.

What square was between the three of them at the end?

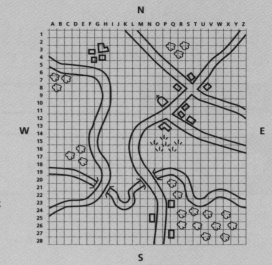

SOLUTION ON PAGE 300

877 WRAPAROUND CROSSWORD

Answers are entered starting at the same number as the clue, and go in a spiral toward the middle. Each answer begins with one or more letters from the end of the previous word.

1 Independent federation of states in SE Asia (8)
2 Former name of an inhabitant of Thailand (7)
3 Music to be played or sung in the evening (8)
4 Port capital of South Australia (8)
5 The study of writing systems that use symbols (10)
6 The study of matter and forces (7)
7 Fish whose eggs are sold as caviare (8)
8 The second largest lake in Europe, close to the Finnish border with Russia (5)
9 The first man in space (7)
10 U.S. state whose chief towns include Fort Wayne and South Bend (7)
11 The world's largest snake (8)
12 The capital of Syria (8)
13 Ill-fated leader of the U.S. 7th cavalry (6)
14 The breastbone (7)
15 The fourth book of the Pentateuch (7)
16 Irish (4)
17 African country, capital Dakar (7)
18 The son of Lancelot in Arthurian legend (7)
19 The king of the underworld in Greek mythology (5)
20 A melody played above another well-known one (7)
21 A beam or girder fixed at one end only (10)
22 Composer of *La Traviata* (5)
23 Style of jazz (9)
24 South American mountain range (5)
25 Biblical elder son of Isaac (4)
26 German cabbage dish (10)
27 Type of non-fixed-wing aircraft (8)
28 Chief port of the Netherlands (9)
29 Type of plum (6)
30 A poem of 14 lines (6)
31 Kingdom of N.W. Europe (11)
32 Art movement that flourished mainly in France between the World Wars (10)
33 Composer of *The Bartered Bride* (7)
34 The youth who, in Greek mythology, fell in love with his own reflection in a pool (9)
35 The male part of a flower (6)

SOLUTION ON PAGE 300

878 CODE BREAKER

Crack the code to find the word:

④ 7 10 ③ ② 11 ⑤ 17 ④

SOLUTION ON PAGE 300

880 COMPLETION

Which piece will connect up this circuit?

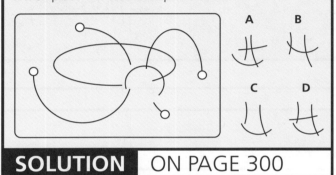

A   B

C   D

SOLUTION ON PAGE 300

879 PATH FINDER

You have apprehended a homicide suspect at the grid reference marked with the "X". Unfortunately, he appears to have thrown away the murder weapon before you caught him. To find it you must discover the square where he started his journey.

Each square is marked with a number of moves, and the direction: ie: N2- north 2 moves.

N

W

E

S

7E	4S	4E	3S	3N	3N	4S	7S	3W	5W
1S	4E	2W	6S	7S	3S	2W	3S	1N	1W
8E	1E	1E	1N	5E	5W	1S	1S	4S	6S
5E	1W	6S	3S	3S	3W	5W	3S	1E	1W
3E	2N	3N	X	4E	5S	2N	2E	4S	3N
1S	6E	3E	5N	4W	2W	4N	4N	4W	1W
5E	1E	1W	3S	2N	2S	3E	2S	3S	6N
2E	2N	1N	2W	5N	1S	3E	3W	1E	1W
4N	1S	4N	1N	4W	3W	2N	6W	5N	3W
7E	8N	4N	3W	6N	7N	2N	7N	4N	2N

SOLUTION ON PAGE 300

881 THEME CROSSWORD

All across answers are the names of musical terms.

Across

1   Quality of a sound (6)
4   Theatrical dancing (6)
9   Music arrangement (13)
12   Percussion instrument (4)
14   Musical composition (4)
16   Harp-like instrument (4)
17   Group of musicians (4)
24   School of music (13)
25   Composition for two performers (6)
26   High-pitched (6)

Down

1   Of designs imprinted on leather (6)
2   Spice (4)
3   Scottish dance (4)
5   Expression of grief (4)
6   Placed down (4)
7   Tints (6)
8   Pig's home (3)
10   The ant (5)
11   Weapons (5)
13   Beam (3)
15   Vase (3)
16   Burst medically (6)
18   Cross out (6)
19   Single time (4)
20   Compass direction (4)
20   Hail (3)
22   Heavenly body (4)
23   Leg (4)

SOLUTION ON PAGE 300

882 PERCENTAGES

If 70% have lost an eye, 75% an ear, 80% an arm, 85% a leg, what percentage, at least, must have lost all four?

SOLUTION ON PAGE 300

883 CITY KILLERS

The map shows the number of homicides in certain American Cities. How many were there in St Louis?.

Seattle 19

Washington DC 235

San Francisco 55

St Louis ?

SOLUTION ON PAGE 300

884 WEDDING

A man married each of his three sisters. However he did nothing to offend against the laws of God or man. How could this be? He did not belong to a religious order which permitted multiple marriages.

SOLUTION ON PAGE 300

885 PREFIX PROBLEM

What word can you put in front of these to make five longer words?

**BIRTH
THOUGHT
EFFECT
CARE
HOURS**

SOLUTION ON PAGE 300

886 SOLE SOLUTION

These eight prints were found at a crime scene. Can you spot the two that are identical and different from the others?

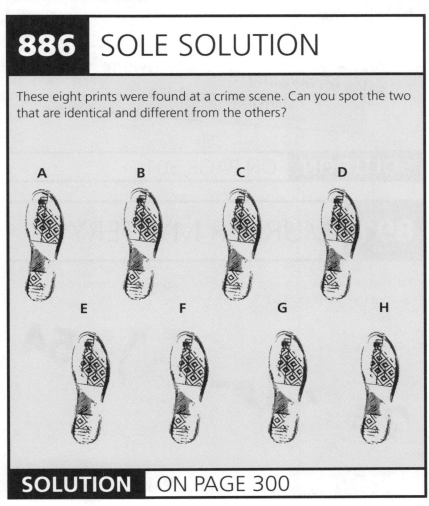

A   B   C   D

E   F   G   H

SOLUTION ON PAGE 300

887 DIAMOND CROSSWORD

Here is a diamond crossword. The aim is to find at least 36 English words (no proper nouns), all of which will start on a number and will go in a straight line without any gaps. Words must have at least three letters.

For example, 1 SE is DEN

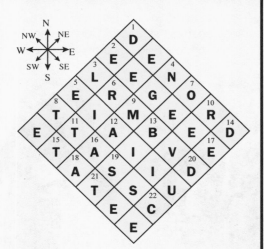

SOLUTION ON PAGE 300

888 PLATE PROBLEM

Which of these car number plates is the odd one out?

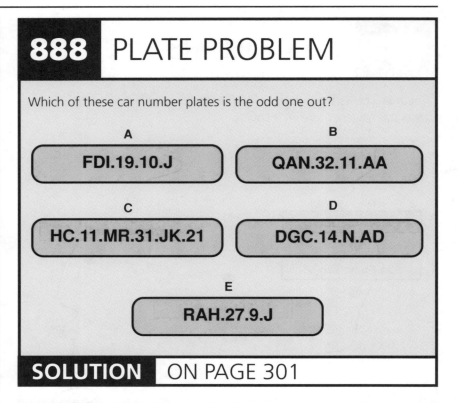

A
FDI.19.10.J

B
QAN.32.11.AA

C
HC.11.MR.31.JK.21

D
DGC.14.N.AD

E
RAH.27.9.J

SOLUTION ON PAGE 301

889 CODE CRACKER

You have been sent this code e-mail, but there is a problem with your encryption software. What does the message say?

eirswaaeyntaoecbotmsm
uumneirceahtte

SOLUTION ON PAGE 301

891 MURDER MYSTERY

If the knife =4, the gun =14 and the rope =9 what is the numerical value of the question mark?

$$? \div \text{🔪} - (\text{🔫} \times \text{🪢}) = 54$$

SOLUTION ON PAGE 301

890 SPY SHEET

One of these agents is a spy. To find out which, unravel the words to discover the one that does not belong with the others.

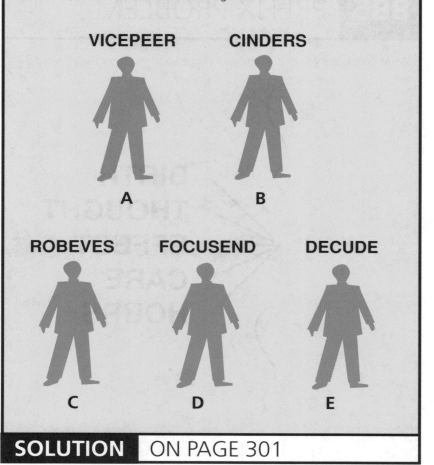

VICEPEER **CINDERS**

A B

ROBEVES **FOCUSEND** **DECUDE**

C D E

SOLUTION ON PAGE 301

892 MAZE MARATHON

FINISH

START

893 TEC PROBLEM

Last night, an FBI agent arrived at his downtown apartment to discover a murder had been committed, and a body was lying by the kitchen door. What was the name of the murder victim.

SOLUTION ON PAGE 301

894 SIMPLEX

A straightforward crossword.

Across

1 Strike a balance (10)
8 Expected (3)
9 Out of date (8)
10 Cloister (5)
11 Obliterate (7)
12 Utter (5)
15 Drying cloth (5)
18 Organize (7)
19 Type of leather (5)
21 Portion (8)
23 Moroccan cap (3)
24 Parentage (10)

Down

2 Globe (3)
3 Plentiful (7)
4 Nervously anxious (2,4)
5 Concept (4)
6 Fit to eat (6)
7 Rebuff (4)
9 Open (5)
13 Acclamation (7)
14 Massage (5)
16 Chesty breath (6)
17 Petty details (6)
19 Cushioned (4)
20 Annotate (4)
22 New and different (3)

SOLUTION ON PAGE 301

895 COUSIN CONUNDRUM

Three cousins have washing pegged out on the line. On each line there is a shirt, a jumper and a towel. Each has one spotted, one plain and one striped item but none of them has the same item in the same design as their cousins. Sandra's jumper is the same design as Paul's towel and Paul's jumper is the same design as Kerry's towel. Kerry's jumper is striped and Sandra's shirt is spotted.

1. Who has a spotted jumper?

2. What design is Sandra's towel?

3. Who has a striped shirt?

4. What design is Kerry's jumper?

5. What design is Paul's towel?

SOLUTION ON PAGE 301

896 TRAFFIC TROUBLE

Here are the number of detectives from different squads, currently being considered for promotion. How many are there in Traffic?

TRAFFIC ?

HOMICIDE SQUAD 17

VICE SQUAD 28

NARCOTICS 24

SOLUTION ON PAGE 301

897 LOST LETTER

What letter should you add to the bottom of the final column to complete the sequence?

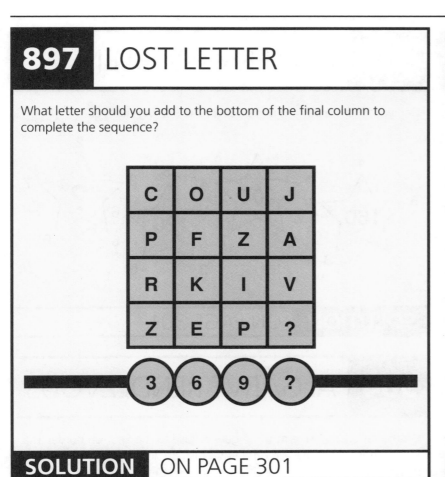

C	O	U	J
P	F	Z	A
R	K	I	V
Z	E	P	?

(3) (6) (9) (?)

SOLUTION ON PAGE 301

898 MISSING NUMBER

Fill in the missing number.

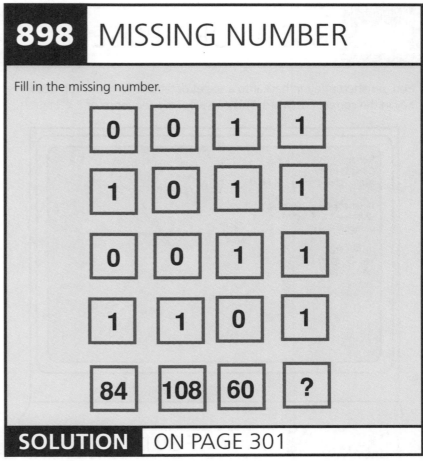

0	0	1	1
1	0	1	1
0	0	1	1
1	1	0	1
84	108	60	?

SOLUTION ON PAGE 301

899 QUICK TEASER

Here is a straightforward crossword for some light relief.

Across

2 Fascinate (9)
7 The fifth brightest star (4)
8 Synthetic material (5)
9 Fragment of cloth (3)
10 Melanesian island group (4)
11 Put in order
14 Newspaper boss (6)
15 Loosen up (6)
16 In proportion (3,4)
19 Smile (4)
20 Obtain (3)
21 Young person (5)
22 Levy (4)
23 Requisite (9)

Down

1 Confuse (8)
2 Container (8)
3 Column (6)
4 Internal (5)
5 Protective clothing (5)
6 Bird of prey (5)
12 Omnipotent (8)
13 Member of irregular armed force (8)
15 Gap (6)
16 Heathen (5)
17 Of the eye (5)
18 Deep gulf (5)

SOLUTION ON PAGE 301

900 LOST NUMBER

Here are the names and telephone numbers of 3 FBI contacts. What is Winston Desmoines' number?

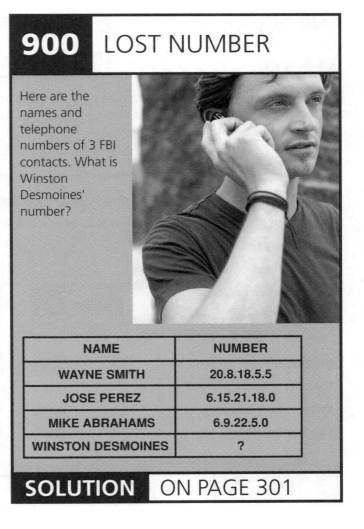

NAME	NUMBER
WAYNE SMITH	20.8.18.5.5
JOSE PEREZ	6.15.21.18.0
MIKE ABRAHAMS	6.9.22.5.0
WINSTON DESMOINES	?

SOLUTION ON PAGE 301

901 PASSWORD POSER

You are attempting to hack into a secret database. To get in you need to key in the correct password. This password is a sequence of 3 x 3 letters.

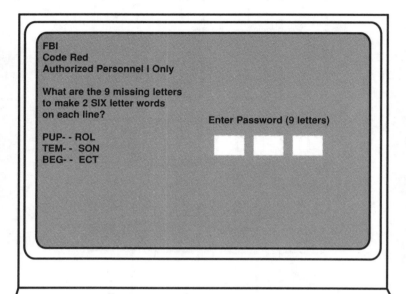

FBI
Code Red
Authorized Personnel I Only

What are the 9 missing letters
to make 2 SIX letter words
on each line?

Enter Password (9 letters)

PUP- - ROL
TEM- - SON
BEG- - ECT

SOLUTION ON PAGE 301

903 NURSERY RHYME CROSSWORD

The narrative below is the story of a nursery rhyme. Solve the eight clues that are highlighted in the narrative, and place the answers in the correct positions in the grid to complete the crossword.

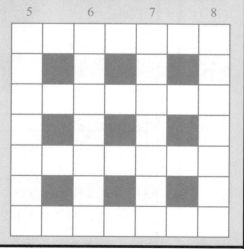

There was an old lady who <u>lived</u>¹ with an <u>American legislator</u>⁶ in a shoe. She was one of the <u>lessees</u>² and <u>no longer worked</u>⁵ for a living. She had so many children that she did not know what to do. She <u>wished for</u>⁸ some peace and quiet, so she <u>gave</u>⁷ them some porridge without any bread, and gave them a ride on a <u>merry-go-round</u>³, whipped them all soundly and put them to bed, because she <u>mocked</u>⁴ them.

SOLUTION ON PAGE 301

902 PATTERN PROBLEM

Can you find the pattern and discover the missing number?

160 · 4 6 6 9 3 8

204 · 6 9 4 1 7

128 · 8 3 6 3 5

? · 2 3 7 6 9

SOLUTION ON PAGE 301

904 ALGARVE RENDEZVOUS

On the far eastern side of the Algarve, close to the Spanish border, is a town whose roads are laid out in grid fashion, like Manhattan. This system was first used in the cities of Ancient Greece. Seven friends live at different corners, marked. ◯

They wish to meet for coffee.

On which corner should they meet in order to minimize the walking distance for all seven?

ROADS

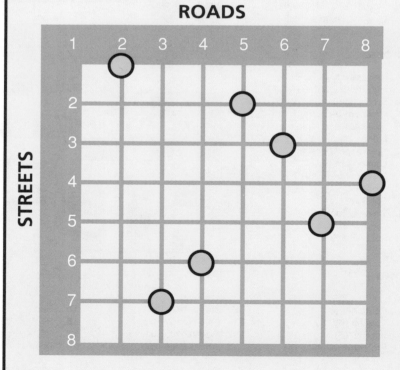

SOLUTION ON PAGE 301

905 SWITCH SOLUTION

Which piece will connect up this circuit?

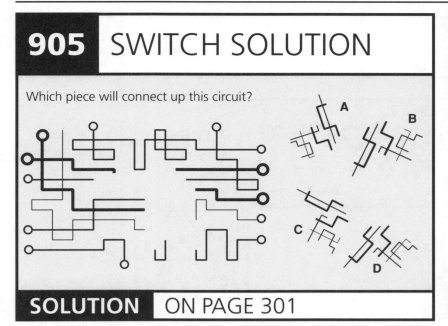

SOLUTION ON PAGE 301

906 CITY CLUES

The following CIA agents were sent to the following cities:

Agent Daniel – Moscow

Agent Newton – Osaka

Agent Macintosh – Istanbul

To which city was Agent Glaister sent?

Washington, Brussels, Seattle, London or Paris?

SOLUTION ON PAGE 301

907 AGENT ANSWER?

Below are the numbers of agents currently undercover in each of these cities. How many are there in Berlin?

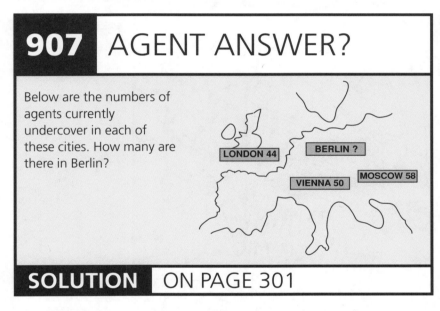

LONDON 44

BERLIN ?

VIENNA 50

MOSCOW 58

SOLUTION ON PAGE 301

908 WORDSEARCH

Find at least 13 types of marine growth in the grid. Words must be in a straight line vertically, horizontally, diagonally, up, down, forward, or back.

V	A	R	E	C	P	R	S	S
E	T	E	P	M	I	L	E	E
G	L	A	R	O	C	A	A	T
N	K	C	A	R	W	S	W	Y
O	E	L	A	E	O	D	R	H
P	L	E	E	N	X	A	A	P
S	P	D	K	J	R	I	C	O
S	W	E	A	G	L	A	K	O
M	U	S	S	E	L	N	B	Z

SOLUTION ON PAGE 301

909 SHAPE SORTER

Which of the following is the odd one out?

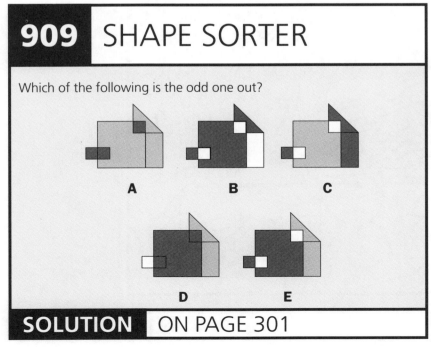

A   B   C

D   E

SOLUTION ON PAGE 301

910 BOX BOTHER

Which of the following is the odd one out?

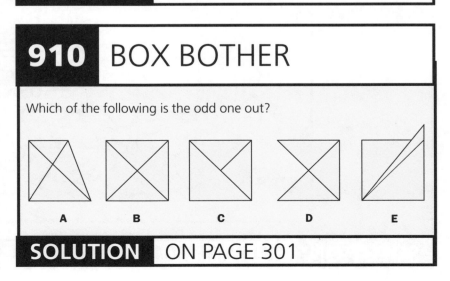

A   B   C   D   E

SOLUTION ON PAGE 301

911 MAZE MARATHON

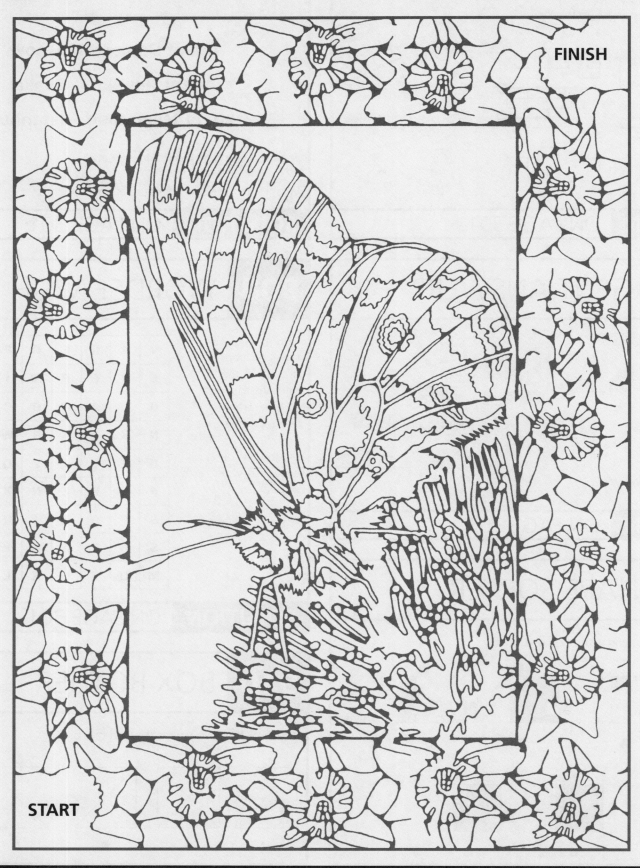

FINISH

START

912 WORD MATCH

Match the word groups below with the given word. Which group completes each line? Answer A, B, C, D or E.

1. TRIANGLE
2. PHYSICS
3. FILE
4. AEROPLANE
5. COPPER

A	B	C	D	E
History	Saw	Train	Beige	Tripod
Biology	Hammer	Bus	Maroon	Trio
Geometry	Chisel	Car	Violet	Triplet

SOLUTION ON 301

913 BABIES

Arthur and Barry were born on the same day and month of the same year in the same room. They have the same mother and the same father. Their appearance is identical. However they are not twins. What is the simplest explanation for this?

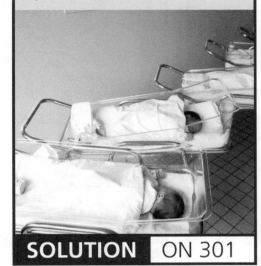

SOLUTION ON 301

914 PET PROBLEM

Maria, Peter and Sarah each have a dog, a cat, and a rabbit, one fluffy-tailed, one short-tailed and one long-tailed. None of the same type of animal has a tail the same as another animal, Sarah's cat has the same type of tail as Peter's rabbit. Maria's rabbit has the same tail type as Peter's cat. Sarah's dog has a long tail, and Maria's cat is fluffy-tailed.

1. Who has a dog with a short tail?
2. Who has a rabbit with a long tail?
3. Who has a dog with a fluffy tail?
4. Who has a cat with a short tail?
5. Who has a cat with a long tail?
6. Who has a rabbit with a short tail?

SOLUTION ON PAGE 301

915 FORMULAS

The numbers on the right are formed from the numbers on the left using the same rules. Discover the rule used and replace the question mark.

$$2 \longrightarrow 10$$
$$3 \longrightarrow 13$$
$$7 \longrightarrow 25$$
$$11 \longrightarrow ?$$

SOLUTION ON 301

916 DISK DILEMMA

Calculate the values of the black, white, and shaded circles and the sum of the final set in each question.

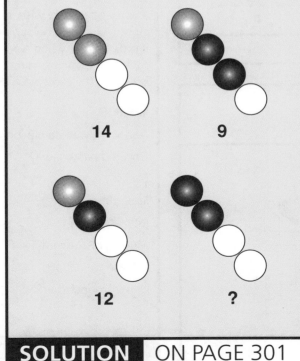

14   9

12   ?

SOLUTION ON PAGE 301

917 RIDDLE

What, or where am I?

My first is in **CASH** and also in **CHEQUE**

My second is in **COLLAR** but not in **NECK**

My third is in **FINGER** and also in **RING**

My fourth is in **SONG** but not in **SING**

My last is in **WATER** but not in **MOAT**

I am a narrow paddle boat.

What am I?

SOLUTION ON 301

918 WORD MATCH

Add the vowels in the following groups of letters to form five words, one of which does not belong with the others. Which word is the odd one out?

	A	B	C	D	E
1.	WLKG	JGGNG	RNNNG	SPRNTNG	STTNG
2.	MSM	MSQ	TMPL	CTHDRL	SYNGG
3.	NSHVLL	SVNNH	LNDN	DTRT	DNVR
4.	MNDY	WDNSDY	JNRY	SNDY	STRDY
5.	RD	YLLW	CRCL	CRMSN	PRPL
6.	ND	TLY	KNY	DLLS	CLND
7.	NGN	CLTCH	GRS	WHLS	LMN
8.	TWNTY	KYBRD	SCRN	MMRY	PRCSSR
9.	CRPHLLY	GRGNZL	STLTN	BR	BLGNS
10.	PLM	PTT	STSM	PRCT	DMSN

SOLUTION   ON PAGE 301

920 SHAPE SORTER

Should A, B, C, or D come next in this series?

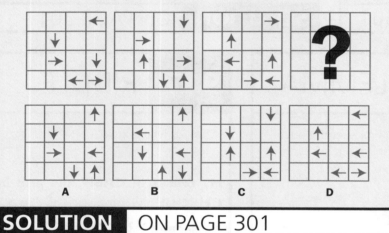

SOLUTION   ON PAGE 301

922 SHAPE SORTER

Should A, B, C, or D come next in this series?

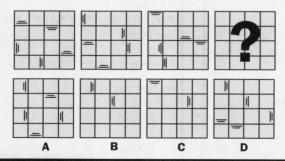

SOLUTION   ON PAGE 301

919 BOX BOTHER

Which of these boxes can be made from the template? Is it A, B, C, D, E, or F? No sign is repeated on more than one side of the box.

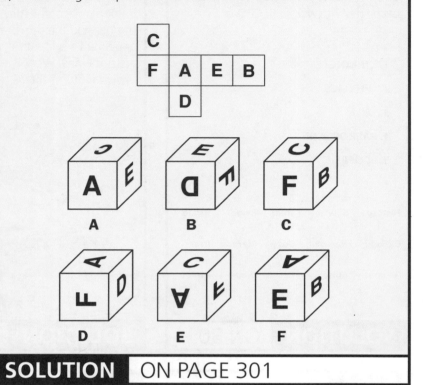

SOLUTION   ON PAGE 301

921 WORD CIRCLE 2

In the small circle below left, the words ONCOST, STRIPE, and PERSON are arranged clockwise, each overlapping by two letters. From the eight clues given below, in no particular order, find eight six-letter words, which, when placed in the correct order around the other circle in a clockwise direction, will each overlap by two letters as shown in the example.

Clues

Abnormally white person

Covered passageway

Foolish

Imbecility

Intimation

Musical instrument

To hate

Underground room

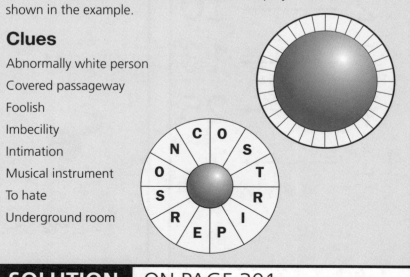

SOLUTION   ON PAGE 301

923 FORMULATION

The numbers on the right are formed from the numbers on the left using the same formula in each question. Find the rule and replace the question mark with a number.

8 ⟶ 99

11 ⟶ 126

26 ⟶ 261

15 ⟶ ?

SOLUTION ON PAGE 301

924 FLUMMOXED BY FRUIT

At a pick-your-own fruit farm, twice as many people are picking raspberries only as plums only. Three more people pick strawberries, raspberries and plums as pick plums only. Four more people pick strawberries only as pick both raspberries and strawberries but not plums. 50 people do not pick strawberries. Eleven people pick both plums and raspberries but not strawberries. A total of 60 people pick plums. If the total number of fruit pickers is 100, can you answer the questions below?

1. How many people pick raspberries?
2. How many people pick all three?
3. How many people pick raspberries only?
4. How many people pick both plums and strawberries but no raspberries?
5. How many people pick strawberries only?
6. How many people pick only two of the three fruits?

SOLUTION ON PAGE 301

925 CARD CAPER

Six children have invented a card game and scoring system. It uses the cards up to 10, at face value, with aces scoring 1. In each round, the value of the card dealt is added to that child's score. Diamonds are worth double the face value. If two or more children are dealt cards with the same face value in one round, they lose the value of that card instead of gaining it (diamonds still doubled). They are each dealt six cards face up as shown below:

Player	Card 1	Card 2	Card 3	Card 4	Card 5	Card 6
1	6 ♥	3 ♠	ACE ♦	9 ♣	10 ♥	4 ♠
2	10 ♠	ACE ♠	7 ♥	6 ♦	5 ♠	8 ♣
3	7 ♦	8 ♥	4 ♣	3 ♥	ACE ♣	5 ♣
4	4 ♥	9 ♦	7 ♠	5 ♦	10 ♣	3 ♦
5	8 ♠	5 ♥	6 ♠	9 ♠	2 ♠	4 ♦
6	3 ♣	2 ♣	9 ♥	7 ♣	10 ♦	8 ♦

When the scores are added up, which player:
1. Came third?
2. Won?
3. Came last?
4. Was winning after the fourth cards had been dealt?
5. Had even scores?
6. Had a score divisible by 3?
7. What was the second highest score?
8. What was the sum of all of the scores?

SOLUTION ON PAGE 302

926 CIRCLES

What is the value of the last string? Black, white and shaded circles have different values.

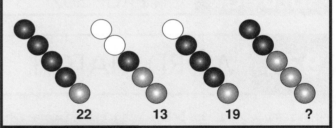

22   13   19   ?

SOLUTION ON PAGE 302

927 MATHS MYSTERY

Start at the top-left circle and move clockwise. Calculate the number that replaces the question mark.

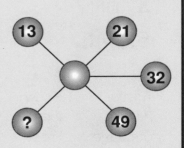

SOLUTION ON PAGE 302

928 THE FIRE

The couple had just finished building their home and because the night would be very cold, they wanted to build a fire to keep warm. The wind outside was gusting at 40 mph and they were soon very cozy and fell asleep. A few hours later they were both dead. What had gone wrong?

Clues

1. The home had not burned down.

2. The house had not blown down.

3. They had not suffocated.

4. They had not been burned to death.

SOLUTION ON PAGE 302

929 FOGGY

This one will have you fuming. What is being described?

**Three fourths of a cross and a circle complete,
Two semi-circles at a perpendicular meet;
Next add a triangle which stands on two feet,
Two semi-circles and a circle complete.**

SOLUTION ON PAGE 302

930 DOTTY DILEMMA

Which of the shapes – A, B, C, D or E – cannot be made from the dots if a line is drawn through all of the dots at least once?

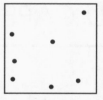

A   **B**   **C**   **D**   **E**

SOLUTION ON PAGE 302

931 WORD MATCH

Match the word groups below with the given word. Which group completes each line? Answer A, B, C, D or E.

1. TRAWLER

2. ARTICHOKE

3. CHICKEN

4. TINY

5. HAIL

A	B	C	D	E
Turnip	Snow	Canoe	Minute	Falcon
Pepper	Ice	Dingy	Small	Puffin
Cabbage	Frost	Barge	Short	Pigeon

SOLUTION ON PAGE 302

932 FORMULATION

The numbers on the right are formed from the numbers on the left using the same rules. Discover the rule used and replace the question mark.

4 ⟶ 18
6 ⟶ 32
9 ⟶ 53
13 ⟶ ?

SOLUTION ON PAGE 302

933 CELTIC CONUNDRUM

FINISH

START

SOLUTION   ON PAGE 302

934 DISK DILEMMA

Calculate the values of the black, white, and shaded circles and the sum of the final set.

14   13   12   ?

SOLUTION   ON PAGE 302

935 RIDDLE

What, or where am I?

My first is in HOT and also in COLD
My second is in BRASH but not in BOLD
My third is in GANG and also in GROUP
My fourth is in ARMY but not in TROOP
My last is in LOAN and also in RENT
I am a musical instrument.
What am I?

SOLUTION   ON PAGE 302

936 THE SWISS DEPOSIT CODE

A man carried a code for his Swiss account engraved in the buckle of his belt until he died. He did not pass on the secret to his family, but in his will he stated that whosoever cracked the code could have the contents of the safe deposit box in the Swiss bank. Can you crack the code?

DID = IIF
BAD = A
CCE = ACCB
HEG = DACC + GG
No F - C - G - B
OPENS THE BOX

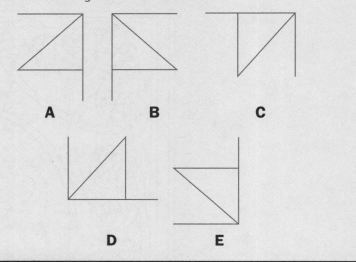

SOLUTION ON PAGE 302

938 FULL CIRCLE

Should A, B, C, or D fill the empty circle?

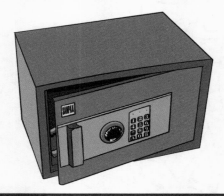

A   B   C   D

SOLUTION ON PAGE 302

937 SHAPE SORTER

Which of the following is the odd one out?

A   B   C

D   E

SOLUTION ON PAGE 302

939 BOX BOTHER

Which of these boxes can be made from the template? Is it A, B, C, D, E, or F? No sign is repeated on more than one side of the box.

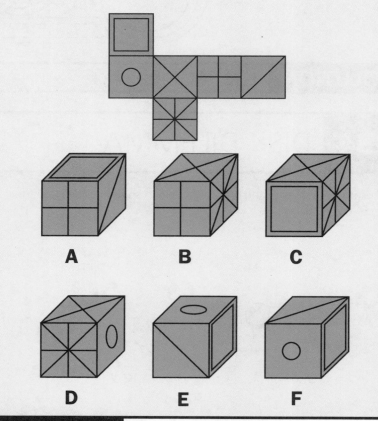

A   B   C

D   E   F

SOLUTION ON PAGE 302

940 SHAPE SORTER

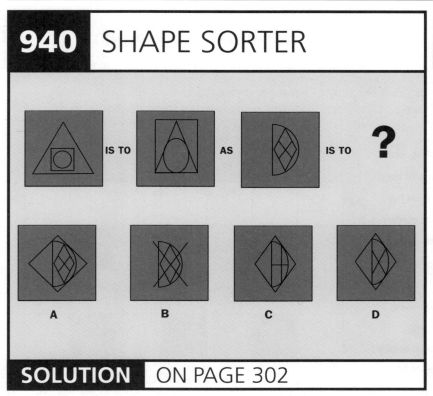

A   B   C   D

SOLUTION ON PAGE 302

941 BOX FILLER

Should A, B or C come next in this series?

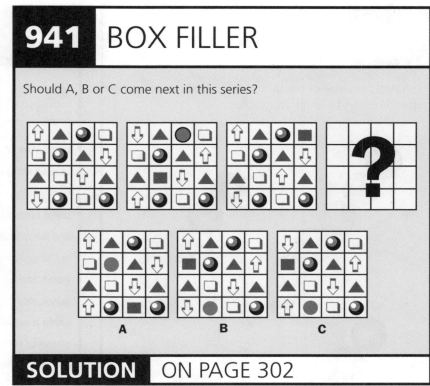

A   B   C

SOLUTION ON PAGE 302

942 DOTTY DILEMMA

Which of these boxes can be made from the template? Is it A, B, C, D, E, or F? No sign is repeated on more than one side of the box.

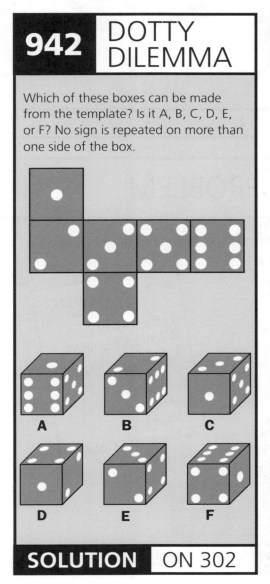

A   B   C

D   E   F

SOLUTION ON 302

943 GENERAL KNOWLEDGE

Answers are entered starting at the same number as the clue, and go in a spiral toward the middle. Each answer begins with one or more letters from the end of the previous word.

Clues

1. Animosity (5)
2. Worth looking at (6)
3. Howling (9)
4. Fruit (3)
5. Drink (3)
6. Let down a rock face (6)
7. Of lower part of back (6)
8. Ancient (7)
9. Funnyman (8)
10. Anxiety (5)
11. Beer mug (5)
12. Tasteless (7)
13. Triangular (7)
14. Worshipper of idols (8)
15. Bursting forth (8)
16. Wild ass (6)
17. Rule (5)
18. Author (8)
19. Sports arena (7)
20. Total shadow cast by eclipse (5)
21. Small wading bird (4)
22. Plant with lilac flowers (8)
23. Unpredictable (7)
24. Crib (3)
25. Mexican pancake (4)
26. Black gold (3)
27. Fluids (7)
28. Sparkling state (13)
29. Surveillance in the dark (10)
30. Waterfall (5)
31. Rigid (5)
32. Showing mental decay (6)
33. Ovum (3)
34. Fruit (6)
35. Elude (6)
36. Wayward person (7)

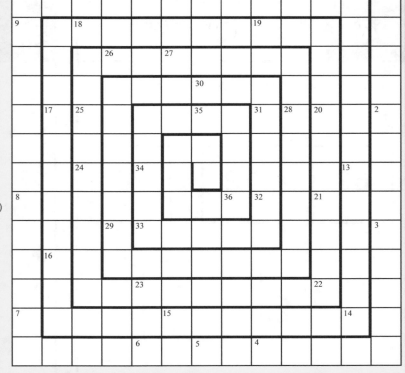

SOLUTION ON PAGE 302

944 DISK DILEMMA

What is the value of the last string? Black, white and shaded circles have different values.

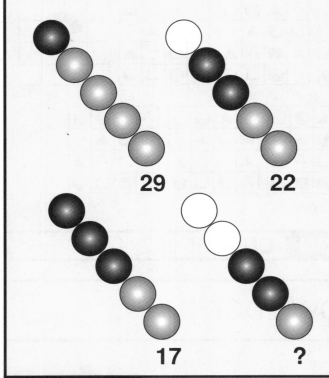

29   **22**

17   **?**

SOLUTION ON PAGE 302

945 NURSERY RHYME CROSSWORD

The narrative below is the story of a nursery rhyme. Solve the eight clues that are highlighted in the narrative, and place the answers in the correct positions in the grid to complete the crossword.

Little Miss Muffet, who was wearing one of her best <u>outfits</u>,[4] sat on her tuffet eating her curds and whey in the <u>open air</u>[6] in the <u>cultivated areas,</u>[7] which had a <u>water shortage</u>.[1] Along came a spider who <u>chose</u>[5] to sit down beside her and frightened Miss Muffet away because it had landed in her <u>hair</u>,[8] so she had <u>chauffeurs</u>[3] take her to her <u>group of friends</u>.[2]

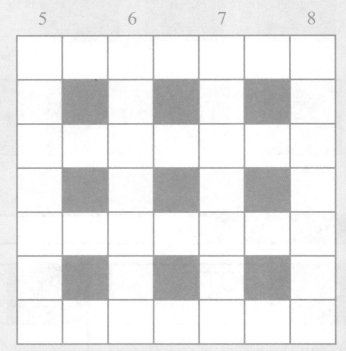

SOLUTION ON PAGE 302

946 CODE CRACKER

What is the next number in this code sequence?

| 63 | 72 | 76 |

| 112 | ? |

SOLUTION ON PAGE 302

947 PENTAGON PROBLEM

You are in Washington DC. While you are there you decide to visit the sights. You make a list, but can't find the Pentagon on your map.

How far away is the Pentagon?

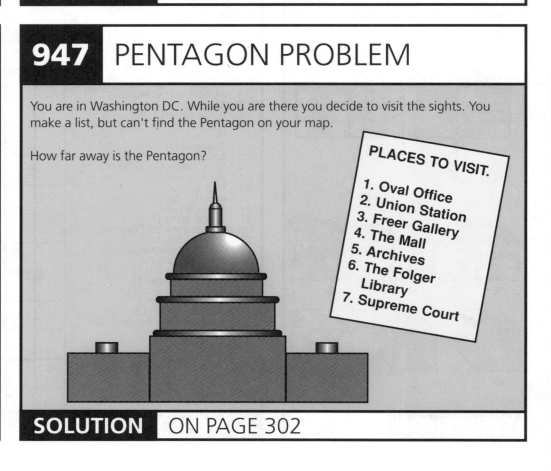

PLACES TO VISIT.

1. Oval Office
2. Union Station
3. Freer Gallery
4. The Mall
5. Archives
6. The Folger Library
7. Supreme Court

SOLUTION ON PAGE 302

948 TRIANGLE TRAUMA

What comes next in this sequence?

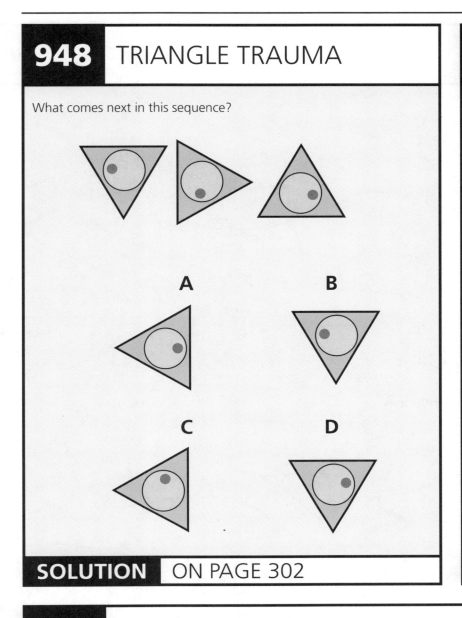

A

B

C

D

SOLUTION ON PAGE 302

949 CRIME SPREE

These 6 words below are associated with violent crime. Can you unravel them?

SONISASASTAIN

EXITONCUE

AMENTALSHRUG

INNERMOSTIMP

DEADPROTEIN

MINTONFENCE

SOLUTION ON PAGE 302

950 A BODY BAG IN THE SUITCASE

Cheryl had just met a new boyfriend, Floyd. They met in Las Vegas and got married after a whirlwind romance. When they loaded up the car she looked into a suitcase that she had not packed, which had been left in the trunk of the car by her new husband. It contained a body bag with a boy's body in it. The suitcase had holes in it so that air could get into it and the body bag was partially open. She did not leave Floyd or report the incident to the police. Why?

Clues

1. He told her that she had found his best friend.

2. The body bag was used for protection.

3. The boy was 7 years old.

4. It was not his son.

5. The body was fully dressed.

6. Foul play was not suspected even though an arm had been broken.

SOLUTION ON PAGE 302

951 PASTA PROBLEM

START

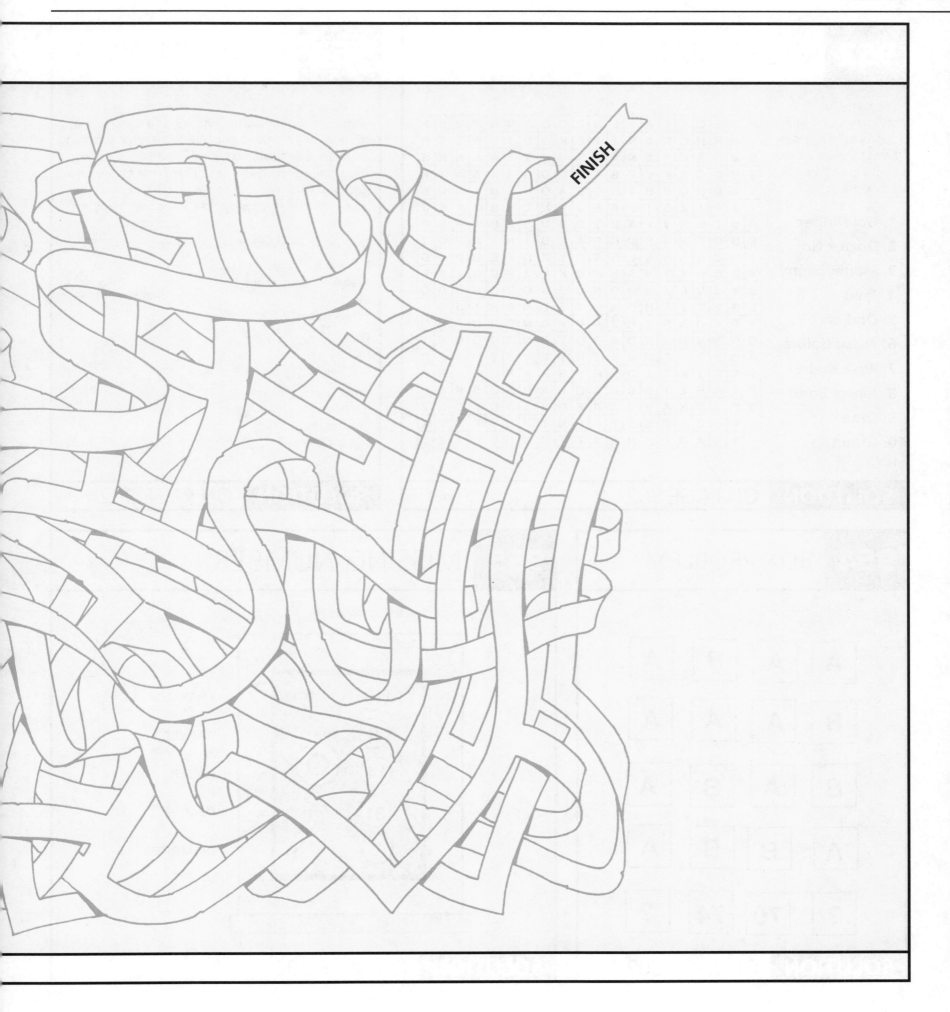

FINISH

952 WORDSEARCH

The names of 10 characters who have appeared in James Bond films are hidden in this grid. Can you find them all?

1. Goldfinger
2. Doctor No
3. Moneypenny
4. Jaws
5. Oddjob
6. Pussy Galore
7. Rosa Klebb
8. James Bond
9. Drax
10. Granitski

H	J	E	C	L	E	A	I	L	H	L	O	O	Y	M	N	P	M	B	F
L	M	R	N	G	R	A	N	I	T	S	K	I	D	T	V	W	S	T	R
S	M	R	E	C	Y	X	N	A	J	T	U	N	X	T	A	S	N	N	S
S	U	O	C	S	K	V	P	B	I	R	E	D	R	A	X	A	W	X	F
L	A	D	N	O	B	B	T	H	O	E	A	O	N	L	H	I	N	U	W
T	X	D	I	E	S	T	J	R	S	J	I	M	C	R	S	Y	V	G	J
R	U	C	B	R	Y	F	A	U	T	D	D	U	S	K	U	I	W	L	P
E	U	Q	F	R	A	P	M	N	F	A	R	D	I	H	I	N	V	O	J
T	R	O	S	A	K	L	E	B	B	O	Y	Z	O	F	E	D	P	O	D
A	S	Q	B	T	T	N	S	N	H	S	K	L	X	R	C	K	I	F	F
S	K	J	V	L	X	J	B	G	N	O	J	W	O	E	O	N	B	D	Q
L	S	L	Z	T	S	H	O	X	M	Y	T	L	N	G	N	I	J	S	I
Y	P	K	O	N	R	A	N	Z	A	F	A	Q	N	O	R	N	F	N	O
Q	R	N	R	N	Z	H	D	A	O	G	L	P	N	Z	O	O	G	V	I
R	Q	S	P	I	F	M	E	K	Y	N	T	F	Y	T	T	M	V	P	O
V	N	W	I	K	T	A	O	S	R	V	F	N	A	E	C	J	F	R	P
P	T	A	E	E	Z	B	S	L	A	O	L	A	B	B	O	S	P	A	D
S	D	J	K	N	A	U	V	G	R	E	G	N	I	F	D	L	O	G	J
H	V	G	B	Y	P	G	E	T	P	E	N	T	R	O	Y	E	Y	V	X
H	S	B	A	D	F	K	N	G	I	T	T	U	S	N	B	W	I	Z	Z

SOLUTION ON PAGE 302

953 COST OF SPYING

The FBI are sending spy satellite equipment to a secret laboratory in Honolulu. In order to keep it secret and not draw any attention, they are sending the shipment as standard air freight in two different packages. The airline company charges 11 cents per mile, with a surcharge of 5 cents per pound on the weight of the package, but 7 cents per pound if it is over 50 pounds.

This surcharge is added to the final cost.

The first package weighs 85 pounds and the second, 27 pounds.

The distance to Honolulu is 4972 miles.

What will be the total cost of sending these two packages?

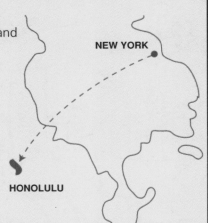

NEW YORK

HONOLULU

SOLUTION ON PAGE 302

954 BOX PROBLEM

Fill in the missing numbers.

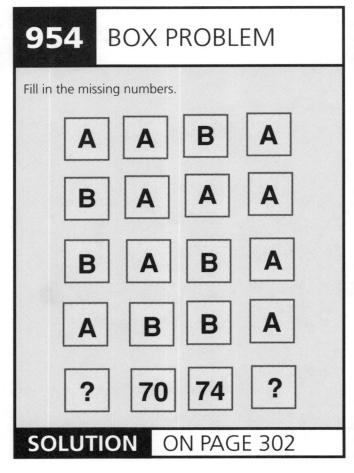

A	A	B	A
B	A	A	A
B	A	B	A
A	B	B	A
?	70	74	?

SOLUTION ON PAGE 302

955 MISSING NUMBER

Find the missing number to crack the safe.

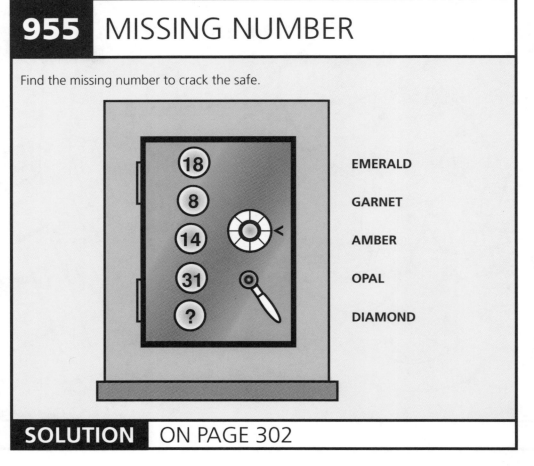

18   EMERALD

8   GARNET

14   AMBER

31   OPAL

?   DIAMOND

SOLUTION ON PAGE 302

956 KEY CRACKER

In which room did Rick find the keys? Crack the code to find out.

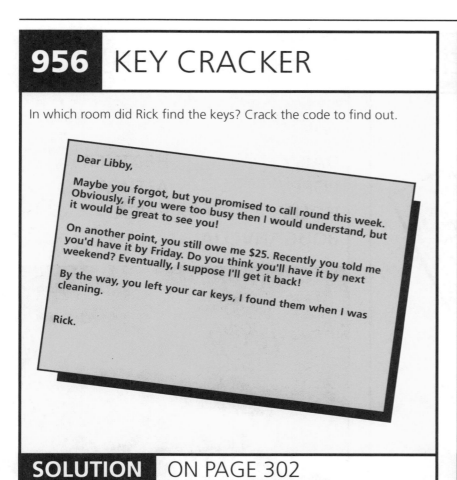

Dear Libby,

Maybe you forgot, but you promised to call round this week. Obviously, if you were too busy then I would understand, but it would be great to see you!

On another point, you still owe me $25. Recently you told me you'd have it by Friday. Do you think you'll have it by next weekend? Eventually, I suppose I'll get it back!

By the way, you left your car keys, I found them when I was cleaning.

Rick.

SOLUTION ON PAGE 302

957 NATO ALPHABET

How well do you know the NATO, or phonetic, alphabet? Can you fill in the blanks and fit the words into the grid? Words already provided do not appear in the grid.

A = ALPHA
B =
C =
D =
E =
F =
G =
H =
I = INDIA
J =
K =
L =
M =
N =
O =
P =
Q = QUEBEC
R = SIERRA
S =
T =
U =
V = VICTOR
W =
X =
Y =
Z = ZULU

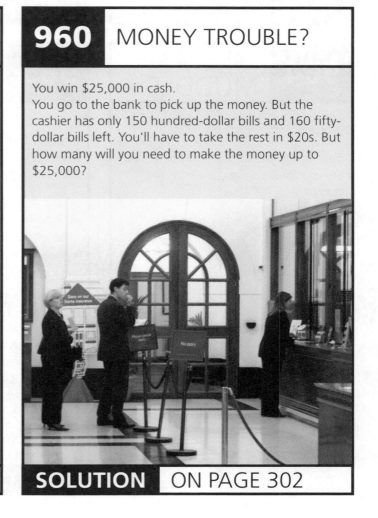

SOLUTION ON PAGE 302

958 MURDER IN MIND

Four suspects – Jack Vicious, Sid Shifty, Alf Muggins and Jim Pouncer – are being interviewed at the scene of a murder. Each of the suspects is asked a question. Their answers are as follows:

Jack Vicious: "Sid Shifty committed the murder."

Sid Shifty: "Jim Pouncer committed the murder."

Alf Muggins: "I didn't commit the murder."

Jim Pouncer: "Sid Shifty is lying."

Only one of the four answers is the truth. Who committed the murder?

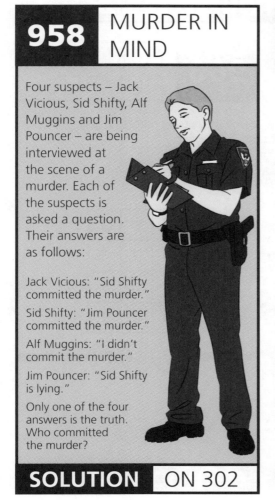

SOLUTION ON 302

959 SHAPE SHIFTER

Which piece will connect up this circuit?

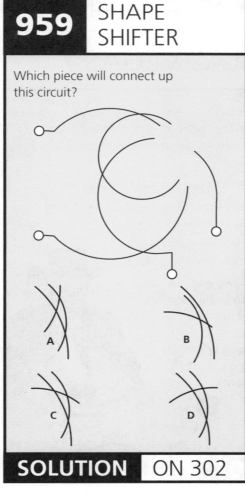

A   B

C   D

SOLUTION ON 302

960 MONEY TROUBLE?

You win $25,000 in cash.
You go to the bank to pick up the money. But the cashier has only 150 hundred-dollar bills and 160 fifty-dollar bills left. You'll have to take the rest in $20s. But how many will you need to make the money up to $25,000?

SOLUTION ON PAGE 302

961 LICENSED

There's something odd about the licence plates below. Find the odd one out.

DJK 40 100 110

HMO 80 130 150

VEY 220 50 250

ACF 10 30 90

SOLUTION ON 302

962 TAKEN

Unravel this word, which means kidnapped.

CUTBADED

SOLUTION ON 302

963 FLOWER FUN

Look at the words below. Which one is the odd one out?

DAISY   **HEATHER**

POPPY   **ALTHEA**

HOLLY   **ERICA**

BOUGANVELIA

SOLUTION ON PAGE 302

964 MESSAGE MUDDLE

This is a clue to an apartment number:

The vowels are missing and the letters are all mixed up. Can you find the number?

HRYTTN

SOLUTION ON 302

965 LAS VEGAS

Three gamblers – Diablo, Scarface and Lucky – attend a convention at Las Vegas. They decide to have a gambling session with six-sided dice, but stipulate unusual rules:

1. Each gambler may select his own numbers.

2. The numbers 1–9 may be selected, but no two numbers may be consecutive.

3. Each die has to have three pairs of different numbers, adding up to 30.

In addition, no two gamblers are allowed to choose the same combination of numbers. In a long run, Diablo's numbers will beat Scarface; Scarface's numbers will beat Lucky; but Lucky's numbers will beat Diablo. How is this possible?

SOLUTION ON PAGE 302

966 LOST NUMBER

Find the missing number to pick the lock.

0	0	1
0	1	1
0	0	1
0	1	1

? 64 76

SOLUTION ON 303

967 BOX BOTHER

Find the missing number in the sequence.

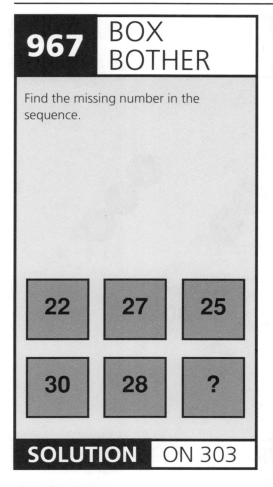

22	27	25
30	28	?

SOLUTION ON 303

968 CASH DOWN

You start out with $25,000 in Vegas. You win some, you lose some and you seem to have less than before. To be exact there are: 138 $100 bills, 147 $50s, and 78 $20s. How much of your original $25,000 has gone?

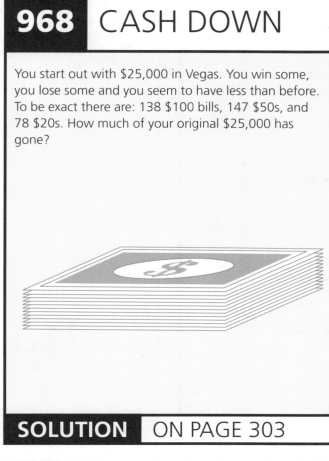

SOLUTION ON PAGE 303

969 LOST LETTER

In each vertical column the letters add up to a number. What should the number be in column 1? Add the correct number to open the lock.

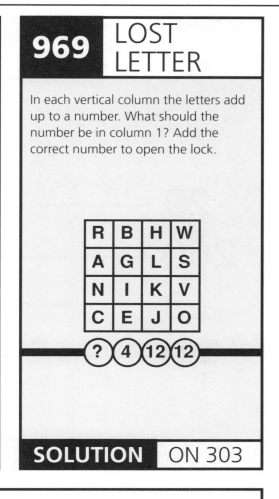

R	B	H	W
A	G	L	S
N	I	K	V
C	E	J	O

(?) (4) (12) (12)

SOLUTION ON 303

970 SHAPE SHIFTER

Which is the odd one out of these shapes?

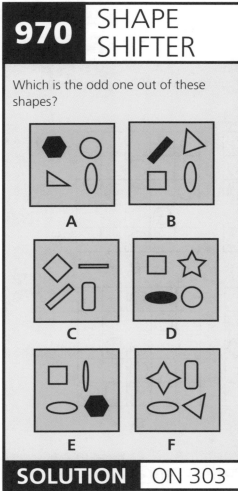

A   B

C   D

E   F

SOLUTION ON 303

971 TARGET PRACTICE

The twins Larry and Pete got up one morning and painted some large targets on the door of the barn. After the paint had dried, they found that their baseball damaged the door if they pitched a fastball. The rubber ball and tennis balls were either lost or of no use because they did not leave a mark to show where they hit the targets. The twins, who were very competitive, did have a solution, one that also pleased their parents. They threw balls at the door for hours and could accurately score every shot without leaving a mess to be cleared away later and without damaging the paintwork. How was this possible?

Clues

1. The balls had no dye and no mud.

2. The balls did not bounce.

3. The twins were told to clear the yard before they could play ball. This instruction was in their best interest.

4. The children kept clean.

SOLUTION ON PAGE 303

972 FORMULATION

The numbers on the right are formed from the numbers on the left using the same formula in each question. Find the rule and replace the question mark with a number.

29 ⟶ 5

260 ⟶ 16

13 ⟶ 3

40 ⟶ ?

SOLUTION   ON PAGE 303

973 DISK DILEMMA

What is the value of the last string? Black, white and shaded circles have different values.

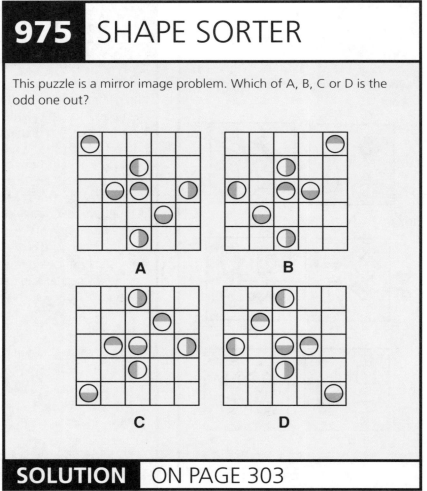

30

18

40

?

SOLUTION   ON PAGE 303

974 MATHS MYSTERY

Start at the top-left circle and move clockwise. Calculate the number that replaces the question mark.

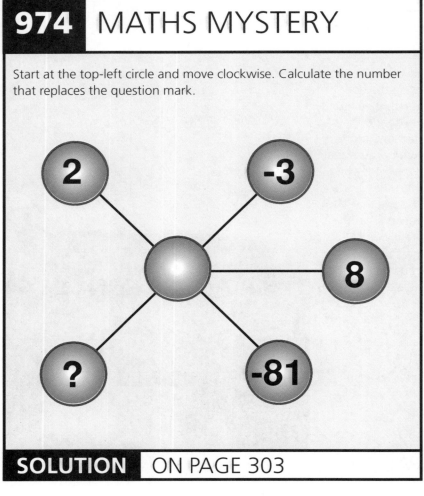

SOLUTION   ON PAGE 303

975 SHAPE SORTER

This puzzle is a mirror image problem. Which of A, B, C or D is the odd one out?

A

B

C

D

SOLUTION   ON PAGE 303

976 BOX BOTHER

Which of the shapes – A, B, C, D or E – cannot be made from the dots if a line is drawn through all of the dots at least once?

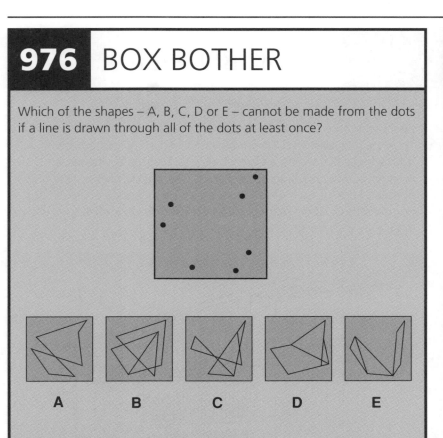

A B C D E

SOLUTION ON PAGE 303

977 ALPHABET CROSSWORD

Using all 26 letters of the alphabet, once only, fill in the blanks to complete the crossword.

A B C
D E F
G H I
J K L
M N O
P Q R
S T U
V W X
Y Z

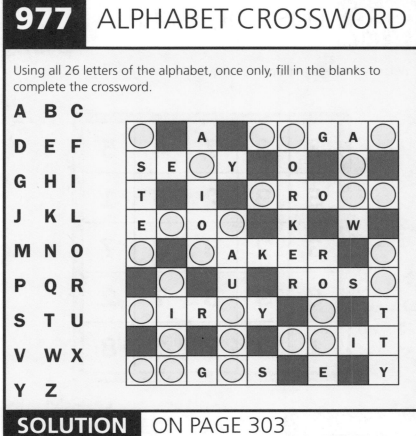

SOLUTION ON PAGE 303

978 DAY DILEMMA

A certain month has five Thursdays in it and the date of the second Sunday is the 13th.

1. What is the date of the third Tuesday?
2. What is the date of the last Friday in the month?
3. What is the date of the first Monday in the month?
4. How many Saturdays are in the month?
5. What is the date of the second Friday in the month?

SOLUTION ON PAGE 303

979 FORMULATION

The numbers on the right are formed from the numbers on the left. Discover the rule used and replace the question mark.

1 ⟶ 1½

4 ⟶ 6

8 ⟶ 12

20 ⟶ ?

SOLUTION ON PAGE 303

980 LOST NUMBER

What number should replace the question mark in this grid?

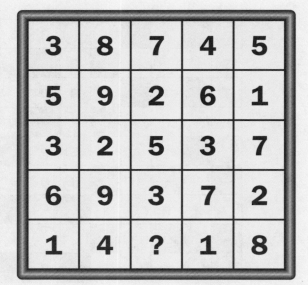

SOLUTION   ON PAGE 303

1. How many biographies were borrowed in total?
2. How many people borrowed only two of the three types?
3. How many people borrowed a thriller, a biography and a science fiction?
4. How many people borrowed a thriller only?

SOLUTION   ON PAGE 303

981 BOOK BOTHER

In a day at the library, 64 people borrowed books. Twice as many people borrowed a thriller only as borrowed a science fiction only. Three people borrowed a biography only and 11 people borrowed both science fiction and a thriller but not a biography. The same number borrowed a biography and a thriller but no science fiction as borrowed one of each of the three types. Twenty-one people did not borrow a thriller. One more person borrowed a science fiction and a biography than borrowed a biography only.

982 SHAPE SORTER

Should A, B, C, or D fill the empty circle?

A   B   C   D

SOLUTION   ON PAGE 303

983 | MAZE MUDDLE

FINISH

START

984 CONFUSED CUBES

Which of these boxes can be made from the template? Is it A, B, C, D, E, or F? No sign is repeated on more than one side of the box.

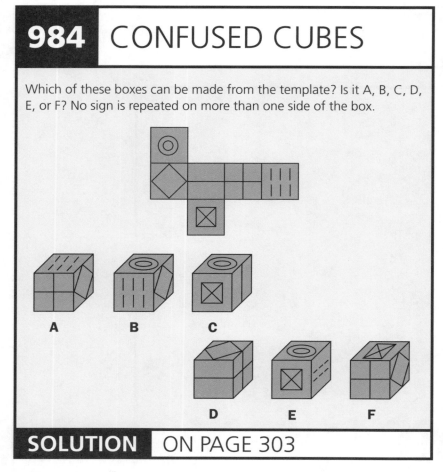

985 SHAPE SHIFTER

Which arrangement is missing?

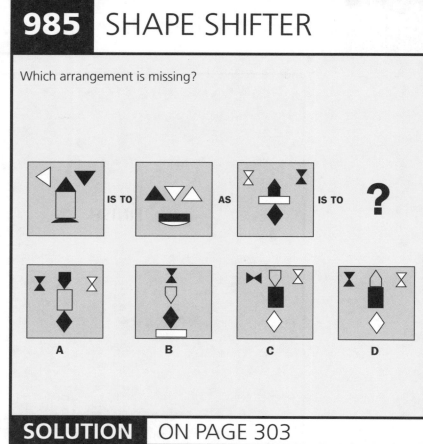

SOLUTION ON PAGE 303

986 SERIES SOLUTION

Should A, B, C, or D come next in this series?

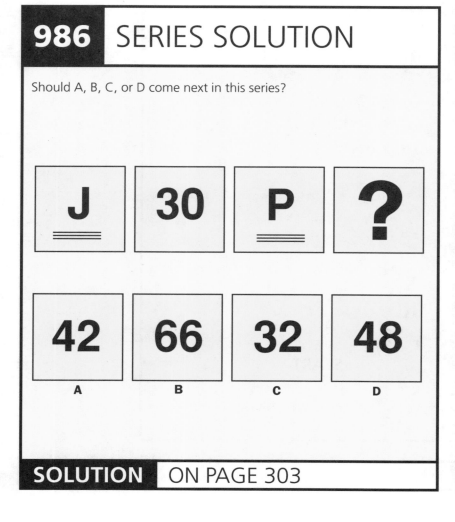

SOLUTION ON PAGE 303

987 BOX BOTHER

Should A, B, C, or D come next in this series?

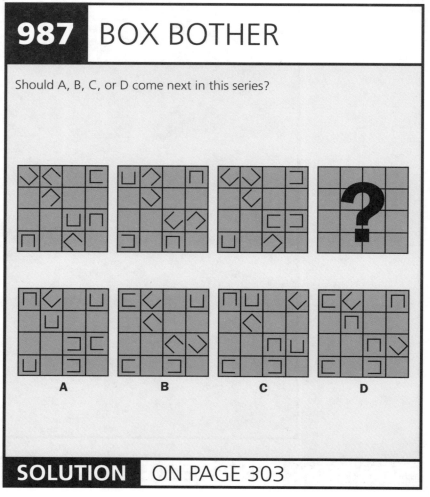

SOLUTION ON PAGE 303

988 G-R-R-RIDDLE

Complete the grid. Clues are given, but in no particular order.

Clues (in no particular order)

Extravagantly odd
Flee from law
Lived in
Man who plays a part

One to whom anything is entrusted
Powdered preparation of tobacco
To consider meditatively

989 JUNGLE JOURNEY

You are on a jungle mission when you reach a river. The only way to cross it is by carefully stepping from stone to stone, from one side to the other. Pick the wrong stones and you'll fall in. The river is full of crocodiles.

Starting at A, and stepping on only one stone from each row, which sequence of stones should you choose?

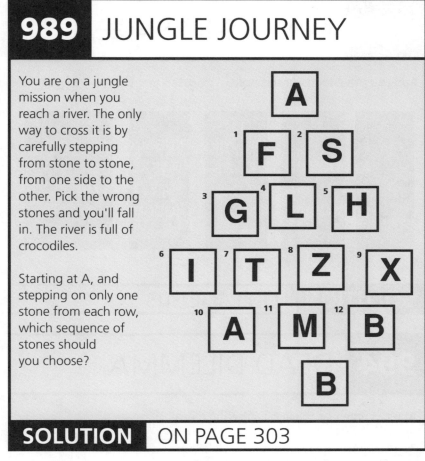

990 SPOT THE SPY

One of these agents is a spy. To find out which, unravel the words to discover the one that does not belong with the others.

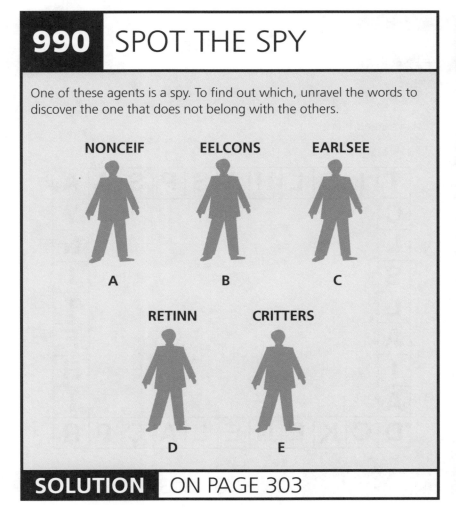

NONCEIF — A
EELCONS — B
EARLSEE — C
RETINN — D
CRITTERS — E

991 WORD WONDER

What do these words have in common?

**GARBED
PRIDES
CORDON
RAPTOR
CORONA
ROGUES**

992 MIXED MESSAGE

Can you piece together this note?

SOLUTION ON PAGE 303

994 DEAD DILEMMA

At what time was the lethal injection given?

A. 11.30am   B. 12.00pm   C. 12.25pm
D. 1.00pm   E. 1.35pm   F. 1.55pm

PATHOLOGY REPORT

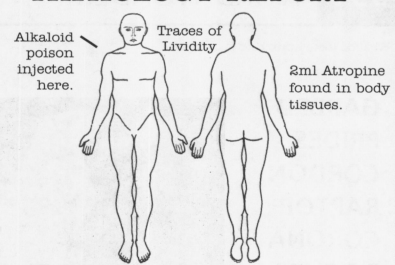

Alkaloid poison injected here.

Traces of Lividity

2ml Atropine found in body tissues.

My examination of the body took place approximately 20 hours after the actual time of death. Consequently, there was some lividity and rigor mortis present. Tests carried out on the tissues revealed evidence of poisoning with a lethal substance which I later discovered to be atropine. Six ml of atropine will kill an adult in twenty minutes. I understand that the last person to see her alive was a neighbour who called round to the house at eleven-thirty that morning.

Time of death was 2pm.

Dr. S. Moffatt
Senior Pathologist.

SOLUTION ON PAGE 303

993 SHELL SHOCK

Which bullet is an exact copy of bullet A?

SOLUTION ON PAGE 303

995 MIXED CITIES

Three American cities are merged together here.

Can you find them?

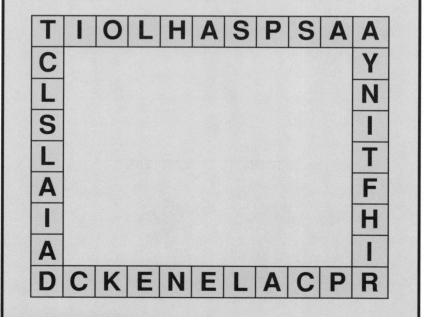

SOLUTION ON PAGE 303

996 THE MESSY EATER

Much to his colleagues' annoyance, Arthur brought fruit to the office each day for his lunch. He would peel his banana and leave the skin lying around, drop apple cores all over the floor, spit the pips from his grapes over other people's desks, and he was forever squirting people in the eye with his orange. Arthur still brings fruit to work but no longer gets complaints from his colleagues. He has not changed his habits, he has not done or said anything to his colleagues, and his colleagues have not changed. Why does he no longer get complaints?

Clues

1. He did not work with animals and the office was normally a clean environment.
2. He no longer uses his fingers to hold the fruit.

SOLUTION ON PAGE 303

997 CRIME CONUNDRUM

A secret agent in Algeria, knowing he was about to be arrested for spying, stole a huge truck and drove off into the desert. After almost a day's driving, and completely lost, he ran out of fuel.

One week later the truck was found. The large metal back doors were open wide and the truck was completely empty. The keys were still in the ignition, and strangely the agent was found lying dead on the trailer roof. It seemed as if there was no way he could have climbed up onto the roof or back down again.

What cargo was the truck carrying and how did the agent get up onto the trailer roof?

SOLUTION ON PAGE 303

998 SAFE SOLUTION

Find the missing number to crack the safe.

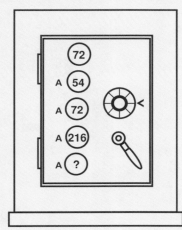

72
A 54
A 72
A 216
A ?

Turn left 180 degrees

Turn right 90 degrees.

Turn right 180 degrees.

Turn left 90 degrees.

SOLUTION ON PAGE 303

999 MISSING NUMBER

Below are the names of some FBI agents, each with their service number.

What is agent Myatt's service number?

NAME	NUMBER
Agent Field	1.4.26.7.25
Agent Shultz	1.16.3.20.2.8
Agent Price	1.3.20.14.16
Agent Myatt	?

SOLUTION ON PAGE 303

1000 CRIME CONUNDRUM

If the rope = 8, the knife = 15, and the gun = 4, what is the numerical value of the question mark?

$$(? \times \text{rope}) - (\text{knife} \times \text{gun}) = 172$$

SOLUTION 0ON PAGE 303

ANSWERS

1

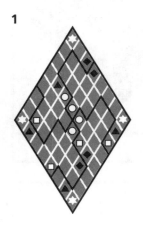

2

E. There are four triangles constantly moving clockwise around the arms and visiting points in sequence.

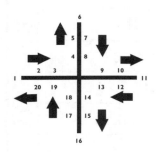

3

There was a stationary car parked 5 m to the robot's right. The program should have said "moving land vehicle".

4

The man was a lighthouse-keeper and it was his responsibility to keep the light shining at all times. He had absent-mindedly turned off the light before going to bed and a ship had ploughed into the rocks with terrible consequences.

5

1. A. 2. D. 3. L. 4. O.
5. N. 6. H. 7. K. 8. R.

9. T. 10. S. 11. V. 12. C.
13. U. 14. I. 15. B. 16. M.
17. G. 18. F. 19. E. 20. P.

6

1. S, to make Allow, Basil.
2. C, to make Pith, Scale.
3. P, to make Ride, Slope.
4. M, to make Swap, Clamp.
5. T, to make Sill, Facet.
6. H, to make Tree, Niche.
   Or R, to make Thee, Nicer.
7. U, to make Vale, Cause.
8. E, to make What, Feast.
9. N, to make Moth, Gland.
10. T, to make Meal, Hotly.
11. R, to make Wing, First.
12. T, to make Wine, Comet.
13. U, to make Prod, Bound.
14. R, to make Dated, Breach.
15. V, to make Cured, Shove.
16. R, to make Cease, Brand.
17. N, to make Bugle, Canter.
18. G, to make Bride, Finger.
19. A, to make Twin, Haunt.
20. O, to make Stop, Float.

7

P	S	E	I	G	R	E	N	E
S	R	U	D	E	E	N	N	E
T	R	O	N	U	O	I	N	T
R	T	E	T	S	M	C	S	A
I	I	A	P	R	H	P	E	L
P	N	E	E	A	U	I	Y	U
E	T	T	N	N	R	D	N	M
S	E	T	I	R	E	D	E	E
D	E	Y	O	R	T	S	E	D

1 – 2   PROTRUDED
2 – 3   DESTROYED
3 – 4   DETERMINE
4 – 5   ENERGIES
5 – 6   SUNSHINE
6 – 7   EMULATE
7 – 8   ENCHANT
8 – 9   TIRED
9 – 10 DRAPERS
10 – 11 STRIPES
11 – 12 STEPSON
12 – 13 NEED
13 – 14 DUMPY
14 – 15 YES
15 – 16 SPUN
16 – 17 NEAT
17 – 18 TIN

8

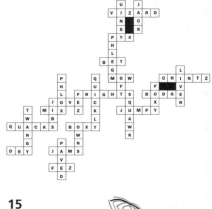

9

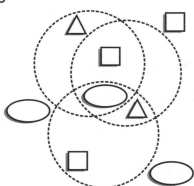

10

Only one weighing operation is necessary. You take one coin from bag one, two coins from bag two and three coins from bag three and weigh all six coins together. If they weigh 305g the first bag contains the counterfeit coins; if they weigh 310g the second bag does; and if they weigh 315g the third bag does.

11

1. Break   2. Base.
3. Rest.   4. Tuba.
5. Real.   6. Back.
7. Ring.   8. Rust.
9. Sand.   10. Strand.

12

1. 14.
2. 7.
3. 2 (using segment numbers 1, 6, 7, 9, 11, 12 and 1, 4, 6, 10, 12).

13

The aisle order is: 1. fruit, 2. tins, 3. washing powder, 4. bottles, 5. meat, 6. bread.

1. Bread.
2. Four.
3. Fruit.
4. Two.

14

15

16

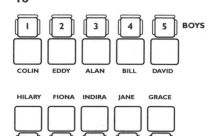

| 1 | 2 | 3 | 4 | 5 | BOYS |
COLIN EDDY ALAN BILL DAVID

HILARY FIONA INDIRA JANE GRACE

| 10 | 9 | 8 | 7 | 6 | GIRLS |

17

D.

There is a sequence occurring from the right eye to the left eye (as we look at them). Look at stages one and two. The contents of the eyes in stage one have merged to form the left eye of stage two and a new symbol has been introduced in the right eye of stage two. Now look at stages two and three. The contents of the left eye in stage two has moved away and does not appear in stage three. The symbol from the right eye in stage two has moved to fill the left eye of stage three and a new symbol has been introduced in the right eye of stage three. This pattern of change is then continued, so that the left eye of stage four contains a merging of both eyes in stage three.

18

From one end or the other, the order is: white, green, black, red, silver, yellow, blue, purple.
1. Silver.
2. Red.
3. Blue.
4. Yellow.

19

C.

The number of right angles in each figure increases by one each time.

20

C.

21

Colonel Present scored 200 (60, 60, 40, 40)
Major Aim scored 240 (60, 60, 60, 60)
General Fire scored 180 (60, 40, 40, 40)

The incorrect statements made by each marksman are as follows:
Colonel Present, statement no. 1;
Major Aim, statement no. 3;
General Fire, statement no. 3.

22

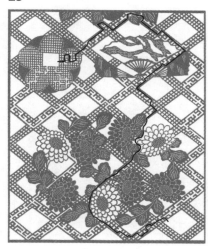

What they say they are	Numbers in the group	What they actually are	What they become
Fibkins	30	30 Switchkins	30 Fibkins
Switchkins	15:15	15 Fibkins	15 Fibkins
		15 Switchkins	15 Switchkins
Truthkins	10:10:10	10 Truthkins	10 Truthkins
		10 Fibkins	10 Fibkins
		10 Switchkins	10 Truthkins

55 Fibkins live in pentagonal houses that night.

Only Switchkins can claim to be Fibkins, as it would be a lie to a Truthkin, and the truth to a Fibkin. So the group which claimed to be Fibkins must be all Switchkins, and so must be the group of 30 x 1. The Switchkins of that group thus become Fibkins, because that's what they said they were. Similarly, only Fibkins or Switchkins can claim to be Switchkins, so the group that claimed to be Switchkins must be 15 Fibkins and 15 Switchkins, and the Switchkins stay as they are. That means that the group that claimed to be Truthkins is made up of all three types – all can claim to be Truthkins. The 10 Switchkins of this group become Truthkins. Therefore, at the end of the day there are 15 Switchkins (the 15 who told the truth about what they were), 20 Truthkins (10 original Truthkins, and 10 former Switchkins), and 55 Fibkins (10 who lied about being Truthkins, 15 who lied about being Switchkins, and the 30 former Switchkins who became Fibkins by claiming that was what they were). Pentagonal houses are used by Fibkins.

23

S	T	I	R			
T	I	D	E			
I	D	E	A			
R	E	A	L	I	S	T
			I	N	C	A
			S	C	A	R
			T	A	R	T

24

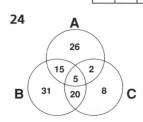

A
26
15 2
5
B 31 20 8 C

A = Hotel, B = Self-Catering, C = Camping.

1. 26.   2. 15.
3. 36.   4. 37.

25

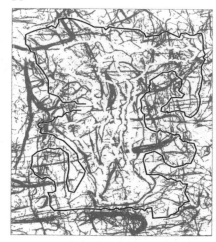

26.
D.

27

Necklace 5 and Rings 4. Each number is the total amount of consonants in each word.

28

If you say the child was a boy then the second speaker must have been the mother, whose first statement must have been a lie and whose second statement was true. But boys in the family do not lie so this option is no good. If you say that the child was a girl and if the first speaker was the father, then the second speaker was the mother whose first statement would be true and whose second statement was a lie. In that case the child would have spoken the truth and would have said, "I am a girl". But this implies that the first speaker lied, but males cannot lie. This option is therefore no good. So by deduction the first speaker was the mother and the child said, "I am a boy." The first statement from both the mother and child were lies. The child was a girl.

29

107. This number is exactly half the difference between 25 and 239.

30

Violence
Killing
Unlawful
Illegal
Agent
Criminal

31

Passport and Revolver.

32

6.

33

2, 5, 6 and 12. The broad ring moves toward the middle on each row.

34

C. Not symmetrical around horizontal axis.

35

Curl.	Barrier.
Camembert.	Calorie.
Dawn.	Dupe.
Epidemic.	Epistle.
Fairyland.	Falter.
Golf.	Grain.
Herringbone.	Hessian.
Immediate.	Joint.
Kipper.	League.
Limerick.	Mediate.

36

2, 5, 7, 10, 12, 15, 17.

37

If number eight did not require repairing the supervisor would have said that five out of the first seven needed repairing.

38

A. There are six triangles, each with their base on one of the sides of the hexagon. Each triangle increases in height by a quarter of the width of the hexagon at each stage. So, showing one triangle only:

39

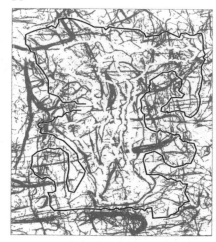

40

1. espionage
2. deception
3. confidential
4. intelligence
5. conspiracy
6. undercover

41
1. Midsummer.
2. Personality.
3. Distance.
4. Antiseptic.
5. Emanate.
6. Remonstrate.
7. Replacement.
8. Dedicate.
9. Intelligence.
10. Enthusiastic.

42
1. D.   2. E.
3. A.   4. C.
5. B.

43
1. B.   2. D
3. E.   4. C.
5. A.

44
1. E.   2. A.
3. D.   4. B.
5. C.

45

A	Z	U	R	E	■	Q	■	S
I	■	E	■	J	U	N	K	■
C	L	E	F	■	I	■	I	■
■	C	■	I	S	L	E	■	M
T	H	A	N	■	A	T	O	P
A	■	B	E	A	T	■	C	■
X	■	O	■	E	W	E	R	■
E	N	V	Y	■	N	■	A	■
D	■	E	■	S	T	I	N	G

46
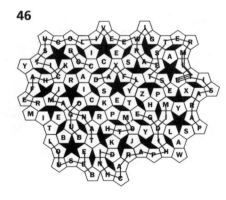

47
22½ miles. Work out how long it takes Russell Carter to walk home. Spot has been running all this time at his given constant speed so it is simple to work out how many miles Spot has covered during this period. Russell walks for 10 miles at 4mph, taking 2½ hours.
Spot is running for 2½ hours too, at 9mph, which means he covers 22½ miles.

48
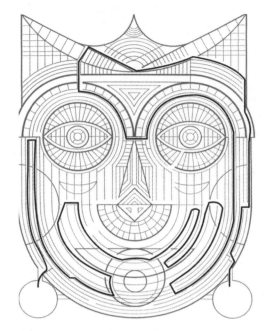

49
1. D.   2. C.   3. B.   4. E.
5. A.

50
1. F.   2. B.   3. E.   4. F.
5. C.

51
1. Four.   2. 26th.
3. 15th.   4. Thursday.
5. Tuesday.

52
The ball was made from frozen mercury, which melted and went through the hole in the base to a glass container. The box was left dry inside.

53
Q.

54
5 and 9. 4x4=16, 6x8=48, 5x9=45. Add them all together to make 109.

55
20 square yards

56
C.

57
20

58
Apartment 35.

59
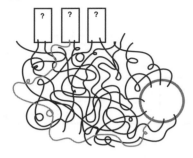

60
19.

61
A.

62
SPYING.

63
10 triangles can be seen.

64
Each letter is replaced with the one after it in the alphabet.

65
2R on row 5, column 3.

66
CODEWORD. Brown stars are vowels. Beige stars consonants. The number is the alpha number of the letter. A=1 and so on, up to five for vowels, and B=1 and so on for consonants.

67
C. The others have alphanumeric values in reverse.

68
$4,500.

69

Name	Occupation	Pastime	Rest day
Smith	Butler	Squash	Friday
Jones	Gardener	Golf	Tuesday
Wood	Chauffeur	Fishing	Wednesday
Clark	Janitor	Chess	Thursday
James	Cook	Bridge	Monday

70
Before you tie the string to the door tie a bow in it. Cut through both loops of the bow and, of course, the cup will stay put.

71
I forgot to mention that my clock was digital. One line was not functioning on the eight lines that make up each digit.

	TIME SHOWED	SHOULD HAVE SHOWN
8.55	5	5
8.56	6	6
8.58	6 ◄ MISSING	8
8.59	5 ◄ MISSING	9
9.00	◄ MISSING	0

72
"F" appears six times. "Of" appears twice and most people look for a "ph" sound.

73
450m.

74
"Push" on one side; "Pull" on the other side.

75
2519 prisoners.
2519 divided by 3 = 839 tables with 2 over
2519 divided by 5 = 503 tables with 4 over
2519 divided by 7 = 359 with 6 over
2519 divided by 9 = 279 with 8 over
2519 divided by 11 = 229 exactly.

76
B. The shape's inside lines have been removed and the shape has been placed in an octagon.

77
24. 77 is a multiple of 7. None of the other numbers are, except when you reverse 24 to 42!

78
A. Looking both across and down, the contents of the third square are formed by merging the contents of the two previous squares as follows:

one white or yellow circle remains; two yellow circles become white; two white circles become yellow.

79
KOJAK.

80

81
28. (x 3) + 1.

82
1. 6. 2. 6. 3. 5.
4. 14. 5. 4.

83
1. A. 2. C. 3. B.
4. C. 4. C.

84
1. Appear. 6. Above.
2. Acquire. 7. Acquit.
3. Acerbity. 8. Absent.
4. Actual. 9. Abbreviate.
5. Airy. 10. Adult.

85
8. Black = 2; white = 1;
shaded = 4.

86
1. The number of letters between the last and the next to last letters of the word.

87
The natural thing to do is to make the field square as the area of a square with the same perimeter as a rectangle will always be larger. The answer, however, is to make it a circle.

π D = circumference of a
    circle
π D = 3000 = 954.80585 meters
    or r (radius)
    = 477.40 meters

π r² = area of circle
    A = 716104.31 square meters

The area of a square would only be 562,500 square meters.

88
February was added to the calendar a little later and nobody knows when he actually did it. The early calendar only had 10 months.

89
Put the pin through the match and pin it to the cork. Strike the match and place on the water so that it floats without getting the match wet. Then put the beaker over the cork and lighted match.

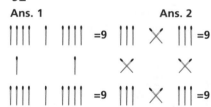

The match burns the oxygen and the water will be drawn into the beaker.

90
8. Black = 2; white = 1;
shaded = 3.

91
Yes. His 18th birthday was yesterday, New Year's Eve. He was speaking on New Year's Day, so he will indeed have another birthday in the current year.

92
Ans. 1   Ans. 2

|||| | |||| =9 ||| ✕ ||| =9

| | ✕   ✕

|||| | |||| =9 ||| ✕ ||| =9

93
a) Remove any two matchsticks from any corner and place as shown. Remember a block of four squares forms a bigger square.
b) Move the remaining match that was left on its own.

Ans. A   Ans. B

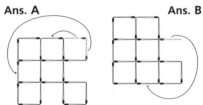

94
The wife of M9 is F10. The male speaker on nuclear fission is M3.

Male	M1	M3	M5	M9	M7
Female	F8	F6	F4	F10	F2
Vehicle	Warp distorter	Galaxy freighter	Space oscillator	Nebula accelerator	Astro carrier
Speech	Time travel	Nuclear fission	Astral transporting	Mind reading	Anti-gravity
Feature	12 fingers	3 eyes	3 legs	4 arms	Webbed feet

95

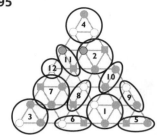

96
A. Each shape rotates in a set sequence.

97
Holes or beams of light.

98
1. DETECTIVE   2. DART.

99
108. Multiply two outer digits of first number to form outer digits of next number. Multiply two inner digits of first number to form two inner digits of second number.

100
3. (A + C) – (D x E) = B or A – B + C ÷ D = E.

101
18.4.18.9.3.11.1 Each number is the alphanumeric value of each letter, but moved forward 2 places.

102
B. Looking both across and down, any lines common to the first two tiles disappear in the third tile.

103
11. (x 2) + 7.

104
1. Humdrum.
2. Humiliate.
3. Headstrong.
4. Hopeful.
5. Hero.
6. Humorous.
7. Hostile.
8. Hold.
9. Hardship.
10. Hungry.

105
Italy and China.
Infancy.
Thought.
Angelic.
Lenient.
Yashmak.

106

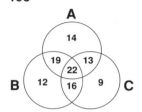

A = Candy, B = Chips, C = Soda.

1. 22.   2. 19.
3. 16.   4. 105.
5. 36.   6. 14.

107

R	U	C	K	S	A	C	K
C	E	R	E	B	R	A	L
N	U	I	S	A	N	C	E
E	L	O	N	G	A	T	E
P	A	R	A	D	I	S	E
F	A	R	E	W	E	L	L
M	O	D	I	F	I	E	D
O	P	E	R	A	T	O	R

The diagonal words are KANGAROO and REINDEER.

108

109
Wednesday=3 and Thursday=6.
The number of letters from z to
the first letter of the day.

110
2, 3, 8 and 10. The circle revolves
90 degrees clockwise on each row.

111
"Abandon the mission and return
to base." a=z, b=y and so on, then
each word is turned back to front.

112
5. The unscrambled words are:
DRESS, OVERCOAT, VEST,
TROUSERS and NECKLACE. Apart
from necklace, they are all items
of clothing.

113
A. Each number has a numerical
value equivalent to its position in
the alphabet. A=1.

114
11. Add the two digits in each circle together. 11 in the 2nd circle:
1+1=2. Add all three; the total
equals 19.

115
The dalmatians are called Andy
(owned by Bill) and Donald
(owned by Colin).

116
Sears Tower.

117
631.

118
2. The unscrambled words are;
YARD, HOUR, FOOT, MILE and INCH.
HOUR is a measurement of TIME.

119
12. Twelve is midway between F
and R in the alphabet.

120
D. It is back to front.

121
17. Multiply the number by 2 then
take 1 off.

122
H.

123
A.

124
1. D.   2. C.   3. B.   4. A.   5. 2. 6.
B.   7. A.   8. None.   9. B.   10. C.
11. C.   12. C.

125
After going forward, you reverse.

126

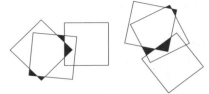

127
He was less than one pace from
the North Pole when he planted
the right foot. His left foot went
over the North Pole and was
therefore pointing south.

128

129
A stallion.

130
Moses.

131
3 hours.

132
1. England.   2. Germany.
3. Square.   4. Cloud.
5. Ankle.   6. Sapphire.
7. Cock.   8. Hair.
9. Saturn.   10. Light.

133
As there are 216 chambers – an
even number – there is no central
chamber. The task is therefore
impossible.

134
1560. Add times as numbers. 200 +
730 = 930; 245 + 445 = 690; 915 +
645 = 1560.

135
Insects: Flea, Slug, Wasp, and
Locust.

136

D. The three squares form four
triangles.

137
The 40-gallon barrel contains beer.
The first customer purchases the
30-gallon and 36-gallon barrels,
giving 66 gallon of wine. The second customer purchases 132 gallons of wine – the 32-gallon, 38-
gallon and 62-gallon barrels. The
40-gallon barrel has not been purchased by either customer and
therefore contains the beer.

138
The words contain: Play, Drama,
Film and Show.

139

2	14	10	7
9	6	1	4
16	3	13	11
12	8	5	15

So that:
1. No two consecutive numbers
appear in any horizontal, vertical or
diagonal line;
2. No two consecutive numbers
appear in adjacent squares.

140
Anne studies algebra, history,
French and Japanese. Bess studies
physics, English, French and
Japanese. Candice studies algebra,
physics, English and history.

141

3	6	3	4	4	6
4	4	7	2	8	3
5	8	5	5	6	7
6	5	3	7	8	2
8	3	1	6	5	4
2	7	8	7	5	3

142

Penny	Piece
Piece	Meal
Meal	Time
Time	Step
Step	Son
Son	Net
Net	Her
Her	Ring
Ring	Worm
Worm	Screw
Screw	Ball
Ball	Cock
Cock	Pit
Pit	Bath
Bath	Bun

143
1. Date.   6. Cost.
2. Cork.   7. Thin.
3. Ball.   8. Bond.
4. Harp.   9. Dial.
5. Slot.   10. Lend.

144
13. (÷ 2) + 6.

145
1. 50.   2. 20.
3. 1280.   4. 1170.

146

 = 3

 = 5

 = 2

 = 7

 = 4

 = 1

= 6

147
1. 66. Two previous numbers
   added.
2. 154. (n + 3) x 2.
3. 9, 20. Two series + 3, + 4, + 5,
   etc., and + 2 each time.
4. 51. (2n – 3).
5. –49. (2n – 15).
6. 70. (2n – 1²), (2n – 2²), etc.
7. 343. (n x previous n) ÷ 2.

148
2. (A x B) – (D x E) = C

149
97. Position of hands (not time) with hour hand, first, expressed as a sum.
113 − 16 = 97.
others are: 51 + 123 = 174
911 + 82 = 993.

150
They were grandmother, mother, and daughter. Two were mothers and two were daughters.

151
2. Make sums: First 2 digits – Second 2 digits, then First – Second.

152

8	7	6	8	7	12	9	1
7	12	7	6	4	3	2	14
8	9	7	8	5	7	11	1
8	8	10	7	6	16	10	1
4	9	13	4	12	2	15	6
8	5	2	2	4	9	8	15
6	9	8	14	14	8	2	1
9	6	10	5	12	1	5	17

153
40.

4	5	12	13
3	6	11	14
2	7	10	15
1	8	9	16

154
37. (Top left + Top right) – (Bottom left + Bottom right).

155
1. 17—19—22—24—28—20 = 130
2. 17—19—22—28—25—20 = 131
    17—23—22—24—25—20 = 131
3. 140. 17—24—26—28—25—20
4. 127. 17—19—22—24—25—20
5. 2 ways:
         17—24—26—24—25—20
         17—23—22—26—28—20

156
Graham is 9 years old and Frederick is 27. Thus, 27 squared is the same as 9 cubed = 729. There are 18 steps, 36 palisades and 243 bricks, which, when added together, gives the door number of 297.

157
29. Black = 7; White = 3;
                 Shaded = 9.

158
A calculating machine: Abacus/Calculator.

159
20. (− 4) x 2.

160
94. (2n + 3), (2n + 6), (2n + 9), etc.

161
You are the train driver, so whatever colour eyes you have.

162

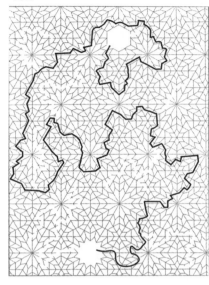

163
The other names contain four vowels each. Roger Moore has five.

164
1U on row 2, column 3.

165
IRONSIDE.

166

60°. If a third face diagonal, BC, is drawn this completes an equilateral triangle. All its sides are equal because they are cube diagonals. Being equilateral, all its angles are 60°.

167

First name	Family name	Room	Appliance
Kylie	Dingle	Conservatory	Computer
Amy	Williams	Bedroom	Television
Clara	Griggs	Living Room	Hi-fi
Roxanne	Simpson	Kitchen	Telephone
Michelle	Pringle	Study	Bookcase

168
26 times + 240° clockwise.

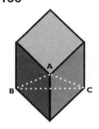

169
2A.

170

Father	Daughter	Father's age	Daughter's age
John	Alison	52	20
Kevin	Diana	53	19
Len	Betty	50	21
Malcolm	Eve	54	18
Nick	Carol	51	17

171
1. 35—34—34—34—35—34—10
2. 35—32—29—28—37—33—10
    35—30—29—35—32—33—10
3. 219. 35—34—34—35—37—34—10
4. 202. 35—30—29—28—37—33—10
5. 4 ways:
         35—32—29—35—37—33—10
         35—30—34—35—32—35—10
         35—33—32—34—32—35—10
         35—33—32—32—35—34—10

172
8. (√) + 3.

173
E.
The two figures merge into one by superimposing one onto the other, except that when two lines appear in the same position they disappear.

174
Two segments: all the triangles do not need to be the same size.

175
E. A is a mirror image of C; B is a mirror image of D.

176

STATEMENT OF WITNESS

At around eleven thirty I was sitting on a wall by the supermarket in Logan Street. I saw the car slowly pull in to the car park and stop over by the fence. Three guys got out. One was a tall black guy in a dark blue suit. The other two wore white. One had a beard and wore a light grey suit, the other wore a brown leather jacket. By the door of the bar they stopped to talk to an older guy with grey hair. He seemed to be in charge. They talked for a few minutes and then they all walked into Garfield Street. I watched them until they turned right in to the park.

177
Aladdin chose one envelope and, without opening it, tore it up into lots of pieces, and asked the king to read what option he had rejected in the other envelope.

178

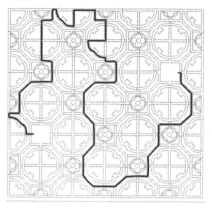

179
Times Square.

180
10. Each number is the amount of letters in the next but one word. So Edinburgh = Birmingham, which contains 10 letters.

181
1D on row 2, column 2.

182
D.

183
B.

184
Each letter is replaced with the one after it in the alphabet. "Your whereabouts has been discovered. Leave the country now if you value your life."

185
HYPNOTISM.

186
Hercule Poirot.

187
18. The alphanumeric value of the first letter.

188
80. (+ 8) x 5.

189
WITNESS

190
33. Add the two digits together and then move on by that amount.

191

| D | B | C | A | C | D | A | B |

| C | MR

| C | MRS

192
D.

193
C

194
1. P21   2. I9
3. M11   4. L7
5. H   6. Q6

195
SUSPICIOUS.

196
Daryl.

197

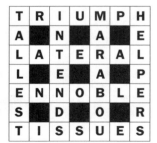

198

T	R	I	U	M	P	H
A		A		N		E
L	A	T	E	R	A	L
L		E		A		P
E	N	N	O	B	L	E
S		D		O		R
T	I	S	S	U	E	S

199

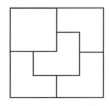

200
a) 15, b) 24, c) 10, d) 34, e) 73.

201
Trains now run 1⅓ times as fast.

202
A. Ans. Cars. Lotus, Fiat, Ford,
    Saab, Audi.
B. Tennis players. Hingis, Cash,
    Henman, Bates.
C. Musical instruments. Tuba, Harp,
    Lyre, Drum.
D. Breeds of Dog: Collie, Basset,
    Boxer, and Beagle.
E. Gems : Amber, Opal, Coral,
    Pearl.

203
Cut the paper as shown.

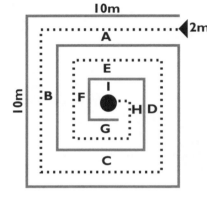

Life flap A vertically
toward you around the
fold line, then twist
section B through
180°.

204
5.

205
C. The letters spell
CAESAR backwards.

206

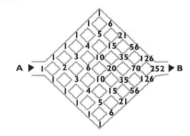

207
62. (x 6) + 8.

208
E. In all the others, if the line
dividing the square is a mirror the
correct mirror image has been
shown.

209
The fact that the man does not see
a door (as in the illustration)
indicates that the door must be on
the other side – the kerb side. As
this is New York, the bus is therefore moving to A.

210
A. At each stage the big hand
moves anti-clockwise first by 10
minutes, then 20 and, finally, by
30 minutes (option A). At each
stage the small hand moves clockwise first by one hour, then two
hours and, finally, three hours
(option A).

211

49m.
A = 9m B = 8m C = 8m D = 6m
E = 6m F = 4m
G = 4m H = 2m I = 2m = TOTAL
49m

212
Major Mustard. Tabulate the results
shown on the board so that each
set equals 71. There are only three
possible ways to do this given the
results: 25, 20, 20, 3, 2,1; 25, 20, 10,
10, 5, 1; and 50, 10, 5, 3, 2, 1. The
first set is Colonel Ketchup's (since
22 cannot be scored in two shots in
the other sets); the third set is
Major Mustard's (as we know that
he scores 3). So Major Mustard hit
the bull's eye.

213
1. In the first bar, 7 x 4 x 8 x 8 x 2
   = 3584.
Similarly, 3 x 5 x 8 x 4 = 480, the
missing number.
Following the same formula, the
missing number in the second bar is
2268 and, in the third, 2688 and
768.
2. In the first bar 58 x 2 = 116.
   In the same vein, 16 x 1 = 16,
   the missing number. Using the
   same formula, the missing number in the second bar is 657
   and, in the third, 162 and 72.

214
Michael Caine and "Live and
Let Die".

215
25. Black = 5; White = 2;
Shaded = 8.

216
A. The figures change places so
that the one in front goes to the
back and vice versa.

217
No. 3.

218
No. The pigeons remain at 200lbs
even whilst flying. Those flying up
would reduce the weight, but
those flying down would increase
the weight, so balancing the total
weight.

219
C. Each horizontal line and vertical
column contains the wavy shape
shown once vertical and once
black. Similarly, each line and column shows the triangle three
times: once pointing left, once
right, once down. Other elements
are similarly repeated.

220

252. Each number represents the
cumulative number of possible
routes to each intersection.

221
Animal X on island A was an ass.
Animal Y on island B was a horse.
Animal Z on island C was a donkey.
The new animal on island B was a
MULE (ass/mare). The new animal
on island C was a HINNEY
(donkey/stallion).

222
"Martini shaken not stirred."

223
Yes. The rule is that no letter may
have an enclosed space within it.

224
9. (Top left x Top right + Bottom left) ÷ Bottom right.

225
C.

The third hexagon is formed by merging hexagons 1 and 2. The fifth hexagon is formed by merging hexagons 4 and 1. In this way, the hexagons build up the shape along vertical lines going from the bottom hexagon upwards. Continuing this trend, the top hexagon is formed by a merging of hexagons 3, 5, 6, and 7: the two straight lines moving upwards to the top hexagon.

226
By lifting the water tank onto its near-side edge. If you cannot see the far edge then the tank is more than half full. If you can just see the far edge then the tank is exactly half full. If you can see below the far edge then the tank is less than half full.

227
10 and 4. The number is the alphanumeric value of the letter halfway between "A" and the letter.

228
6. (– 5) x 2.

229
D. Each pair of circles produces the circle above by carrying forward only those elements that are different. Similar elements disappear.

230
90. You can buy nine tickets from each of the 10 stations:
9 x 10 = 90.

231
C. The striped and green segments move in the following sequences: the striped segments move two anti-clockwise then one clockwise in turn, and continue in this way. The green segments move two clockwise then one anti-clockwise in turn, and continue in this way too.

232
J is option 4; N is option 6. The orange segments move from top to bottom and right to left in sequence, then rise in the same way. However, when an arrangement has occurred previously it is omitted from the sequence.

233
E. Each symbol is linked to the two below it. No symbol ever appears above an identical one. The symbols are produced as follows:

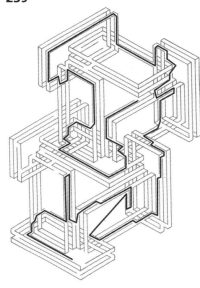

so that ▦ + ♛ must equal something completely different to anything else in the pyramid. Of the options shown, this can only be: ♧

234
4. In the first pentagon 5 x 5 x 125 = 3125 or 5^5. In the second pentagon, 3 x 9 x 9 = 243 or 3^5. In the same way, 16 x 8 x 8 = 1024 or 4^5.

235

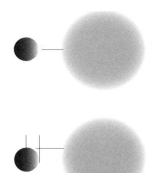

Any valley on or near the equator, owing to the revolution of the Earth.

236
E. The others all have rotated symmetry. In other words, if they were rotated through 180° they would appear exactly the same.

237
The number of empty squares on the card is impossible to calculate, and irrelevant to the question. The odds are always 2:1 against.

238
24. In the first circle, 56 + 79 divided by 5 = 27. The same formula applies to circles two and three.

239

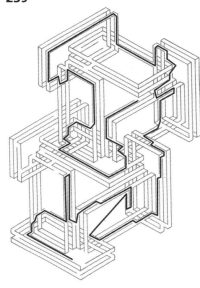

240
1. Alice + 3. Alice's sister is married to Alice's husband's brother. The mother of both men is Alice's mother's sister and to be married to Alice's paternal uncle.

241
Zero, (t - t) = 0 and anything multiplied by zero is zero.

242
If the customer chose red, he would choose blue.
If the customer chose blue, he would choose yellow.
If the customer chose yellow, he would choose red.
He should win 5 in every 9 rolls

Red vs Blue		Blue vs Yellow	
Red Score	Blue	Blue score	Yellow
2	3 - 5 - 7 wins	3	6 - 8 wins
4	5 - 7 wins	5	6 - 8 wins
9	Nil wins	7	- 8 wins

Yellow vs Red	
Yellow Score	Red
1	2 - 4 - 9 wins
6	9 wins
8	9 wins

243
a) 15   b) 3
c) 24   d) 20
e) 12

244
Just turn it upside down to get 81 + 19 = 100

245
25. Black = 4; White = 5; Shaded = 6.

246
156. (Top left x Bottom right) + (Bottom left x Top right).

247
120. Sum of left x sum of right.

248
1. A6, C5, G6.   2. D2.
3. 12.   4. 117, occurs 3 times.
5. 91, G1.   6. E4.
7. None.   8. None.

249
175. (Window + Window) x Door.

250
3. Opposite segments total 30.

251
The other half are boys too – all five of the children are boys.

252
60851. Top row + bottom row + letter values = middle row.

253
–25. (2n – 9).

254
13. (÷ 4) + 3.

255
68. (Top left^2 – Bottom right) + (Bottom left^2 – Top right).

256
22. (x 2) – 2.

257
1. C.	2. B.	3. D.	4. D.
5. A.	6. B.	7. D.	8. E.
9. C	10. C.	11. D.	12. A.
13. D.	14. B.	15. C.	16. C.
17. B.	18. D.	19. C.	20. D.

258

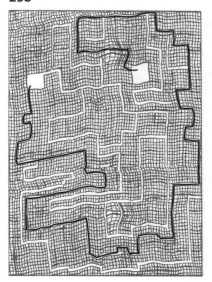

259

One child fell on his feet, and his face was not covered with dust to make his face dirty. When he saw his friend's face covered in dust, he thought his own must also be dirty; his friend only saw his friend's clean face. The dirty child did not think that he needed to wash.

260

261

Michelle had SALMONELLA.

262

2C.

263

I am 40 and my daughter is 10.

264

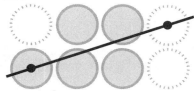

265

B.There are three sizes of rectangle. In the next three stages A moves from left to right one stage at a time. Then it is the turn of B to do the same.

266

C. The square turns 90° clockwise at each stage. Similarly, the shading also moves one segment clockwise at each stage.

267

D. The smallest number is dropped each time and the remaining numbers appear in reverse order.

268

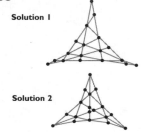

Both solutions produce nine rows of five trees per row.

269

12. The third number, 27, is obtained by adding the digits of the two preceding numbers – 7 + 2 + 9 + 9. This formula applies throughout the puzzle.

270

44. 28 huskies with four legs each plus 44 penguins with two each, making 200 in all.

271

B. The figures are flipped vertically.

272

Strong, weak, strong. He will always beat the weak player, so playing this way gives him two chances to beat the strong one.

273

8679. Turn the page upside-down and add up the two numbers.

274

33. Multiply diagonally opposite squares and subtract the smaller product from the larger:
(13 x 5) - (8 x 4) = 33.

275

Name	Airport	Destination
Mike	Heathrow	JFK
Nick	Gatwick	Vancouver
Paul	Cardiff	Berlin
Robin	Manchester	Roma
Tony	Stansted	Nice

276

He isn't dead.

277

29.

278

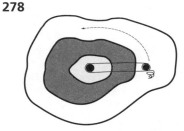

He ties the rope to the tree, then walks around the lake carrying the rope. As he reaches half-way, the rope wraps itself around the tree on the island. He then ties the rope to the tree on the mainland and hauls himself across to the island.

279

CARPET
CELLAR
FENDER
GARDEN
INFORM
JESTER

MONDAY
PARTED
QUEENS
RULERS
SYSTEM
TENDON

280

Abbie.

281

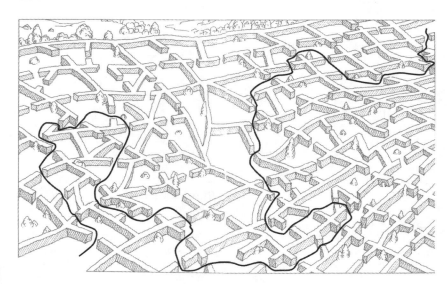

282

4. The unscrambled words are; CARROT, POTATO, TURNIP, ORANGE and ONION. ORANGE is a fruit (or you might have discovered ONAGER, which is an animal).

283

ESPIONAGE.

284

No. All the words contain a creepy crawlie of some sort (ANT, BUG, GRUB, TICK, LOUSE, FLY).

285

ALEP gives PALE, PEAL, LEAP, PLEA.

286

Columbo, Murder She Wrote, The X Files, Charlie's Angels.

287

Harry Palmer.

288

Name	Rank	Ship	Location
Perkins	Steward	Aircraft carrier	Malta
Ward	Seaman	Cruiser	Portsmouth
Manning	Commander	Submarine	Falklands
Dewhurst	Purser	Frigate	Gibraltar
Brand	Captain	Warship	Crete

289

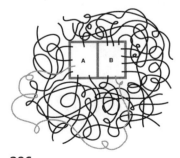

290

17. (– 7) ÷ 2.

291

Dana Scully.

292

"Don't pay anything, I'm going to escape tonight."
The co-ordinates give the line up and then the word in, worked out from the bottom of the text.

293

"Seattle is in Washington State". Each vowel is replaced by the one after it; i=o and so on.

294

E.

295

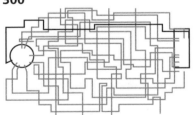

296

Reagan
Lincoln
Roosevelt
Johnson
Eisenhower
Nixon.

297

The total number of dollars that they receive for their cattle must be an odd number. They buy an odd number of sheep at $10 each, so the tens figure in the total square number must be an odd number. The only square numbers with an odd "tens" figure have "6" as their "units" figure. The number 256 is one such number, equalling the price of 16 steer at $16 a head as well as 25 sheep at $10 a head with $6 for the goat. Because the square number must end in 6, the goat is always worth $6, no matter how many sheep they bought (16, 36, 256, etc). Bully Bill evens up the takings by giving Dynamo Dan the goat and Colt.45 to equal his own share of the sheep ($10) minus the Colt.45. Therefore the gun is worth half the difference between a sheep and a goat, or $2.

298

299

Bonnie and Clyde.

300

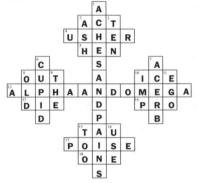

301

12. 7 - 4 = 3. 3 x 4 = 12.

302

24. The number of letters in the first word are multiplied by the number of letters in the second.

303

DO, TO, ZE.

304

305

Only if they can express the number to base 9, which gives $7,000,000 or $1,000,000 each.

306

307

1. Relaying, Layering, Yearling.
2. Owners, Worsen, Rowens.
3. Bounders, Rebounds, Suborned.
4. Decimals, Medicals, Declaims.
5. Retraces, Terraces, Caterers.
6. Wrestle, Swelter, Welters.
7. Serrated, Treaders, Retreads.
8. Paled, Pedal, Plead.
9. Earnest, Eastern, Nearest.
10. Remolds, Smolder, Molders.

308

1. Owl, Rail, Gull, Jay.
2. Gold, Jade, Opal, Amber.
3. Sea, Tide, Wave, Reef.
4. Rome, Nice, Lima, Bonn.
5. Barn, Hut, Shed, Tent.
6. Coo, Hoot, Crow, Cry.
7. Arrow, Lance, Axe, Gun.
8. Sue, Kim, Pam, Anne (or Ann).
9. Bat, Ox, Rat, Pig.
10. Star, Sky, Moon, Sun.

309

1. Cost, which makes Costlier, Costumes, Costliest.
2. Stud, which makes Studhorse, Studied, Student.
3. Bean, which makes Beanfeast, Beanpole, Beanery.
4. Tend, which makes Tendons, Tenderly, Tendered.
5. Dam, which makes Damned, Damages, Damsels.
6. Tea, which makes Teapot, Tearoom, Teasels.
7. Dan, which makes Dander, Dangle, Dandier.
8. Time, which makes Timetable, Timelist, Timelier.
9. Horse, which makes Horseshoe, Horseflies, Horseflesh.
10. Coal, which makes Coaling, Coalesced, Coalfield.

310

Three chances in four. Look at the possible combinations of drawing the balls. There are black–black; white–black; black–white; and white–white. The only one of the four possible combinations in which it does not occur is the fourth one. The chances of drawing at least one black ball are, therefore, three in four.

311

36.

16	9	8	1
15	10	7	2
14	11	6	3
13	12	5	4

312

5	7	8	15	4	7	5	6
11	6	9	8	16	12	10	10
7	12	10	12	3	11	6	8
6	7	2	5	7	7	15	10
12	15	10	8	5	12	8	7
6	7	11	13	9	6	9	6
9	8	10	6	8	8	1	2
3	6	4	10	10	10	15	15

313

280. First digit x Fourth digit = First and Fourth digits, Second digit x Third digit = Second and Third digits.

314

	21	
15		34
	22	

Move clockwise by the given number minus 1.

315
6. (BC) + A = DE.

316
The two trains pass each other at 14.00, 75 miles from Brotherton.

317
The structure would enclose the largest area if it was built 22 m wide and 46m long, giving an area of 1,012m^2.

318
45. Black = 3; White = 8; Shaded = 13.

319
35. (n + 3), (n + 6), (n + 9), etc.

320
–18. (Left numbers multiplied) – (right numbers multiplied).

321
1. A6, C5, G6.
2. D2.
3. 12.
4. 117, occurs 3 times.
5. 91, G1.
6. E4.
7. None.
8. None.

322
175. Left window + right window x door.

323
B. 25. (a x b) – c = d.

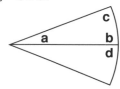

324
1. Doughnut, Fruitcake, Gingerbread, Flapjack, Macaroon.
2. Chest, Dresser, Settee, Table, Wardrobe.
3. Daffodil, Snowdrop, Sunflower, Fuchsia, Begonia.
4. Cairo, Seoul, Athens, Baghdad, Bangkok.
5. Karate, Golf, Rugby, Judo, Badminton.
6. Bowie, Ross, Jackson, Streisand, Presley.
7. Iran, Chile, Paraguay, Israel, Holland.
8. Pepperoni, Risotto, Pizza, Salami, Pasta.
9. Stuttgart, Dortmund, Berlin, Bonn, Heidelberg.
10. Turmeric, Cinnamon, Cayenne, Cumin, Oregano.

325
1. Bracelet. Others are Glove, Hat, Scarf, Shawl.
2. Khaki. Others are Denim, Nylon, Silk, Wool.
3. China. Others are Plate, Dish, Saucer, Beaker.
4. Garden. Others are Bungalow, Flat, House, Maisonette.
5. Quartet. Others are Guitar, Zither, Trombone, Piano.
6. Student. Others are Dancer, Grocer, Sailor, Driver.
7. Arizona. Others are Baltimore, Phoenix, Chicago, Houston.
8. Gravy. Others are Vodka, Bourbon, Advocaat, Brandy.
9. Harpsichord. Others are Diminuendo, Allegro, Fortissimo, Crescendo.
10. Boston. Others are Maryland, Indiana, Nevada, Georgia.

326

327
AMETHYST
BERYL
COAL
EMERY
GYPSUM
IRON
MAGMA
MARBLE
MARL
ONYX
RUBY
SPAR
TIN
ZINC

328
Thursday

329
4. (squared) – 5.

330
The bottom half of the wheels.

331
Take alternate outside cocktail sticks to produce a separate triangle.

332
Move 2 from any one of A B C or D to form squares at E and F.

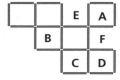

333
Number moves clockwise by original number.

334
48. (a x b) – (c x d) = ef

335
It was a sleeping policeman (traffic-calming road bump).

336
A. Seat Seam Team Tram
B. Head Heal Teal Taal Tail
C. Stone Shone Shine Thine Think Thick Trick Brick
D. White Whine Chine Chink Clink Blink Blank Black (also Clank, Clack, Black)
E. Here Hare Hark Hank Hunk Junk
F. Fair Fail Fall Fill Rill Rile Ride
G. Write Writs Waits Warts Wards Cards
H. Brown Brows Brews Trews Trees
I. Glass Class Clans Clank Clink Chink China
J. Green Breen Bleed Blend Bland Blank Black

337
21. A + B + E + F = CD

338
976. Take 2 to the power of 10, which gives you the lowest number above 1000.
$2^{10} = 1024$
Then use the formula 1024 – 2 (1024 – 1000) = 976

339
A seahorse

340
S = 0   T = 6
A = 1   O = 7
C = 2   R = 8
P = 3   L = 9
E = 4

341
8 male plus 6 female.

342
Letter moves clockwise by one less than its alphabetical position.

343
m, x. 2a – b + c = d. Use alphabetical values of each letter.

344

1)

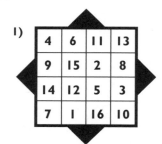

2)

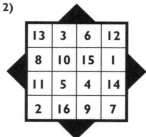

345
20. (squared) + 4.

346
Any hybrid, such as a jackass, hinney, etc.

347
Halfway between A and C. This would give a maximum distance of 10 minutes to any town.

348
Again, remove alternate outside cocktail sticks and overlay them on the others.

349
They suggested drawing a line on the tall man's chest level to where the short man stood. Any shot above that line was not to count.

350

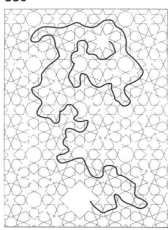

351
Rain, for which Iran is an anagram (as Nepal is an anagram for plane, and China for chain).

352

Name	Age	Ride	Food
Sam	14	Dodgems	Hot dog
Joe	11	Big dipper	Fries
Don	12	Whirligig	Candy floss
Len	15	Crocodile	Gum
Ron	13	Mountain	Ice cream

353
E. The contents of each hexagon are determined by merging the contents of the two hexagons immediately below, except that two identical lines disappear.

354
D. The large circle moves 180°; the small white circle moves 180°; the black circle moves 90°; and the black dot moves 180°.

355
1. If you don't believe this, hold the book up to a mirror. You will see that with the inclusion of the above, the numbers 1, 2, 3, 4, 5 appear in sequence.

356
B. A and F are the same, as are C and D, and E and G.

357

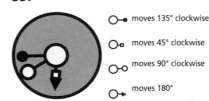

moves 135° clockwise
moves 45° clockwise
moves 90° clockwise
moves 180°

358
B.

359

Name	Country	Birds	Collective Noun
Albert	Belgium	Owls	Parliament
Roger	France	Crows	Murder
Harold	Germany	Ravens	Unkindness
Cameron	Scotland	Plovers	Wing
Edward	England	Starlings	Murmuration

360
1. Pampered.
2. Medieval.
3. Seashell.
4. Farewell.

361
36. (− 11) x 4.

362
.5. (Top row − 3rd row) + 2nd row = 4th row.

363

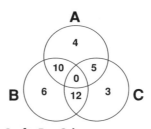

17		6
9		3

Move clockwise by the given number plus 1.

364
28. First digit x Second digit = First and Second digits, and Third digit x Fourth digit = Third and Fourth Digits.

365
41. The grid values are the same as for answer 37.

16	9	8	1
15	10	7	2
14	11	6	3
13	12	5	4

366
54. (Top left x Bottom left) − (Top right x Bottom right).

367
17. Black = 4; White = 7; Shaded = 2.

368
a) 14, b) 4, c) 18, d) 7, e) 8

369
10. (Outside top x outside bottom) − Inside). Left side − right side.

370
42. (Left window x Right window) − Door.

371
1. Sha.   2. Pur.   3. Mat.
4. Gri.   5. Far.

372
1. Clairvoyant.   6. Cruelty.
2. Correct.   7. Counter.
3. Casual.   8. Chastise.
4. Catapult.   9. Cheap.
5. Cherub.   10. Child

373
18. Outside pair added = opposite one inside.

374
71. (x 4) − 13.

375

A = Craft, B = Science,
C = Humanities.
1. 12.   2. 12.   3. 27.
4. 13.   5. 20.   6. 4.

376
12. (Bottom left x Bottom right) − (Top left + Top right).

377
20. Black = 5; White = 3; Shaded = 4.

378
1125. Multiply the previous two numbers.

379

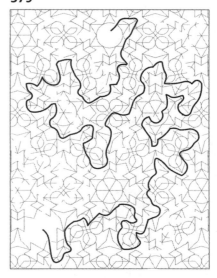

380
The jewels were thrown on to quicksand. Little Joe had forgotten about it, but Big Al made him try to get the jewels. Little Joe tried and sank without trace. The police did not even know that Little Joe was dead.

381
4. (squared) − 5.

382

T	C	R	O	B	I	N	M
H	R	I	P	A	K	O	Y
R	A	E	U	T	S	C	C
U	N	E	P	Q	B	H	O
S	E	T	U	U	I	O	K
H	I	I	C	C	O	W	C
T	T	K	K	O	O	R	E
O	W	L	I	B	R	E	G

BAT   GECKO   PUP
BUCK   GERBIL   ROBIN
CHICK   GROUPER   ROC
CHOW   KITE   ROOK
COB   MOSQUITO   THRUSH
COW   OKAPI   TIT
CRANE   OWL

383
7^2 = 49. The 6 has been turned over to convert it into a 9 and the 2 becomes a square.

384
B. There are four different symbols grouped ABC, ABD, BCD and, in answer B, ACD, which completes the set of symbols which are in order and that have one ommision.

A   B   C   D

385
B. It is a straight-sided figure within a curved figure. The rest are curved figures within a straight-sided one.

386
20. Start at 10 and jump to alternate segments, adding 1, then 2, then 3 and so on.

387
D. The small circle moves two on and then one back. The middle-size circle moves one back and then two on. The large circle moves one on and then two back.

388
Divide the central number by 5 to give the top number. Add the digits of the central number to give the bottom left number. Reverse the digits of the central number and divide by three to give the bottom right number.

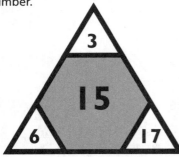

389
25 minutes. As the man leaves home according to his normal schedule it is earlier than 6.30 pm when he picks up his wife. As the total journey saves 10 minutes, that must be the same time it takes the man from the point he picks up his wife to the station and back to the same point. Assuming that it takes an equal five minutes each way he has therefore picked up his wife five minutes before he would normally, which means 6.20pm. So his wife must have walked from 6.00pm to 6.25pm, that is for 25 minutes.

390
1536. First two digits x second two digits form next number.

391

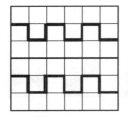

392
An American gallon is equal to about 0.833 imperial (UK) gallons.

393
Three cheques of $20. Penny, Mary, and Claire should give Ann $20.

394
425. Alphabetical value of each letter is squared and added together by line.

395
The second player copies every move made by Player 1.

396

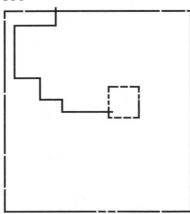

397
4-digit numbers made from 1, 4, 6 and 7 will always be divisible by 9 and 3, so the answer is no in both cases, except if the 6 is turned upside down into a 9. If the numbers were 1, 4, 7 and 9, it would never be divisible by 9 but still always divisible by 3.

398
Miss Marple.

399
110. Add the numbers on opposite corners of each square and multiply these results to get the number in each square.

400
81. The number of letters in the word, squared.

401
Inspector Morse and Sherlock Holmes

402
Mr Smith only managed to run 1.8 miles before he had to hail the taxi.

403
1. 5.   2. 3.
3. Orange Juice.   4. Apple, Pizza,
   Potato and Tomato.
5. 2.   6. Wednesday.
7. 4.   8. 2pm.
9. 29.   10. Bushes.

404
AL, IN, IT.

405
Washington   Denver
Dallas   Baltimore
Cincinnati   New Orleans.

406
SEARCH.

407
36 yards of tape.

408
Chianti.

409
"The sun was setting over the city as it started to rain. I pulled up the collar of my coat, and shuddered."

410
"Be on the train to Belgrade at five" Each vowel is replaced by the one before it, e=a and so on.

411
8.

412
Third Ave. The first letter of each food spells it out.

413
S. All the other letters contain a closed space.

414
GEORGE LAZENBY.

415
By throwing the ball straight up in the air.

416
71. (Left window x Door) + Right window.

417
1. C & E.   2. A & D.
3. B & D.   4. B & C.
5. A & E.

418
C. Others rotate into the same shape.

419
C.

420
E.

421
She lives on the 27th floor. The elevator came down from the 36th to the 28th floor – nine floors; or it came up from the first to the 27th floor – 27 floors, so there is a 3:1 chance of it going up than down.

422
104. (3n – 1), (3n – 2), (3n – 3), (3n – 4), etc.

423
360. All digits multiplied.

424
60. (Right window – Door) x Left window.

425
C. Others are Roman numerals rotated 90° anti- (counter) clockwise.

426
CAMEL.

427
F.

428
1st, E; 2nd, C; 3rd, F; 4th, D; 5th, A; 6th, B.

429
1st, Rick; 2nd, John; 3rd, Alex; 4th, Sean; 5th, Anne; 6th, Liam; 7th, Sandra; 8th, Robert.

430
1. I. (Wave – Noise).
2. Y. (Hone – Yeast).
3. O. (Live – Coast).
4. F. (Rile – Flake).
5. S. (Wait – Shoot).
6. A. (Pint – Bloat).
7. T. (Rust – Deter).
8. T. (Vial – Table).

431
1. 3.   2. 12 and 13.   3. 4.
4. –21.   4. 4.

432
1. B.   2. D   3. A.
4. E.   5. C.

433
1. C.   2. D
3. F.   4. A.
5. B.   6. None.

434
EAS to give PEARS, REAPS, SPARE, SPEAR.

435
The man was an native American chief and he used the blanket for smoke signals to start a battle.

436
They were working on a long bridge with no spare room at the side of the tracks. It was a much shorter distance to the end of the bridge where the train was coming from. They were able to get to the end and jump to one side.

437
He had bought a round-trip ticket for himself but not for his wife. The clerk thought this odd. When the police checked, the policeman had taken insurance out for his wife's life. He confessed to everything.

438
It was a library and she had to pay a fine for being overdue.

439

11 + 12 + 1 + 2 = 26
10 + 3 + 9 + 4 = 26
5 + 6 + 7 + 8 = 26.

440
If the shorter pieces, placed end to end, are longer than the largest piece, then they will form a triangle.

441
C. B and D, and A and E are the same, with large and small circles reversed.

442
D. Each pair of circles produces the circle above by carrying on elements that they have in common. Different elements disappear.

443
Mr Allen had a vacation of 15 days, but with a little more careful planning it could have lasted 20 days.

444
The friend was male and his name was Michael.

445

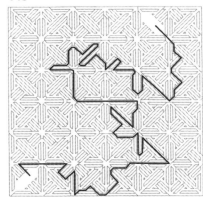

446

S	C	A	R	L	E	T
C		B		A		E
A	N	A	G	R	A	M
L		T		G		P
E	L	E	M	E	N	T

447

					L		
				M	O	W	
			C	A	V	E	S
		H	O	N	E	D	
	T	E	N	O	R		
	S	I	X	E	R		
P	A	L	E	D			
M	A	T	E	D			
M	O	V	E	D			
D	A	T	E	S			
R	O	D					
R							

448

S		A		R	A	D	I	O
T	A	M	E		N		D	
A		A		S	T	I	L	L
C	A	S	T		L		E	
K		S	I	N	E	W		S
	C		M		R	A	P	T
D	O	U	B	T		L		O
	I		E		S	T	A	R
S	N	O	R	E		Z		M

449
Undercover

450
PER.

451
ASSASSINATION

452
IN, RE, AT.

453
Brooklyn Bridge.

454

Name	Class	Subject	Sport
Alice	6	Algebra	Squash
Betty	2	Biology	Running
Clara	4	History	Swimming
Doris	3	Geography	Tennis
Elizabeth	5	Chemistry	Basketball

455
"Meet me near the old bridge at nine". The alphanumeric number of each letter is worked out from z. So, e = 5, 5 from z = v.

456
TER.

457
AE, OW, ST.

458
D. P is six letters away from J in the alphabet. So is D.

459
Caught.

460

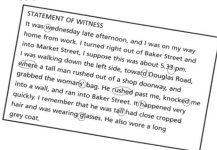

STATEMENT OF WITNESS
It was wednesday late afternoon, and I was on my way home from work. I turned right out of Baker Street and into Market Street, I suppose this was about 5.33 pm. I was walking down the left side, toward Douglas Road, where a tall man rushed out of a shop doorway, and grabbed the woman's bag. He rushed past me, knocked me into a wall, and ran into Baker Street. It happened very quickly. I remember that he was tall, had close cropped hair and was wearing glasses. He also wore a long grey coat.

461
P. In each pair of letters, P is middle way between them in the alphabet.

462
22 square yards

463
Each has exactly the same number of vowels in their name as in the place name.

464
1. 175   2. 140   3. 7.

465

466
It is possible but there has to be a compensating factor. Jim has $8 at the start so Bill can win only $8 even if he wins all 10 frames. Jim, however, can win a large sum if he wins every frame: $8, $12, $18, $27, etc. However, Bill can win a small amount overall even if he wins two fewer frames than Jim. The order of Jim's winning and losing frames makes no difference to the final total.

Frame	Jim	Jim has $8
1	win	$12.00
2	lose	$6.00
3	lose	$3.00
4	win	$4.50
5	win	$6.75
6	lose	$3.38
7	win	$5.07
8	win	$7.60
9	win	$11.40
10	lose	$5.70 = loses $2.30 from starting $8.00

467
B.

468
"I will arrive tomorrow. Check no one is watching the house." The initial "C" is the clue. C becomes I, D becomes J, and so on.

469
A.

470
D. The last letter in the sequence should have been Z.

471
5.30am on the next day.

472

473
The lock is of the Yale type (which explains why there is no keyhole on the inside of the door). Fred simply turned the latch and walked out.

474
Lucky Mr Thrifty can expect to receive $83,026.73 from the sale of the land.

475
F. Column 1 is added to column 2 to make column 3. Similarly, line 1 is added to line 2 to make line 3. In both cases, repeated symbols disappear.

476
3A.

477
Arrange them into groups of three, each totalling 1000.
457 + 168 + 375 = 1000
532 + 217 + 251 = 1000
349 + 218 + 433 = 1000
713 + 106 + 181 = 1000

478
C. The squares become circles and all segments remain in the same positions, but dark becomes light and vice versa.

479
A D G H F B E C.

480
D. Only when an orange or white triangle appears three times in the same position in the four surrounding triangles is it transferred to the central circle.

481
A. Instead of being joined at the top, the two bars are joined at the middle segment. In addition, dark becomes light and vice versa.

482

CREATURE	COUNTRY	APPEARANCE	TREASURE
ELF	NORWAY	MALEVOLENT	DIAMONDS
GOBLIN	WALES	REPULSIVE	GOLD
TROLL	SCOTLAND	OBNOXIOUS	RUBIES
LEPRECHAUN	IRELAND	MISCHIEVOUS	EMERALDS
IMP	ENGLAND	UGLY	SILVER

483
D. One dot is in a circle only, with the other dot in both a triangle and a square.

484
37: The worst case is all 21 blue, all 14 striped, and two black.

485
Numbers 1 and 3.
Most people turn 1 & 4 but this is not correct. 1 must be turned; if it has a triangle the answer is yes; if not, it is no. 2 does not need to be turned. If 4 is turned green the answer is yes; if white, it is no.

This does not help as it gives no information about 3. Card 3 needs to be turned to see if its other side is black. If it is black, the answer is no; if white, then it is yes. Therefore 1 and 3 must be turned.

486
$27.

487
B. Top circle gets smaller. Bottom curved rectangle gets larger then starts again. Central circle gets larger. Torpedo shape gets smaller. Right hand circle alternates.

488

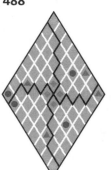

489

NAME	TEAM	POSITION	SHIRT
DAVID	GREEN BAY PACKERS	QUARTERBACK	YELLOW
CLAUDE	DALLAS COWBOYS	TACKLE	BLUE
VICTOR	CLEVELAND BROWNS	RUNNING BACK	RED
SAMUEL	OAKLAND RAIDERS	CORNERBACK	BLACK
BILL	CAROLINA PANTHERS	KICKER	PURPLE

490

FIRST NAME	SURNAME	HOUSE NAME	FRONT DOOR
MABEL	STEVENS	ROSE COTTAGE	BLUE
DOROTHY	HILL	HILL HOUSE	RED
GRACE	SULLIVAN	VALLEY VIEW	WHITE
TRACY	PETERS	RIVERSIDE	BLACK
PEGGY	RIVERS	WHITE HOUSE	GREEN
CHERYL	MANBY	CHEZ NOUS	ORANGE

491
Ernie Black.

492
E. Others rotate into the same shape.

493
A. Others rotate into the same shape.

494
93. Right window^2 – Left window^2 – Door.

495
360. (n x 5), (n x 4), (n x 3), etc.

496
360. All digits multiplied.

497
36. (– 13) x 6.

498

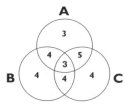

A = Sprint, B = Hurdles, C = Relay.
1. 27.   2. 4.   3. 12.
4. 12.   5. 4.   6. 13.

499

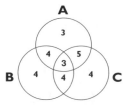

A = Labrador, B = Alsatian,
C = Greyhound.
1. 9.   2. 7.   3. 10.
4. 3.   5. 4.   6. 21.

500

501

CATGUT	KENNEL
DAMSEL	MANNER
DISMAL	PILLAR
FELLOW	REBUTS
GEEGAW	ROBUST
JEWELS	SILVER

502

G	L	A	R	E
L	O	N	E	R
A	N	G	E	R
R	E	E	V	E
E	R	R	E	D

503
Eric is a teacher.

504
D. 224 X $5 and 53 X $10.

505
B.
$339 X $1 and $63 X $20. TOTAL= $1599.

506
29. There are four numbers between 3-8, five between 8-14, and so on.

507
C.

508
L. Clockwise, the number of the following letter.

509
B.

510
4. All rows and columns add up to 10.

511
C.

512
33. Each number is added to itself, then 1 is subtracted.

513
23. All the other numbers added together equal 8.

514
N.

515
317.

516
1R on row 3, column 1.

517
18 days. If it takes a man 27 days to drink one barrel, he drinks 0.037 of a barrel each day. Similarly, a woman drinks 0.0185 of a barrel each day. Added together, a day's combined drinking consumes 0.0555 of a barrel. In this case, to drink the whole barrel takes 18.018 days.

518
8. The number of consonants in the words in the box.

519
"CORNER OF MADISON AND MALL." "D" is a clue to the code. O=A, P=B, and so on.

520
1. The unscrambled words are: HESITANT, BRAVE, COURAGEOUS, INTREPID, and FEARLESS. All of the words mean fearless except Hesitant, which means fearful.

521
Only Ed McBain begins with a vowel.

522

523

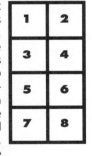

524
D. In the example, the two circles become one big circle. The remaining figure then goes inside the large circle, the triangles attached to the arms. Green figures/lines become pale and vice-versa. Similarly, the two squares turn into a large square and from pale to green; the green circles attached to the green arms go inside the square and turn pale.

525
Charlie was a cuckoo. The punctuality refers to a cuckoo clock.

526
B. There are eight different patterns within the rectangle. Between stages one and two, patterns one and two swap places, then continue to swap at each stage. In stage three patterns three and four start swapping, therefore in stage four patterns five and six start to swap too. Once a pair starts to swap places it continues to swap at each stage.

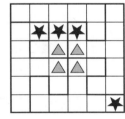

527
1:5. There are six possible pairings of the four balls:
1. Red/red
2. Red no. 1/white
3. Red no. 1/black
4. Red no. 2/white
5. Red no. 2/black
6. Black/white.
The black/white combination has not been drawn out. This leaves five possible combinations; therefore the chances that the red/red pairing has been drawn out are 1:5.

528
He was cleaning the inside of the windows.

529
He was sky-diving and his parachute failed to open.

530
15 consecutive days.

531
a) Cow – Cattle or   Ox – Oxen
b) Pig – Piglet or   Cat – Kitten
c) Sheep – Sheep or   Swine –
Swine.

532
a) 91
b) The easy way is to start with a square of 1 x 1, then 2 x 2 and so on until you see the sequence.

1 x 1 = 1
2 x 2 = 5
3 x 3 = 14 (3 x 3) + 5
4 x 4 = 30 (4 x 4) + 14
5 x 5 = 55 (5 x 5) + 30
6 x 6 = 91 (6 x 6) + 55
7 x 7 = (7 x 7) + 55 = 104.

533
They are the binary alphabetic positions of the vowels.
A = 1 E = 5 I = 9 O = 15 U = 21

534

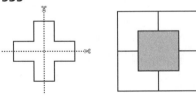

535

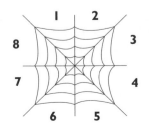

536
A.

537
Plum (Add the B-line to Plum to make Plumb line)

538
With the lights in the house dimmed she held a glass to the wall covering the hole and shone a beam of light through the glass into the hole. When the insect moved out of the hole and into the glass she slid a card over the end of the glass.

539
She had a mains-operated electric clock. The power to her house had been cut off for just over 30 minutes while she slept. As a result the buzzer was late.

540
32 : It follows the formula 2^{n-1} where n equals the number of folds. $2^{6-1} = 2^5 = 32$

541
πr^2 = Area of a circle
The area of a tarus (washer-shaped item) = πh^2

542
Flowers: Iris, Pansy, Orchid, and Aster.

543
The words contain: Tie, Shoe, Hat, and Belt.

544
41. Consonants are worth 5, vowels 7. Caspian = 21+21.

545
100 = 16 + 16 + 17 + 17 + 17 + 17, only one solution.

546

3 - 6	2 - 6	2 - 5	3 - 3	0 - 0
3 - 5	0 - 2	0 - 1	4 - 6	4 - 5
1 - 1	5 - 6	5 - 5	1 - 3	1 - 2
2 - 4	1 - 4	2 - 2	0 - 3	6 - 6
2 - 3	0 - 4	4 - 4	3 - 4	1 - 5

547
a) 4   b) 5   c) 7   d) 11   e) 18

548
A = 99m²   G = 34m²
B = 78m²   H = 9m²
C = 21m²   I = 16m²
D = 77m²   J = 25m²
E = 43m²   K = 41m²
F = 57m²

549
(A + B) – (C + D) = E.
The answer is 4.

550
36. Feet positions in web.

551
Jupiter.

552
While the family were out, a pipe had burst and the floor was under two inches of water on which the balloons were floating.

553

G	E	L	I	D	#	T	#	L	O	P	E	S
U	#	I	#	E	L	O	P	E	#	O	#	E
L	I	N	E	N	#	T	#	V	A	L	I	D
C	#	E	#	I	R	A	T	E	#	E	#	A
H	A	R	E	M	#	L	#	R	I	S	E	N
#	S	#	D	#				#	S	#	M	#
S	T	R	I	P		5		A	S	T	I	R
#	E	#	C	#				#	U	#	T	#
G	R	A	T	E	#	S	#	F	E	A	S	T
A	#	L	#	N	I	C	E	R	#	L	#	A
P	O	I	N	T	#	O	#	E	A	T	E	R
E	#	V	#	E	X	U	D	E	#	E	#	N
S	T	E	E	R	#	T	#	D	A	R	T	S

554
Since three people buy all three papers, 14 buy the *Echo* and the *Moon*, 12 buy the *Moon* and the *Advertizer*, and 13 buy the *Echo* and the *Advertizer*. Since 70 buy the *Echo*, the number who buy the *Echo* only must be 70 – 14 – 13 – 3 = 40. 60 buy the *Moon*, so the number who buy the *Moon* only is 60 – 12– 14 – 3 = 31. 50 buy the *Advertizer*, so the number who buy the *Advertizer* only is 50 – 12 – 13 – 3 = 22. Thus the newsagent has 40 + 14 + 31 +12 + 3 +13 + 22 customers, that is 135.

555
361. + 2, then squared.

556

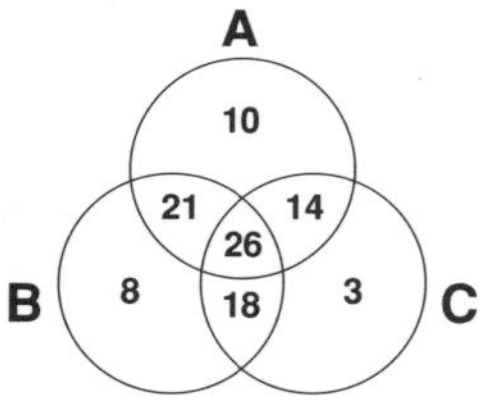

A = Soaps, B = Movies, C = Documentaries.

1. 21. 2. 10. 3. 18.
4. 8. 5. 53. 6. 21.

557
126. (Top left + Top right + Bottom left) – Bottom right.

558
82. (Bottom left x Top right) + Top left + Bottom right.

559
153. Door^2 – (Left window + Right window).

560
T. The series is formed from the initial letters in the Fibonacci series.

561
E. Number the alphabet backwards (Z=1, A=26). Top row added to middle row equals number in bottom row. Therefore Y(2)+G(20)=E(22).

562
1. C. 2. E. 3. D.
4. B and C. 5. C.
6. Nobody.

563
TARSE, giving EARST, RATES, RESAT, TARES, TEARS, TERAS.

564
1. 3.87. 116 passes for 30 students. 2. 3.32. 83 passes for 25 students. 3. 58.

565
42.

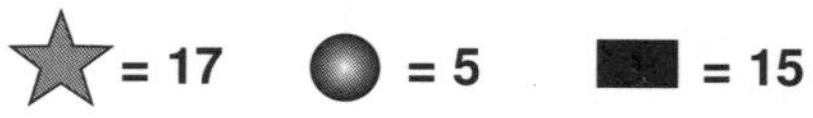

566
1. 500, 1000. Two methods. Either consecutive Roman numerals or an alternating series, x 5, x 2.
2. 203. Two methods. Either multiply previous number by 3 and deduct 1, or + 5, + 15, + 45, + 135.
3. 603. (previous + 3) x 3.
4. 6, 3, 2. Numbers 1 to 9 in alphabetic order.
5. 190. (+ 1 (x 2).
6. 41. Two methods. 5 + 1^2 , 5 + 2^2, 5 + 3^2, or series + 3, + 5, + 7, etc.

567
328. Along each row multiply first two digits of first number to get first two digits of second number. Multiply last two digits of first number to get last two of second number and join them. 4 x 8 = 32, 2 x 4 = 8; 328.

568

North ◄—— Pier ——► South

Name	Joe	Fred	Dick	Henry	Malcolm
Occupation	Banker	Electrician	Professor	Plumber	Salesman
Town	L.A.	Orlando	Tucson	New York	St Louis
Bait	Worms	Bread	Maggots	Shrimps	Meal
Catch	6	15	10	9	1

569
960. (Top left x Top right x Bottom left) ÷ Bottom right.

570

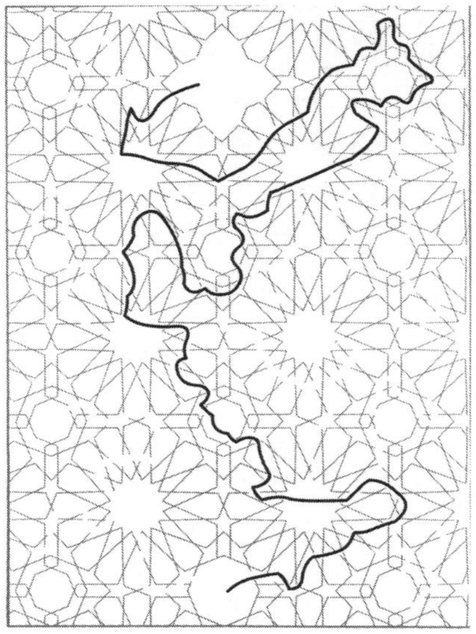

571
–37. (3n – 7).

572
100. (Bottom left x Bottom right) + Top left + Top right.

573
Shapes with straight sides have names of letters with no curves. Only the list under the circle has names with curved letters so that is where ROBERT fits.

574
E. The others are made of two shapes.

575
4752. In each number the first two digits are multiplied by the last two digits to give the next number along the row.
54 x 88 = 4752.

576
The simplest way is to read the label on the end of the reel.

577
The probability that it will be fine on Sunday is found by working out the total number of combinations of weather changes for the next three days. They are:
Fine, fine, fine.
Wet, fine, fine.
Fine, wet, fine.
Wet, wet, fine.
Then take the probability for each combination and add them together:
$\frac{3}{4} \times \frac{3}{4} \times \frac{3}{4} + \frac{1}{4} \times \frac{1}{3} \times \frac{3}{4} + \frac{3}{4} \times \frac{1}{4} \times \frac{1}{3} + \frac{1}{4} \times \frac{2}{3} \times \frac{1}{3}$, which equals $\frac{347}{576}$ – so I think I'll go walking on Sunday!

578

						P						
					D	A	Y					
				M	A	N	E	S				
			S	U	L	T	A	N	A			
		P	I	L	E	#	R	O	P	E		
	S	A	N	E	#	#	#	W	O	R	D	
E	P	I	C	#	#	#	#	#	L	O	O	M
	A	N	E	W	#	#	#	N	O	D	E	
		T	R	I	P	#	R	A	G	E		
			E	C	O	N	O	M	Y			
				K	N	A	V	E				
					D	I	E					
						L						

579
Rivers: Seine, Rhone, Congo, Ganges, and Wear.

580
The words contain: Cod, Roe, Pike, and Hake.

581
Yes, the words are all anagrams of European cities: Oslo, Cork, Paris, Basle, Siena, Sedan, Reims. Born is an anagram of Brno.

582
a) 19 b) 22 c) 3 d) 45 e) 8.

583
Edward Peters; Robert Edwards; Peter Roberts. Mr Peters must be Edward because the man who spoke last is Robert and he is not Mr Peters.

584
California.

585
D. The five symbols run along the top row, then along the second row, etc.

586
85426. Replace the letters with their alphabetical value (A=1, B=2, etc.), then add them to lines 1 and 2 of the previous box to create line 3.

587
Chrysanthemum.

588
Brontosaurus.

B S R B	R R T U	O T N A
B U O T	U O A S	A A T O
T R O U	S O B A	O B O S

589
2S on the 2nd row 2nd column.

590

591

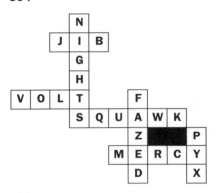

592
1. SICKNESS   2. IGNORANT.

593
Patricia Cornwell
Ed McBain
Elmore Leonard
John Grisham
Carol O'Connell

Each letter is replaced with the one following it in the alphabet.

594
Any vowel. Vowels are worth 2 and consonants 1. Columns with vowels add up to 5, and those without to 4

595
Her name is an anagram of GIRL ON AN EAGLE.

596
Professions: Chef, Miner, Driver and Joiner.

597
The letters form an anagram of JUST ONE WORD.

598
A stitch in time saves nine.

599
B. The six symbols run down the first column, then spiral round to the middle of the grid.

600
76652. Replace the letters with their alphabetical value, then deduct them from the sum of lines 1 and 2 of the previous box to create line 3.

601
Phantom of the Opera.

602
San Francisco

S	A	N		N	
O	E	F	M	N	F
B		H		H	
A		I		I	
C	I	J	F	G	R
L		D		A	
M		E		B	
S	M	N	E	F	A
I		C		N	

603
Move both outside cocktail sticks from B or C and complete the squares on E and F. This creates 10 squares of 1 x 1, 4 squares of 2 x 2, and one square of 3 x 3.

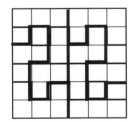

604
32. (A x B) divided by C = D.

605

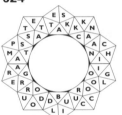

606
Six of one and half a dozen of another.

607
At first glance the best option seems to be the first. However, the second option works out best.

First option	($500 increase after each 12 months)
First year	$10,000 + $10,000 = $20,000
Second year	$10,250 + $10,250 = $20,500
Third year	$10,500 + $10,500 = $21,000
Fourth year	$10,750 + $10,750 = $21,500

Second option	($125 increase after each 6 months)
First year	$10,000 + $10,125 = $20,125
Second year	$10,250 + $10,375 = $20,625
Third year	$10,500 + $10,625 = $21,125
Fourth year	$10,750 + $10,875 = $21,625

608
Each contains a girl's name: MAY, SUE, KIM, GRACE, GINA.

609
Herring (her ring).

610
1A on the inner circle at the 4 o'clock position.

611
S to give Haste, Laser, Miser, and Nasty.

612
1. DIARY and DAIRY.
2. PEACH and CHEAP.
3. TALE and LATE.
4. STOP and POTS.
5. EAT and TEA.

613
Marina, Abduct, Tanker, Raisin, Normal, Lasted, Decide, Embalm.

614

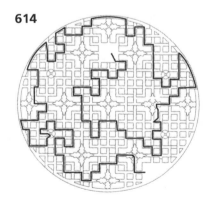

615
The nightwatchman was fired for sleeping on the job.

616

617
It has been written without the letter 'E'.

618
F and 4. Each vertical column is an anagram of a number.

619
8 hours.

620
19. Each vowel in a name is given 2 points. Each consonant gets 1 point. These are then added together to give the service number.

621
You need roman numerals V(5) and IX(9) and EN (two thirds of ten) to make VIXEN.

622
Trap, lived, regal, and bats all create another word when read backward.

623
a) 20, b) 12, c) 21, d) 18, e) 122.

624

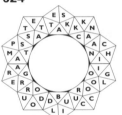

625
Pear, Plum and Lime.
People
Eyelid
Autumn
Rhymes.

626
Pause, lulls, islet, and tests.

627
40. The formula is (n x 3) – 5.

628
9. $(3n + 0^2)$, $(2n + 1^2)$, $(n + 2^2)$, $(0 + 3^2)$.

629
A. Binary system, start at 5 and add 3 each time. You can also find the answer by treating the images as a negative and mirror-imaging them.

630
B. Numbers rotate clockwise by the number given.

631
1. French.   2. A.
3. A.   4. Two.
5. D.

632
1. Lunar.
2. Millet.
3. Eternal.
4. Deplete.
5. Herbivore.
6. Content.
7. Bagpipes.
8. Nullify.
9. Secure.
10. Magnate.

633
39. (x 4) + 3.

634
Add the two digits of each number together to give the number of places the numbers move round.

635
Eleven. The values are totalled in each grid to give the number shown. The sum of the values of triangles and circles gives the answer. Δ = 2, O = 1.

636
1. There are 4: B3, F4, C6, F6.
2. D4 and D5. Both have 81.
3. E2. 109.
4. F. 102.
5. 7. 85.
6. Col F. 6.
7. Col C and Row 5. Both add up to 636.

637
63. Reading clockwise, the upper half numbers are multiplied by 4, 5, 6, 7, respectively to equal the diagonally opposite lower sector.

638

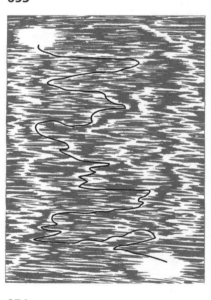

639
Horse racing.

640

M	A	L	L	E	T			S	A	B	R	E	S
A		I			H			A			E		E
S	A	M	P	L	E			B	A	N	G	E	R
T		I			S			L			A		V
E				G	E	N	E	S	I	S		R	
R	I	S	E	R		A			O	L	D	E	R
				A	N	V	I	L					
C	A	S	E	S		A			V	A	L	V	E
L			L		L				O			E	D
I			N		E				L			C	
M	E	D	I	A	L			S	C	R	A	P	E
B			A		O				T			L	R
S	A	L	L	O	W			S	T	E	E	D	S

641

I	S	L	E	T				A	B	O	D	E
S	T	O	V	E				B	E	V	E	L
L	O	S	E	R				O	V	O	I	D
E	V	E	N	S				D	E	I	C	E
T	E	R	S	E	R	A	S	E	L	D	E	R
					R	O	M	A	N			
					A	M	P	L	E			
					S	A	L	E	M			
P	L	A	T	E	N	E	M	Y	E	A	S	T
L	A	T	E	R				E	E	R	I	E
A	T	T	A	R				A	R	I	E	L
T	E	A	S	E				S	I	E	G	E
E	R	R	E	D				T	E	L	E	X

642
Pussy Galore.

643
There were three male agents and four female agents.

644
The first man places a $1 bill on the counter. The second man puts down three quarters, two dimes and a nickel – amounting to one dollar. Had he wanted a 90-cent beer he had the change to offer the exact amount.

645
433.

646
51. In all the other numbers the first is smaller than the second.

647
B. The inside elements rotate at 30 degrees anti clockwise each time.

648
X. If the alphabet was joined together in a circle, X would be exactly halfway from K.

649
"The Lincoln Memorial. Saturday. Noon." The first letter in the message is replaced with the last, and so on.

650
RHYME, because it has no vowels.

651
1. GUN 2. DISTRESSED.

652
1. Parson St.
2. South St.
3. Parson St. & Loftus Rd.
4. 2
5. Car Parts Shop
6. Carol Jennings
7. Philip Capewell
8. 2
9. Methodist
10. Carol Jennings
11. 15
12. Parson St.
13. 10, Parson St.
14. Joan Fox
15. John Allen
16. Shoe Shop
17. Valley Road
18. By the Sports Shop
19. 1
20. 3

653

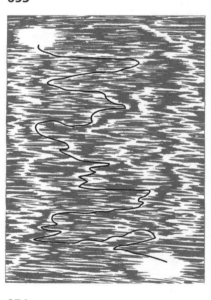

654
He keeps ducks.

655
50. (Window + window) – door = roof. (37 + 28) [65] – 15 = 50.

656
30. (Arm x arm) – (leg x leg) = head. (8 x 9) [72] – (6 x 7) [42] = 30.

657
359. Top number + lower number = middle number. 462 + 197 = 659.

658
1. B. Talent.
2. C. Genuine.
3. D. Dry.
4. C. Unruly.
5. C. Bequeath.
6. C. Weak.
7. D. Degrade.
8. C. Vouch.
9. C. Ruminate.
10. E. Flaccid.
11. A. Feral.
12. E. Pungent.
13. D. Combine.
14. A. Constant.
15. B. Fast.
16. B. Kindliness.
17. C. Plead.
18. D. Inactive.
19. D. Obscurity
20. B. Maintenance.

659
1625. Add times as numbers. 135 + 600 = 735; 245 + 1215 = 1460; 520 + 1105 = 1625.

660
Mr Carter is the drover.

661
−15. The sum of the values of white and black squares gives the answer.

 = 5   = −5

662
MEXICO:
M=1,000
C=100
X=10.

663
3. Sum of diagonally opposite segments equals 11.

664
4. (Left arm x right leg) – (right arm x left leg) = head. (12 x 7) [84] – (4 x 20) [80] = 4.

665
−272. Top number – lower number = middle number.

666
E. The figures rotate one sector at a time.

667
B. Shapes rotate in sequence.

668
294. Add numbers on hands and complete the sum. (6 + 9) [15] x (1 + 6) [7] = 105; (6 + 3) [9] x (9 + 3) [12] = 108; (12 + 9) [21] x (2 + 12) [14] = 294.

669

18	6	4	30	47	29
45	30	6	18	17	2
1	21	1	42	23	5
3	28	7	17	1	6
44	4	32	43	30	40

670

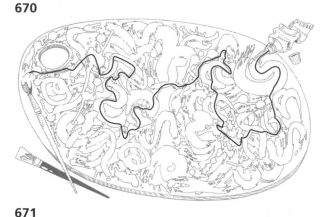

671

672

673
The cat. Fred and Ginger were goldfish, and the cat had knocked their bowl over.

674
25.22.14.12
The alphanumeric values of the first 2 letters of the name are added together. Then the next 2 are taken, and so on. The last letter in each name is ignored.

675
C.

676
O. The blood group letter is the one before the first letter of each name.

677
Martin has blood group "O".

678
B.

679
15 square yards

680
Bangkok

681
P. In each column, the alphanumeric values are added together and divided by 5.

682
Dial 2 and Code 1. Each number is the total amount of letters in the alphabet between A and the first letter of the word.

683
Mel Gibson. Bruce Willis. Clint Eastwood. Eddie Murphy. Harrison Ford. Danny Glover

684

685

686

687

6	2	3	4	4	3
3	5	5	2	6	2
5	3	1	3	5	0
2	4	5	3	0	5
3	3	4	6	6	5

688
15.

689
–61. (27 – 2n).

690
A. Shapes rotate in sequence.

691
B. All use three lines.

692
1. R.   2. C.   3. L.   4. O.
5. G.   6. M.   7. H.   8. T.
9. N.   10. U.

693
1. L. (PATE – GLOAT).
2. L. (FEET – GOLD).
3. R. (PICE – BREAM).
4. G. (RIND – GAMBLE).
5. D. (DOGE – ABIDED).
6. O. (LIVE – FLOAT).
7. A. (PINT – BLOAT).
8. R. (GAPE – BERET).

694
1. G. Makes Ruing and Grant.
2. H. Makes Booth and Heel.
3. K. Makes Tank and Knot.
4. T. Makes Leant and Thigh.
5. E. Makes Theme and Every.
6. D. Makes Seed and Draft.
7. N. Makes Pawn and Never.
8. T. Makes Event and Teach.
9. E. Makes Lunge and Eland.
10. O. Makes Cameo and Open.

695
16. (x 2) ÷ 3.

696
1. 6.   2. 24.   3. 9.
4. 12.   5. 18.

697
1. C.   2. A.
3. B.   4. A and C.
5. 55 silver, 25 bronze.

698
1. Retentive.   2. Random.
3. Regular.   4. Ready.
5. Release.

699
Charlie puts the handkerchief under a door and stands on the corner at the other side.

700
4752. In each number the first two digits are multiplied by the last two digits to give the next number along the row.
54 x 88 = 4752.

701
3. (A + B) x C = D + E.

702

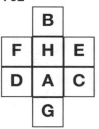

703

3	6	4	4	8	6
9	6	6	7	9	2
5	6	5	6	2	7
7	6	7	5	9	3
8	9	4	8	9	7
4	9	6	8	4	6

704
22. The grid values are shown and the sum of the positions gives the answer.

4	3	2	1
5	6	7	8
12	11	10	9
13	14	15	16

705

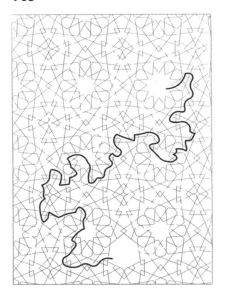

706

707

708

The lady had suffered a heart attack and her heart had stopped. The man was a doctor. The punch to her chest had restarted her heart, after which he carried her to his car and took her to the hospital where she made a full recovery.

709

Foods: Bran, Flan, Bun and Toast.

710

The words contain : Lark, Rook, Owl and Rail.

711

1001.

712

Opal ring. The first two letters of the woman's name followed by the first two letters of the man's name give the gem.

713

Pyrenees.

714

```
    9 8 7 6 5
  +   1 2 3 4
  ───────────
    9 9 9 9 9
```

715

Each line describes the one above. The final line is:
3 1 1 3 1 2 1 1 1 3 1 2 2 1.

716

717

A = Hat, B = Scarf, C = Gloves.

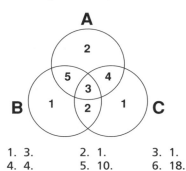

1. 3.   2. 1.   3. 1.
4. 4.   5. 10.   6. 18.

718

Aroma, today, amaze, layer.

719

Penguin, manor, long, toy, tan, you.

720

3D on row 1, column 1.

721

The detective had noticed an impression on the latest blackmail note. He lightly rubbed pencil over the note to reveal the impression of a recently written letter, including the culprit's signature!

722

1. Agatha Christie
2. Ellery Queen
3. Ruth Rendell
4. Arthur Conan Doyle
5. Raymond Chandler

723

Internet and Email.

724

"WE'LL DO THE JOB TONIGHT. LEAVE KEY IN DESK." In the main text there are words that have capital letters when they shouldn't have. Each of these words in order spells out the message.

725

Spencer prunes three more trees than Don.

726

"Someone was creeping out of the building on 34th street, taking furtive glances behind him. It all seemed very suspicious."

727

1, 4, 8 and 12. The spiral grows by 90 degrees each time from B to A.

728

All the letters which make up the place name are contained within the agent's name.

729

SLEUTH.

730

$95.07.
Pistol bullets cost $57.84, shotgun cartridges cost $4.95 and rifle bullets cost $32.28.

731

B.

732

"New York is my favorite city."
a=d, b=e and so on.

733

CONCEALED.

734

Nebraska	Texas
Tennessee	Alabama
Minnesota	Illinois.

735

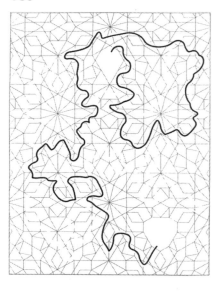

736

1. CURTSY   2. CHURCH
3. ARCHED   4. EXTORT
5. COVERT   6. HOVELS
7. SLIVER   8. REVERT
9. TOWARD   10. TENDED
11. VENDOR   12. VICTOR
13. SECTOR   14. PENCIL
15. CARTON   16. TORPOR

737

738

The surgeon is the patient's mother.

739

C. Rotates and lines are subtracted from one and added to the other.

740

D. Rotating shapes.

741

PRE.

742

D. First number is alphanumeric position (eg, A=1).

743

1. B.   2. C.   3. D.
4. A.   5. E.

744
1. Paul.   2. Fred.   3. Paul.
4. Paul.   5. Harry.   6. Fred.

745
15. (÷ 3) + 7.

746
184. In each row the two outer digits of the first number are multiplied to give the two outer digits of the second number. The two middle of the first number are multiplied to give the middle digits of the second number. 7 x 2 =14; 4 x 2 = 8; 184.

747
2. If all 49 women wore glasses then 21 men wore glasses too. If 11 of these men were under 20 years of age, only 10 men older than 20 years of age wore glasses. Then 10 – 8 = 2 men is the minimum number.

748
32. Multiply the hands by their sector values and complete the sum.
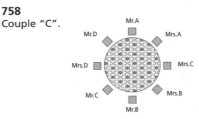
(1 x 2) [2] + (3 x 4) [12] = 14;
(3 x 3) [9] + (2 x 2) [4] = 13;
(4 x 4) [16] x (1 x 2) [2] = 32.

749
88. Sum of top three numbers x sum of bottom three numbers = middle number.

750
1. Derives, Diverse, Revised.
2. Limes, Miles, Slime, Smile.
3. Deltas, Lasted, Salted, Slated.
4. Bared, Beard, Bread, Debar.
5. Resort, Roster, Sorter, Storer.
6. Danger, Gander, Garden, Ranged.
7. Capers, Pacers, Parsec, Recaps, Scrape.
8. Canter, Carnet, Nectar, Recant, Trance.
9. Coasting, Agnostic, Coatings.
10. Parings, Parsing, Rasping, Sparing.
11. Claret, Cartel, Rectal.
12. Arcing, Caring, Racing.

751

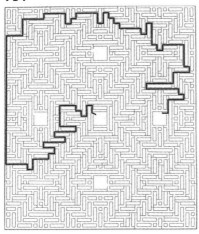

752
Belgium.

753
G to give Anger, Eager, Bight, and Regal.

754
McLaren and Ferrari.
Mindful
Closest
Liberty
Admiral
Radiant
Emperor
Nourish.

755
BIB   GIG
BOB   MAM   REVIVER
BOOB   MARRAM   ROTATOR
DAD   MINIM   SEXES
DEED   NOON   TAT
EKE   NUN   TENET
EVE   RADAR   TIT
EYE   REDDER   TOT
GAG   REFER

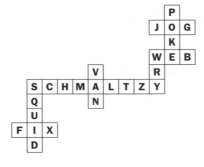

756
Too, elm, thaw, the, koala.

757
Partridge, Chaffinch, Ptarmigan.

758
Couple "C".

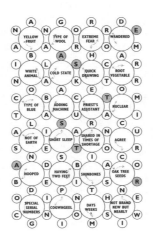

759
Valet   Above   Lobes
Event   Testy.

760
East Star.

761
DRONE, OASIS, TENSE, RESIN, SIXTY, LYRIC, MAGMA, ITCHY.

762

Tree	Elm	Ash	Beech	Lime	Poplar
Person	Bill	Jim	Tony	Sylvester	Desmond
Club	Squash	Golf	Tennis	Bowling	Soccer
Bird	Owl	Blackbird	Crow	Robin	Starling
Year	1970	1971	1972	1973	1974

763
24. Each vowel is worth 8.

764
Gary. The last letter of each capitalized word gives the names.

765
Right. All the words on the left have their letters in alphabetical order. The words on the right have their letters in reverse alphabetical order.

766

```
                              P
                         J  O  G
                              K
                         W  E  B
                   V          R
          S  C  H  M  A  L  T  Z  Y
          Q          N
          U
       F  I  X
          D
```

767
Richard Gere.

768
Trifle and Toffee.
Talent
Robust
Inform
Fulfil
Ladder
Empire.

769

770
1. Squirrel, Mongoose, Chipmunk.

771
Chest
Hello
Elver
Sleds
Torso.

772
a) Horse.

773
a) Taps.
b) Tabs.
c) Type.
d) Wept.

774
Kathleen Turner and Jamie Lee Curtis.

775
Drop the egg from a height of four feet. It falls three feet without anything happening – 12 inches later, you have a mess on the floor.

776
1. B   2. A
3. E   4. D
5. C   6. D
7. B   8. E
9. C   10. E
11. B   12. D
13. D   14. A
15. B   16. A
17. 2   18. B
19. C   20. C

777
2. The number of vowels in each name subtracted from the number of consonants.

778
Print D.

779
The victim had been hit over the head with the same boot that had made the print.

780

781

"I made my way through a series of underground passages. Eventually I arrived in an overgrown courtyard that was open to the sky."

782

She was his mother.

783

12. The number of the precinct multiplied by the number of vowels in that number.

784

A.

785

The three ages, when multiplied, must be one of the following combinations:

	When added, they equal
72 x 1 x 1	74
36 x 2 x 1	39
18 x 4 x 1	23
9 x 4 x 2	15
9 x 8 x 1	18
6 x 6 x 2	14
8 x 3 x 3	14
12 x 6 x 1	19
12 x 3 x 2	17
18 x 2 x 2	22
6 x 3 x 4	13
3 x 24 x 1	28

The census-taker should have known the number of the house, as he could see it, but he did not know their ages, therefore the house must be number 14. He needed more information to decide whether their ages were 6, 6, 2 or 8, 3, 3. When the woman says "eldest" daughter, he knows they were 8, 3, 3.

786

London
Paris
Amsterdam
Washington
Hong Kong
Cairo.

787

Six and a half gallons. The plane had travelled 390 miles at 60 mpg.

788

2. The number of consonants in each word, minus the number of vowels.

789

B. The circle and its contents turn 90 degrees clockwise.

790

791

GUAVA
APPLE
PEACH
PRUNE
PECAN
KEY anagram:
GRAPE.

792

B.

793

D. Small circles move left to right and bottom to top.

794

Let us assume that 240 fingers could be 20 aliens with 12 fingers each or 12 aliens with 20 fingers each, etc. This does not provide a unique answer so eliminates all numbers that can be factorized (ie non-prime numbers).

Now consider prime numbers: there could be one alien with 229 fingers (not allowed, according to sentence one); or 229 aliens with one finger (not according to sentence two). Simple primes are therefore not allowed, so the rules eliminate all prime numbers – except those squared. There is only one of these between 200 and 300 and that is 289 (172). So in the room are 17 aliens each with 17 fingers.

795

D. Matched opposite pairs.

796

A. Whole figure rotates 90° anti-(counter) clockwise and circles are reversed at end of lines.

797

F.

798

E.

799

Yes, Mandy liked places with an 'O' in the name.

800

E. • = (numbers of stars x 2) + numbers of stars = number of stars in column 3.

801

The "housebreaker" was her husband and they had locked their keys inside the house.

802

124. $n^2 + 3$.

803

0 and 6. B + D = E ; E – A = C.

804

4.The two-digit number on the left minus the two-digit number on the right gives the middle number.

805

806

Square = 10, asterisk = 18, triangle = 24.

	A	B	C	D	E	F
1	19	31	31	26	12	12
2	28	■	57	43	29	17
3	37	★	78	△	46	22
4	53	77	94	81	■	22
5	39	★	△	64	34	22
6	30	42	47	38	17	5

807

83. Sum of all numbers in outer circles.

808.

Ja COB-ALT	Cob	=	Cobalt
Alter	Al	=	Aluminium
Augusts	Au	=	Gold
Germany	Ge	=	Germanium
UnfaIR	Ir	=	Iron
ONE	Ne	=	Neon
Nile	Ni	=	Nickel

809

1. Port, Cola, Sake, Tea.
2. Nut, Fish, Bun, Pie.
3. Pan, Dish, Tin, Pot.
4. Wine, Sage, Rust, Rose.
5. Ant, Fly, Moth, Bee.
6. Actor, Vet, Spy, Tutor.
7. Bran, Corn, Oats, Rice.
8. Cent, Dime, Rand, Yen.
9. Lima, Bari, Nice, Cork.
10. Sock, Dress, Hat, Coat.

810

Fruit.

811

1. B. SUB. Subtle, Sublime, Suburb, Subtend.
2. E. TOP. Toparch, Topmast, Topside, Topspin.
3. D. PIT. Pithiness, Pithier, Pitied, Pitons.
4. C. PAL. Palate, Palest, Palpate, Palmate.
5. E. TEN. Tenant, Tenpin, Tendon, Tensile.
6. E. COR. Cordial, Coronet, Cornish, Corsets.
7. C. WAR. Wardens, Wartime, Warmest, Wariness.
8. D. NOT. Nothing, Notary, Notable, Noticed.
9. B. BUS. Busiest, Bussing, Bustles, Busied.
10. C. POT. Pottage, Potash, Potent, Potato.

812

1. Handmaiden, Newsvendor, Shipmaster.
2. Liveryman, Paymaster, Pawnbroker.

3. Signwriter, Sharpshooter, Housemaster.
4. Screenplay, Newsreel, Footlight.
5. Whenever, Domesday, Whitetail.
6. Larkspur, Snowdrop, Waterlily.
7. Listless, Earthquake, Ransack.
8. Rampart, Password, Peaceable.
9. Wisecrack, Blockage, Forward.
10. Kidnap, Falsehood, Troublesome.
11. Deadlock, Peacemaker, Boyfriend.
12. Setback, Topmost, Carefree.
13. Wholesale, Batten, Haywire.
14. Eyesore, Breakable, Bottleneck.
15. Beloved, Wildlife, Goodwill.
16. Handsome, Foolhardy, Barrage.
17. Reflection, Brigand, Knowledge.
18. Contribute, Signpost, Guesswork.
19. Bondage, Slipshod, Showman.
20. Windfall, Rotten, Rumour.

813
A. Square becomes circle, triangle becomes square, circle becomes triangle.

814
E. Backwards from the bottom left: THREE HUNDRED THOUSAND.

815
E.

816
F.

817
Freight: $789.82 Surcharge: $9.25
Total cost: $799.07

818
Anastasia tells a lie when she says that the number is below 500. The only square and cube between 99 and 999 whose first and last digit is 5, 7 or 9 is 729.

819

820
Z. Add the alphanumeric values of the two letters in each row from left to right to make the next letter.

821
3.

822
The area of a circle can be found by multiplying the radius of the circle by the circumference and then dividing by two. In other words, the area of a circle is exactly the same as the area of a triangle whose base is the radius of the circle and whose height is the circumference.

823
Forensic. Homicide. Arrested. Detective. Investigator.

824
18. Each is the same as the alphanumeric value of the last letter of the word.

825
"I'll be at the old mill at midnight." In this code g=a, h=b and so on throughout the alphabet.

826

827
Morgan Freeman and Clint Eastwood.

828
The knife has a value of 1.

829
HOPE ST. Each address has a house number. Count in from the end of the address the number of letters in the house number.

830

831
17.

832
None. The clock has four faces each with two hands, but Big Ben is the name of the bell inside the clock tower and not the clock itself.

833
"The enormous significance of fingerprints in establishing personal identity has been recognised for more than a century."

834

835
G.

836
Second letters of the numbers 1 to 7. Missing letter is E.

837
Richards. The first letter of the name equals the sixth letter of the task.

838
FRANC=1, POUND=9. All the vowels in each word have a value. These are added together. A=1, E=2 and so on.

839

	1	2	3	4	5	6	7	8	
1	W	L	B	G	T	S	S	N	BETWEEN
2	S	N	D	T	S	S	R	S	SERENE
3	N	R	T	B	R	R	R	L	BEETLE
4	S	M	H	H	H	H	C	S	SCHEME
5	T	T	T	S	C	S	D	L	SETTLE
6	T	Y	S	N	T	N	R	H	TEETER
7	L	C	T	T	M	H	G	C	THEME
8	M	S	N	L	P	D	L	T	SPENT

ELEMENTS · CELERY · SHEETED · LENGTH · CHEERS · SENDERS · LEDGERS · CHEESES

The circled consonants are those used in the words reading across.

840
MATA HARI.

841
D. In the complete sequence the black dots and open circles in their respective rows occupy each square only once.

842
"OUTSIDER". W - H = O. (23 - 8 = 15) and so on.

843

844
Night.

845
45. With 17 and 89, the first digit is smaller than the second. Only 45 is the same.

846
Designer. The alphanumeric value of each letter of the name corresponds to the number of the letters in the code. (J=10, the 10th letter is D.)

847
C and G.

848
T. All the letters in the sequence are made up of two straight lines.

849
12. 6x12=72 (27 reversed) 2x12=24 (42 reversed) 8x12=96 (69 reversed).

850
1, 4, 9 and 11. All the other symbols are symmetrical.

851
The family had to sail across the sea before they could begin climbing. Upon boarding the ship, they went straight to their sleeping quarters. Unfortunately, their cabin dipped below the waterline once the ship was fully laden, and a faulty porthole had caused it to fill with seawater. The water pressure had held the door shut and the crew had been unable to save the family.

852
G.

853
F.

854
1. Swimming.
2. A and C.
3. Four.
4. Tennis.
5. Three.

855
1. Mint.
2. Nest.
3. Mist.
4. Deal.
5. Corn.
6. Ball.
7. Fight.
8. King.
9. Lamp.
10. Wide

856
1. E.
2. C.
3. D.
4. A.
5. B.

857
$171\frac{1}{2}$. $n^3 \div 2$.

858
4. Reading clockwise, the lower half numbers are multiplied by 2, 3, 4, 5, respectively to equal diagonally opposite upper sector.

859
6. Sum of diagonally opposite numbers is middle number.

860

1 Step 1
Hook to load B, reverse to A, and move into position shown and unhook.

2 Step 2
Hook to A and unhook in position shown, then go through the tunnel to collect B.

3 Step 3
Hook to B and reverse.

4 Step 4
Move forward to connect all three together.

5 Step 5
Move all three to position shown.

6 Step 6
Unhook train, go around loop, and hook up to load A.

7 Step 7
Move both loads to position shown and unhook B.

8 Step 8
Reverse load A into position shown.

9 Step 9
Unhook train and go around the loop to position shown.

10 Step 10
Collect load B and reverse toward load A.

11 Step 11
Move load B to position shown, and return train to the original position.

861
Clock.

862
They are all anagrams of occupations: FARMER, CATERER, DIRECTOR, TEACHER, DESIGNER, FARRIER.

863

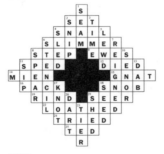

864
1. "The ends of the earth"; 2. "Six feet under"; 3. "Bedspread"; 4. "Painless operation"; 5. "Unfinished business"; 6. "Broken promises".

865

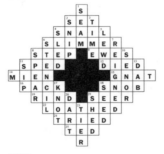

866
B. Others rotate into each other.

867
D. Others rotate into each other.

868
D. Letter reverses, stick moves to the left.

869.
B. First letter contains two straight lines, second letter contains three straight lines, and third letter contains four straight lines.

870

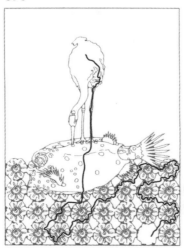

871
A. Box rotates 90° anti- (counter) clockwise.

872
Joanna has a cat on her pen, a rabbit on her crayon and an elephant on her pencil-case; Richard has a rabbit on his pen, an elephant on his crayon and a cat on his pencil-case; Thomas has an elephant on his pen, a cat on his crayon and a rabbit on his pencil-case.
1. Joanna.
2. Elephant.
3. Thomas.
4. Rabbit.
5. Joanna.

873
Blameless.

874
25 square yards.

875
15. The alphanumeric value of the first vowel in the name.

876
1. Q17
2. R14
3. R2
4. O12
5. J9
6. Q12

877

1. Malaysia
2. Siamese
3. Serenade
4. Adelaide
5. Ideography
6. Physics
7. Sturgeon
8. Onega
9. Gagarin
10. Indiana
11. Anaconda
12. Damascus
13. Custer
14. Sternum
15. Numbers
16. Erse
17. Senegal
18. Galahad
19. Hades
20. Descant
21. Cantilever
22. Verdi
23. Dixieland
24. Andes
25. Esau
26. Sauerkraut
27. Autogyro
28. Rotterdam
29. Damson
30. Sonnet
31. Netherlands
32. Surrealism
33. Smetana
34. Narcissus
35. Stamen.

878
ESPIONAGE. Circles are vowels, squares consonants. The numbers correspond to the alpha value of each letter, but they are reversed. Z=1, U=1.

879
4N. Row 6, Column 7.

880
D.

881

882
10%.

883
31. The prime divisor(s) of the alphanumeric sum of each of the city's capital letters.

884
The man was a priest who presided over the marriage ceremonies of each of his sisters.

885
After.

886
B and H

887

1.	S.	DEMISE	12.	E.	ABED	
1.	S.E.	DEN	12.	N.	ARE	
1.	S.W.	DELETE	12.	W.	ATE	
2.	S.	ERASE	13.	E.	BED	
2.	S.	ERAS	13.	W.	BATE	
2.	S.	ERA	13.	W.	BAT	
3.	S.W.	LET	14.	N.W.	DRONED	
3.	N.E.	LED	14.	N.W.	DRONE	
4.	N.W.	NED	14.	S.W.	DEDUCE	
4.	S.E.	NOR	14.	W.	DEBATE	
5.	E.	ERGO	15.	S.E.	TAT	
5.	S.	ETA	16.	N.	AIL	
6.	S.	RASE	16.	S.E.	ASS	
7.	N.W.	ONE	17.	S.W.	EDUCE	
7.	W.	OGRE	18.	N.	ATE	
8.	E.	TIMER	18.	N.W.	ATE	
8.	E.	TIME	18.	S.E.	ATE	
9.	S.	MISE	19.	N.W.	SAT	
10.	S.W.	REVISE	20.	S.W.	DUCE	
10.	W.	REMIT	21.	N.	TAIL	
11.	E.	TAB	21.	N.W.	TAT	
11.	N.E.	TIRE	21.	S.E.	TEE	
11.	S.E.	TASS	22.	N.E.	CUD	

888
E. 9 = I not J.

889
"There must be an easier way to communicate." Start 2nd letter from the end, then read alternate letters to the beginning and back.

890
D. Confused. The others were: Perceive, Discern, Observe, Deduce.

891
80.

892

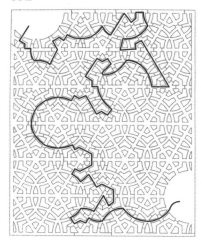

893
It is a statement, not a question. His name is What.

894

895
Kerry has a striped jumper, plain shirt and spotted towel; Paul has a spotted jumper, striped shirt and plain towel; Sandra has a plain jumper, spotted shirt and striped towel.
1. Paul.   2. Striped.   3. Paul.
4. Striped. 5. Plain.

896
13. The number of letters in the word, added to the alphanumeric value of the middle letter.

897
L and 12. Diagonally across from the left, C is the 3rd letter of the alphabet, F the 6th and so on.

898
36. 1 = 9, 0 = 33.

899

900
19.9.24.0.0. Count the number of vowels in each name, then find the alphanumeric value of each letter of the number, ie: THREE: T=20, H=8 and so on.

901
PET, PER, INS.

902
74. Add together the two right-hand numbers, take away the bottom left from the bottom right, and multiply the two left hand numbers. Add together the three totals, and multiply this with the top number.

903

5	6	7	8
R E S I D E D
E   E   O   E
T E N A N T S
I   A   A   I
R O T A T O R
E   O   O   E
D E R I D E D

904
On the corner of road 5, street 4. Draw a line down the person who is in the middle of the roads axis. Then draw a line across the person who is in the middle of the streets axis.

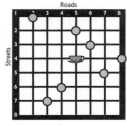

905
B.

906
Seattle. The first letter of the city follows the last letter of the name in the alphabet.

907
52. Sum the positions of the consonants in the alphabet.

908

ALGAE
BARNACLE
CORAL
KELP
LIMPET
MUSSEL
NAIADS
SEAWEED
SEAWRACK
SPONGE
VAREC
WRACK
ZOOPHYTE

909
E. Has only two segments shaded; the others have three.

910
D. Others have six lines.

911

912
1. E.   2. A.   3. B.
4. C.   5. D.

913
Arthur and Barry, along with their brother Charlie, are triplets.

914
1. Maria.   2. Maria.   3. Peter.
4. Sarah.   5. Peter.   6. Peter.

915
37. (x 3) + 4.

916
10. Black = 1; white = 4; shaded = 3.

917
Canoe.

918
1. E. Sitting. The others are Walking, Jogging, Running, Sprinting.

2. A. Museum. The others are Mosque, Temple, Cathedral, Synagogue.
3. C. London. The others are cities in the USA: Nashville, Savannah, Detroit, Denver.
4. C. January. The others are days of the week: Monday, Wednesday, Sunday, Saturday.
5. C. Circle. The others are colours: Red, Yellow, Crimson, Purple.
6. D. Dallas. The others are India, Italy, Kenya, Iceland.
7. E. Lemon. The others are car parts: Engine, Clutch, Gears, Wheels.
8. A. Twenty. The others are computer parts: Keyboard, Screen, Memory, Processor.
9. E. Bolognese. The others are Caerphilly, Gorgonzola, Stilton, Brie.
10. B. Potato. The others are Plum, Satsuma, Apricot, Damson.

919
D.

920
B. Each segment rotates 90° anti-(counter) clockwise.

921
The order is:

CELLAR
ARCADE
DETEST
STUPID
IDIOCY
CYMBAL
ALBINO
NOTICE

The start point does not matter.

922
D. Short and long lines swap places and rotate clockwise.

923
162. (+ 3) x 9.

924

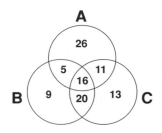

A = Raspberries,
B = Strawberries, C = Plums.

1. 58.   2. 16.   3. 26.
4. 20.   5. 9.   6. 36

925
1. Player 2.   2. Player 3.
3. Player 6.   4. Player 3.
5. Players 1, 2 and 6.
6. Players 1, 2, 4 and 6.
7. 21.   8. 51.

926
16. Black = 5; White = 2; Shaded = 2.

927
78. (2n – 5), (2n – 10), (2n – 15),
(2n – 20).

928
They were explorers who had built
an igloo. The fire was too big and
melted the walls when they fell
asleep. They both suffered
extreme hypothermia and died.

929
TOBACCO.

930
A.

931
1. C.   2. A.   3. E.
4. D.   5. B.

932
81. (x 7) – 10.

933

934
12. Black = 3; white = 4;
shaded = 2.

935
Organ.

936
1 - 5 - 6 - 2 opens the box
Letter values A=4, B=2, C=5, D=3,
E=8, F=1, G=6, H=7, I=9.
DID = IIF (3x9x3) = (9x9x1) etc.

937
A. Others rotate into each other.

938
B. Vertical object moves 45° clockwise, then a further 45° clockwise,
then doubles.

939
A.

940
D. Shapes get longer and outside
shape moves.

941
C. Arrows reverse direction.
Shading moves one place.

942
E.

943

O	M	E	D	I	A	N	G	S	T	E	I	P
C	G	N	O	V	E	L	I	S	T	A	N	I
I	I	C	O	I	L	I	Q	U	I	D	S	Q
A	E	A	W	A	T	C	H	U	D	I	I	U
H	R	T	T	A	P	E	S	T	S	U	P	E
C	E	O	H	R	E	R	C	E	C	M	I	Y
R	G	C	G	G	V	T	A	N	I	B	D	E
A	A	I	I	G	R	E	P	S	N	R	E	F
B	N	T	N	E	L	I	N	E	T	A	L	U
M	O	A	O	I	T	A	L	L	I	I	T	L
U	I	R	R	E	D	N	E	V	A	L	O	U
L	T	P	U	R	E	T	A	L	O	D	I	L
I	E	S	B	A	E	T	U	N	O	I	T	A

1. Pique	10. Angst	19. Stadium	28. Scintillation
2. Eyeful	11. Stein	20. Umbra	29. Nightwatch
3. Ululation	12. Insipid	21. Rail	30. Chute
4. Nut	13. Deltoid	22. Lavender	31. Tense
5. Tea	14. Idolater	23. Erratic	32. Senile
6. Abseil	15. Eruption	24. Cot	33. Egg
7. Lumbar	16. Onager	25. Taco	34. Grapes
8. Archaic	17. Reign	26. Oil	35. Escape
9. Comedian	18. Novelist	27. Liquids	36. Pervert

944
21. Black = 1; White = 6; Shaded = 7.

945

	5	6	7	8
1	D R O U G H T
2	C O T E R I E
3	D R I V E R S
4	D R E S S E S

946
116. The last number is multiplied
by itself, the result is then added
to the original number, ie: 3 x 3 =
9 + 63 = 72.

947
One Mile. The first item on the
list, the first letter. The second, the
second letter, and so on.

948
C. The triangle rotates 30 degrees
each time; the orange circle 90.

949
Assassination
Execution
Manslaughter
Imprisonment
Depredation
Confinement.

950
He was a part-time ventriloquist
and it was his dummy.

951

952

953
Freight: $1093.84 Surcharges:
$7.30 Total cost: $1101.14.

954
72 and 68. A = 17 and B = 19.

955
13. The alphanumerical values of
the two first letters of the word
are added together.

956
Bedroom. The first letter of each
sentence put together spells
bedroom backwards.

957

958
Alf Muggins. If it was Jack Vicious,
the statements of Alf Muggins and
Jim Pouncer would be true. If it
was Sid Shifty, the statements of
Jack Vicious, Alf Muggins and Jim
Pouncer would be true. If it was
Jim Pouncer, the statements of Sid
Shifty and Alf Muggins would be
true. Therefore it is Alf Muggins,
and only the statement of Jim
Pouncer is true.

959
C.

960
You would need 100 $20 bills.

961
Each letter is repeated as its
alphanumeric value multiplied by
10, but in ACF, F times 10 is not 90.

962
ABDUCTED.

963
They are all plants that are
commonly used as girls' names.
Only BOUGAINVELLIA is not used.

964
Thirty One.

965
Each gambler's die was numbered
as follows:
Diablo: 6 – 1 – 8 – 6 – 1 – 8
Scarface: 7 – 5 – 3 – 7 – 5 – 3
Lucky: 2 – 9 – 4 – 2 – 9 – 4
In a long run:
Diablo would win against Scarface
10 times in 18;
Scarface would win against Lucky
10 times in 18;
Lucky would win against Diablo 10
times in 18.

Diablo v Scarface: 6–7; 1–7; 8–7

win; 6–5 win; 1–5; 8–5 win;
6–3 win; 1–3; 8–3 win, which,
when repeated, gives 10 wins and
8 losses for Diablo.
Scarface v Lucky: 7–2 win; 5–2 win;
3–2 win; 7–9; 5–9; 3–9;
7–4 win; 5–4 win; 3–4, which,
when repeated, gives 10 wins and
8 losses for Scarface.
Lucky v Diablo: 2–6; 9 – 6 win;
4–6; 2–1 win; 9–1 win; 4–1 win;
2–8; 9–8 win; 4–8, which, when
repeated, gives 10 wins and
8 losses to Lucky.

966
52.

967
33. Move on by 5, go back 2, and
so on.

968
There is $22,710 left. $2,290 is
missing.

969
3. In each column vowels = 0,
and consonants in column 1 =1,
in column 2=2, and so on.

970
A. It's the only one to contain an
asymmetrical shape.

971
It had snowed overnight so they
cleared the yard and made snow-
balls, which stuck to the barn and
melted away afterwards.

972
6. – 4, then √.

973
47. Black = 0.8; White = 12.8;
Shaded = 7.8.

974
1312. –1(n + 1), –2(2n + 2),
–3(3n + 3), –4(4n + 4).

975
B.

976
D.

977

978
1. 15th.　　2. 25th.
3. 7th.　　4. Four.
5. 11th.

979
30. (x 6) ÷ 4.

980
4.The two-digit number on the
right minus the two-digit number
on the left gives the middle
number.

981

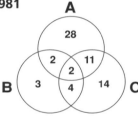

A = Thriller, B = Biography,
C = Science Fiction.

1. 11.　　　2. 17.
3. 2.　　　4. 28.

982
C. Horizontal object moves down,
small shape moves down then up
again.

983

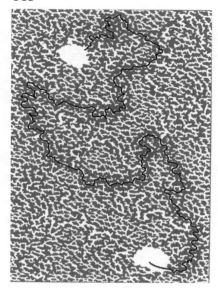

984
B.

985
C. White shapes turn 90° clockwise. Black shapes turn 180°. Black
becomes white and white becomes
black.

986
D. Alpha position multiplied by
the number of lines.

987
B. Each shape moves clockwise, 45°
with one line, 90° with two.

988

989
1, 5, 8 and 10. Each letter is made
up of three straight lines.

990
C. Release. The others were
Confine, Enclose, Intern, Restrict.

991
They are all anagrams of
creatures:
BADGER
SPIDER
CONDOR
PARROT
RACOON
GROUSE.

992
"I caught the mid-afternoon flight
to Dallas. I was met at the airport
by a guy driving a red convertible."

993
Q.

994
D. 1pm. If 6ml of poison would kill
an adult in 20 minutes, then the 2ml
that was injected would take 1 hour.

995
SAN FRANCISCO, PHILADELPHIA
and SALT LAKE CITY.

996
He brings tinned fruit or pre-
prepared fruit.

997
The truck was a refrigerated ice
truck. The agent had climbed onto
the roof to try to see where he
was. He'd done this by placing ice
blocks on top of one another.
Once he was up there the ice had
melted, and he'd been trapped.
He died of thirst and sunstroke.

998
63. From the last number, if left, it
is half the amount between the
angle and the number. If right it is
double.

999
1.13.15.8.8. The first letter of each
name becomes the first letter of the
alphabet. Then each number is the
alphanumeric value of each letter.

1000
29.

The publishers would like to thanks the following sources for their kind permission to reproduce the pictures in this book. The page numbers for each of the photographs are listed below, giving the page on which they appear in the book.